£3

Traffic-Free Cycle Trails

Nick Cotton

CYCLECITY

GUIDES

D0230958

Traffic-Free Cycle Trails

Traffic-Free Cycle Trails

Author: Nick Cotton

Publisher: CycleCity Guides

Mapping: Mark Fordham

Printer: Victoria Litho

Maps in this publication are based upon Ordnance Survey Mapping with permission of the Controller of Her Majesty's Stationery Office © Crown Copyright. CycleCity Guides.

OS Licence No: 100015871.

© Nick Cotton and CycleCity Guides 2010.

Third edition 2010.

ISBN 978-1900623216

CycleCity Guides, The Welsh Mill, Park Hill Drive, Frome, Somerset, BA11 2LE.

info@cyclecityguides.co.uk
www.cyclecityguides.co.uk

Acknowledgements and thanks to:

Tim Roe: www.auburndesign.co.uk

The Forestry Commission for use of its images, which appear in the Scotland and North-East sections.

Andy McCandish for permission to use his images on pages 396 and 397.

Sustrans for permission to use various images throughout the book (photographers: Alexandra Allen, Julia Bayne, Jonathan Bewley, John Grimshaw, David Hall, Andy Hazell, Tim Snowdon and Andy Syme).

Martin Whitfield for permission to use his images in the North-East section.

All other photographs by Nick Cotton, Howard Cotton, Chas Thursfield, Ralph Hughes, Tom Burslem, Mike Hams and Eve Kelly-Jones.

Cover image:
Jason Patient, jason@cycling-images.co.uk

TRAFFIC-FREE CYCLE TRAILS

While every attempt has been made to include the vast majority of traffic-free cycle trails in mainland Britain, there will inevitably be omissions. We apologise if we have missed your favourite ride. Please tell us if this is the case, letting us know details of start and finish and cafés and pubs along the way, and we'll try to include it next time. Likewise, if you know of any other routes not listed in this third edition of *Traffic-Free Cycle Trails* please contact CycleCity Guides at the address on the left.

Contents

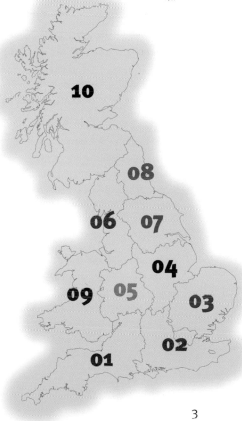

How to use this guide

In this book, you will find more than 400 traffic-free trails from Cornwall to the Scottish Highlands, including railway paths, forestry routes, canal towpaths, round-reservoir routes, purpose-built cyclepaths and some easier ridge rides on byways and bridleways.

How do I find a trail near me?

The country has been divided into ten regions, each with a map showing all the trails in the area. So simply look at the map then look up the numbers of the trails nearest to you. Under the entry for each ride number, you will find details of starting point, distance, refreshments and useful publications such as leaflets and maps. The nearest Tourist Information Centre is also mentioned, enabling you to find out about nearby bike shops, bike hire or accommodation.

What if I know the name of a trail but don't know where it is?

The index at the back will help you to find the Granite Way, the Phoenix Trail or the Innocent Railway, for example. Then look up the entry.

How do I get to the start of the ride?

We have included details of the closest railway station and of convenient car parking places (including grid references). A grid reference pinpoints on an Ordnance Survey map exactly where a trail starts. To find out how to use these, see page 6.

What sort of bike should I use?

Few of the trails have sealed surfaces so it is best to use mountain or hybrid bikes. Children's bikes are normally built to withstand knocks and will cope with all of the easier trails. A small number of the trails are out-and-out mountain bike rides and may get quite muddy in winter. Be prepared for this, or enjoy them after a dry spell in summer.

Do I need special clothes?

Ordinary clothes are fine for all the easier rides. Waterproofs are always useful, and gloves and a hat will stop your hands and ears getting cold (a common problem on a bike). If you discover you really love cycling, it is worth investing in cycling shorts and padded gloves, which make riding more comfortable. A top made of 'wicking' fabric will help prevent you getting too clammy.

How long will each trail take to ride?

We have deliberately avoided giving a time as there are so many variables, the most important of which is YOU! A ride that takes a fit cyclist half an hour could take all day with a group of children. Other variables are the quality of the surface, hills, wind and type of bike. These rides are for enjoyment! Indeed, many of the trails are shared with walkers and horseriders, and you should slow down when there are other users around. Most people of average fitness should cover 5–9 miles in an hour, discounting any stops (this type of cycling is two or three times as fast as walking).

Are all the rides 100 per cent traffic-free?

Most of the trails have long sections of traffic-free cycling but inevitably, many have to cross roads, and some routes also use quiet lanes. You are given a warning if there are any busier roads to cross.

Will I find somewhere to eat?

If there is a convenient pub, teashop or cafe along the trail then we have mentioned it. This is more likely on canal towpath rides and round-reservoir routes. Forestry routes are the least likely to have refreshments along the way, but many start from visitor centres where you can buy a snack. It is always worth carrying a bar of something and a bottle of water.

What if I break down?

None of these rides is so long or remote that you couldn't walk back to the start or somewhere where your bike can be fixed. The usual problem is a puncture, so carry a spare tube and a pump. Multitools, with screwdrivers, allen keys and spanners, can be used to tighten up nuts, bolts and screws that rattle loose, and can adjust saddle height.

Does the book include trails on the National Cycle Network?

The National Cycle Network is a mixture of cycle lanes, quiet streets, country lanes and traffic-free trails. Traffic-free sections over 3 miles are included. You will know you are on the National Cycle Network by the red and white route number signs. You will find a section on the National Cycle Network in each region, listing the maps that cover the area. These maps highlight all traffic-free sections and – who knows? – you may be tempted to do an entire long-distance route, such as the famous Sea to Sea (C2C) from Cumbria to the North Sea coast.

What about mountain biking?

Most of the Forestry Commission rides are tougher than railway paths and some areas have purpose-built singletrack mountain bike trails, particularly in Wales and Scotland. There are also long-distance trails such as the Ridgeway, South Downs Way or Peddars Way, which are more of a challenge. At the beginning of each section there is a map with details of good mountain biking areas or centres. Most good bookshops will stock a range of cycling guides, including ones covering mountain biking.

Where else can I ride, traffic-free and legally?

You have a right to ride on bridleways and byways, all shown on Ordnance Survey maps, but these are a bit hit-and-miss in terms of quality. You are NOT allowed to ride on footpaths. The majority of canal towpaths are too narrow, rough, muddy or overgrown to be much fun. The best option is to go to the nearest Forestry Commission holding where you can explore the broad stone tracks (forestry operations permitting). There is a map of the Forestry Commission holdings at the start of each regional chapter.

What about riding on lanes?

After you have built up your confidence there is no reason why you should not explore Britain's fantastic network of quiet country lanes by bike. At the start of each region there are details of good areas, with suggested bases from which to start. Many of the waymarked long-distance routes on the National Cycle Network are also good options for longer rides.

Useful information

Finding a Grid Reference

What is a grid reference?

A grid reference is a number that allows you to pinpoint a place on a map. It looks and sounds technical, but is easy to learn. Grid references can be enormously helpful, saving the need for heaps of directions you would otherwise need.

Why is it called a grid reference?

If you look at any Ordnance Survey map there are numbered blue lines running across and down the map – these form a grid. In the case of the Landranger maps, which we refer to a lot in this book, there are 40 vertical and 40 horizontal lines, creating 1,600 squares on each map, each of which represents one square kilometre (just over half a mile by half a mile).

So how does it work?

There are times when you want to direct people to a point in one of the squares formed by the grid to find a feature (a pub, a train station etc) contained in that square. Within the six-figure grid reference, the first set of three numbers gives you an imaginary line running up and down the map (north–south), the last set of three numbers gives you a line running across the map (east–west). Where these imaginary lines cross is the place on the map you want to pinpoint.

How do you work out the first three figures of a grid reference?

The first two numbers of the six-figure grid reference refer to the vertical line on the left of the chosen square. These double-digit numbers can be found along the top and bottom edges of the map. For the third number in the series, imagine the chosen square, the one to the right of the vertical line, divided into ten vertical strips, numbered from '1' on the left to '9' on the right. The third number locates one of these strips so, for example, '2' would be towards the left of the square and '8' would be towards the right.

What about the last three numbers?

These refer to the horizontal lines. Instead of starting at the left of the chosen square, start from the bottom and work towards the top. (To find the numbers, look at the left- or right-hand edges of the map.) The line at the bottom of the chosen square gives you the fourth and fifth numbers in the six-figure grid reference.

To calculate the sixth number, imagine the chosen square above the horizontal line divided into ten horizontal strips, numbered from '1' at the bottom to '9' at the top. The sixth and final number of the six-figure grid reference locates one of these strips. For example, '2' would be towards the bottom of the square and '8' would be towards the top.

Put the vertical numbers together with the horizontal and you have a six-figure grid reference, and can locate a point on the map to a high degree of accuracy. To help you remember which set of numbers goes first, always remember the saying 'Along the corridor and up the stairs' – ie work along the map from left to right, then up the map from bottom to top.

Towpath Cyclists' Safety Code

- Give way to other people on the towpath and warn them politely of your approach. A 'hello' and a 'thank you' mean a lot.

- Access paths can be steep and slippery – join the towpath with care.

- Dismount if the towpath is busy with walkers or anglers.

- Get off and push your bike:
  - if the path gets very narrow
  - beneath low bridges
  - alongside locks
  - if you encounter any other danger.

- Ride at a gentle pace, in single file and do not bunch. Never race – remember you have water on one side of you.

- If you are a young or inexperienced cyclist, always go with a responsible adult.

- Watch out for hidden mooring spikes or ropes across the path beside moored boats.

- Take particular care on wet or uneven surfaces, and don't worsen them by skidding.

- Never cycle along the towpath in the dark.

- You are responsible for your own and others' safety.

- Your bike should have a bell or hooter.

- Watch for trimmings that can cause a puncture.

For more information about towpath cycling visit: *www.waterscape.com*

Forestry Code

The Forestry Commission has, by and large, adopted an enlightened approach to cycling in its woodlands. The broad rule of thumb is that you are welcome to use the hard, stone-based forestry roads that provide excellent opportunities for safe, traffic-free cycling. In certain woodlands there are also waymarked trails on 'singletrack' paths, which are often more testing. You should pay attention to any signs that may indicate a temporary or permanent restriction on cycling (usually on walkers' trails or where forestry operations are in progress).

The best maps to use for exploring Forestry Commission woodland are the most up-to-date Ordnance Survey Explorer maps, which are at 1:25,000 scale with an orange cover.

Follow the forest cycling code

1. Expect the unexpected – keep your speed down.

2. Remember other vehicles use forest roads as well as you!

3. Give way to walkers – be friendly towards other forest users.

4. Hail a horse and avoid an accident.

5. Keep away from forest operations such as tree felling.

6. Do not pass any vehicle loading timber until you have been told to do so.

7. Footpaths are for walkers only.

8. Cycle with care and come back again.

For more information about forest cycling visit: *www.forestry.gov.uk/recreation*

South-West Trails

1 Flat Lode Trail, Camborne
2 Cornish Mineral Tramways Coast to Coast Trail
3 Camel Trail: Padstow to Wadebridge and Bodmin
4 Pentewan Valley, St Austell
5 Clay Trails, Bugle
6 Cardinham Woods, Bodmin
7 Tarka Trail: Braunton to Barnstaple
8 Tarka Trail: Barnstaple to Bideford
9 Tarka Trail: Bideford to Meeth
10 Granite Way, south of Okehampton
11 Plym Valley Trail, Plymouth
12 Princetown Tramway, Dartmoor
13 Eggesford Forest, north-west of Exeter
14 Dunster Woods, south of Minehead
15 Haldon Forest, south-west of Exeter
16 Exeter along the River Exe
17 Grand Western Canal, east of Tiverton
18 Exmouth to Budleigh Salterton
19 Bridgwater & Taunton Canal
20 Willow Walk, west of Glastonbury
21 Strawberry Line: Yatton to Cheddar
22 Colliers Way: Radstock to Frome

23 Severn Bridge Cyclepath
24 Bristol to Pill Riverside Path
25 Forest of Dean Family Trail, south-west of Gloucester
26 Coleford to Parkend & Cannop Wharf, Forest of Dean
27 Gloucester & Sharpness Canal, south of Gloucester
28 Stroud Valleys Cycle Trail, south of Gloucester
29 Bristol & Bath Railway Path
30 Kennet & Avon Canal: Bath to Bradford-on-Avon
31 Kennet & Avon Canal: Bradford-on-Avon to Devizes

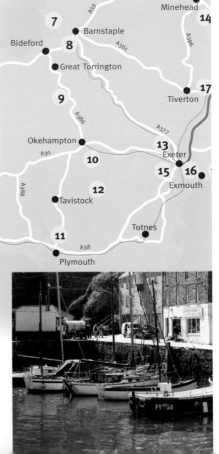

32 Chippenham to Calne Railway Path

33 Cotswold Water Park, south of Cirencester

34 Marlborough to Chiseldon Railway Path, south of Swindon

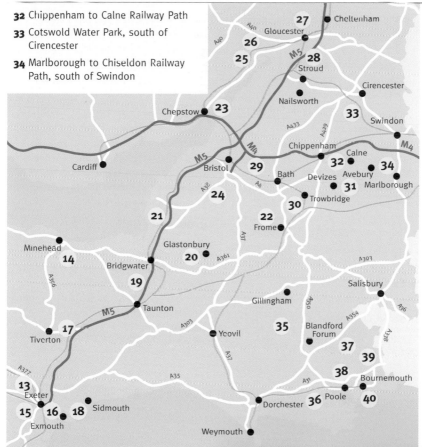

35 North Dorset Trailway from Sturminster Newton

36 Sika Trail, near Wareham

37 Castleman Trail: Stapehill to Ringwood

38 Castleman Trail: Upton Country Park to Merley, near Poole

39 Moors Valley Country Park, west of Ringwood

40 Bournemouth Promenade

South-West Mountain Biking

The South-West is blessed with a wide mixture of mountain biking possibilities on bridleways and byways. Dartmoor, Exmoor and the Quantocks can be ridden pretty much all year round as the underlying soil tends not to get too sticky. By contrast, the trails in the Cotswolds and on the chalk downlands of Wiltshire and Dorset are much better enjoyed from May to October, when the trails are drier and easier to ride; they can become impassable in the depths of winter.

1. Dartmoor

Although Dartmoor is much larger than Exmoor, it is not nearly so well provided with legal, rideable tracks. Some of the bridleways shown on Ordnance Survey maps run across the open moorland and are barely visible on the ground. The best areas for mountain biking are around Princetown in the centre of the moor, and on the east of the moor around Lustleigh.

2. Exmoor

Despite being the UK's smallest National Park, Exmoor is one of the best in the country for mountain biking with a plethora of well-waymarked and generally well-maintained trails. For a taster, try the 11-mile descent from Dunkery Beacon down to Winsford via the Exe Valley. Most of the best tracks lie within a circle drawn 10 miles around Exford.

3. Quantock Hills

For a range of hills that is only 10 miles long by 5 miles wide, the Quantock Hills boast an astonishing range of mountain bike rides, from the broad, undulating track along the ridge to some very testing technical singletrack down through the combes.

3 Quantock Hills

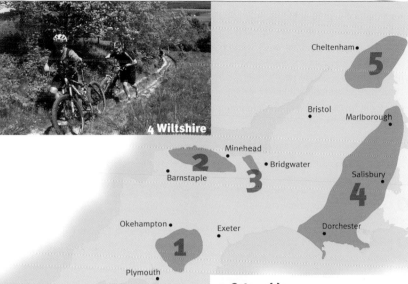

5. Cotswolds

There is a surprising quantity of rideable tracks in among the picturesque honey-coloured villages of the Cotswolds. The best riding lies in a 20-mile arc to the north-east, east and south of Cheltenham.

4. Chalk downlands of Wiltshire, Salisbury Plain & Dorset

Wiltshire and Dorset have a higher proportion of bridleways and byways than anywhere else in the country. The most well known of all is the Ridgeway. It can be ridden along its whole length from West Kennet (near Avebury) to Goring on Thames, a distance of 43 miles. Further south in Wiltshire the village of Wilton, to the west of Salisbury, is a good base from which several excellent ridge tracks can be followed for many miles. In Dorset the finest tracks are found in the triangle formed by Bridport, Blandford Forum and Weymouth.

Websites:
www.forestry.gov.uk and search 'Haldon Forest Park' for a singletrack trail near to Exeter or 'FODCA Trail' for a red-grade route in the Forest of Dean.
www.forestofavon.org and click on 'Cycling' for a route near Bristol.
www.moredirt.co.uk and follow links from 'Trails & Tracks' to 'United Kingdom' to 'South West'.

Guidebook:
South-West Mountain Biking: Quantocks, Exmoor, Dartmoor – Nick Cotton

This guidebook features 25 rides of varying lengths and difficulty through the beautiful scenery of two National Parks and one Area of Outstanding Natural Beauty. Go to *www.v-graphics.co.uk* for more details.

South-West Forestry

The Forest of Dean is the only large forestry holding in the region (the New Forest is described in the South-East section). However, there are some smaller holdings which have waymarked trails and others where it is possible to devise your own route. The relevant Ordnance Survey map is mentioned. It is highly recommended that you take a map for the larger woods as it is very easy to get lost. Local bike shops and the Forestry Commission website (*www.forestry.gov.uk*) may point you towards the best spots.

Forests & woods with waymarked trails

These are shown with a corresponding ride number and page reference:

❸ Cardinham Woods, Bodmin (see Ride 6, page 22)

❾ Haldon Forest, south-west of Exeter (see Ride 15, page 33)

❿ Heywood Wood, north-west of Exeter (see Ride 13, page 31)

⓫ Dunster Woods, south of Minehead (see Ride 14, page 32)

⓰ Wareham Forest, north-west of Wareham (see Ride 36, page 56)

⓲ Moors Valley Country Park, west of Ringwood (see Ride 39, page 61)

㉑ Forest of Dean, east of Coleford (see Ride 25, page 44)

The Forestry Commission's website, *www.forestry.gov.uk* is a good source of information. Click on 'Explore, Experience, Enjoy' then 'Cycling' and you can find out details of hundreds of waymarked trails throughout the UK. You can search by forest name or by the nearest town / city. The search will tell you the grade, length and waymarking details of the trails. Alternatively, by clicking on the map you can see the nearest forest to where you live.

Smaller Forestry Commission woodlands

These are numbered on the map opposite:

1. **St Clement Woods**, north of Truro (OS Explorer Map 105)

2. **Great Grogley & Hustyn Woods**, north-west of Bodmin (OS Explorer Map 106 / 109)

4. **Halvana Plantation** north-east of Colliford Lake on Bodmin Moor (OS Explorer Map 109)

5. **Halwill Moor Plantation** east of Holsworthy (OS Explorer Map 112)

6. **Cann Wood**, north of Plymouth (OS Explorer Map 108)

7. **Soussons, Bellever & Fernworthy**, north-east of Princetown (OS Explorer Map OL 28)

8. **Abbeyford Woods**, north of Okehampton (OS Explorer Map 113)

12. **Great Wood** (Quantocks) south-west of Nether Stowey (OS Explorer Map 140)

13. **Several small woodlands** south of Taunton, either side of the B3170 (OS Explorer Map 128)

14. Blandford Forest, west of Blandford (OS Explorer Map 117)

15. Affpuddle Heath, east of Dorchester (OS Explorer Map OL 15)

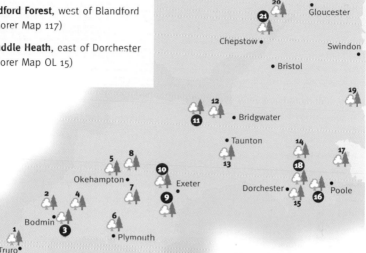

20
21 Gloucester
Chepstow •
Swindon
• Bristol

19

12
11 • Bridgwater

• Taunton
14
13
17

5 8
Okehampton • 10
7 Exeter
2 4
9 Dorchester • Poole
Bodmin • 18
3 6 16
1 • Plymouth 15
Truro •

11 Dunster Woods

17. Cannon Hill Plantation, West Moors Plantation and Hurn Forest north of Bournemouth (OS Explorer Map OL 22)

19. Savernake, West Woods & Collingbourne Wood, south-west and south-east of Marlborough (OS Explorer Map 157)

20. Wye Valley between Chepstow and Monmouth (OS Explorer Map OL 14)

It is also worth contacting the following Forest District Offices for further information:

Forest of Dean
Bank House
Bank Street
Coleford
Gloucestershire
GL16 8BA
Tel: 01594 833057
email: enquiries.dean@forestry.gsi.gov.uk

Peninsula Forest District (Devon & Cornwall)
Bullers Hill
Kennford
Exeter
Devon
EX6 7XR
Tel: 01392 832262
email: enquiries.peninsula@forestry.gsi.gov.uk

South-West National Cycle Network

A map for this route is available from www. sustrans.org. uk *or* 0845 113 0065.

Cornish Way

123 miles from Land's End to Bude (with two options between Truro and Bodmin). Highlights include: Land's End, Lamorna Cove, the traffic-free coastal route through Penzance, Cornish Mineral Tramways, the Camel Trail, King Harry Ferry from Falmouth, the Lost Gardens of Heligan and the Eden Project.

Traffic-free sections over 3 miles long:
- Crofthandy to Devoran, east of Redruth (NCN 3).
- The Camel Trail from Padstow to Bodmin (NCN 32).

Cornish Way

West Country Way

240 miles from Padstow to Bristol (or Bath). Highlights include the Camel Trail, the Tarka Trail, Exmoor, Knighthayes Court, the Grand Western Canal, the Bridgwater & Taunton Canal, Glastonbury, Wells, the Mendips and the Bristol & Bath Railway Path.

Traffic-free sections over 3 miles long:
- The Camel Trail from Padstow to Blisland (NCN 32).
- The Tarka Trail from Petrockstowe to Barnstaple (NCN 3).
- Grand Western Canal east of Tiverton (NCN 3).
- Bridgwater & Taunton Canal (NCN 3).
- Bristol & Bath Railway Path (NCN 4).

Devon Coast to Coast

102 miles from Ilfracombe to Plymouth via Barnstaple, Bideford, Okehampton and Tavistock. Highlights include the North Devon Coast at Ilfracombe, the Tarka Trail, Meldon Viaduct and the Granite Way, Dartmoor views, the handsome town of Tavistock, Plym Valley Trail and Plymouth.

Traffic-free sections over 3 miles long:
- The Tarka Trail from Barnstaple to Meeth (NCN 3 & 27).
- The Granite Way from Okehampton to Lake Viaduct (NCN 27).
- The Plym Valley Trail from Clearbrook to Plymouth (NCN 27).

Devon Coast to Coast

Severn & Thames Cycle Route

141 miles from Gloucester to Newbury via Bristol. Highlights include Gloucester Cathedral, the Severn Vale, the Gloucester & Sharpness Canal, Avon Gorge, Clifton Suspension Bridge, Bristol & Bath Railway Path, Bath, the Kennet & Avon Canal, Avebury and Marlborough.

Traffic-free sections over 3 miles long:

• Gloucester & Sharpness Canal (NCN 41).

• Riverside path from Pill to Bristol (NCN 41).

• Bristol & Bath Railway Path (NCN 4).

• Kennet & Avon Canal from Bath to Devizes (NCN 4).

• Marlborough to Chiseldon Railway Path (NCN 45).

Severn & Thames Cycle Route

Other good areas for lane cycling

For such popular tourist areas there is very little good, easy cycling on the lane networks of Cornwall, Devon and Dorset: the narrow, hilly lanes are often set between high hedgerows with poor visibility. The exceptions are those right on the top of Exmoor and Dartmoor. By contrast, the **Somerset Levels** offer some very easy cycling alongside the rhynes (drainage ditches) bordered by weeping willows. There are good bases at Somerton, Glastonbury and Mark. The **Severn Vale** is bypassed by both the A38 and the M5, and there is a gentle charm to the network of quiet lanes that run north from Thornbury to Gloucester, linked at times by the Gloucester & Sharpness Canal towpath. Try starting from Berkeley or Frampton on Severn. As for the **Cotswolds**, think of them like a wedge of cake on its side: the edge of the cake represents the steep escarpment overlooking the Severn Vale where the cycling is strenuous; east from here (the flatter part of the cake!), the land slopes gently down towards the Thames and there is a wonderful network of quiet lanes linking together the honey-coloured stone villages and towns. Northleach, Malmesbury, Bourton-on-the-Water and Burford are all good starting points.

West Country Way

15

Ride 1 Flat Lode Trail, Camborne

Category
Linked mineral tramways, quiet lanes.

Distance
8-mile circuit.

This well-waymarked circuit is a real celebration of the area's mining heritage and at every turn it seems there is another atmospheric ruin, characterised by the typical tall chimney. The trail is predominantly on improved gravel tracks with occasional short sections of lane. There are one or two short, steep climbs where you may wish to push, rewarded with fine views out into the surrounding countryside, dotted with clumps of yellow gorse and even the occasional glimpse of the sea.

Starting point & parking

The main car park for the trail is on the minor road south-west of Carnkie, a hamlet lying 3 miles **south-west of Redruth** (grid reference SW 681395). There are a few much smaller parking spots around the course of the route.

On your bikes!

There are too many junctions to describe in detail but the route is very well waymarked, either as 'Flat Lode Trail' or with a black icon of a mining chimney. There are several short climbs, two of them quite steep.

Station: Camborne.

TIC: Redruth, 01209 219 048.

Other nearby trails: Cornwall Coast to Coast (Portreath to Devoran). There are plans to continue extending the Mineral Tramway network in the area.

Useful publications & websites: OS Landranger Map 203. The website covering the tramways is *www.cornwall.gov.uk/mineral-tramways*. Various leaflets about cycling in Cornwall are available as downloads at *www.visitcornwall.com/site/activities/cycling*

Refreshments: Brea Inn, Carn Brea. Lots of choice in Camborne and Redruth.

Cornish Mineral Tramways Ride 2
Coast to Coast Trail

The Mineral Tramway route, which runs from the north coast of Cornwall at Portreath to the south coast at Devoran, is one of Cornwall's most popular cycle trails. The result of many years of patient negotiation, the trail uses several sections of old tramroad that once served the mines that are scattered around this part of Cornwall. Many of the old ruins and chimneys are still visible. The route climbs gradually from the attractive seaside resort of Portreath through Cambrose to Wheal Rose and Scorrier. From this highpoint the trail drops down into the Poldice Valley and along the Carnon River down to Devoran, passing beneath the soaring railway viaduct. The route is generally well waymarked with handsome granite stones, but there are a couple of places (particularly in Scorrier) where you should keep a sharp eye out for signposts.

Starting points & parking

1. The car park by the beach in **Portreath**, on the B3300 to the north of Camborne / Redruth (grid reference SW 655454).

2. The car park by **Bissoe Cycle Hire**, about 5 miles south-west of Truro (grid reference SW 772415).

3. The car park by the village hall on Quay Road in **Devoran**, just south of the A39 between Truro and Falmouth (grid reference SW 792393).

Category
Railway path, mineral tramways and quiet lanes.

Distance
12 miles each way.

NB There are a few climbs and a few rougher sections so this is a tougher ride than a railway path like the Camel Trail. The easiest bit is between Devoran and Bissoe.

Ride 2 Cornish Mineral Tramways, Coast to Coast Trail

2

On your bikes!

1. Exit the car park by the beach in Portreath and follow the B3300 towards Redruth. At the Portreath Arms, bear left onto Sunnyvale Road signposted 'Portreath Tramroad'. After 1/2 mile, just before rejoining the B3300, bear left uphill onto the start of the traffic-free trail. Continue in the same direction on a generally level track at several minor junctions.

2. The route is well signposted in both directions, with 'Devoran' or 'Portreath' as destinations. Also look out for the granite cairns with a black symbol of an old mining chimney. Go past The Plume pub in Scorrier and descend into the Poldice Valley, passing Bissoe Cycle Hire.

3. If you continue on the quiet lane through Devoran you will come to the estuary (Restronguet Creek), and a chance of refreshment at the Old Quay Inn (just up the hill from the water).

> **Station:** Perranwell Station.
>
> **TIC:** Falmouth, 01326 312300.
>
> **Other nearby trails:** The Flat Lode Trail.
>
> **Useful publications & websites:** OS Landranger Maps 203 & 204. Various leaflets about cycling in Cornwall are available as downloads at *www.visitcornwall.com/site/ activities/cycling*
>
> **Refreshments:** Pubs in Portreath, Scorrier and Devoran. Café at Bissoe Cycle Hire.

Ride 3 The Camel Trail
Padstow to Wadebridge & Bodmin

3

Category
Railway path.

Distance
Wenfordbridge to Bodmin –
7 miles each way.

Bodmin to Wadebridge –
5 miles each way.

Wadebridge to Padstow – 6 miles each way.

The most popular recreational ride in the country, visited by over 500,000 people a year, the Camel Trail runs along the course of a dismantled railway. From Wenfordbridge and the wooded countryside of the upper Camel Valley, the trail runs down past Bodmin to Wadebridge and alongside the picturesque Camel Estuary as far as Padstow. The route is very busy in July and August. There are many cycle hire centres in Padstow, Wadebridge and Bodmin with a huge variety of bikes to cater for every combination imaginable, many of which you will see on your way along the ride!

Starting points & parking

There are several possible starting points and car parks. The car parks are free at the north-east end of the trail, and Pay & Display in the towns:

1. Wenfordbridge, 7 miles east of Wadebridge (grid reference SX 085751).

2. Poley's Bridge, 6 miles east of Wadebridge (grid reference SX 083742).

3. Bodmin, Scarlett's Well Road, near the Jail (grid reference SX 061675).

4. Wadebridge (grid reference SW 990723).

5. Padstow (grid reference SW 920751).

The Camel Trail, Padstow to Wadebridge and Bodmin   Ride 3

Station: Bodmin Parkway Station, 6 miles south-east of the trail.

TIC: Padstow, 01841 533449. Wadebridge, 01208 813725 and Bodmin, 01208 76616.

Other nearby trails: There are several miles of forest tracks in Cardinham Woods, east of Bodmin. The Clay Trails start at Bugle, 8 miles south-west of Bodmin.

Useful publications & websites: OS Landranger Map 200. Various leaflets about cycling in Cornwall are available as downloads at *www.visitcornwall.com/site/activities/cycling*

Refreshments: Lots of choice in Bodmin, Wadebridge and Padstow. Camel Valley Tea Garden near Poley's Bridge and Potters Barn Tearooms at Wenfordbridge (01208 850471).

NB There is a ¾-mile section on roads through Wadebridge and you will need to use roads from the western end of the trail to get into the heart of Padstow.

Pentewan Valley & Mevagissey   Ride 4
near St Austell

This route forms part of the Cornish Way (National Cycle Network Route 3), the 180-mile cycle route that runs from Land's End to Bude. The traffic-free section starts on a cycletrack parallel with the B3273 just south of St Austell, and follows the river valley down towards the seaside village of Pentewan. At a footbridge over the river you have the choice of continuing on the flat down towards the beach, or climbing for 300ft up past the Lost Gardens of Heligan and down the other side of the hill to the popular fishing village of Mevagissey. The descent to Mevagissey is quite steep so you may well prefer to walk up the hill on the way back. As you are surrounded by wildflowers and fine views this hardly constitutes hardship!

Category
Railway path and specially-built cyclepath.

Distance
London Apprentice to Mevagissey: 4 miles each way. London Apprentice to Pentewan: 2 miles each way. London Apprentice north towards St Austell: 1¹/₂ miles each way.

Ride **4** **Pentewan Valley & Mevagissey, near St Austell**

NB If you wish to go right into the heart of Mevagissey or visit the Lost Gardens of Heligan, you will need to use roads for about ¹/₂ mile.

Starting points & parking

1. London Apprentice: the car park in Shepherdshill Woods about 2 miles south of St Austell (grid reference SX 008498). Follow the B3273 towards Mevagissey. Just after London Apprentice turn left signposted 'Retail Leisure Warehouse'. Follow the lane round to the right and park in the woods.

2. Mevagissey: park in the main car park on the B3273 just north of Mevagissey (grid reference SX 011455) and once on your bikes follow the road towards St Austell. Shortly after passing a park on the left, turn left by a 'Heligan Bike Trail' signpost. The gradient steepens soon after the start of the traffic-free section.

On your bikes!

1. From the start point in London Apprentice follow the tarmac lane through the woods. As the road swings left uphill, bear right onto the lower, broad woodland track soon running alongside the river. After 1 mile, at a bridge and a Millennium signpost, you have a choice: straight on for Pentewan (1 mile) or turn right across the bridge for Mevagissey (3 miles).

2. (Towards Mevagissey). After crossing the bridge, turn left at the B3273 along the shared-use pavement, cross the road via the traffic island and continue as the track swings right away from the road and begins to climb. At a junction of tracks shortly after passing under the road bridge, turn left for Mevagissey (or go straight ahead for the Lost Gardens of Heligan).

3. Descend, climb, then descend again. At the T-junction (with a footpath to the left), turn right. There is a steep descent to the road on the edge of Mevagissey. Turn right to visit this popular fishing village. Retrace your steps.

Pentewan Valley & Mevagissey, near St Austell Ride **4**

Station: St Austell.

TIC: St Austell, 01726 879500. Truro, 01872 274555.

Other nearby trails: The Clay Trails run north from St Austell via the Eden Project to Bugle. The Camel Trail runs from Padstow through Wadebridge to Bodmin and Wenfordbridge.

Useful publications & websites: OS Landranger Map 204. The Cornish Way Cycle

Route Map produced by Sustrans shows this and several other traffic-free routes in Cornwall including the Camel Trail, the Mineral Tramway from Bissoe to Devoran and the route through Penzance from Mousehole to Marazion. It costs £5.99 and is available from www.sustrans.org.uk. Also try: *www.visitcornwall.com/site/activities/cycling*

Refreshments: Lots of choice in Mevagissey and in Pentewan.

Clay Trails Ride **5**
Bugle to St Austell

At every point on this ride you get the impression of man shaping nature – either scooping out great white clay pits, or creating volcano-shaped hills and deep green lakes or, more recently, tree-planting on a massive scale to cover the mining scars. It is a quite extraordinary landscape, at times almost lunar, at times reassuringly wooded. There are several hills to climb but these give you ever better views of the massive reworking of the landscape. The highpoint (66oft / 200m) is reached as you contour around the rim of Baal Pit, to the south of Penwithick.

Starting points & parking

1. Bugle: the car park at the start of the trail is about ¹/₂ mile from the centre of Bugle along the B3374 Rosevean Road towards Penwithick, on the left-hand side by a white sculpture of a horse lying down (grid reference SX 020586).

2. The China Clay Museum, **Ruddlemoor**, on the B3274 north of St Austell (grid reference SX 005554).

3. A road called Tremena Gardens to the west of St Austell railway station (grid reference SX 011529). Follow Market Hill from the centre of **St Austell**, climb steeply and turn left after crossing the railway line.

Category
Mineral tramways, quiet lanes.

Distance
10 miles each way.

Ride 5   Clay Trails, Bugle to St Austell

5

NB *This is not a ride for young children as there are many climbs, some steep.*

On your bikes!

1. (Starting from Bugle). The trail is well-signposted as 'Clay Trails' or with an elongated red triangle carved into large boulders located along the course of the trail. Follow signs for 'Eden Project' on track and lane for almost 4 miles, then just before arriving at the Eden Project turn right following a sign for 'Trethurgy'.

2. Follow signs for 'Wheal Martyn' and 'St Austell' up hill and down dale for a further 4$\frac{1}{2}$ miles, ignoring the 'Sky Spur' to the right. The China Clay Museum (Wheal Martyn) is reached by crossing the footbridge over the B3274 and climbing north for $\frac{2}{3}$ mile.

3. For St Austell, do not descend to cross this footbridge but continue south on

a wide smooth trail, ending at Tremena Gardens on the west side of St Austell (near the railway station). A long descent via Market Hill takes you into the heart of the town.

Station: St Austell.

TIC: St Austell, 01726 879500.

Other nearby trails: St Austell to Mevagissey, Camel Trail at Bodmin, Cardinham Woods near Bodmin.

Useful publications & websites: OS Landranger Map 200. Various leaflets about cycling in Cornwall are available as downloads at *www.visitcornwall.com/site/activities/cycling*

Refreshments: Lots of choice in Bugle and St Austell. Café at the China Clay Museum on the B3274 in Ruddlemoor (north of St Austell).

6

Ride 6   **Cardinham Woods Bodmin**

Category
Forest trails.

Distance
Two 3-mile circuits (with plenty of opportunities to extend).

There are few Forestry Commission holdings of any real size in Cornwall. With the exception of Idless Woods to the north of Truro there is only a scattering of small holdings along the A389 and A38 between Wadebridge, Bodmin and Liskeard. Of these, Cardinham Woods is the largest (650 acres) and it is possible to devise several short rides within the woodland. The Forestry Commission bought Cardinham Woods in 1922. Today their fertile soils produce fine timber, saw logs for house building from the impressive old Douglas Firs, and pulp for newsprint from the younger thinnings. Nearly 80 years of

careful management has created a varied and attractive forest. Each age of tree is home to a different range of wildlife. Look out for ravens and buzzards soaring above the forest. Catch the occasional glimpse of grey squirrels, rabbits or foxes. Red and roe deer are here but melt away into the forest at the first hint of danger.

Starting point & parking

The car park in **Cardinham Woods** (grid reference SX 100666). From Bodmin take the A38 towards Liskeard for 2 miles. Cross the bridge over the A30 dual carriageway then after $\frac{1}{4}$ mile turn left along a road signposted 'Cardinham, Fletchersbridge'. Shortly after a sharp right-hand bend, turn left and follow signs for the Cardinham Woods car park.

On your bikes!

Lady Vale & Lidcutt Valley Walk

1. Go to the end of the car park, cross the stone bridge and turn right at a wooden barrier by a tall wooden signpost. Take the right-hand of the three tracks, signposted 'Lady Vale Walk'.

2. Climb steadily on the wide forest track. At the track junction immediately after crossing the stream, turn left gently uphill. Go past the Scots Pine picnic area on a right-hand bend by an exposed rock cliff.

3. At the highest point follow the main wide forest road as it swings sharp left to descend on the other side of the valley. Keep bearing left, **ignoring** a wide forest road off to the right after crossing a stream.

4. At the bottom turn left to cross the stream then right towards the 'Lady Vale Bridge' sign. Cross a second bridge and turn right. Join a minor road to return to the start.

Callywith Wood Walk

This is a tougher 3-mile route with more climbing. It starts from the same point as the Lady Vale Walk. Follow the blue signs.

Station: Bodmin.

TIC: Bodmin, 01208 76616.

Other nearby trails: The Camel Trail starts west of Bodmin. The Clay Trails run south from Bugle to St Austell.

Useful publications & websites: OS Landranger Map 200. For further information contact Forest Enterprise, Peninsula Forest District, Bullers Hill, Kennford, Exeter, Devon EX6 7XR (01392 832262) or visit *www. forestry.gov.uk* and enter 'Cardinham' in the search engine.

Refreshments: Woods Café at the far end of the car park, near the start of the trails (01208 78111).

Ride 7 Tarka Trail from Braunton to Barnstaple

7

Category
Railway path.

Distance
6 miles each way.

Forming part of Sustrans' West Country Way (Padstow to Bristol), the Tarka Trail is one of the longest railway paths in the country, running north from near the edge of Dartmoor down to the coast, then following the estuaries of the Rivers Torridge and Taw through Bideford, Barnstaple and Braunton. The trail has been split into three easily-managed sections. The section described below runs right alongside the estuary and links Braunton to the handsome town of Barnstaple with its famous Pannier Market, passing brightly painted boats and yellow RAF Rescue helicopters on its way.

Starting points & parking

1. Braunton: the trail starts by the Police Station at the far end of the main car park in the centre of Braunton, signposted 'Museum, Tourist Information Centre, Countryside Centre' (grid reference SS 487366). Braunton is on the A361 to the west of Barnstaple.

2. Barnstaple: the old bridge in the centre of town (grid reference SS 558330). The trail is signposted along the north side of the River Taw. There are car parks on the north side of the river off The Strand / Castle Street / North Walk.

On your bikes!

Exit the Braunton car park following signs for 'The Burrows, Barnstaple'. Briefly join the road past Otter Cycle Hire then turn right onto Station Close and left onto the cyclepath.

Station: Barnstaple.

TIC: Barnstaple, 01271 375000. Braunton, 01271 816400.

Other nearby trails: The Tarka Trail continues west from Barnstaple to Bideford then south to Great Torrington and Meeth.

Useful publications & websites: OS Landranger Map 180. Go to *www.devon. gov.uk/tarkatrail* for a download of the trail leaflet or *www.devon.gov.uk/cycling* for a more general overview of what is happening in Devon.

Refreshments: Lots of choice in Braunton and Barnstaple.

Tarka Trail Ride 8
from Barnstaple to Bideford

This ride forms part of the longest railway path in the South-West, running over 30 miles from Braunton to Meeth. In its entirety the trail encompasses a range of vistas from the broad flat expanses of the Taw / Torridge estuary to the intimacies of wooded riverbanks. The trail threads its way alongside the River Torridge, passing the port of Instow where there is a fine sandy beach and a ferry across to Appledore on the western banks of the Torridge. It continues to East-the-Water, the settlement opposite Bideford. There is plenty of wildlife along the route and a good café at the cycle hire centre at Fremington Quay. Barnstaple is famous for its Pannier Market, held on Tuesdays and Fridays. It would be easy to extend this ride in both directions, ie to continue west from Barnstaple to Braunton on the north side of the River Taw, or south from Bideford towards Meeth.

Starting points & parking

1. Barnstaple: the old bridge in Barnstaple (grid reference SS 558329). There is a convenient large car park by the Leisure Centre to the south-east of the old bridge.

2. Bideford: the Old Bideford Station on the east side of the River Torridge in East-the-Water, just east of the A386 bridge (grid reference SS 457263).

Category
Railway path.

Distance
9 miles each way.

NB Care should be taken if you cross the (busy) road bridge over the River Torridge into Bideford or if you go north into Barnstaple itself, which also involves crossing a busy road bridge.

Station: Barnstaple.

TIC: Barnstaple, 01271 375000 and Bideford, 01237 477676.

Other nearby trails: The Tarka Trail continues south from Bideford to Great Torrington and Meeth, and west from Barnstaple to Braunton. You can use the cyclepath on the new bridge if you are cycling from Bideford to Braunton but you will miss out Barnstaple town centre.

Useful publications and websites: OS Landranger Map 180. Go to *www.devon. gov.uk/tarkatrail* for a download of the trail leaflet or *www.devon.gov.uk/cycling* for a more general overview of what is happening in Devon.

Refreshments: Lots of choice in Barnstaple, Instow and Bideford. Café at Fremington Quay (adjacent to the cycle hire centre).

Ride 9 Tarka Trail from Bideford to Meeth

9

Category
Railway path.

Distance
15 miles each way.

NB *Care should be taken if you cross the (busy) road bridge over the River Torridge from East-the-Water into Bideford.*

The final ride on the Tarka Trail runs south from Bideford to Meeth, on the A386 near Hatherleigh. There is a steady 400ft (120m) climb on the stone and gravel railway path over 5 miles from the Puffing Billy pub, west of Great Torrington, to the highpoint near to East Yarde. The railway used to carry clay from the quarries at Petrockstowe down to the ships at Bideford. The trail runs past the pretty village of Weare Giffard, where Tarka the Otter was born and fought his last battle, and on to Meeth. There is a very different feel to the ride compared to the other two sections described as it is largely wooded with several river crossings. Keep an eye out for the wooden and mosaic sculptures on this stretch of the trail.

Starting points & parking

1. The Old Bideford Station in East-the-Water near **Bideford** (grid reference SS 457263).

2. The Puffing Billy pub on the A386 to the west of **Great Torrington** (grid reference SS 480197).

3. In **Meeth** on the A386 to the north of Hatherleigh (grid reference SS 547079). There is limited parking in Meeth in the layby opposite the start of the trail – if full follow signs to Petrockstowe car park (grid reference SS 507105).

Station: Barnstaple or Eggesford.

TIC: Bideford, 01237 477676.

Other nearby trails: The Tarka Trail continues from Bideford to Barnstaple and Braunton. The Granite Way, Okehampton.

Useful publications & websites: OS Landranger Maps 180 & 191. Go to *www. devon.gov.uk/tarkatrail* for a download of the trail leaflet or *www.devon.gov.uk/cycling* for a more general overview of what is happening in Devon.

Refreshments: Lots of choice in Bideford. Puffing Billy pub to the west of Great Torrington. Bull & Dragon pub in Meeth.

Granite Way Ride 10
south of Okehampton

The Devon Coast to Coast Route (part of the National Cycle Network) will before long offer a largely traffic-free route all the way from Ilfracombe on the north coast down to Plymouth on the south coast. The ride described here forms part of the middle section, along the course of an old dismantled railway linking Okehampton station via the magnificent Meldon Viaduct, to a picnic spot beyond Lake Viaduct. There are superb views into the heart of Dartmoor and across to the west over the rolling patchwork of fields and hedgerows so typical of Devon. A steam engine runs between Okehampton station and Meldon Viaduct, so it would be easy to combine the bike ride with a trip on the wonderfully restored old train. Another short section of railway line has been converted to recreational use closer to Lydford but you will need to use some steep lanes to connect the two sections.

Starting point & parking

Okehampton station car park (grid reference SS 593944). Follow signs for the station from the traffic lights at the crossroads in the centre of Okehampton. There is also a car park beyond the railway bridge near the station, on the left-hand side.

On your bikes!

Exit Okehampton station car park and cross onto the minor road opposite, signposted 'National Cycle Network Bike Route 27. Tavistock'. Shortly, turn sharp left to join the path running alongside the railway line. Follow this for 6½ miles to the picnic spot (granite seats) about ³/₄ mile beyond Lake Viaduct (the second viaduct). The highest point of the railway is about halfway along.

Station: Okehampton (seasonal).

TIC: Okehampton, 01837 53020.

Other nearby trails: The Tarka Trail starts from Meeth, a few miles to the north on the A386 (north of Hatherleigh). There is a mountain bike trail on the old tramway at Princetown.

Useful publications & websites: OS Landranger Map 191. Go to *www.devon.gov. uk/granite_way-2.pdf* for a download of the trail leaflet or *www.devon.gov.uk/cycling* for a more general overview of what is happening in Devon.

Refreshments: Café at Okehampton railway station. The Bottle Neck Inn, Sourton Down (just off the route). The Highwayman Inn, Sourton (just off the route). The Bearslake Inn, Lake (just off the route).

Category
Railway path.

Distance
6½ miles each way.

Ride 11 **Plym Valley Trail Plymouth**

11

Category
Railway path.

Distance
9 miles each way.

This popular railway path climbs steadily as it runs north from Plymouth (Laira Bridge) over a series of spectacular stone viaducts through the Plym Valley to Clearbrook on the edge of Dartmoor. The ride follows the course of the old Great Western Railway, which started its life as the South Devon & Tavistock Railway – yet another engineering project of Isambard Kingdom Brunel. In addition to the magnificent viaducts mentioned there is also the 300-yd Shaugh Tunnel towards the northern end of the ride. It is the southern start of the Devon Coast to Coast Cycle Route, a National Cycle Network route that runs north from Plymouth to Ilfracombe on the north coast.

NB At the northern end of the trail there is a short, steep, stony climb up to the pub in Clearbrook. You can return back to the trail gently downhill on road.

Starting point & parking

The ride starts at **Laira Bridge, Plymouth,** where the A379 crosses the River Plym (grid reference SX 502543). You can park at:

1. Coypool Road by B&Q near **Coypool Park & Ride** (SX 520569)

2. Plym Bridge (SX 524587)

3. Clearbrook (SX 525656)

On your bikes!

1. From the east side of Laira Bridge (A379) head north along the road passing static caravans and through a gate into woodland. Follow the estuary path (Route 27) onto the bridge over the railway line.

At the end of the railings, turn sharp right under the A38 viaduct aiming towards a narrow stone path running parallel with the railway line.

2. Cross a road and continue in the same direction, rejoining tarmac and passing alongside the Coypool Park & Ride car park (keep this to your left).

3. Leave behind houses and factories, cross Plym Bridge Woods car park to climb up to the railway path and follow this as it climbs steadily for 4 miles to the end of the tunnel.

4. At the end of the tarmac, bear left then turn sharp left up a steep rough track. At the T-junction with a better track turn left and follow up to the Skylark pub in Clearbrook.

5. As an alternative return to the cyclepath, continue on the road uphill from the pub and take the first lane to the left towards Goodameavy. After almost 1 mile and just after passing a left turn to Goodameavy, bear left onto the railway path and follow it back to Plymouth.

Station: Plymouth.

TIC: Plymouth, 01752 306330.

Other nearby trails: The Granite Way starts from near Lydford, to the north of Tavistock.

Useful publications & websites: OS Landranger Map 201. For a map download go to *www2.plymouth.ac.uk/PlymValley*. For a more general overview of cycling in Devon, try *www.devon.gov.uk/cycling*

Refreshments: Skylark pub in Clearbrook.

Princetown Tramway Ride **12**
Dartmoor

The trail uses a remote stretch of dismantled railway (formerly part of the Yelverton to Princetown line) in the heart of Dartmoor, running around King's Tor and past old granite quarries where vast blocks of granite were taken to build bridges, including the widening of London Bridge in 1903. The ride starts from near the infamous Dartmoor Prison, which was originally built to house French prisoners of war in Napoleonic times. The trail is also known as the Tyrwhitt Trail, after Thomas Tyrwhitt who founded Princetown and built the prison. The stone and gravel path drops 500ft (150m) as it meanders west and south-west from Princetown to the suggested turn-around point at the stile just before the junction of the railway with the B3212 (just east of Dousland), so be aware that the return part of the journey will take far longer than the first half. As the going is fairly rough and because of the drop, this is not a ride for the unfit or for young children. Princetown is also one of the best bases for mountain biking on Dartmoor, with a wide variety of bridleways leading off in all directions. These tend to be strenuous and should not be undertaken by the inexperienced, particularly if visibility is poor.

Category
Rough railway path, only suitable for mountain bikes.

Distance
6 miles each way.

Ride **12** **Princetown Tramway, Dartmoor**

Starting point & parking

Princetown lies in the heart of Dartmoor, at the junction of the B3357 and the B3212. The ride starts from the main car park (with an honesty box) in the centre of Princetown and leaves the car park by the Fire Station signposted 'Disused Railway' (grid reference SX 589734).

On your bikes!

1. At a three-way fork of tracks after about 1¹/₂ miles, take the left-hand of the three tracks to go around King's Tor.

2. After a further 4¹/₂ miles of gentle downhill you will come to a stile. It is

suggested you turn around here. The alternative is to go over the stile and follow the ever rougher tramway to the B3212 and turn left, climbing back to Princetown. This road can be busy.

Station: Nowhere nearby.

TIC: Tavistock, 01822 612938.

Other nearby trails: Plym Valley Trail from Plymouth. Granite Way, Okehampton.

Useful publications & websites: OS Explorer Map OL 28 (or three OS Landranger maps – 191, 201 & 202). Go to *www.dartmoor-npa. gov.uk* and click on 'Cycling'. Also try *www. devon.gov.uk/cycling*

Refreshments: Several options in Princetown.

Heywood Wood Ride **13**
Eggesford Forest, north-west of Exeter

There are very few Forestry Commission holdings in the South-West and even fewer waymarked routes. This short circuit in Heywood Wood is waymarked with round wooden posts marked with a red band at the top: the only cycle signs you are likely to see are those telling you where you **cannot** go. Mountain bikes are essential for this route as there are occasionally rough sections. Overall, the route is undulating with some steeper sections. There is another nearby Forestry Commission holding, called Flashdown Wood, which you are welcome to explore – although some of the tracks turn from stone to grass then earth so be prepared for mud. The trail through Heywood Wood goes past the remains of a motte and bailey, which can be accessed via steps.

Starting point & parking

The small car park on the eastern edge of **Heywood Wood** at grid reference SS 672119. From Eggesford Station (on the A377 halfway between Exeter and Barnstaple) take the road signposted 'Wembworthy, Winkleigh' and shortly turn right (same sign). After climbing for 1 mile, on a sharp left-hand bend, turn right signposted 'Bridge Reeve'. Go past the Wembworthy Outdoor Centre then after ¹/₂ mile you will come to a small car parking area, off the road to the left.

On your bikes!

1. From the car park, return to the minor lane, turn right, then shortly after passing Eggesford Farm on your left, turn right downhill onto a wide forestry track (signposted 'Footpath'). Shortly, bear left onto a narrower track, marked with a red-banded round wooden post.

2. At a T-junction by a wooden barrier with a wider track, turn right. Follow this main track in the same direction, crossing a minor road onto the wide stone track opposite.

3. Follow the main track as it curves around the humped remains of the motte and bailey to return to the car park.

Category
Forestry trail (mountain bikes recommended).

Distance
3 miles.

Station: Eggesford.

TIC: Exeter, 01392 665700.

Other nearby trails: The Tarka Trail starts in Meeth, 12 miles to the west. Granite Way, Okehampton.

Useful publications & websites: OS Landranger Maps 180 & 191. For further information contact Forest Enterprise, Peninsula Forest District, Bullers Hill, Kennford, Exeter, Devon EX6 7XR (01392 832262) or visit *www.forestry.gov.uk* and enter 'Eggesford' in the search bar. For a map, go to *www.enjoyeggesford.co.uk/map.htm*

Refreshments: At Eggesford Garden Centre.

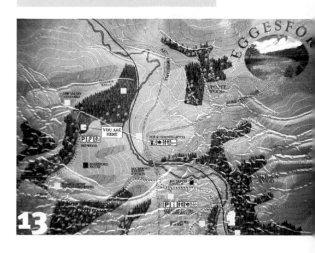

Ride 14   Dunster Woods south of Minehead (3 routes)

Category
Woodland trails.

Distance
From 1- to 9-mile circuits.

There are three waymarked trails in the forestry to the south of Dunster. One is described as a Family Route and is a relatively flat circuit; a second, more intermediate route involves a lot more climbing but is on good broad stone-based forest roads, which will not deteriorate in the winter months. The third (Explorer) is a tougher challenge. It would be easy to combine Dunster Woods with a trip to Dunster Castle or a journey on the steam railway that runs between Minehead and Bishops Lydeard.

Grade	Distance	Waymarks	Starting point
Family	1 mile	Green	Nutcombe Bottom Car Park
Intermediate	6 miles	Orange	Nutcombe Upper Car Park
Explorer	9 miles	Brown	Nutcombe Bottom Car Park

Starting point for Family & Explorer Routes:
From Dunster take the A396 towards Tiverton. Less than a mile after the end of the village (and shortly after crossing a bridge over the River Avill), take the next lane to the left. **Nutcombe Bottom Car Park** is on the left, about 3/4 mile up this steep and narrow lane (grid reference SS 978424).

Starting point for Intermediate Route:
Nutcombe Upper Car Park (grid reference SS 974420) is about 3/4 mile up the hill, on the right, from the Nutcombe Bottom Car Park. Just as the gradient starts to ease, opposite a 'Dunster Woods Mountain Biking' signpost, turn sharp right onto a broad track into the car park.

On your bikes! The Family Route
Exit Nutcombe Bottom Car Park, cross the road onto the track opposite and turn right following the green arrows, climbing steadily. **Ignore** the first major track to the left. Continue straight ahead at this point but keep bearing left and look out for the green arrow pointing you left onto a grassier track. Rejoin the outward route and return to the car park.

Station: Taunton or Tiverton Parkway.

TIC: Minehead, 01643 702624.

Other nearby trails: The towpath of the Grand Western Canal, near Tiverton.

Useful publications & websites: OS Landranger Map 181 or OS Explorer Map OL9. Leaflet called 'Exmoor: Bike it / Dunster Woods' available from *www.nationalparks. gov.uk/exshop* and click on 'Cycling leaflets'. See also *www.everythingexmoor.org.uk*, search 'Cycling' then click on 'Dunster Forest'.

Refreshments: Lots of choice in Dunster.

Haldon Forest Ride 15
south-west of Exeter

There are three options for cycling in Haldon Forest – the Family Trail and the Adventure Trail are both 3-mile waymarked circuits that are fairly easy explorations of the tracks near to the visitor centre. The third option is the Freeride area where there is a chance for more skilful mountain bikers to practise their skills.

Starting point & parking
Haldon Forest Park

From Exeter follow the A38 towards Plymouth. Turn off for the racecourse and Dunchideock, then follow signs for 'Haldon Forest' and 'Gateway' (grid ref SX 883847).

On your bikes!
Family Trail

Pick up the 'Family Cycle Trail' signs from near the visitor centre. The trail runs gently downhill for about 1.3 miles on a broad forest track before a sharp left turn and a steep climb on a narrower track. The trail then undulates with more ups and downs and twisty sections.

Adventure Trail

Oddly, this is probably easier than the Family Trail as there is less climbing. The trail is a bit narrower with a lot more twists and turns.

> **Station:** Exeter.
>
> **TIC:** Exeter, 01392 665700.
>
> **Other nearby trails:** Exe Valley through Exeter.
>
> **Useful publications & websites:** OS Landranger Map 192. Visit *www.forestry.gov. uk/haldonforestpark* or *www.haldonfreeride. org/index.php*
>
> **Refreshments:** None on route. The nearest pub is at Kennford, 3 miles to the north-east.

Category
Waymarked forest trails.

Distance
Two 3-mile circuits.

Exeter Ride 16
along the River Exe

A traffic-free route starts in the very heart of Exeter, and follows a combination of the River Exe and the Exe Canal down past the Double Locks Inn to the wide expanse of the Exe Estuary at Turf Locks. The River Exe and its tributary, the River Culm, drain much of Exmoor and the Blackdown Hills, making Exeter prone

to flooding: weirs and defence works have reduced the risk, creating at times a bewildering amount of water channels and possible paths to follow. All paths lead south to Turf Locks! The section through the town centre passes the attractive marina where brightly coloured dinghies tack and jibe. Further south there is an option of

Category
Riverside path and specially-built cyclepath.

Distance
7 miles each way.

33

Ride 16   Exeter, along the River Exe

following the river or the canal, the latter passing the popular Double Locks Inn. Beyond the major road bridge the cyclepath drops down onto a tarmac path parallel with the towpath as far as the Turf Locks.

Starting point & parking

Station Road car park, Exeter, just across the river from St David's railway station, off the Cowley Bridge Road (the A377 on the north-west side of Exeter).

On your bikes!

1. From the car park off Station Road, follow signs for 'Exe Bridges, City Centre'. The route passes beneath a railway bridge then rejoins the river. Keep the river to your left.

2. At the start of the canal (just past the Maritime Museum) you have a choice of

following a route through the Riverside Valley Park or alongside the canal. The canal route will take you past the Double Locks Inn.

3. Both routes rejoin at Bridge Road (A379) where there is a pelican crossing to enable you to follow the canal towpath further south.

4. The path drops down onto a wide tarmac path parallel with and below the canal towpath. Continue on under the M5 bridge to the Turf Inn. Retrace your steps.

Station: Exeter St David's.

TIC: Exeter, 01392 665700.

Other nearby trails: Exmouth to Budleigh Salterton. There are waymarked trails in Haldon Forest, south-west of Exeter.

Useful publications & websites: OS Landranger Map 192. A leaflet called *Exeter Cycle Guide* and a map is available from the Tourist Information Centre (01392 665700). This is also available online at *www.devon. gov.uk/exetcycleguideleaflet.pdf*. Try also *www.devon.gov.uk/cycling* and *www. cycleexeter.org.uk*.

Refreshments: Lots of choice in Exeter. The Double Locks Inn, halfway between the city centre and Bridge Road (the A379). Turf Inn, at the end of the canal where it joins the Exe estuary (south-east of Exminster).

Ride 17   Grand Western Canal east of Tiverton

Category
Canal towpath.

Distance
12 miles each way.

Built between 1810 and 1814, this section of the Grand Western Canal was part of a grand coast-to-coast scheme to link Exeter (and the River Exe) to Bridgwater (and the River Parrett), thus enabling ships and their cargoes to avoid the treacherous Cornish coast. The scheme was never fully realised and this is one of the fragments that remain. It runs between Tiverton and Whipcott in mid-Devon. The

Grand Western Canal, east of Tiverton Ride **17**

towpath has been brought up to a uniform standard along its whole length. At the eastern end the water is amazingly clear, fed by underground springs. In the distance there are views of the patchwork of red earth fields and green pastures so characteristic of Devon.

Starting point & parking

The Grand Western Canal Visitor Centre, **Tiverton** (grid reference SS 963123). From the A361 North Devon Link Road follow the A396 towards the centre of Tiverton for 1¹/₂ miles. At a sign for 'Police Station, Butterleigh, Grand Western Canal' turn left onto Old Road (leading to Canal Hill). Keep following the brown signs for 'Grand Western Canal'. Start climbing the hill, ignore 'The Avenue' to the left and take the next left signposted 'Grand Western Canal'. Park here and go to the end of the car park to join the towpath.

On your bikes!

From the end of the Grand Western Canal car park bear right onto the towpath. Follow the towpath for up to 12 miles,

stopping for refreshments at any of the places signposted from the canal: Halberton, Sampford Peverell, Burlescombe or Holcombe Rogus.

> **Station:** Tiverton.
>
> **TIC:** Exeter, 01392 665700.
>
> **Other nearby trails:** The Bridgwater & Taunton Canal.
>
> **Useful publications & websites:** OS Landranger Map 181. See also *www.devon. gov.uk/grand_western_canal.htm*. Map download available.
>
> **Refreshments:** Lots of choice in Tiverton. Tea shop at the start of the ride (at the end of the car park). Pubs in Halberton and Sampford Peverell just off the route.

NB The towpath under almost all the bridges is very narrow so take great care at these points. Give plenty of warning to walkers with a 'Hello', a ring of your bell, a whistle or start talking loudly amongst yourselves!

Exmouth to Ride **18**
Budleigh Salterton

Starting conveniently from Phear Park in the centre of the seaside town of Exmouth, this ride heads east along the course of the railway path towards Budleigh Salterton. The trail climbs gradually up through woodland on a good-quality path, then drops down towards

Knowle. If you wish to visit the attractive seaside town of Budleigh Salterton you will need to use a map to work out the combination of quiet lanes and residential streets to reach the shops, cafés and pubs. If it is a hot summer's day and a swim in the sea beckons, there is an excellent

Category
Railway path.

Distance
4 miles each way.

beach at Sandy Bay, to the south-east of Exmouth.

Starting point & parking

The free car park in Phear Park (grid reference SY 007816) to the north-east of the centre of **Exmouth**. If approaching from the north on the A376 you should turn left off the Exeter Road onto Gipsy Lane before reaching the town centre. Gipsy Lane comes shortly after Hulham Road (also on the left).

On your bikes!

1. Return past the café in Phear Park, go over the bumps and exit the park through the opening with bollards and eagle-topped stone pillars. Turn left on the pavement up Marlpool Hill and shortly, take first left signposted 'Littleham Cycle Route' then follow signs for Budleigh Salterton.

2. (On to Budleigh Salterton by road.) At the T-junction with the minor lane (Bear Lane), at the end of the traffic-free trail, turn right then at the next T-junction (with the busier B3178) turn left then right onto Bedlands Lane. At the T-junction at the end of Bedlands Lane, turn right and follow the road around to the left.

3. At the T-junction at the end of Moor Lane turn right and follow this downhill into the centre of Budleigh Salterton. If you wish to visit the beach, turn left at the traffic lights along the High Street for $^1/_4$ mile. From wherever you choose to finish the outward ride, retrace your steps back to Exmouth via Station Road – Moor Lane – Bedlands Lane – Bear Lane – cyclepath – Phear Park.

Station: Exmouth.

TIC: Exmouth, 01395 222299.

Other nearby trails: Exe Valley through Exeter.

Useful publications & websites: OS Landranger Map 192. Try also *www.devon. gov.uk/cycling-maps-exmouth.pdf* or go to *www.cornwall-devon.com* and click on 'Things to do' then 'Cycling' to get to 'Cycling Routes'.

Refreshments: There is a café in Phear Park in Exmouth. There is plenty of choice in Budleigh Salterton beyond the end of the railway path.

Ride **19** **Bridgwater & Taunton Canal**

Category
Canal towpath.

Distance
15 miles each way.

Forming part of Sustrans' West Country Way, which runs from Padstow to Bristol, the fine stone and gravel towpath of the Bridgwater & Taunton Canal runs along the western edge of the Somerset Levels and links the two historic Somerset towns of Bridgwater and Taunton. There is plenty of wildfowl to be seen on the water and there is also a series of stone sculptures of the planets set back in the hedgerows. The route starts from Town Bridge, Bridgwater and passes through Huntworth, North Newton, Creech St Michael and Bathpool to reach the County Cricket Ground in Taunton. There are short road sections from the centres of Bridgwater and Taunton to the start of the towpath, and a short stretch on quiet lanes in the middle of the ride.

Starting points & parking

1. From **Bridgwater**, the West Country Way (National Cycle Network Route 3), which includes the canal towpath, is signposted from Town Bridge in the centre of Bridgwater (grid reference ST 302368).

2. You may prefer to join the towpath on the outskirts of town at the Boat & Anchor pub, **Huntworth**, just north of the M5 Jct 24 (grid reference ST 313350).

3. From **Taunton**, the ride starts from Coal Orchard car park, right next to Somerset County Cricket Ground in the centre of town, near to the junction of Bridge Street with St James Street (grid reference 227248).

Station: Taunton or Bridgwater.

TIC: Taunton, 01823 336344 or Bridgwater, 01278 436438.

Other nearby trails: The Willow Walk to the west of Glastonbury.

Useful publications & websites: OS Landranger Maps 182 & 193. Try *www.somerset.gov.uk* and search 'Cycle Routes'.

Refreshments: Lots of choice in Taunton and Bridgwater. There are pubs at Huntworth, Creech St Michael and North Newton. Café at Lower Maunsel Lock.

Willow Walk   Ride **20**
west of Glastonbury

This ride runs through a lovely nature reserve full of swans and other wildfowl. There are glimpses of dark, rich peat fields – characteristic of the Somerset Levels – the wildflowers are prolific, and there is a real indication of how the area would return to dense and impenetrable vegetation if left to its own devices for a few decades. The ride starts from the Peat Moors Visitor Centre, which has recreated some of the wooden huts that people used to live in a few thousand years ago. At the other end of the ride it is easy to go right into the heart of the mystical town of Glastonbury on relatively quiet roads. There is a short road section from the car park at the start to the beginning of the trail. There are two

Category
Railway path.

Distance
5 miles each way.

Ride **20** **Willow Walk, west of Glastonbury**

½-mile road sections close to Glastonbury. These can be avoided if you turn around at the end of the traffic-free section.

Starting point & parking

The Peat Moors Visitor Centre, west of Glastonbury. This is located on the minor road between the B3151 at Westhay and the A39 near to Ashcott (grid reference ST 426415).

On your bikes!

1. Exit the Peat Moors Visitor Centre car park and turn left along the lane. **Ignore** the first track to the left. Cross the bridge over the drainage channel and turn immediately left into Shapwick Heath Nature Reserve.

2. Follow for 3½ miles to the end of the traffic-free section (grid reference ST 472392); then if you wish to visit Glastonbury, keep following signs for

National Cycle Network Route 3 and Glastonbury town centre for 2 miles on a mix of quiet lanes and a short section of traffic-free trail to emerge in Market Place at the end of Benedict Street.

3. (Start / return from the centre of Glastonbury.) Follow Benedict Street, a continuation of the High Street, to cross the A39 bypass via the toucan crossing. Go past Bradfords Building Suppliers and take the first lane to the right after Snows Timber Yard. Shortly turn left following signs for the Peat Moors Visitor Centre via Nature Reserve.

4. Easy to miss: about 2 miles from Glastonbury, and shortly after passing a peat business on the right, leave the road (and also leave National Cycle Network Route 3) and turn right onto the broad stone track through the nature reserve.

Station: Bridgwater.

TIC: Glastonbury, 01458 832954.

Other nearby trails: Bridgwater & Taunton Canal.

Useful publications & websites: OS Landranger Map 182. Visit *www.isleofavalon. co.uk/avalon-moors.html*

Refreshments: The Railway Inn, about halfway along the route. Lots of choice in Glastonbury.

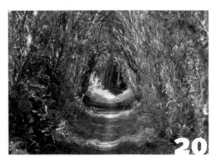

Strawberry Line Ride 21
Yatton to Axbridge and Cheddar

The Strawberry Line gets its name from the fields of strawberries planted around Axbridge and Cheddar on the sunny south side of the Mendips, which have traditionally produced some of the country's finest strawberries. The railway ran for almost a century between 1869 and 1965. The wooded hills of the Mendips form a fine backdrop to the ride as you cycle south from Yatton. The ride passes through a mix of arable land, pasture and cider orchards, climbing to a highpoint near Winscombe and the Shute Shelve Tunnel, where the lights along the trail switch on magically as you pass through. The route into Axbridge itself will involve some time spent on road but it makes an attractive destination with many fine timbered houses.

Starting points & parking

1. Yatton Station car park (grid reference ST 425660).

2. Winscombe recreation ground (grid reference ST 420574).

3. King John's Hunting Lodge, **Axbridge** (grid reference ST 431546).

4. Valley Line Industrial Park on the west side of **Cheddar** (grid reference ST 450534).

On your bikes!

1. From Yatton station follow the railway path south for just over 1 mile. The trail bears right away from the line of the old railway and crosses a bridge over the River Yeo. At the T-junction with the A370, turn left along the shared-use pavement then cross via the toucan crossing onto a continuation of the trail.

2. After 3 miles there is a second road section near to the cider orchards. Turn

left uphill on the lane and keep an eye out after $^1/_2$ mile for a right turn onto a track.

3. Cross the A368 via a toucan crossing and follow the railway path past Winscombe and through the tunnel.

4. Shortly after the tunnel you may wish to turn around at the junction with the A38 as there are more road sections after this point. To continue to Axbridge, cross the A38 via the traffic island and bear to the right of the small car park, descending on a lane and following National Cycle Network Route 26 signs into the centre of Axbridge.

5. Another traffic-free section starts at the junction of the road through Axbridge with the A371 and finishes on the edge of Cheddar at the Valley Line Industrial Park.

Category
Railway path.

Distance
9 miles each way.

Station: Yatton.

TIC: Cheddar, 01934 744071 or Axbridge, 01934 750833.

Other nearby trails: Willow Walk near Glastonbury. Bridgwater & Taunton Canal.

Useful publications & websites: OS Landranger Map 182. A Strawberry Line leaflet is available from *www.sustrans.org.uk*. See also *www.thestrawberryline.co.uk*

Refreshments: Sousta pub on the A370 west of Congresbury. Pubs just off the route in Winscombe. Lots of choice in Axbridge.

Ride 22 Colliers Way from Radstock to Midsomer Norton, Shoscombe Vale & Frome

22

Category
Railway paths.

Distance
Radstock to
Midsomer Norton:
2 miles each way.

Radstock to
Shoscombe Vale:
2 miles each way.

Radstock to
Frome:
6 miles each way.

Known as the Colliers Way, indicating the area's connection with coal mining, the trail uses two old railways – one between Midsomer Norton and Shoscombe Vale, the other between Radstock and Frome – offering some wonderful, easy cycling on good-quality surfaces with views out over the gently rolling countryside to both sides. There are many boulders placed along the course of the trail with plaques showing the names of apple varieties. The old iron tracks of the railway to Great Elm are still in place, now overgrown with brambles and trees. There are signs indicating where to leave the trail for refreshments at Kilmersdon, Vobster and Mells. If you are prepared to use some lanes and tackle the odd hill, the Colliers Way can be followed right into Frome to the south-east and to Wellow, Midford and Dundas Aqueduct to the north-east.

Starting points & parking

1. Car park at Tom Huyton children's play park on the north side of the A362 just west of the centre of **Radstock,** near the Co-op (grid reference ST 688550).

2. For the trail from Radstock to Frome there is a car park in Radstock closer to the start of the traffic-free section on **Fortescue Road,** just past the library on the right. Fortescue Road lies off the A367 Shepton Mallet Road, immediately south of its junction with the A362 (grid reference ST 689547). Turn right out of the car park then left onto Meadow View to join the railway path.

3. Great Elm, 2 miles north-west of Frome (grid reference ST 752498).

NB There is no parking here, at the eastern end of the trail.

On your bikes!

From the Radstock start there are three options:

1. Access the trail and turn left (west) to Midsomer Norton. The trail ends somewhat abruptly after 2 miles on the B3355 (grid reference ST 658548).

2. Access the trail and turn right (east) to Shoscombe Vale. Shortly, at the junction with the road by the tall wheel / mining sculpture, continue straight ahead on Waterloo Road for almost 1/2 mile. Just before the start of the hill turn right onto the railway path for 1 1/2 miles as far as Shoscombe Vale.

3. As per (**2**) above but keep an eye out for a signpost on the 'green' indicating that National Cycle Network (NCN) Route 24 goes right. Follow NCN 24 signs

22

Colliers Way from Radstock to Midsomer Norton, Shoscombe Vale & Frome Ride **22**

carefully, crossing roads and dismounting as necessary to arrive at Victoria Hall / the Public Library. Turn left, go past the church and primary school, and shortly turn left onto Meadow View following signs for Kilmersdon and Frome. Follow the railway path for 5½ miles to its end at the minor road in Great Elm (grid reference ST 752498).

Station: Frome or Freshford.

TIC: Frome, 01373 467271.

Other nearby trails: Kennet & Avon Canal between Bath and Bradford on Avon.

Useful publications & websites: OS Landranger Maps 172 and 183. A Colliers Way leaflet can be downloaded from *www.sustrans.org.uk*. See also *www.colliersway.co.uk*

Refreshments: Lots of choice in Radstock. Pubs off the route in Kilmersdon, Vobster and Mells.

23

Severn Bridge Cyclepath Ride 23

The first Severn Bridge, opened in 1967, saw its traffic flows slashed with the opening of the Second Severn Crossing, a few miles further south. As a result, as you cycle high above the swirling brown waters of the River Severn, you are more aware of a sense of space and height than noise and traffic fumes. There are cycleways on both the north and south sides of the bridge, climbing to a highpoint in the middle. At the Chepstow end these are connected via a conveniently located subway. At the Gloucestershire end it is a bit more complicated! This is a ride best undertaken on a bright sunny day when the wind is not too strong: what may be a gentle breeze elsewhere can be funnelled by the shape of the Severn Estuary into a strong and gusty crosswind.

Starting points & parking

1. (English side, **near Aust.**) Follow the M4 / M48 towards Chepstow. At Jct 1, just before the old Severn Bridge, turn left on the A403 towards Avonmouth then first right towards 'St Augustine's Vineyard, Severn Bridge Maintenance Department'. Park along this minor road (grid reference ST 569891).

2. (Welsh side.) On the **south-west edge of Chepstow.** There is a long layby with parking on the east side of the A466, just north of M48, Jct 2. Follow the cyclepath parallel with the A466 towards the Severn Bridge. **Take care** crossing the road at the roundabout. Go to Instruction **4.**

Category
Cyclepath on motorway bridge.

Distance
8-mile circuit using cyclepaths on both sides of the bridge.

41

Ride **23** **Severn Bridge Cyclepath**

23

On your bikes!

1. (Start from Aust.) Climb on the minor road that leads towards Old Passage and take the first right, signposted 'No entry except access. Bridge Maintenance Unit'. After 200yds take the first left signposted 'National Cycle Network Route 4'.

2. Cross the bridge on the cyclepath running along its south side and follow the track downhill away from the motorway.

3. At the T-junction turn right through the subway under the M48 signposted 'Caldicot, Usk', then at the end of the tunnel turn left uphill and sharp left* at the top.

* or if you have started from Chepstow turn right at this point to return to the A466.

4. Cross the bridge on the cyclepath along its north side. Go past the toll booths and under the footbridge. Descend to the roundabout by Aust Services then turn sharp left uphill (use the pavement / concrete track parallel to the road). Keep bearing left.

5. Go past the services following 'Lodge' signs, then turn left opposite the fuel station and go down the steps that lead to the bridge running across the top of the toll booths, signposted 'Aust, Chepstow'. At the other side of the bridge turn left** signposted 'Aust', then shortly at the T-junction turn right to return to the start.

** or if you have started from Chepstow turn right here and join Instruction 2.

> **Station:** Chepstow or Severn Beach (via Bristol).
>
> **TIC:** Chepstow, 01291 623772.
>
> **Other nearby trails:** Forest of Dean, Gloucester & Sharpness Canal.
>
> **Useful publications:** OS Landranger Map 172.
>
> **Refreshments:** Aust Services. Lots of choice in Chepstow.

Ride **24** # **Bristol to Pill Riverside Path**

24

Category
Riverside path.

Distance
6$\frac{1}{2}$ miles each way.

Explore the broad riverside path running beneath the Clifton Suspension Bridge, one of Isambard Kingdom Brunel's finest creations. The path runs along the bottom of the gorge. The tidal rise and fall of the Bristol Channel is one of the highest in the world, so do not be surprised to see the river flowing strongly in the wrong direction! The path can easily be linked to the trails in Leigh Woods above the gorge or via quiet lanes to form a circuit returning to Bristol via Ashton Court.

Starting points & parking

1. The Industrial Museum in **Bristol** city centre (grid reference ST 586723).

2. Leigh Woods. Cross the Clifton Suspension Bridge away from Clifton Village then take the first right on to North Road. Follow this for $\frac{1}{2}$ mile then just after the third turning on the left, the traffic-free trail starts by wooden barriers to the right signposted 'National Cycle Network Route 41' (grid reference ST 555731).

On your bikes!

From Bristol city centre

1. With your back to the Industrial Museum, turn left and follow the docks with the water to your right. After 700yds, opposite a curved grey metal dockside crane, turn left between black and white barriers to cross the railway lines to your left and follow the wide path at the base of a high wall. Pass beneath a road bridge and bear right on the cobbled riverside path.

2. Shortly after passing huge red-brick buildings on your right, turn left to cross the grey steel bridge over the river then turn right along the stone and gravel riverside path for a further 4 miles to Ham Green (Pill).

3. The trail climbs and joins a tarmac lane. At the T-junction at the top of Chapel Pill Lane, bear right onto the gravel path across the 'green'. At the far end jink right then left onto Watchhouse Hill and descend on the cyclepath to Pill, emerging near a red-brick railway bridge and the creek.

From Leigh Woods

A. From the Leigh Woods starting point described left, the trail starts with a short, steep climb into woodland. Shortly, at a T-junction near a house, turn right then left following the blue-handed posts and 'NCN 41' signs. After 200yds turn left through a gap in the wall, following signs.

B. At the T-junction with tarmac by a line of copper beeches, turn right. Continue in the same direction as tarmac turns to stone track and descends steeply.

C. Easy to miss: after ¾ mile keep an eye out for a right turn off this broad stone track signposted 'NCN 41'. This will drop you down via a narrow stone path onto the wider riverside path. Turn left for Pill, right for Bristol. If you plan to return to Clifton via Leigh Woods, remember this junction with the riverside path for the return route.

Station: Temple Meads, Bristol.

TIC: Bristol, 0906 711 2191 (premium rate).

Other nearby trails: The Bristol & Bath Railway Path starts from the other side of the city from Midland Road. The Kennet & Avon Canal runs from Bath east towards Devizes.

Useful publications & websites: OS Landranger Map 172. Several free cycle maps cover Bristol and the surrounding area. Contact Life Cycle UK, The CREATE Centre, Smeaton Road, Bristol BS1 6XN (0117 353 4580) or email: post@lifecycleuk.org.uk. Website: *www.lifecycleuk.org.uk* and go to 'Maps & info' then 'Resource centre' then 'Maps & guides'.

Refreshments: Lots of choice in Bristol city centre. Café at the CREATE Centre. Pubs in Pill, at the end of the path.

Ride 25 Forest of Dean Family Cycle Trail east of Coleford

25

Category
Railway path and forestry tracks.

Distance
9-mile circuit.

The Forest of Dean lies on an area of higher land between the River Severn and River Wye, and provides spectacular views of the borderland of England and Wales. It represents one of the best areas for recreational cycling in the region. A combination of enlightened thinking by the Forestry Commission in their largest holding in the West Country, and co-operation with local authorities and Sustrans, has created an integrated recreational cycling network linking towns with woodland over a large area. The flagship route is the 9-mile Family Cycle Trail which follows disused railway lines for much of its course, providing mostly easy gradients that are ideal for family cycling. There are challenges at all levels in other parts of the forest.

Starting point & parking

Pedalabikeaway Cycle Hire Centre in the centre of the Forest of Dean. This lies just north of the crossroads of the B4226 and B4234 **between Cinderford and Coleford**, about 15 miles south-west of Gloucester (grid reference SO 608124).

On your bikes!

1. Facing the Pedalabikeaway Cycle Centre go to the right past the Cannop Colliery

signpost to join the yellow 'tyre track' bike trail waymarks. Descend, cross the road with care onto the path opposite, go up a short steep climb and turn left. Shortly, at a T-junction by a tall wooden signpost, turn left again signposted 'Drybrook Road Station'.

2. Keep following the yellow tyre track signs in the direction of Drybrook. At a fork, with Lydbrook signposted left, bear right to Drybrook. Long, steady climb up to Drybrook Road Station. Shortly after passing Lightmoor Colliery ruins there is a short, steep climb, then turn left on a long descent. Go past Spruce Ride and Central Bridge.

3. Follow signs for Cannop Wharf and Cycle Centre, at one point turning right where 'Mallards Pike' is signposted straight ahead.

4. After ¹/₂ mile, cross a road then after a further ¹/₂ mile descend steeply from Three Brothers to Cannop Wharf. At the T-junction at the bottom, turn right for the Cycle Centre. The route runs briefly along a road near to Cannop Ponds then bears off right, soon returning to the Cycle Centre.

Station: Lydney.

TIC: Monmouth 01600 713899.

Other nearby trails: Coleford to Parkend. Sharpness & Gloucester Canal. Severn Bridge Cyclepath.

Useful publications & websites: OS Landranger Map 162 or better still OS Explorer Map OL 14. Try the following websites: *www. forestry.gov.uk* and search 'Forest of Dean' *www.active.visitforestofdean.co.uk*

Refreshments: At the Cycle Centre. Otherwise you will need to use a map to find your way to the various pubs located in the villages nearest to the cycle trail. There is an ice-cream van near Cannop Ponds at busy times.

Coleford to Parkend & Cannop Wharf Ride 26
Forest of Dean

A 5-mile traffic-free trail leads from Coleford to join the Forest of Dean Family Cycle Trail, running through woodland, between rock cuttings and past the ruins of Darkhill Ironworks, a reminder of the industrial past of the area. Be warned that it is almost all downhill from Coleford to Parkend so almost all uphill on the way back. Starting and finishing at Coleford, together with the Family Cycle Trail, would form a lollipop-shape ride, 19 miles in length.

Starting point & parking

The Railway Museum in the main central car park in **Coleford** (grid reference SO 577105). Coleford lies 15 miles south-west of Gloucester.

On your bikes!

1. From the Railway Museum you will see a bike route signpost with 'Milkwall, Parkend' on it. Cross the road with care and follow the obvious cyclepath now signposted 'Parkend'.

2. After a short climb, descend to cross the road then continue downhill past the ruins of Darkhill Ironworks. At the next road go straight ahead and continue in the same direction through a rock cutting following signs for 'Parkend' then 'Cannop Wharf'.

3. Follow a cyclepath parallel to the road, then turn left along Hughes Terrace for a brief lane section. Cross the busy B4234, go past Coleford Junction and, if you wish, join the Family Cycle Trail at Cannop Wharf. Remember this point if you do the family circuit for your return to Coleford.

Station: Lydney.

TIC: Monmouth 01600 713899.

Other nearby trails: Forest of Dean Family Cycle Trail, Severn Bridge Cyclepath.

Useful publications & websites: OS Landranger Map 162 or better still OS Explorer Map OL 14. Visit *www.forestry.gov. uk* and search 'Forest of Dean' or *www. active.visitforestofdean.co.uk* or *www. visitforestofdean.co.uk*

Refreshments: Lots of choice in Coleford. Otherwise you will need to use a map to find your way to the various pubs in the villages nearest to the cycle trail. There is an ice-cream van near Cannop Ponds at busy times.

Category
Railway path.

Distance
5 miles each way.

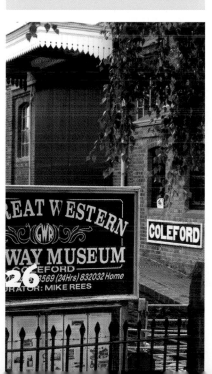

Ride 27 Gloucester & Sharpness Canal from Saul to Sharpness

27

Category
Canal towpath.
Mountain bikes
recommended.

Distance
8 miles each way.

The Gloucester & Sharpness Canal performs the curious function of joining the River Severn to ... the River Severn! The tidal rise and fall of the Bristol Channel and the Severn Estuary is one of the highest in the world and makes navigation up the River Severn to Gloucester very tricky. The canal was opened in 1817 and at the time it was the broadest and deepest canal in the world. The towpath is of varying standard: the section which is undoubtedly the jewel in the crown is the 2-mile stretch south of Frampton on Severn to Shepherd's Patch (near Slimbridge), which forms part of the National Cycle Network Route 41, on its way from Gloucester to the old Severn Bridge. Here the surface is excellent. Either side of this section the towpath is more grass and earth: mountain bikes with wide tyres to absorb the bumps are highly recommended. There are long-term plans to improve the quality of the whole towpath. The route described here runs from Saul (near Frampton on Severn) to Sharpness. North of Saul towards Gloucester the towpath is a lot rougher.

Starting point & parking

The car park by Wycliffe College Rowing Club in **Saul**, on the Gloucester & Sharpness Canal, about 7 miles south-west of Gloucester. Leave the M5 at Jct 13, follow the A419 / A38 / B4071 into Frampton on Severn. Just before the Bell pub turn right onto Whitminster Lane, signposted 'Whitminster'. At the end of the houses, turn left signposted 'NCN Route 41' then immediately after crossing the canal, turn right. Park at the far end of the large car park (grid reference SO 754090).

On your bikes!

1. From the car park by Wycliffe College Rowing Club, follow the tarmac lane alongside the canal (with the water to your left). Cross the road at Sandfield Bridge onto the towpath straight ahead. The track is good as far as Fretherne Bridge then soon becomes grassy for less than a mile.

2. At Splatt Bridge, at the southern end of Frampton on Severn, the quality of the towpath improves dramatically: the next 2-mile section, as far as Patch Bridge, forms part of NCN Route 41.

3. At Patch Bridge you may wish to retrace your steps, as the track becomes grassy once again as it heads west to Sharpness. The Tudor Arms pub and Black Shed Cafe are located on the other side of the bridge. You have two other options: **(a)** continue along the towpath through Purton as far as the marina in Sharpness (the most interesting section is the 2-mile stretch from Purton to Sharpness with wide views of the Severn Estuary); **(b)** return to the start by following the quiet road through the attractive village of Frampton on Severn. To do this, leave the canal towpath at Splatt Bridge.

From the start in Saul you can also follow the towpath north-east for 7 miles towards Hempsted Bridge and Gloucester. There are several rough sections on this stretch.

Station: Cam & Dursley.

TIC: Gloucester, 01452 396572.

Other nearby trails: The Stroud Valleys Cycle Trail, Bristol & Bath Railway Path, Forest of Dean.

Useful publications & websites: OS Landranger Map 162. Visit *www.waterscape. com/canals-and-rivers/gloucester-and-sharpness-canal/cycling.* Also try *www.gloucestershire.gov.uk* and follow links through 'Travel and Transport' to 'Private Transport' to 'Cycling in Gloucestershire'.
www.gloucester.gov.uk/VisitGloucester/ TravelInformation/cycle.aspx

Refreshments: The Stables Café at Saul (by the canal). The Bell Inn and the Three Horseshoes pub in Frampton on Severn. The Tudor Arms pub, Black Shed Café at Shepherd's Patch.

Stroud Valleys Cycle Trail Ride **28**
from Stroud to Nailsworth

This attractive, largely wooded ride follows a disused railway along the bottom of the Stroud Valley, passing close to many of the settlements that grew up in the late Middle Ages as the valley became the centre of a flourishing cloth trade. Although the path extends further west, from Dudbridge to Stonehouse, it runs at this stage alongside the busy bypass and can hardly be deemed a recreational route. By contrast, the course of the route from Nailsworth west to Dudbridge appears to be one of those secret hidden passages tucked between

the edge of the built-up areas and the surrounding countryside.

Category
Railway path.

Distance
4 miles each way.

47

Ride **28**   **Stroud Valleys Cycle Trail from Stroud to Nailsworth**

Starting points & parking

1. Near Egypt Mill, **Nailsworth.** From the roundabout by the clocktower in the centre of Nailsworth take Bridge Street (the A46) towards Stroud and Woodchester. Shortly, turn first right signposted 'Egypt Mill'. Go past the entrance to Egypt Mill and the fire station, and follow this road to the end for the small car park (grid reference ST 850999).

2. The Bell Hotel in the centre of **Stroud**, near the railway station and the roundabout at the junction of the A46 and the A419. There is a car park on Cheapside (near the railway station) along the no-through-road that leads off the mini-roundabout near the Bell Hotel. Once on your bike, go downhill from The Bell through the subway then uphill past Kwik Fit and the Vet Hospital, following cycle signs for Woodchester (grid reference SO 848050).

3. **Dudbridge**, at the roundabout at the junction of the B4066 and the A419 to the south-west of Stroud, near to the Sainsbury's store (grid reference SO 834045).

On your bikes!

From the start near Egypt Mill in the centre of Nailsworth, follow the railway path towards Stonehouse and Stroud for almost 4 miles, crossing several minor roads. You arrive in Dudbridge immediately after passing through a round concrete tunnel about 20yds long. At this point you have a choice of turning around and returning to Nailsworth, or going into Stroud.

For the Stroud option, come back through the tunnel and at the Millennium Milepost go downhill through the housing estate, crossing a bridge over a stream. Continue in the same direction, cross the A46 using the traffic island, climb the steps opposite (use the wheeling ramp) and follow the railway path to its end. If you wish to go right into the centre of Stroud you will need to use a mixture of cycle lanes, a subway and quiet streets, taking you past the Bell Hotel.

Station: Stonehouse.

TIC: Stroud, 01453 760960.

Other nearby trails: The Gloucester & Sharpness Canal starts at Sharpness, west of Stroud.

Useful publications & websites: OS Landranger Map 162. See also *www. stroudvalleyscyclecampaign.org.uk/cyclemap.htm*

Refreshments: Lots of choice in Stroud and Nailsworth. The Egypt Mill at the Nailsworth end of the ride serves coffees, lunches and teas.

Ride **29**   **Bristol & Bath Railway Path**

Category
Railway path.

Distance
13 miles each way.

One of Sustrans' first railway path trails, the route now carries over a million visitors a year. The flat, tarmac path runs from the heart of Bristol to the outskirts of Bath, running through the (lit) tunnel at Staple Hill, passing old steam trains at Bitton Station and crossing the River Avon on a series of bridges as you approach Bath. In springtime, the broadleaf woodland of Kelston Woods is

Bristol & Bath Railway Path Ride 29

carpeted with bluebells. There are many remarkable sculptures along the way such as a fish standing on its head and a drinking giant.

Starting points & parking

1. From the centre of **Bristol**, there is a signposted link route from Bristol Bridge / Castle Green via Gardiner Haskins to St Philips Road (off Midland Road, near Old Market) where the railway path starts (grid reference ST 600730). The route runs from here to Brassmill Lane Trading Estate on the western edge of Bath, passing through Fishponds, Staple Hill, Warmley, Bitton and Saltford.

2. There is a waymarked link along the riverside path from the centre of **Bath** to the start of the railway path in Brassmills Lane Trading Estate (grid reference ST 722653).

3. The car park at **Bitton** steam railway station on the A431 on the eastern edge of Bristol (grid reference ST 670704).

Station: Bristol Temple Meads or Bath.

TIC: Bristol, 0906 711 2191 or Bath, 0906 711 2000.

Other nearby trails: The Bristol to Pill Riverside Path starts from the Industrial Museum, Bristol. The Kennet & Avon Canal Towpath starts in Bath and runs east towards Reading.

Useful publications & websites: OS Landranger Map 172. Several free cycle maps cover Bristol and the surrounding area. Contact Life Cycle UK, The CREATE Centre, Smeaton Road, Bristol BS1 6XN (0117 353 4580) or email: post@ lifecycleuk.org.uk. Website: *www.lifecycleuk. org.uk* and go to 'Maps & info' then 'Resource centre' then 'Maps & guides'. See also *www. bristolbathrailwaypath.org.uk*

Refreshments: Pubs at Saltford and Warmley. Café at Bitton steam railway station.

Kennet & Avon Canal Ride 30
(1) Bath to Bradford-on-Avon

Linking Bath to Reading (and ultimately, via the River Avon and the River Thames, linking Bristol to London) the Kennet & Avon Canal was completed in 1810 but from the start encountered problems with water supply in the top plateau section where it reaches 474ft at Savernake. It has been much restored in the last 40 years. Large parts of it are used in National Cycle Network Route 4. Keep an eye out for the spectacular viaducts at Avoncliff and Dundas.

Starting points & parking

1. From the **centre of Bath** the canal towpath is reached at Beckford Road by following National Cycle Network Route 4, signposted along the streets from Pulteney Bridge.

Category
Canal towpath.

Distance
9 miles each way.

2. It is also possible (just!) to follow the river from the back of **Bath railway station** to the start of the canal, although this is a fairly bitty route and involves steps.

3. The George pub in **Bathampton**, east of Bath (grid reference ST 777665).

4. Pound Lane car park in **Bradford-on-Avon**, off the B3109 Frome Road (grid reference ST 826604).

Station: Bath or Bradford-on-Avon.

TIC: Bath, 0906 711 2000 or Bradford-on-Avon, 01225 865797.

Other nearby trails: The towpath continues east from Bradford-on-Avon to Devizes. The Bristol & Bath Railway Path runs from the west side of Bath to the east side of Bristol.

Useful publications & websites: OS Landranger Map 172 & 173. A map of the Kennet & Avon Canal is available from *www.sustrans.org.uk/assets/files/leaflets/ KAcycleguide.pdf* or from *www.waterscape. com/media/documents/20589.pdf*

Refreshments: Lots of choice in Bath and Bradford-on-Avon. The George pub at Bathampton. Pub and teashop at Avoncliff.

Ride **31**   **Kennet & Avon Canal (2) Bradford-on-Avon to Devizes**

Category
Canal towpath.

Distance
12 miles each way.

One of the most extraordinary sights on this section of the towpath is the Caen Hill flight of locks: 29 locks in 2 miles make it look like a veritable hill of water, lifting boats up onto the higher section across the chalk downland before the canal drops down to the east to Hungerford and Newbury. The completion of the locks in 1810 signalled the end of the canal project that started in Bradford-on-Avon and Newbury in 1794. This is a pleasant, open stretch of the canal, far less busy than the Bath to Bradford-on-Avon section. There are pubs conveniently situated every few miles along the towpath. Beyond Devizes, National Cycle Network Route 4 follows lanes almost to Newbury where it rejoins the canal towpath.

31

Starting points & parking

1. The Pound Lane car park in **Bradford-on-Avon**, off the B3109 Frome Road (grid reference ST 826604).

2. The Canal Centre in **Devizes** (grid reference SU 005618).

> **Station:** Bradford-on-Avon.
>
> **TIC:** Bradford-on-Avon, 01225 865797.
>
> **Other nearby trails:** The Kennet & Avon Canal can also be followed west to Bath from Bradford-on-Avon.
>
> **Useful publications & websites:** OS Landranger Map 173. Download a map from *www.waterscape.com/media/documents/20589.pdf*
>
> **Refreshments:** Lots of choice in Bradford-on-Avon and Devizes. Canalside pubs at Hilperton, Semington, Seend Cleeve and Sells Green.

32

Chippenham to Calne   Ride 32
Railway Path

The ride links the two handsome Wiltshire towns of Chippenham and Calne via a dismantled railway, neatly avoiding both the busy A4 and the hills either side of the valley formed by the River Marden. The attractive exit from Chippenham runs by the river and through parkland, with a brief zig-zag climb up onto the railway path. A wonderful, new, eccentric-looking bridge carries you safely over the A4 and through a wooded corridor to the outskirts of Calne. There are traces of the old Wiltshire & Berkshire Canal (now disused) alongside the path, which leads right into the heart of Calne – once an important staging post on the A4 from Bristol to London.

Starting points & parking

1. The Olympiad Leisure Centre car park, **Chippenham** (grid reference ST 925737). From the centre of town, follow signs for the railway station up Station Hill. Go past the station and turn right opposite the car park onto Sadlers Mead (by Wiltshire College), signposted 'Olympiad, Golf Course'.

2. The trail starts in **Calne** near to the Lansdowne Strand Hotel. Follow Patford

Category
Railway path.

Distance
6 miles each way.

Ride **32**   **Chippenham to Calne Railway Path**

Street to its end in the park and bear right to join the path that soon crosses the old canal and river (grid reference ST 997710).

On your bikes!

1. From the entrance to the Olympiad car park in Chippenham, turn sharp left through the car park towards the house with green tiles and skylights to go downhill on a tarmac path past trees to the river, and turn left.

2. Keep the river to your right and the golf course to the left. After $^1/_2$ mile, at a crossroads of paths (with a blue metal bridge to your right), turn left for 100yds then right, skirting round the edge of the housing estate.

3. Join Riverside Drive and turn right, keeping the parkland to your right. Follow the road to the end and climb up the zig-zag path onto the railway path. **Remember this point for the return trip**. Turn right to cross the bridge.

4. Follow the railway path for 2 miles. Join a lane and turn left for $^3/_4$ mile. Keep an eye out for a Millennium Milepost and turn left through a small parking area to rejoin the railway path.

5. Follow the path for 3 miles, crossing an interesting bridge over the A4. Go through an ornate metalwork arch, cross the river and the canal, turn right then keep bearing left to emerge on Patford Street in the centre of Calne (the Lansdowne Strand Hotel is just to your left).

Station: Chippenham.

TIC: Chippenham, 01249 665970.

Other nearby trails: Marlborough to Chiseldon Railway Path, Kennet & Avon Canal Towpath (Bath to Devizes).

Useful publications & websites: OS Landranger Map 173. *www.gocalne.org.uk/ travel_options_bike.asp*

Refreshments: Lots of choice in Chippenham and Calne.

Cotswold Water Park south of Cirencester

Ride **33**

The Cotswold Water Park covers an area of 40 square miles with over 140 lakes formed as a result of gravel extraction. The trail marked with a black and white drawing of a bittern is a linear route running alongside some of the many lakes and along the course of a dismantled railway. Some sections will be muddy from late autumn through to spring, and after prolonged rain. If you explore South Cerney in search of refreshments, keep an eye out for a street called 'Bow Wow'! Although waymarked, an Ordnance Survey map and/or the *Cotswold Water Park Access Map* (see right) is highly recommended.

Starting points & parking

1. The car park on the B4696 Spine Road at its junction with the railway path (by a large red-brick bridge) to the **south-east of South Cerney** (grid reference SU 064964).

2. The car park by Waterhay Bridge on the minor road **south-east of Ashton Keynes** (grid reference SU 060933).

On your bikes!

The route is waymarked with black and white bittern signs. It follows a meandering course through the lakes on its southern section and joins the railway path for the northern section at grid reference SU 080949. From this point the railway path can be followed north-west to the edge of South Cerney, or south east to the edge of Cricklade. Both places offer a variety of refreshments.

Station: Kemble.

TIC: Cirencester, 01285 654180.

Other nearby trails: The Stroud Valleys Trail and the Marlborough to Chiseldon Railway Path.

Useful publications and website: OS Landranger Map 163. *www.waterpark.org/general/water_park_map.html*

Refreshments: Three pubs in South Cerney. Lots of choice in Cricklade at the south-east end of the railway path.

Category
Railway path and bridleways.
(Mountain bikes recommended).

Distance
4 miles each way.

Ride 34 Marlborough to Chiseldon south of Swindon

34

Category
Railway path.

Distance
7$\frac{1}{2}$ miles each way.

Marlborough is a handsome town with a wide High Street and many Georgian buildings. The ride starts one mile east of the town centre on the A4 towards Hungerford, and runs through Ogbourne St Andrew and Ogbourne St George (where there is a short section on lanes) to Chiseldon. The railway path uses the course of the old Midland & South Western Junction Railway that used to run between Cheltenham and Southampton. There are fine views of the rolling Marlborough Downs either side of the path.

Starting points & parking

1. Marlborough High Street (grid reference SU 188692).

2. The car park just off the A346 to the south of **Chiseldon**, near M4, Jct 15 (grid reference SU 193793).

On your bikes!

1. From Marlborough's High Street, pass to the left of the imposing town hall then shortly after a left-hand bend turn right onto Silverless Street, signposted 'Ramsbury'. At the crossroads continue straight ahead (same sign).

2. After 750yds, shortly after the 'End of speed limit' and a 'Road narrows' sign, take the next lane to the left signposted 'Rabley, Poulton'. After 150yds and immediately before the bridge, turn right up the gravel access ramp to the railway path and sharp left at the top along the course of the old railway line.

3. After 3$\frac{1}{2}$ miles there is a short section on lanes through Ogbourne St George. Keep following signs for 'National Cycle Network Route 45' and 'Chiseldon'.

Station: Great Bedwyn, 7 miles to the south-east.

TIC: Marlborough, 01672 513989.

Other nearby trails: Chippenham to Calne railway path. The Kennet & Avon Canal towpath can be ridden to the west of Devizes.

Useful publications & websites: OS Landranger Maps 173 & 174. The northern part of the trail is shown on *www.forestweb. org.uk/gwf-leisure.pdf*

Refreshments: Lots of choice in Marlborough. Old Crown Inn, Ogbourne St George.

North Dorset Trailway from Sturminster Newton to Shillingstone

Ride **35**

There are grand plans for the North Dorset Trailway to run as a continuous recreational path along the Stour Valley all the way from Stalbridge to Spetisbury. It uses the course of the old Somerset & Dorset Railway that used to run from Bournemouth to Burnham and was closed in 1966. At present, there are five sections open to the public, four of which are quite short but one of which is over 4 miles long and is described here. The ride from Sturminster Newton to Shillingstone takes you through the rich agricultural countryside of Dorset with views towards the distinctive bulk of Hambledon Hill. Along the way you will pass the old railway station at Shillingstone, which is in the process of being restored to its former glory.

Starting points & parking

1. Station car park on the eastern edge of **Sturminster Newton** (grid reference ST 789142).

2. Holloway Lane, at the western end of **Shillingstone** off the A357 (grid reference ST 834106). There is no parking along the lane. There is a large layby / parking area on the A357 about 1/2 mile east of Holloway Lane, but the A357 is a busy road and not recommended for children.

On your bikes!

The trail is easy to follow and well signposted as the North Dorset Trailway. This section at present runs from the edge of Sturminster Newton to a point just to the east of Shillingstone, but there are plans for it to be extended south-east into Blandford.

Station: None nearby.

TIC: Blandford Forum, 01258 454770.

Other nearby trails: Sika Trail in Wareham Forest, north of Wareham. Castleman Trail, Wimborne. Bournemouth Promenade.

Useful publications & websites: OS Landranger Map 194. Go to *http://www.north-dorset.gov.uk/north_dorset_trailway_leaflet_2009_-2.pdf*

Refreshments: Lots of choice in Sturminster Newton.

Category
Railway path.

Distance
4$\frac{1}{2}$ miles each way.

Ride 36 Sika Trail Wareham Forest

36

Category
Waymarked forest trail.

Distance
7-mile circuit.

This is an easy, undulating ride through the sandy pinewoods and heathland of Wareham Forest. Although there are around 40 waymarked posts along the course of the route, it is still helpful to get hold of a leaflet or download a map as the course of the route can be a bit confusing! It is certainly better on a second and subsequent visits when you remember whether to turn right or left at each junction. The trail is named after Sika deer, which were first introduced from Asia to Britain in the 19th century. Many escaped and formed wild populations like the herd in Wareham Forest today.

Starting point & parking

The Sika Trail car park to the north-west of **Wareham**, on the minor road towards Bere Regis (grid reference SY 906894).

On your bikes!

It will be considerably easier to follow this route if you get hold of a paper copy of the Sika Trail leaflet or at least download the basic map from the website (see below). The route is signposted with numbered posts, which should always be on your right when you pass them. However, there are occasions where the outward and return routes overlap, which can be a bit confusing.

Station: Wareham.

TIC: Wareham, 01929 552740.

Other nearby trails: North Dorset Trailway at Sturminster Newton. Castleman Trail, at Wimborne Minster. Bournemouth Promenade.

Useful publications & websites: OS Landranger Map 195. For more details go to *www.forestry.gov.uk* and search 'Sika Trail'. For a downloadable map go to *www.purbeck.gov.uk* and search 'Sika Trail', following links to get to 'Northport Greenway and Sika Cycle Trail leaflet'.

Refreshments: None on the route; the nearest are in Wareham.

Castleman Trail Ride 37
from Stapehill to Ringwood

This woodland trail runs between Ringwood and Stapehill, partly on purpose-built woodland trails and partly on the course of the old Dorchester to Southampton railway. Because of its twists and turns the railway was nicknamed 'Castleman's Corkscrew' after Charles Castleman, the Wimborne solicitor who was chiefly responsible for the building of the line. There is a chance of diverting off the course of the railway path at its eastern end to explore the trails in Moors Valley Country Park – and the excellent cafe in the visitor centre. Unfortunately there is no safe connection through Wimborne Minster to the other section of the Castleman Trail. You will need to do this as a separate ride from a different starting point (see the next ride).

Starting points & parking

1. Several small car parking areas on Uddens Drive, **Stapehill**, to the east of Wimborne Minster. From the roundabout at the junction of the A31 and B3073 to the west of Wimborne, follow the road towards Stapehill and Ferndown. At the Old Thatch pub, turn left onto Uddens Drive and park on the left at one of several small car parks at or just beyond the signpost at the start of the Castleman Trail (grid reference SU 052008).

2. West Moors Memorial Hall car park, opposite St Mary's Primary School, on the B3072 about ³/₄ mile north of the A31 and just north of the Castleman Trail (grid reference SU 079031).

3. The car park just to the south of the junction of the B3081 with the A31 to the west of **Ringwood** (grid reference SU 139048).

Category
Railway path and forest trails.

Distance
8 miles each way.

Ride **37** **Castleman Trail from Stapehill to Ringwood**

On your bikes!

1. Start from Uddens Drive, Stapehill, at the sign for 'Castleman Trail, Ameysford & Colehill', and follow the track into the woodland. Cross the bridge over the A35 and turn right signposted 'Dodmans Crossing'.

2. After ¹/₂ mile, cross a road following signs for Castleman Trail and Ameysford. There are too many junctions to list but the route is well signposted through woodland.

3. After almost 3 miles, at a junction with a busier road (B3072) in West Moors, turn right (**take care**) for 300yds then left opposite the Tap & Railway pub onto Newcombe Road. After 100yds bear right following Castleman Trail signs through the residential streets to the start of the next traffic-free section.

4. Follow the wooded railway path for almost 4 miles, with one road crossing using a toucan crossing. At the end of this traffic-free section, at the T-junction with the B3081 (near the A31), you may wish to turn around.

5. If you decide to continue to the end of the trail on the edge of Ringwood, turn right on the pavement and cross the next road carefully. Pass through the subway under the A31. Go through the car park (off Hurn Lane) and continue for ³/₄ mile to the end of the trail on Bickerley Road at the south-western edge of Ringwood. Retrace your steps.

Station: Christchurch.

TIC: Wimborne Minster, 01202 886116.

Other nearby trails: The second section of the Castleman Trail starts in Merley to the south of Wimborne Minster. There are waymarked trails in the Moors Valley Country Park itself and lots more in the New Forest. Bournemouth Promenade.

Useful publications & websites: OS Landranger Map 195. A map can be downloaded from *www.dorsetforyou.com/castlemantrailway*

Refreshments: Tea rooms in the visitor centre at Moors Valley Country Park. The Old Thatch pub at Stapehill.

Castleman Trail from Upton Country Park to Merley (Wimborne Minster)

Ride **38**

This is the second part of the Castleman Trail – there is no safe route through Wimborne Minster that links this section to the one described in the previous ride. There are good refreshment stops at either end of this ride: the Willett Arms pub in the north and the Peacock Tearooms at Upton Country Park in the south. In between is a very attractive, easy ride on a wide, smooth track through broadleaf woodland. There is also a brief section on an old Roman Road. From Upton Country Park you have another option of a traffic-free ride along the shoreline of Holes Bay, a stretch of water that is a real magnet for wildfowl.

Starting points & parking

1. Upton Country Park, off the A35 just east of Upton, near Poole (grid reference SY 992931). Park just inside the entrance gates on the left.

2. The Willett Arms pub, **Merley,** lies on the B3073 south of Wimborne Minster (grid reference SZ 017984), just off the more southerly of the two roundabouts near the junction of the A31 / A349 / B3073. The best parking at the north end of the ride is on Harrier Drive. To get here: from the traffic lights by the Willett Arms, turn right on Oakley Lane, turn first right onto Oakley Straight and shortly right again onto Harrier Drive. Park just along on the left beyond the school. The trail lies at the end of Harrier Drive through the metal barriers.

Category
Railway path and shoreline path.

Distance
Upton Country Park to Merley (Wimborne Minster) – 4 miles each way.

Upton Country Park around Holes Bay – 2$\frac{1}{2}$ miles each way.

Ride **38**   **Castleman Trail from Upton Country Park to Merley (Wimborne Minster)**

On your bikes!

South to north

1. Exit Upton Country Park and turn left onto the waymarked route along the pavement.

2. Follow the pavement round to the right, pass through the subway under the A35, cross two roads at the roundabout at the designated crossing points (**take care**). Follow the path downhill to the left, through a second subway and up alongside the road.

3. Go through a gate and onto a narrow path with woodland to your left, soon joining the Castleman Trail and bearing right by a 'Roman Road' sign. Remember this point for your return.

4. After almost $1/2$ mile keep an eye out for a path leading up to the right immediately before a large red-brick bridge (grid reference SY 992943). Join the railway path and turn right. Again, remember this point for the return.

5. Follow for $1^1/2$ miles, go through three subways in quick succession, following signs for Wimborne. **Easy to miss**: after

$1/2$ mile, turn right across a metal bridge and follow the path through fine broadleaf woodland to the Willett Arms at Merley.

Holes Bay route

A. Ride to the far end of the car park just inside the Upton Country Park entrance gates to join a stone path that soon runs through woodland and alongside Holes Bay.

B. Follow for $2^1/2$ miles to the end of the trail near to Asda, the RNLI station and a block of brightly painted flats. Retrace your steps.

Station: Poole.

TIC: Wimborne Minster, 01202 886116.

Other nearby trails: The other section of the Castleman Trail. Bournemouth Promenade. There are waymarked trails in the Moors Valley Country Park itself and lots more in the New Forest.

Useful publications & websites: OS Landranger Map 195. A map can be downloaded from *www.dorsetforyou.com/ castlemantrailway*

Refreshments: Peacock Tearooms at Upton Country Park. Willett Arms pub in Merley.

Moors Valley Country Park west of Ringwood

Ride **39**

This is an absolute model of how recreational cycling for families should be developed in Forestry Commission holdings. The routes start from an excellent visitor centre with a good cafe attached, there are plenty of other activities for children of all ages, and the routes themselves are well laid out so that at almost any point you have the option of extending the ride or following a more direct route back to the start. The broad stone and gravel tracks through tall pines and heather heathland are gently undulating so you have a few climbs and descents. If only it were all this simple! The only drawback is the steep cost of the Pay & Display car park but when you realise that you have the potential of a full day's entertainment in addition to the cycling, it puts the cost into context.

Starting point & parking

The Moors Valley Country Park Visitor Centre, signposted off the A31 to the west of Ringwood, is located just north of Ashley Heath (grid reference SU 106057).

Station: Christchurch.

TIC: Ringwood, 01425 470896.

Other nearby trails: New Forest, Castleman Trail, Bournemouth Promenade.

Useful publications & website: OS Landranger Map 195. A much more useful map is the one available at the visitor centre which shows all the waymarked routes and how they connect one to another, or go to: *www.moors-valley. co.uk/download/Cycle-map.pdf*

Refreshments: Good café at the visitor centre.

Category
Forest trails.

Distance
Four circuits of between 2 and 6 miles.

61

Ride 40 Bournemouth Promenade between Hengistbury Head & Poole Head

Category
Seafront promenade.

Distance
9$^{1}/_{2}$ miles each way.

*NB Cycling is **NOT** allowed from 1000 - 1800 hrs in July and August. Please also note that there is a 10mph speed limit for cyclists and you should always give way to pedestrians. Be particularly aware of young children who may suddenly run out in front of you.*

The wide sweep of Poole Bay offers a wonderful flat ride alongside fine sandy beaches, with views west to the outcrop of Ballard Down above Studland Bay and east to the sandy hill of Hengistbury Head. This is an out-and-out seaside ride and if it is a hot day, travelling by bike is the perfect way to find an uncrowded section of the 10-mile-long beach. Be warned that even outside the peak season (when restrictions apply) the whole promenade does become crowded on hot days, so it is best to choose a time when there are fewer people around – ie early morning, early evening or mid-week. Hengistbury Head has an abundance of traditional beach huts, brightly coloured dinghies in Christchurch Harbour and a ferry across to Christchurch itself. The ride is a gentle glide alongside the sandy beaches with plenty of chances to stop for refreshments. The prevailing wind is from the west so if you have started at the eastern end of the ride you are likely to be blown back to Hengistbury Head.

Starting points & parking

The cheapest parking seems to be at the Poole Head end of the ride, inland from the coast. There are car parks all along the promenade – the closer to the piers, the more expensive. Another alternative is to catch the Mudeford passenger ferry from Christchurch to Hengistbury Head.

1. Hengistbury Head, south of Christchurch (grid reference SZ 182910).

2. Poole Head, south-west of Bournemouth (grid reference SZ 050884). Follow signs for Sandbanks from Poole via the B3369.

On your bikes!

1. (From Poole Head). Follow the promenade east alongside the beaches. Do not exceed 10mph. After 3 miles you will need to dismount to walk past Bournemouth pier.

2. The cycle route follows the road / long parking strip for 1$^{1}/_{4}$ miles as far as Boscombe pier.

3. The promenade finishes 7 miles after leaving Poole Head and turns inland, briefly joining roads. Follow 'National Cycle Network Route 2' and 'Hengistbury Head' signs, turning right at the road.

4. After ¹/₂ mile, on a sharp left-hand bend, turn right following 'Hengistbury Head' signs. After a further ¹/₂ mile, as the road swings left, bear right onto a tarmac path towards Hengistbury Head.

5. The trail ends after 1¹/₂ miles at the Beach House Café. Alternatively you may wish to catch the Mudeford Ferry and continue towards Christchurch.

Station: Bournemouth.

TIC: Bournemouth, 0845 051 1700.

Other nearby trails: There are many miles of traffic-free trails in the New Forest, east of Bournemouth.

Useful publications & websites: *Area Cycle Map – Poole, Bournemouth & Christchurch* is available from Bournemouth Tourist Information Centre (0845 051 1700). Or search 'Bournemouth Cycle Map' on *www. bournemouth.gov.uk*. Try also *www. boroughofpoole.com* and *www.dorsetforyou. com*

Refreshments: Beach House Café, Hungry Hiker Café in Hengistbury Head. Lots of cafés all along Bournemouth promenade.

40

South-East Trails

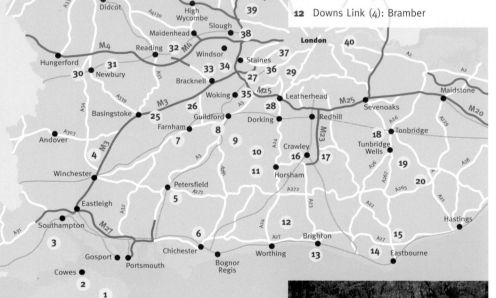

1 Newport to Sandown, Isle of Wight

2 Cowes to Newport Cycleway

3 New Forest, Hampshire

4 Test Way, Stockbridge

5 Queen Elizabeth Country Park

6 Centurion Way, Chichester

7 Alice Holt Forest, Farnham

8 Wey Navigation, Guildford

9 Downs Link (1): Bramley

10 Downs Link (2): Cranleigh

11 Downs Link (3): Southwater

12 Downs Link (4): Bramber

5 Queen Elizabeth Country Park

40 Thames: Greenwich to Erith

South-East Mountain Biking

Mountain biking in the South-East is almost exclusively on the chalk and flint tracks that abound in the area. These are best enjoyed in the summer months from May to October when the trails are drier and easier to ride: they can become impassable in the depths of winter. The main exception to the chalk is the area lying just south of the North Downs, where there are many sandy tracks – often easier when they are wet and harder-packed (imagine riding on a wet beach or a dry beach!). This sandy area extends east from Alton in Hampshire across towards Dorking, Reigate and Oxted in Surrey, and on to Maidstone and Ashford in Kent.

1. Isle of Wight
There are many miles of excellent tracks on the Isle of Wight, particularly the Tennyson Trail on the western half of the island between Freshwater Bay and Newport.

2. Hampshire Downs
As with Wiltshire and Dorset, Hampshire is blessed with many hundreds of miles of chalk and flint byways and bridleways.

Some of the waymarked long-distance trails such as the Wayfarer's Walk and the Test Way, both of which start on Inkpen Hill to the south of Hungerford, have long bridleway and byway sections. Winchester is also the start of the South Downs Way, one of the premier long-distance bridleways in the country that runs east for 100 miles to Eastbourne. Hampshire County Council publishes two packs of off-road cycling leaflets. Go to *www3.hants.gov.uk/ cycling/cycling-maps-leaflets.htm*

3. Berkshire Downs (Ridgeway)
There are a plethora of fine tracks to the south of the Ridgeway and to the north of the M4 through West Berkshire and South Oxfordshire. Lambourn is an excellent base with tracks radiating off in every direction.

4. Chilterns
The beechwoods of the Chilterns offer splendid woodland rides on well-maintained and well-waymarked bridleways and byways. The best tracks lie to the west and north of Henley.

5. North Downs
Unlike the South Downs Way or the Ridgeway, where you are allowed to cycle from one end to the other, the North Downs Way – running along the chalk ridge from Farnham to Canterbury and Dover –

6 The South Downs

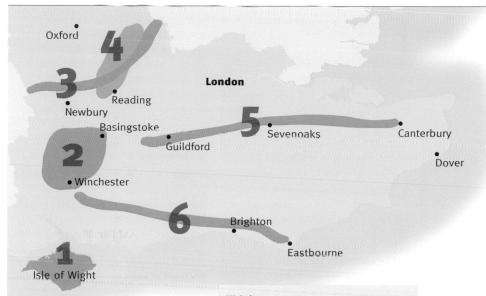

is mainly a footpath and you are **not** permitted to cycle on footpaths. There are, however, several long bridleway and byway sections that are open to cyclists, easily found by looking at the relevant Ordnance Survey map. There are many good bases from which to explore the North Downs bridleway and byway network: Gomshall, Peaslake, Leith Hill, Walton on the Hill, Limpsfield and Wye.

6. South Downs

The South Downs Way is a 100-mile linear bridleway from Winchester to Eastbourne. A few miles either side of the trail there are many other bridleways and byways enabling you to devise all sorts of circular rides. The South Downs tracks are very definitely best ridden in summer, on mountain bikes, after a few dry days; the chalk and clay can be depressingly sticky in winter.

Websites:

www.moredirt.co.uk and follow links from 'Trails & Tracks' to 'United Kingdom' to 'South East & London'.

www.forestry.gov.uk and search 'Bedgebury', 'Aston Hill', 'Queen Elizabeth Country Park' or 'Friston Forest'.

www.mudtrail.co.uk

Guidebooks:

South-East Mountain Biking: North & South Downs – Nick Cotton

Features 25 rides of varying lengths and difficulty through the beautiful scenery of the North Downs and South Downs, featuring rides in Kent, Surrey, Sussex and Hampshire. Go to *www.v-graphics.co.uk* for more details.

South-East Mountain Biking: Ridgeway & Chilterns – Nick Cotton

Features 25 rides of varying lengths and difficulty through the chalk downland and steep beechwoods of the Ridgeway and the Chilterns, featuring rides in Oxfordshire, Berkshire, Hampshire and Buckinghamshire. Go to *www.v-graphics.co.uk* for more details.

South-East Forestry

For such a densely populated area, the South-East of England has, surprisingly, more woodland than either the South-West or the Midlands. The largest forestry holding is the New Forest but there are also large swathes of woodland along the South Downs. In some forests and woods there are no waymarked routes, but you are free to explore the tracks. The relevant Ordnance Survey map is mentioned. It is highly recommended that you take a map for the larger woods as it is very easy to get lost. Local bike shops and the Forestry Commission website (*www.forestry.gov.uk*) may point you towards the best spots.

Forests & woods with waymarked trails

These are shown with a corresponding ride number and page reference. There are five Forestry Commission holdings with waymarked family trails in the South-East region:

Mention should also be made of the waymarked trails from The Look Out near to Bracknell (Ride 33, page 107): these are on Crown Commission land but to you or me they are waymarked woodland trails!

5 **Queen Elizabeth Country Park**, Petersfield (Ride 5, page 75)

6 **Alice Holt Forest**, Farnham (Ride 7, page 77)

9 **Friston Forest**, Eastbourne (Ride 14, page 85)

11 **Bedgebury Forest**, Cranbrook (Ride 20, page 92)

43 **Wendover Woods**, Aylesbury (Ride 43, page 119)

The New Forest *(shown as **2** on the map)*

Although this is by far the largest forest in the South-East, there is no set list of waymarked circular rides; instead, you will find a large network of excellent, broad, gravel-based trails waymarked with green and white disks that enable you to make up your own rides. Key to this is the map produced by the Forestry Commission called *Cycling in the New Forest – The Network Map*. See Ride 3, page 73 for further details.

In some forests and woods there are no waymarked routes, but you are free to explore the tracks. The relevant Ordnance Survey map is mentioned. It is highly recommended that you take a map for the larger woods as it is very easy to get lost.

The woodlands below correspond with the numbers on the map shown top right:

1. Brighstone & Parkhurst Forests, Isle of Wight (OS Explorer Map OL 29)

3. Farley Mount, west of Winchester (OS Explorer Map 132)

4. West Walk, north of Fareham (OS Explorer Map 119)

7. Charlton Forest & Eartham Wood, south-east of Midhurst (OS Explorer Map 121)

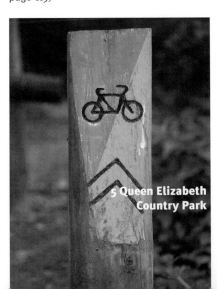

5 Queen Elizabeth Country Park

The Forestry Commission's website, *www.forestry. gov.uk* is a good source of information. Click on 'Explore, Experience, Enjoy' then 'Cycling' and you can find out details of hundreds of waymarked trails throughout the UK. You can search by forest name or by the nearest town / city. The search will tell you the grade, length and waymarking details of the trails. Alternatively, by clicking on the map you can see the nearest forest to where you live.

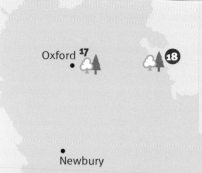

8. Rewell Wood, west of Arundel (OS Explorer Map 121)

10. Wilmington Wood & Abbot's Wood, south-west of Hailsham (OS Explorer Map 123)

12. Hemsted Forest, east of Cranbrook (OS Explorer Maps 125 & 137)

13. King's Wood, north of Ashford (OS Explorer Map 137)

14. West Wood, Elhampark & Covert Wood, east of Ashford (OS Explorer Map 138)

15. Denge Wood, north-east of Ashford (OS Explorer Map 137)

16. Clowes Wood, north of Canterbury (OS Explorer Map 150)

17. Shabbington Wood & Waterperry Wood, east of Oxford (OS Explorer Map 180)

It is also worth contacting the following Forest District Offices for further information:

New Forest
The Queen's House
Lyndhurst, Hampshire SO43 7NH
Tel: 02380 283141
Website: *www.forestry.gov.uk/newforest*
Email: enquiries.new.forest.@forestry.gsi.gov.uk

Downs and Chilterns
Bucks Horn Oak
Farnham
Surrey GU10 4LS
Tel: 01420 23666
Email: enquiries.seefd@forestry.gsi.gov.uk

South-East National Cycle Network

A map for this route is available from www.sustrans. org.uk or 0845 113 0065.

Thames Valley Cycle Route

97 miles from Oxford to London via Reading and Windsor. Highlights include Oxford, the Chiltern Hills, Windsor Castle and Great Park, the Thames Towpath east of Weybridge, Hampton Court, Richmond Park and Barnes Wildfowl & Wetlands Centre.

Traffic-free sections over 3 miles long:
- Teddington to Weybridge along the Thames (NCN 4).
- Windsor Great Park (NCN 4).
- Kennington to Oxford along the Thames (NCN 5).

Thames Valley Cycle Route

Downs & Weald Cycle Route

159 miles from London to Brighton and along the coast to Hastings, with an alternative route from Crawley via East Grinstead and Heathfield to Eastbourne. Highlights include Greenwich, the Waterlink Way through South London, the North Downs, the three traffic-free railway paths – the Worth Way and Forest Way near East Grinstead and the Cuckoo Trail south of Heathfield – the South Downs and Brighton.

Traffic-free sections over 3 miles long:
- Worth Way from Crawley to East Grinstead (NCN 21).
- Forest Way from East Grinstead to Groombridge (NCN 21).
- Cuckoo Trail from Heathfield to Polegate (NCN 21).

Garden of England Cycle Route

180 miles from London to Canterbury then along the coast to Sandwich, Deal, Dover, Rye and Hastings. Highlights include Greenwich, the traffic-free Thames-side route to Erith, Whitstable, the Crab & Winkle Way railway path south from Whitstable, Canterbury Cathedral, Dover Castle and Rye.

Traffic-free sections over 3 miles long:
- Crab & Winkle Way between Canterbury and Whitstable (NCN 1).
- Thames Riverside between Greenwich and Erith (NCN 1).

Other good areas for lane cycling

From a cyclist's point of view, the South-East has a high population density and high levels of car ownership, filling the roads with traffic. The concept of 'quiet lane networks' is somewhat alien in this region. The best rule of thumb is that the further away you go from London, the quieter the roads will become – for example, try **west** or **north Oxfordshire** with good bases at Burford or Hook Norton; North Buckinghamshire from Winslow or Buckingham; **south Hampshire** has networks of lanes between the M3 and the A3; and in the **eastern half of Kent** it is worth exploring lanes south-west, south and south-east of Canterbury.

Downs & Weald Cycle Route

Garden of England Cycle Route

OS Cycle Tours: Each guide features 15 lane rides (25 – 35 miles) and five off-road rides (10 – 20 miles), using highlighted Ordnance Survey mapping with clear route instructions.

Ride 1 **Newport to Sandown Isle of Wight**

Category
Railway path.

Distance
8 miles each way.

This ride forms part of what might be considered the easiest coast-to-coast ride in the country: from Cowes on the north coast of the Isle of Wight to Sandown on the east coast. The section from Cowes to Newport is described in Ride 2; the middle section is a complicated route on streets through Newport; the final part, described here, follows a railway path south and east across the island through rich agricultural land and clumps of broadleaf woodland, to arrive in Sandown and a chance for a paddle on the beach.

Starting points & parking

1. Newport: the trail starts close to the junction of the A3056 with the B3401 Shide Road at the south-east edge of Newport (grid reference SZ 503882).

2. From **Sandown railway station**, turn right to go under the subway, turn right on Perowne Way, then after 400yds turn left just before the shops on to the start of the traffic-free trail (grid reference SZ 593850).

Station: Sandown (connects with the ferry from Portsmouth to Ryde).

TIC: Newport, 01983 813818.

Other nearby trails: Cowes to Newport. The Tennyson Trail is a chalk and stone bridleway along the ridge from Freshwater Bay to Newport, excellent for mountain bikes in the summer months. There are two other short railway paths on the Isle of Wight: Shanklin to Wroxall and Yarmouth to Freshwater Bay.

Useful publications & websites: OS Landranger Map 196. Visit *www.cyclewight.org.uk*

Refreshments: Lots of choice in Sandown and Newport.

Ride 2 **Cowes to Newport Cycleway Isle of Wight**

Category
Railway path.

Distance
4 miles each way.

The Isle of Wight is a great place to explore by bike and as taking a car on the ferry is so expensive, it is well worth leaving the car on the mainland and catching the ferry with just your bikes. In this way you will also avoid adding to the vehicle traffic on the island. This ride from Cowes to Newport is one of four railway paths on the Isle of Wight. The three others run from

Freshwater to Yarmouth, from Shanklin railway station to Wroxall and south-east from Newport to Sandown (see Ride 1). The Cowes to Newport Cycleway runs for 4 miles alongside the River Medina, a wide expanse of water with hundreds of moored yachts. Cowes is of course a famous yachting centre, and during Cowes Week the whole of the Solent is filled with bright sails.

2

Starting points & parking

1. From the clocktower in the centre of **Newport,** follow Quay Street / Little London / Hurstake Road / Manners View and signs for 'Cowes Cycle Route'. There is a small car park on the trading estate on the north side of Newport, just beyond the Royal Mail building (grid reference SZ 501902).

2. The trail starts / ends on the **south side of Cowes** on the Medina Industrial Estate, Arctic Road (grid reference SZ 498948). From the ferry terminal take the first left and keep following 'Cowes to Newport Cycleway' signs.

On your bikes!

Starting from the centre of Newport

1. From the Guildhall / Clocktower in the centre of Newport, turn along Quay Street. Follow round a sharp left-hand bend then turn second right onto Little London, signposted 'Cowes Bike Route'.

2. Follow this road around a left-hand bend. At the T-junction at the end of Hurstake Road, turn right signposted 'Cowes'. Continue straight ahead at the roundabout onto Manners View, passing a large Royal Mail building.

3. Join the trail proper. Follow for 4 miles alongside the River Medina.

4. The trail ends in Cowes at the Medina Court Industrial Estate, Arctic Road.

> **Nearest ferry terminal:** Cowes.
>
> **TIC:** Newport, 01983 813818.
>
> **Other nearby trails:** Newport to Sandown. There are two other short railway paths – Yarmouth to Freshwater lies at the western end of the island, Shanklin to Wroxall at the eastern end. The chalk ridge of the Tennyson Trail from Freshwater to Carisbrooke (Newport) is a superb, challenging mountain bike ridge ride, best done in summertime.
>
> **Useful publications & websites:** OS Landranger Map 196. Visit *www.cyclewight.org.uk*
>
> **Refreshments:** Plenty of choice in Cowes and Newport.

3

New Forest
Hampshire

The New Forest's gravel forest tracks link villages and the main tourist sites. The vast majority of the tracks and trails lie either side of an imaginary line drawn between Beaulieu in the south-east and Fordingbridge in the north-west, passing through Bolderwood. The A31 can be crossed via an underpass near to Bolderwood. Great care should be taken crossing roads in the New Forest as many can get busy, especially at the weekends and through the summer holidays.

Category
Wide, gravel-based forest tracks. See: *www.forestry.gov. uk/newforest*

Ride 3 New Forest, Hampshire

Distance
As short or as long as you want. There are over one hundred miles of waymarked routes. You are encouraged to make up your own routes, as long as you stay on the gravel roads waymarked with green and white disks.

Starting points & parking

There are many car parks that form suitable starting points, particularly to the south and west of Lyndhurst.

Station: Brockenhurst.

TIC: Lyndhurst, 02380 282269.

Other nearby trails: There are over a hundred miles of tracks to explore in the New Forest.

Useful publications & websites: OS Landranger Maps 195 & 196. Much more useful is the excellent leaflet called *Cycling in the New Forest – The Network Map* produced by the Forestry Commission and available from the New Forest Visitor Information Centre in Lyndhurst (02380 282269). Or try *www.new-forest-national-park.com/new-forest-cycling.html*

Refreshments: Lots of choice in Lyndhurst and Brockenhurst.

Ride 4 Test Way, Stockbridge
north-west of Winchester

Category
Railway path.

Distance
5 miles each way.

This 5-mile section of the Test Way runs south from the attractive, large village of Stockbridge parallel with and occasionally crossing the delightfully clear, shallow, fast-flowing River Test, one of the best fishing rivers in England. The old railway track has been converted into a good, stone-based trail. There is a traffic-free connection from the end of the railway path to the lane leading to Mottisfont Abbey, a National Trust property with a tearoom (*www.nationaltrust.org.uk* and search 'Mottisfont'). The Test Valley railway line was also known as the 'Sprat & Winkle Line'. It was unusual in that it was built on the bed of an old canal that linked Andover and Southampton. The waterway was first used in 1794 but had fallen into disuse within 50 years. The railway began service in 1865 and was used in both

world wars to move troops and supplies to Southampton Docks. It closed in 1964 and has since become part of the Test Way, a long-distance footpath from Inkpen to Totton. Short sections of it are also open to cyclists.

Starting point & parking

Trafalgar Way, off the roundabout at the eastern end of **Stockbridge** at the junction of the A30 and A3057 (grid reference SU 359351). The White Hart pub is situated on the roundabout. Stockbridge is about 10 miles north-west of Winchester.

Test Way, Stockbridge, northwest of Winchester   Ride **4**

Station: Mottisfont.

TIC: Winchester, 01962 840500.

Other nearby trails: The long-distance bridleway, the South Downs Way, starts in Winchester, 10 miles south-east of Stockbridge.

Useful publications & websites:

OS Landranger Map 185. Go to *www3.hants. gov.uk/cycling/cycling-route-finder/cycling-testway.htm*

Refreshments: Lots of choice in Stockbridge. The John of Gaunt pub by the River Test at Horsebridge. Tearoom at Mottisfont Abbey, a National Trust property.

Queen Elizabeth Country Park   Ride **5**
Petersfield

Queen Elizabeth Country Park is certainly not flat but there is an excellent waymarked woodland circuit (purple waymarks), as well as plenty of other attractions in the park and at the visitor centre. For the more adventurous there is a technically challenging mountain bike circuit (orange waymarks). There are also trails leading out of the park onto the network of bridleways and lanes that criss-cross the South Downs, the great chalk ridge stretching from Winchester to Eastbourne. The park is part of the landscape of the South Downs and is in an Area of Outstanding Natural Beauty. It covers 1,400 acres and is dominated by the three hills of Butser, War Down and Holt Down, which provide a contrast between the dramatic downland and beautiful woodland. With 38 species of butterfly and 12 species of wild orchid, it is a naturalist's paradise, a large area of which is designated as a Site of Special Scientific Interest. The many Roman and Iron Age sites in the park are also preserved as Scheduled Ancient Monuments.

Starting point & parking

Queen Elizabeth Country Park is well signposted off the A3 to the **south-west of Petersfield**, on the way to Portsmouth. There is a Pay & Display car park by the visitor centre (grid reference SU 718185).

On your bikes!

The routes are well signposted. The trails start from the corner of the car park to the left of the visitor centre by a large, colourful wooden signpost, or alternatively go through the first car park and onto the Gravel Hill car park. In general terms, the purple (easier) route climbs steadily for the first half of the route and descends for the second half.

Category
Forest trails.

Distance
3.7 miles (Family trail) and 3.2 miles (Mountain bike trail).

75

Ride **5**   Queen Elizabeth Country Park, Petersfield

Station: Petersfield.

TIC: Petersfield, 01730 268829.

Other nearby trails: The South Downs Way passes through Queen Elizabeth Country Park.

Useful publications & websites: OS Landranger Map 197. Much better is the excellent A2 full-colour *Queen Elizabeth*

Country Park Trails Guide produced by Hampshire County Council / Forest Enterprise and available from: Queen Elizabeth Country Park, Gravel Hill, Horndean, Waterlooville, Hampshire PO8 0QE (01705 595040). Visit *www3.hants.gov.uk/qecp* and follow links through 'Activities' to 'Cycling'.

Refreshments: Café at the visitor centre.

Ride **6**   **Centurion Way Chichester**

Category
Railway path.

Distance
6 miles each way.

The railway path between Chichester and West Dean passes some extraordinary metal sculptures of Roman centurions and 'surveyors'. The route runs through woodland and arable land with a profusion of wildflowers along the verges. The name Centurion Way was suggested by a local schoolboy and is based on the fact that the path crosses the course of a Roman Road. From the southern end the path it is easy to visit Chichester Cathedral, to link to a short section of the Chichester Canal towpath or to the longer route known as the Salterns Way, which is a mixture of quiet lanes and traffic-free sections (*see www.conservancy. co.uk/uploads/user_documents/ salternsway.pdf*). The Chichester to Midhurst Railway was opened in 1881 and was finally closed in 1991. In 1994 the County Council purchased the railway line and the old railway line was converted to recreational use.

Starting points & parking

1. Turn east (downhill) off the A286 between Midhurst and Chichester in **West Dean** onto the minor road by the Selsey Arms pub towards West Dean Stores. At the bottom, turn right and park along here (grid reference SU 858122).

2. The southern end of the path is on the **west side of Chichester**. Follow West Street from the centre of Chichester, straight over a roundabout signposted '7.5-ton weight

6

limit'. Continue in the same direction along Westgate. Just before the level crossing, bear right onto a tarmac path by the school then shortly turn left onto the Centurion Way (grid reference SU 848047).

On your bikes!

From West Dean, heading south

1. Follow the minor road to join the A286 and turn left onto the cyclepath alongside the main road.

2. After 1 mile, at the end of the cyclepath, with a red letter box set in a brick wall ahead, turn left downhill on a rough track, soon joining the railway path running along the valley.

3. At the houses in Mid Lavant, aim for the far right-hand corner of the 'green' then turn left. Continue in the same direction, ignoring turns to the left. Pass between concrete bollards and as the road swings

right, bear left onto Churchmead Close, signposted 'Chichester'. Take the next left on Warbleheath Close, signposted 'Chichester', to rejoin the railway path for a gentle descent over almost 3 miles to Chichester. You may wish to turn around at the end of the traffic-free section but if you want to go into the centre of Chichester, turn left and follow Westgate and West Street to the cathedral.

Station: Chichester or Fishbourne.

TIC: Chichester, 01243 775888.

Other nearby trails: The South Downs Way is a long-distance bridleway between Winchester and Eastbourne.

Useful publications & websites: OS Landranger Map 197. A leaflet called Cycle Chichester is available via *www.westsussex.gov.uk* (put 'Cycle Chichester' in the 'Search' box).

Refreshments: Selsey Arms pub in West Dean. Earl of March pub in Mid Lavant. Lots of choice in Chichester.

Alice Holt Forest Ride **7**
south-west of Farnham

7

A n easy, well designed route on the sandy soils south of Farnham, part of the greensand strata that runs east from Alton between the chalk of the North Downs and the clay of the Weald, providing well-drained, all-year-round tracks. The well-waymarked circular route starts from the visitor centre and uses stone and gravel paths with the occasional gentle hill. From the Middle Ages onwards, timber from Alice Holt was being used to build ships for Britain's navy. Hundreds of mature oaks

Category
Forest trail.

Distance
4-mile circuit.

Ride 7   Alice Holt Forest, south-west of Farnham

were needed to build a single ship and the forest was periodically stripped of its large trees to supply the naval shipyards dotted along the south coast.

Starting point & parking

At the **Alice Holt Visitor Centre**, 4 miles south-west of Farnham just off the A325 Farnham to Petersfield road at Bucks Horn Oak (grid reference SU 812417).

Station: Bentley.

TIC: Farnham, 01252 715109.

Other nearby trails: The Basingstoke Canal runs from Odiham to Weybridge and passes through Fleet, 5 miles north of Farnham. The Downs Link runs from near Guildford south to Shoreham.

Useful publications & websites: OS Landranger Map 186. Go to *www.forestry.gov. uk/aliceholt*

Refreshments: Café at the visitor centre.

Ride 8   **Wey Navigation from Godalming to Guildford**

Category
Canal towath.

Distance
4^1/$_2$ miles each way.

Two sections of the Wey Navigation are suitable for cycling – both are described in this guide (see also Ride 35, page 109). The canal was part of a series of waterways connecting London to Portsmouth via the River Arun and Chichester Harbour. Barges transported large quantities of government stores and ammunition to Godalming, from where it was taken on to the naval arsenal at Portsmouth. The 1830s were the highpoint of the waterways when tonnage carried was at its highest. Competition from the railways began to take away trade from the waterways from the 1840s onwards. The quality of the towpath is variable and mountain bikes are recommended. It is easy to link this ride to the Downs Link at a point close to where the railway crosses the canal to the west of Shalford. Look out for the extraordinary cliffs of yellow sand at the northern end of the trail.

Starting points & parking

1. Guildford: Mill Mead car park, by the council offices, off the High Street between the A3100 Portsmouth Road and the A281 Shalford Road (grid reference SU 995493).

2. Godalming: in the main car park by Waitrose in the centre of town (grid reference SU 973440). Walk your bike across the bridge over the River Wey and turn right onto the towpath by the Godalming United Church.

On your bikes!

1. From the south end of Mill Mead in Guildford (by the council offices and the Britannia pub), cross the river into the park and follow the path alongside the Wey Navigation, keeping the water to your left, soon passing the Guildford Rowing Club.

2. The quality of the towpath varies. After about 1½ miles, pass under a railway bridge.

If you wish to join the Downs Link, about 100yds after the railway bridge keep an eye out for an old World War II pill box up

to your right. This is the start of the Downs Link. The surface quality improves after about ½ mile.

3. Stay on the towpath and cross the busy A248 (take care), then after a further mile cross the next road by Farncombe Boat House and Hectors Tearoom.

4. The towpath ends near the Godalming United Church just north of the bridge over the river in Godalming.

Station: Guildford or Godalming.

TIC: Guildford, 01483 444333.

Other nearby trails: Downs Link from Bramley to Cranleigh.

Useful publications & websites: OS Landranger Map 186. The Surrey Cycle Guides provide more detail: go to *www.surreycc.gov.uk* and put 'Surrey Cycle Guide' into the 'Search' box to find out how to order copies. Try also *www.weyriver.co.uk/theriver/wey_nav_1.htm* or *www.nationaltrust.org.uk* and search for 'Wey Navigation'.

Refreshments: Lots of choice in Guildford. Hectors Tearoom at Farncombe. Lots of choice in Godalming.

Downs Link (1) Ride **9**
from Bramley to Cranleigh, south of Guildford

As its name suggests, this railway path route links the North Downs Way with the South Downs Way. The Downs Link, which is over 30 miles long, has been split into four sections. There is a short 1-mile railway path stretch to the north of Bramley, as far as the A281, but the trail described below heads south from Bramley to Cranleigh. This section of

the trail is owned and managed by Surrey County Council. Small areas of trees are periodically cut back (coppiced) to diversify the woodland structure and encourage the growth of wildflowers. This also benefits butterflies, small mammals and bird life. The railway was built in two sections: the southern part, from Christ's Hospital to Shoreham, was completed in 1861 and the

Category
Railway path.

Distance
6 miles each way.

Ride 9 Downs Link (1) from Bramley to Cranleigh, south of Guildford

northern part, from Guildford to Christ's Hospital, was built in 1865. The railways served the local communities and industries like the Southwater Brickworks but were not profitable and were shut in 1966.

Starting points & parking

1. Bramley & Wonersh Old Station car park, south of Guildford. At the junction of the A281 and B2128, exit the roundabout towards 'Wonersh, Shamley Green'. After

200yds turn left signposted 'Bramley Business Centre, Bramley and Wonersh Railway Station' (grid reference TQ 010451).

2. In **Cranleigh**, at the far corner of the main car park, off the High Street, near the NatWest Bank (grid reference TQ 056391).

Station: Shalford.

TIC: Guildford, 01483 444333.

Other nearby trails: The Downs Link can be followed southwards beyond Cranleigh. There is a waymarked trail in Alice Holt Forest, south-west of Farnham. The Worth Way and Forest Way start in East Grinstead.

Useful publications & websites: OS Landranger Maps 186 & 187. The Surrey Cycle Guides provide more detail: go to *www.surreycc. gov.uk* and put 'Surrey Cycle Guide' into the 'Search' box to find out how to order copies. A leaflet can also be downloaded from *www. westsussex.gov.uk* – follow links through 'Leisure & Tourism' then 'Walking, Cycling and Horseriding' to get to 'Downs Link'.

Refreshments: Pub in Bramley. Lots of choice in Cranleigh.

Ride 10 Downs Link (2) from Cranleigh south to Slinfold

Category
Railway path.

Distance
7 miles each way.

It is worth cycling this section in May when the woods south of Baynards are carpeted with a magnificent display of bluebells. The stone-based track will become muddy in winter or after prolonged rain. There is one hill south of Baynards where the trail has to climb up over the blocked tunnel that the railway used to use. There are a couple of minor lanes to cross and one busy road – the A281 south

of Rudgwick – where you should take GREAT CARE.

Starting points & parking

1. In Cranleigh, at the far corner of the main car park, off the High Street, near the NatWest Bank (grid reference TQ 056391).

2. There is a small car park near the Downs Link on Spring Lane, just off The Street, to the west of Slinfold. **Slinfold** lies due west of Horsham, just off the A29 (grid reference TQ 114310).

On your bikes!

1. Exit the far corner of the main car park in Cranleigh and turn left. After 300yds cross the road towards the houses then shortly turn right by low wooden posts, signposted 'Downs Link'. Follow the track/lane between playing fields. Continue for 3½ miles to the old station at Baynards.

2. At a tarmac lane just beyond the old station turn left then right, signposted 'Downs Link'. Go under the first bridge, turn sharp left uphill onto the road, cross the bridge then go first left through a gate signposted 'Downs Link'. In order to avoid the old tunnel you now have a steep climb. After 400yds, at a crossroads of tracks at the top, turn left and go steeply downhill.

(Remember this point for the return trip.)

3. About 1 mile after rejoining the course of the railway line you have to cross the busy A281. **TAKE GREAT CARE.**

4. After 2 miles, and about 200yds after going through a short round tunnel beneath the A29 and past a factory on your right, turn left by an information board onto tarmac to go into Slinfold. At the T-junction at the end of the lane, turn right for the pub in the village.

Station: Horsham.

TIC: Horsham, 01403 211661.

Other nearby trails: The Downs Link can be followed north from Cranleigh to Bramley (described in the previous ride). To the south, the next good section of the Downs Link runs from Southwater Country Park (described in the next ride). The Worth Way and Forest Way start from East Grinstead.

Useful publications & websites: OS Landranger Map 187. A leaflet can be downloaded from *www.westsussex.gov.uk* – follow links through 'Leisure & Tourism' then 'Walking, Cycling and Horseriding' to get to 'Downs Link'.

Refreshments: Lots of choice in Cranleigh. King's Head pub just off the route in Slinfold.

Downs Link (3) Ride **11**
from Southwater to Bramber

South from Southwater, the views open up with the whaleback ridge of the South Downs looming on the horizon. One suggested turn-around point is the pub at Partridge Green. If you wish to continue further south you should take care along the B2135 as far as the next traffic-free section. A mixture of railway path, stone-based track and minor lanes is used south to Bramber with its fine castle and pub.

Category
Railway path.

Distance
5 miles each way.

Ride 11   Downs Link (3) from Southwater to Bramber

11

Starting points & parking

1. Lintot Square, **Southwater,** or Southwater Country Park (grid reference TQ 160258).

2. The car park in **Bramber**, a village signposted off the A283 roundabout at the south end of the Steyning bypass. The ride itself starts at the roundabout with the A283. There is a 'Downs Link' sign at the north-east corner of the roundabout (grid reference TQ 186106).

On your bikes!

South from Southwater

1. Start by the silver bike sculptures in Lintot Square in Southwater, by the war memorial and opposite the Lintot pub.

2. Go past Southwater Country Park, cross a minor road. Leave tarmac by a red-brick pumping station, bearing right to join the railway path.

3. Views of the South Downs open up. About 5 miles after leaving Southwater you will come across a sign for the Partridge pub in Partridge Green. You may wish to turn around here.

4. To continue south on the Downs Link, join the B2135 (take care, it is sometimes busy), turn right, ignore the first left to the Star Trading Estate and take the next left signposted 'Downs Link'. Tarmac turns to track. At a crossroads turn right to rejoin the railway path.

5. After almost 2 miles, at the end of the railway path, turn left then right downhill opposite the Cat & Canary pub. As the road swings left at the bottom, turn right (Holland Lane) then shortly left to rejoin the railway path. There is one short section across a field.

6. After 2 miles, cross the river and follow the track as it swings right uphill. At the T-junction at the top turn left downhill and keep following 'Downs Link' signs onto tarmac and into Bramber, turning left onto King Stone Avenue and left again onto Castle Lane (keep a close eye out for signs).

Station: Horsham or Shoreham.

TIC: Horsham, 01403 211661.

Other nearby trails: The Downs Link to the north and south.

Useful publications & websites: OS Landranger Map 198. A leaflet can be downloaded from *www.westsussex.gov.uk* – follow links through 'Leisure & Tourism' then 'Walking, Cycling and Horseriding' to get to 'Downs Link'.

Refreshments: Lots of choice in Southwater. Lakeside Teas at Southwater Country Park (May to September). Partridge pub at Partridge Green.

12

Downs Link (4) Ride 12
from Bramber to Old Shoreham

The most southerly section of the Downs Link, this part of the trail crosses the South Downs Way and continues south to Old Shoreham. Bramber is an attractive village at the foot of the South Downs, located on the banks of the tidal River Adur, one of only three rivers that flows south from the Weald, cutting a course through the chalk hills of the South Downs. The ride runs south from Bramber alongside the river to Old Shoreham, where there is a choice of refreshment stops. There is plenty of wildlife to see along the river, and fine views of Lancing College from the southern end of the ride.

Starting point & parking

The car park in **Bramber**, a village signposted off the A283 roundabout at the south end of the Steyning bypass. The ride itself starts at the roundabout with the A283. There is a 'Downs Link' sign at the north-east corner of the roundabout (grid reference TQ 186106).

On your bikes!

1. Exit the car park in the centre of Bramber and turn right on the road as far as the roundabout with the A283. There is a 'Downs Link' sign immediately **before** the roundabout directing you onto a track running parallel with the southbound A283. Follow for $^1/_2$ mile.

2. TAKE EXTREME CARE crossing the A283 to the other side. Wait patiently until there is a clear gap in the traffic for you to cross. After $^3/_4$ mile at the T-junction of tracks turn left, signposted 'South Downs Way, Eastbourne'. Cross the river bridge then turn right, signposted 'Coastal Link'.

3. Follow the track alongside the river for 3 miles, passing under a large road bridge, ignoring a wooden bridge to the right, passing under a railway bridge and alongside a new riverside development. The surface varies in quality.

4. The path ends at the Bridge Inn on the roundabout at the junction of the A283 / A259 in Old Shoreham. Retrace your steps.

Station: Shoreham-by-Sea.

TIC: Worthing, 01903 221066.

Other nearby trails: The Downs Link continues north from Bramber to Henfield and Southwater. There is a traffic-free cyclepath along Brighton & Hove Seafront Promenade. The Dyke Railway Trail runs north from Hove. Nearby ridge sections of the South Downs Way are fine in the summer months on mountain bikes.

Useful publications & websites: OS Landranger Map 198. A leaflet can be downloaded from *www.westsussex.gov.uk* – follow links through 'Leisure & Tourism' then 'Walking, Cycling and Horseriding' to get to 'Downs Link'.

Refreshments: Bramber Castle Hotel, Old Tollgate pub in Bramber. Lots of choice in Old Shoreham.

Category
Railway path.

Distance
$4^1/_2$ miles each way.

NB There is one difficult road crossing near the start of the ride. Please take **EXTREME CARE** crossing the A283 just south of Bramber. Alternatively start from the church in Old Shoreham and ride north as far as the A283.

Ride 13 Brighton Promenade

13

Category
Seafront promenade.

Distance
6 miles each way.

Ever more seaside resorts in the South of England are creating cyclepaths along the wide promenades that run parallel with the coast, offering cyclists the chance to glide along from one end of a resort to the other with fine views out to sea, and myriad opportunities to stop for refreshments. The route through Brighton passes the famous Brighton Pier and continues on to Rottingdean, where you've the option of a high-level route along the clifftop or a route at sea level beneath the towering chalk cliffs. Why not go out on one option and return on the other?

Starting points & parking

If you live in the Brighton / Hove area the seafront cyclepath can be joined at any point between **Hove Lagoon** and **Brighton Marina**. If you are arriving by car from outside the area, parking in central Brighton can be very expensive. It would be better either to start from **Rottingdean** in the east or to park at the Southwick Bay

car park / Carat Café **near Shoreham docks** at the western end of the spit of land beyond Portslade-by-Sea (grid reference TQ 243047).

On your bikes!

East from Hove Lagoon towards Rottingdean

1. The route is well waymarked as National Cycle Network Route 2. Signs on the ground, painted cycle lanes and 'No Cycling' signs will all give you a clear indication of the course of the route, at times right by the seafront, at other times set back from it.

2. Go past Brighton Pier and towards the marina. The route climbs up away from the seafront. At the top of the climb you have a choice:

(a) bear left through the subway under the A259 to join the clifftop path past the windmill to Rottingdean to finish at the White Horse Hotel.

(b) bear right downhill to join the Undercliff Path running beneath the towering chalk cliffs on a wide concrete path that also leads to Rottingdean.

NB Please ride responsibly along the promenade, especially during busy summer weekends: pay attention to the cycling signs and be aware that the paths are shared with pedestrians.

Station: Brighton.

TIC: Brighton, 0906 711 2255.

Other nearby trails: The Downs Link runs north from Shoreham to Bramber. Nearby ridge sections of the South Downs Way are fine in the summer months on mountain bikes.

Useful publications & websites: OS Landranger Map 198. The Brighton & Hove Cycle Map is available from *www.brighton-hove.gov.uk* – put 'Brighton & Hove Cycle map' into the 'Search' box.

Refreshments: Lots of choice all along the seafront and in Rottingdean.

Friston Forest west of Eastbourne

Ride 14

There are two rides starting from Exceat, where the River Cuckmere has cut a course through the chalk ridge of the South Downs. The short ride goes to the coast and back; the longer ride is a waymarked forest route. The visitor centre for the Seven Sisters Country Park is housed in a converted 18th-century barn at Exceat Farm.

Starting point & parking

Forestry Commission car park in **Exceat**, on the minor lane towards Litlington, just off the A259 to the east of Seaford (grid reference TV 519995).

On your bikes!

Route to the sea

Push your bike past the café and visitor centre. Cross the busy A259 by the bus stop, signposted 'To the beach, Foxholes'. **TAKE GREAT CARE**. Follow the track through Seven Sisters Country Park for ³/₄ mile then as the concrete track swings left towards Foxholes, bear right onto a gravel track for fine sea views. Retrace your steps.

Waymarked forest route

1. From the car park by the visitor centre, go back towards the exit then turn right at a square wooden post, signposted 'Bridleway to West Dean'. Join the family cycle trail at a green and white 'Friston Forest' sign.

2. At the track junction with brick & flint Pond Cottage ahead, bear right to join a better gravel track. Follow this long, wide, straight forest road passing flint houses on the left and going round a metal barrier across the road. At the crossroads of wide tracks by tall red and white poles, go straight ahead.

3. After almost ¹/₂ mile the path narrows then swings left and starts climbing. Shortly turn left uphill off the wide gravel track onto a stone and earth track, soon turning left again (all signposted).

4. Long, gentle descent on earth and grass track. At a crossroads with smooth forest road turn right gently uphill. After ¹/₄ mile turn left on a similar broad forest road. Climb to the highpoint with the option of turning right up to the viewpoint (rough and steep). For the main route continue straight ahead downhill.

5. At the T-junction with a forest road at the bottom of a fun, grassy descent, turn right to rejoin the outward route back to the start.

Station: Berwick or Polegate (between Lewes and Eastbourne).

TIC: Eastbourne, 0871 663 0031.

Other nearby trails: The Cuckoo Trail starts at Polegate, 4 miles north of Eastbourne. The South Downs Way is a long-distance bridleway that runs from Winchester to Eastbourne with some easier 'plateau' sections. (Mountain bikes only, best done in the summer.)

Useful publications & websites: OS Landranger Map 199. Go to *www.sevensisters.org.uk* (click on 'Cycling') or *www.forestry.gov.uk* and search 'Friston Forest'.

Refreshments: Café at the start. Pubs nearby in Friston, Jevington and Litlington.

Category

Forest trail / stone track through Seven Sisters Country Park.

Distance

Forest circuit 5 miles.

To the coast and back – 2¹/₂ miles.

85

Ride 15 Cuckoo Trail north of Eastbourne

15

Category
Railway path.

Distance
11 miles each way.

The Cuckoo Trail is one of the longest and most popular railway paths in the South-East. The line gained its name because of a Sussex tradition that the first cuckoo of spring was released each year at Heathfield Fair. It offers superb traffic-free cycling through a mixture of broadleaf woodland, open grassland, arable farmland and pasture. As you head down towards Polegate there are views of the rolling chalk hills of the South Downs ahead of you. Along the way are metal sculptures, an arch in the form of a Chinese Pagoda roof and plenty of carved wooden seats with a variety of motifs, made from local oaks blown down in the Great Gale of 1987. The verges are thick with wildflowers. There is a gentle climb up from Polegate to Heathfield so that you can look forward to a gravity-assisted return journey! In several places along the way, bridges have been dismantled and houses built on the course of the railway requiring you to cross several minor roads and use short sections of estate roads through Hailsham and Horam to regain the railway path.

Starting points & parking

Heathfield, Hailsham, Horam or **Polegate**. The car parks are all close to the trail (with the exception of Polegate where there is no specific car park for the Cuckoo Trail). For more details of car parks, download the map mentioned below under 'Useful publications & websites'.

On your bikes!

1. From Polegate, follow the railway path for 3 miles into Hailsham. At this point the route follows estate roads so look out for 'Cuckoo Trail (bikes)' signs.

2. Rejoin the railway path and follow for 5 miles through to Horam. There is a second, short section on estate roads.

3. The trail ends after a further 3 miles in Heathfield. In this final section there are several roads to cross – mainly quiet lanes, but care should still be taken if you are with young children.

Station: Polegate, less than $^1/_2$ mile from the start of the route.

TIC: Eastbourne, 0871 663 0031.

Other nearby trails: Friston Forest lies 5 miles to the south-east of Polegate. The South Downs Way has some 'plateau' sections, best enjoyed on a mountain bike, in the summer.

Useful publications & websites: OS Landranger Map 199. Go to *www.eastsussex. gov.uk,* click on 'Leisure and tourism' then 'Cycling' then 'Cycle routes and maps', and on the right-hand side there is a link to 'The Cuckoo Trail'.

Refreshments: Lots of choice in each of the towns. Tea shop on the trail at the Old Loom Mill Craft Centre (2 miles north of Polegate, just before crossing the B2104).

Worth Way
west of East Grinstead
Ride 16

One of two railway paths that start in East Grinstead, the Worth Way whisks you away from commuter land into a wooded landscape in the twinkling of an eye. There is a ½-mile section along roads through Crawley Down before you dive back into woodland once again. The route ends at Worth (on the eastern edge of Crawley). As with the Forest Way, this forms part of National Cycle Network Route 21, the Downs & Weald Cycle Route between London and the South Coast.

Starting points & parking

The car park at the back of the **railway station in East Grinstead**. Follow the one-way system out of town on the A22 (A264) towards London and Crawley. After passing the railway station on your left, just before a major junction with the A264 Tunbridge Wells road, turn left onto Park Road, then first left onto Grosvenor Road. Turn right into the station car park. The Worth Way starts by a wooden signpost on the right (grid reference TQ 388383). *If this is full there is another car park on Railway Approach, about ½ mile east of the railway station.*

On your bikes!

1. Follow the Worth Way for 2½ miles at which point the track turns to tarmac. Three T-junctions! At the first, at the end of Cob Close, turn left; at the second, at the end of Hazel Way, turn right; then at the third, at the end of Woodland Drive, turn left.

2. At the offset crossroads at the end of Burleigh Way, go straight ahead onto Old Station Close. The tarmac turns to track. Continue in the same direction at the next crossroads.

3. At the next road, by a brick and slate building, turn left then shortly right through Rowfant car park.

4. The railway path ends at the third road (by Keepers Cottage) but it is possible to continue a further mile to the church at Worth on a good, stone-based bridleway. Cross the road and turn left onto the track along the verge. On a sharp left-hand bend after 200yds, turn right and follow this track in the same direction for a mile, past a farm and over the M23 as far as Worth, perhaps visiting its lovely Anglo-Saxon church.

Category
Railway path.

Distance
6½ miles each way.

Station: East Grinstead.

TIC· Horsham, 01403 211661.

Other nearby trails: The Forest Way runs south-east from East Grinstead.

Useful publications & websites: OS Landranger Map 187. Go to *www.westsussex. gov.uk* then click on 'Leisure & Tourism' then 'Walking, Cycling and Horseriding'. Scroll down the list to 'Worth Way / Forest Way'.

Refreshments: Lots of choice in East Grinstead. Royal Oak pub, Crawley Down.

Ride **17** **Forest Way**
east of East Grinstead

Category
Railway path.

Distance
10 miles each way.

The countryside around Hartfield is the setting of A. A. Milne's *Winnie the Pooh* stories, so watch out for Tiggers and Heffalumps! This fine ride passes through woodland and arable land lying between East Grinstead and Groombridge. There are picnic tables along the way and the broad, good-quality track makes an ideal ride for exercise and conversation. The railway path forms part of National Cycle Network Route 21, the Downs & Weald Cycle Route between London and the South Coast. The railway line was opened by the London, Brighton & South Coast Railway in 1866 as an extension of the Three Bridges to East Grinstead branch line. Forest Row was the busiest of the intermediate stations, dealing in minerals and general goods. It was finally closed as part of the Beeching cuts in 1966.

Starting points & parking

1. East Grinstead – the trail starts at the east end of the High Street, at the junction of Lewes Road (B2110) with Old Road by the roundabout with the A22 (grid reference TQ 401379). The nearest car park is on De La Warr Road, off College Lane (B2110). This is more easily seen by looking up East Grinstead street mapping on the internet.

2. Groombridge, to the south-west of Tunbridge Wells. There is a free car park by the Post Office and bakery (grid reference TQ 531373).

On your bikes!
East Grinstead to Groombridge

1. From the car park, return to De La Warr Road and turn right. At the T-junction with

17

College Lane, turn right for 100yds then turn first left downhill by a stone wall. At the end of Old Road, cross to the opposite pavement, turn left then right through the fence onto the path. At the next road go straight ahead onto Forest Way.

2. After 2 miles, use the toucan crossing to cross the busy A22 and continue straight ahead onto a tarmac drive signposted 'Tablehurst Farm'. After 400yds, shortly after passing Forest Row Pumping Station on your left, near the end of a line of cypress trees, turn right onto a narrow path signposted 'Forest Way Country Park'.

3. After 4 miles, at a T-junction, just after going through a large yellow stone bridge under the B2026, turn left then right past Hartfield Station, which is now a private house.

4. The Forest Way continues for a further 3$^1/_2$ miles to the edge of Groombridge, crossing several minor roads. To visit the pub, shop or bakery turn left at the T-junction with the lane (by a pumping station) and follow up and down for $^1/_2$ mile into the village.

Station: East Grinstead.

TIC: Tunbridge Wells, 01892 515675.

Other nearby trails: The Worth Way starts from East Grinstead railway station car park.

Useful publications & websites: OS Landranger Maps 187 & 188. Go to *www. eastsussex.gov.uk,* click on 'Leisure and tourism' then 'Cycling' then 'Cycle routes and maps', and on the right-hand side there is a link to 'Forest Way Country Park'.

Refreshments: Lots of choice in East Grinstead. Good pubs just off the route in Hartfield, Withyham and Groombridge.

18

Tonbridge Ride **18**
to Penshurst Place

The bike route between Tonbridge Castle and Penshurst Place offers an excellent, almost entirely traffic-free ride from the heart of Tonbridge alongside the River Medway, out into the countryside as far as the glorious buildings of Penshurst Place, some five miles to the west. The ride takes you past playing fields on the edge of Tonbridge and into Haysden Country Park, running around the edge of Barden Lake with its wide variety of birdlife. Shortly after passing beneath the A21 you enter a delightful secret kingdom of lush broadleaf woodland, carpeted with wildflowers in the spring and a delight in autumn as the colours change. The one noticeable climb of the day comes between the bridge over the River Medway and Well Place Farm, giving you wide-ranging views of the surrounding countryside and setting you up for a fine descent past two lakes to arrive at Penshurst Place, the finest and most complete example in England of 14th-century domestic architecture.

Starting point & parking

Tonbridge Swimming Pool car park, near the castle (grid reference TQ 588465).

Category
Stone-based cyclepath.

Distance
5 miles each way.

Ride **18** Tonbridge to Penshurst Place

On your bikes!

1. From the entrance to Tonbridge Swimming Pool car park, by a 'Children' road sign, take the access road to the overflow car park, keeping the rugby clubhouse to your left. The cycle path starts at the end of the overflow car park, running around the edge of the playing fields. Follow National Cycle Network Route 12 signs into woodland and over a series of bridges with metal railings.

2. Emerge at Barden Lake, turn left and keep the water to your right. At the end of the lake turn left to go under a railway bridge then at the T-junction, with the car park to the right, turn left. At the next T-junction, at the end of the approach road to Haysden Country Park, turn right signposted 'Penshurst Bike Route'.

3. Follow this lane through the village of Lower Haysden, past the pub, under the A21, turn first right then left onto a stone track signposted 'Public Bridleway'. Follow the excellently signposted track through lovely broadleaf woodland.

4. At the end of the track, at the T-junction with a road, turn right then shortly after crossing the bridge take the first concrete track to the left, signposted 'Penshurst 1^1/$_2$'.

5. Climb on this broad concrete track then descend past Well Place Farm towards the magnificent buildings of Penshurst Place.

Station: Tonbridge.

TIC: Tonbridge, 01732 770929.

Other nearby trails: The Forest Way starts in Groombridge, about 5 miles south of Penshurst.

Useful publications & websites: OS Landranger Map 188. A *Tonbridge Castle to Penshurst Place Map & Guide* is available from Tonbridge Tourist Information Centre (01732 770929) or can be downloaded from: *www.sevenoaks. gov.uk/documents/ tonbridgeleaflet.pdf*

Refreshments: Lots of choice in Tonbridge. If you wish to use the tearooms at Penshurst Place you will need to pay the entrance fee to visit the building.

Bewl Water
Lamberhurst
Ride **19**

The only round-reservoir route south of London, Bewl Water offers a fine, challenging summer ride through woodland and pasture on a mixture of tracks and quiet lanes. Be warned that there are some steep hills on the lane sections and that on some of the off-road stretches the surface can be rough. The route should be avoided after prolonged rain. It is shut from November to the end of April. As a full 13-mile circuit it is not suitable for young children. The dam is made from local clay and faced with concrete slabs to prevent erosion. Holding back 6,900 million gallons of water, Bewl Water is the largest reservoir in the South-East. Nearby Chingley Wood is a mixed coppice woodland once used for fuelling ironworks in the valley. Several willow plantations around the lake produce timber for the manufacture of cricket bats.

Starting point & parking

Bewl Water Visitor Centre, near Lamberhurst, off the A21 between Tunbridge Wells and Hastings (grid reference TQ 677338). There is a charge to use the car park. There is limited free parking on the causeway across the reservoir at its eastern end (grid reference TQ 700320).

On your bikes!

From the visitor centre, head down towards the dam and follow bike signs. The route is waymarked with 'Round Water Route' signs but the waymarking is patchy and it is not sufficient to say 'Follow the edge of the lake' as the route veers away from the water's edge on the southern part of the ride. A map is useful for the first time you ride the circuit. On the tarmac sections, keep an eye out for 'Round Water Route' signs at each junction.

Station: Wadhurst.

TIC: Tunbridge Wells, 01892 515675.

Other nearby trails: There are waymarked routes in Bedgebury Forest, just to the east of the reservoir. The Cuckoo Trail runs from Polegate to Heathfield.

Useful publications & websites: OS Landranger Map 188. A map is available at the visitor centre (01892 890661) or go to *www.bewl.co.uk*

Refreshments: At the visitor centre or the Bull pub at Three Leg Cross, about halfway around the circuit.

Category
Round-reservoir route.

Distance
13-mile circuit.

NB This is a very popular route with walkers and horses – please give way to them and ride with consideration for others at all times.

Ride 20 Bedgebury Forest near Hawkhurst

20

Category
Forest trail.

Distance
5 miles.

NB *There is a £7 charge to use the car park. This goes down to £3 for visits after 1700hrs.*

Bedgebury Forest is the only Forestry Commission holding in Kent with waymarked bike routes. There is a 5-mile circuit aimed at families and an 8-mile, tougher singletrack course for more experienced mountain bikers. Bedgebury is mixed woodland and in amongst the fir and conifers you will find sweet chestnut, birch, oak and sycamore, not to mention bright yellow ragwort, purple willowherb and foxgloves. The forest lies adjacent to Bedgebury Pinetum, which contains a magnificent collection of rare trees and flowering shrubs. There is a lovely picnic spot by the lakes that you pass along the route.

Starting point & parking
Bedgebury Forest lies off the B2079 about 1 mile north of its junction with the A21 **between Lamberhurst and Hastings** (grid reference TQ 715336).

On your bikes!
The route is well signposted with marker posts 1-63. The only choice you have to make is whether to do it clockwise, following the numbers in ascending order, or anti-clockwise, following the numbers down from 63 to 1. Louisa Lake is about halfway around the circuit.

Station: Etchingham, south-west of Hawkhurst.

TIC: Tunbridge Wells, 01892 515675.

Other nearby trails: Bewl Water lies just to the west.

Useful publications & websites: OS Landranger Map 188. A *Bedgebury Trail Map* is available from the visitor centre (01580 879820) or go to *www.forestry.gov.uk/ bedgebury*

Refreshments: Café at the visitor centre.

Ride 21 Hythe Seafont

21

Category
Seafront promenade.

Distance
East to Folkestone –
5 miles each way.

West along the Military Canal –
1¹/₂ miles each way

This is surely one of the finest seafront cycle routes on the English south coast. Other cycling promenades such as Bournemouth or Brighton may be full of things to see, but they are also very popular with pedestrians and much of your time is spent looking out for other people. Here, for much of the time you can enjoy the views out over the English Channel without fear of the crowds. There are two very contrasting ways of extending this ride: continuing east along National Cycle Network Route 2 you will be faced with a climb of almost 600ft up onto the famous white cliffs between

Folkestone and Dover; to the west the Military Canal leads to the amazing network of quiet flat lanes that criss-cross Romney Marsh, an area as flat as the Somerset Levels or the Fenland of East Anglia.

Starting point & parking

There is a free car park at the back of the Dukes Head pub, on Portland Road, off the A259 Dymchurch Road in the centre of **Hythe**, near the junction with the A261 (grid reference TR 147137).

On your bikes!
East from Hythe to Folkestone

1. From the car park at the back of the Dukes Head pub (Portland Road), drop down to join the canal towpath and turn right (ie keep the water to your left), following National Cycle Network Route 2 signs.

2. At the end of Portland Road, cross Stade Street onto a tarmac drive alongside the canal. Shortly, opposite a blue metal bridge on the left, turn right onto Ladies Walk (NCN 2) by the Hythe Bowling Club. Cross the road onto Moyle Tower Road to join the wide red tarmac promenade. Turn left.

3. The promenade turns from red tarmac to white concrete. It ends after almost 5 miles

just before Folkestone pier. You may prefer to turn around at this point and return to Hythe. If you wish to visit Folkestone, bear left away from the sea towards the fringe of woodland and follow National Cycle Network Route 2 signs along residential roads into town.

West from Hythe along Royal Military Canal

Heading west from the Dukes Head pub in Hythe, the Military Canal can be followed for 1^1/$_2$ miles through parkland then along Green Lane as far as a metal bridge, which drops you opposite Peregrine Close (and then a further 1^1/$_2$ miles on a quiet road for refreshments at the Botolphs Bridge Inn or the chance to explore the quiet flat lane network of Romney Marsh).

Station: Folkestone.

TIC: Hythe, 01303 266421 or Folkestone, 01303 258594.

Other nearby trails: Folkestone to Dover along the clifftop.

Useful publications & websites: OS Landranger Map 179. Go to *www.whitecliffscountryside.org. uk* and click on 'Cycling'.

Refreshments: Lots of choice in Hythe and Folkestone.

Ride 22 Chalk & Channel Way from Dover to Folkestone

22

Category
Clifftop path.

Distance
5 miles each way.

On a fine, clear day, the views across to France from the top of the cliffs between Folkestone and Dover are quite extraordinary. It is a superb, airy ride high up above the English Channel, with some interesting artworks along the way. As it is a climb of over 500ft up from Folkestone or from Dover, the suggested starting point is on the top of the cliffs above Folkestone. Samphire Hoe was created from the chalk that was excavated from under the sea to create the Channel Tunnel. It is already beginning to grass over and there is a circular ride around this new piece of England.

Starting point & parking

Old Dover Road, **Capel-le-Ferne**, between Folkestone and Dover. Turn off the B2011 just east of the Battle of Britain memorial (grid reference TR 246383).

On your bikes!
East towards Dover

1. From the Cliff Top Café follow the road east towards Dover (with the sea to your right).

NB National Cycle Network Route 2 drops over 550ft from the cliffs down to the sea at Folkestone (via residential streets), so the climb back up from here should only be undertaken by fit cyclists.

2. Go past the Lighthouse Inn and join a cyclepath alongside the B2011. After about $^{1}/_{4}$ mile bear right, soon joining a superb gravel path along the clifftop.

3. After $2^{1}/_{2}$ miles the path emerges alongside the A20. Here you have three choices:

(a) turn back

(b) continue on into Dover, bearing in mind that after crossing the footbridge over the A20 the rest of the route is a long descent on residential streets or cyclepaths alongside busier roads

(c) drop down to the right to explore the cyclepaths on Samphire Hoe

West towards Folkestone

From the Cliff Top Café it is possible to go west for about 1 mile on the Chalk & Channel Way while still maintaining your height, offering fine views out over the channel. Turn left on the cyclepath along the B2011 then bear right onto Crete Road. This can be followed for 1 mile to its junction with the A260, north of Folkestone (grid reference TR 223384).

Station: Folkestone, 01303 258594 or Dover, 01304 205108.

TIC: Folkestone or Dover.

Other nearby trails: Folkestone to Hythe along the promenade.

Useful publications & websites: OS Landranger Map 179. A Chalk & Channel Way leaflet is available from *www.sustrans.org.uk*. Click on 'Sustrans near you' then 'South-east' then scroll down to 'Chalk & Channel Way leaflet'.

Refreshments: Cliff Top Café at the start. Lighthouse Inn, about 1 mile east of Capel-le-Ferne. Valiant Sailor pub on the B2011 west of Old Dover Road.

The Viking Coastal Trail Ride 23
from Reculver to Margate

The Viking Coastal Trail is the name given to a 27-mile ride around the shoreline of the Isle of Thanet, at the north-eastern tip of the coast of Kent. It is a mixture of traffic-free trails, quiet roads and traffic-calmed streets in the coastal towns. The section from Reculver to Margate is the one with the highest traffic-free proportion. It starts from the distinctive towers of the ruins of Reculver Church and proceeds east along a wide concrete sea wall, with a shingle beach to your left with many breakwaters made of huge boulders. Away to the right are flat fertile fields dedicated to arable farming. Coastal resorts at Birchington and Westgate are interspersed with sandy bays. Shingle beaches turn to low chalk cliffs and before long you can sample the delights of Margate.

Starting point & parking
Reculver Country Park car park by the King Ethelbert pub and the church ruins in Reculver, on the north Kent coast, to the east of Herne Bay (grid reference TR 226693).

On your bikes!
1. The route is signposted as the Viking Trail from Reculver on a wide concrete path along the sea wall.

2. After almost 4 miles, this first traffic-free section ends in a car park near Minnis Bay. Go around the edge of the car park, descend to the promenade and turn right (follow signs).

3. Go past a series of low chalk cliffs. Almost 2 miles after the car park and about 200yds before the end of the path (there are steps ahead with railings), keep an eye out for a right turn uphill on a cobbled path cut through the chalk.

4. Follow the cycle lane on the road for almost 1 mile then descend back down to the promenade. **Dismount** in front of the beach huts as indicated by the signs.

5. The trail leads into the heart of Margate where you may turn around after finding some refreshments or continue along the Viking Coastal Trail (which has more road sections beyond this point) to North Foreland, Broadstairs and Ramsgate.

Station: Margate or Birchington.

TIC: Margate, 08702 646111.

Other nearby trails: The Viking Trail can be followed east beyond Margate although there are more road sections. The Crab & Winkle Way runs between Whitstable and Canterbury.

Useful publications & websites: OS Landranger Map 179. Download the Viking Coastal Trail leaflet at www.visitthanet.co.uk/viking/

Refreshments: King Ethelbert pub, Reculver. Lots of choice from Minnis Bay eastwards to Margate.

Category
Seafront promenade.

Distance
9 miles each way.

NB In the Margate area there are several short sections where cyclists must dismount in front of the rows of the beach huts between 1000-1800 hrs from May to September. Young children might easily run out of the huts or cross without looking from the beach back to the huts, hence the need for this measure.

Ride 24 Crab & Winkle Way from Canterbury to Whitstable

24

Category
Purpose-built cyclepath and railway path.

Distance
8 miles each way.

The ride starts from the centre of the beautiful, historic city of Canterbury and uses traffic-calmed roads and specially-built cyclepaths to link town to countryside, following the course of a dismantled railway through broadleaf woodland to the attractive seaside town of Whitstable. The streets around Canterbury Cathedral are best explored on foot and there is in any case a restriction on cycling here between 1030hrs and 1600hrs. The route climbs steadily out of the city with wonderful views opening up behind you. After passing close to the university the route soon joins a traffic-free section that runs for over 4 miles, past fruit farms and through woodland to South Street on the edge of Whitstable. Cyclepaths and traffic-calmed streets lead right into the heart of this fine coastal town.

Starting points & parking

1. Westgate in the centre of **Canterbury** (grid reference TR 146580).

2. Whitstable town centre (grid reference TR 108670).

On your bikes!

1. From Westgate, at the junction of Pound Lane and St Peter's Street in the centre of Canterbury, use the cycle facility to cross the main road and follow the route waymarked 'Route 1, Whitstable' along Westgate Grove and Whitehall Road.

2. The route runs eastwards, parallel with the A2050, then turns north through a more rural setting and climbs steadily. Look behind you and to your right for fine views of Canterbury and the cathedral.

3. Go past a tall white water tower. Use the toucan crossing to cross the busy Whitstable Road (A290) onto the shared-use pavement. Opposite Kent College turn right onto a tarmac lane that goes past a car park and turns to track as it continues northwards.

4. Descend to cross a stream then climb again, passing fruit orchards and farms. Follow the obvious track into woodland, turning right at the first crossroads then left at a T-junction of forestry tracks. To your left is a pond which was used to cool the winding gear on the old Canterbury & Whitstable Line.

5. After $3/4$ mile bear left away from the wide forestry track, descend to cross the bridge over the new A299 and follow the farm track to the road near Brooklands Farm, South Street.

6. Turn left on the road for 300yds then immediately **after** passing Millstrood Road to the left bear left onto the red tarmac cyclepath signposted 'Station, Town Centre Cycle Route'. At the end of the cyclepath turn left then right downhill through the residential road with sea views ahead.

7. Follow the waymarked route into the heart of Whitstable. It is well worth visiting the harbour. Follow: All Saints Close, railway station, Stream Walk, Albert Street, town centre and harbour.

Station: Whitstable or Canterbury.

TIC: Canterbury, 01227 378100.

Other nearby trails: Reculver to Margate along the Viking Trail.

Useful publications & websites: OS Landranger Map 179. A cycling leaflet for the trail is available from *www.canterbury.gov. uk* – search 'Crab and Winkle'. Also try *www. kent.gov.uk* and follow 'Transport and streets' to 'Travel by bike'.

Refreshments: Lots of choice in Whitstable and Canterbury.

Basingstoke Canal (1) Ride 25
from Odiham to Fleet

The Basingstoke Canal runs from near Odiham in Hampshire to the junction with the Wey Navigation near West Byfleet. It has been split into three sections, each about 10 miles long. This westernmost section runs from the Greywell Tunnel, near Odiham, past the ruins of Odiham Castle and on to Fleet. The Basingstoke Canal was completed in 1794. It was 37 miles long with 29 locks and a 1,230-yd tunnel through Greywell Hill.

The canal was built to boost agricultural trade in central Hampshire, carrying coal and fertilizers from London, returning with timber, corn and other produce to the capital. The canal was never a commercial success and by the mid-1960s it was lying semi-derelict. All the locks were decaying, the towpath was overgrown and the water channel choked by weed, refuse and silt. Efforts to stop the rot were made by the Surrey & Hampshire Canal Society.

Category
Canal towpath.

Distance
10 miles each way.

Ride 25   **Basingstoke Canal (1) from Odiham to Fleet**

Restoration work was completed and the canal reopened in 1991.

Starting points & parking

1. Fleet – small car park at the traffic lights at the junction of the B3013 with the A323, just south of the centre of Fleet (grid reference SU 809537). This is at the junction of Reading Road South, Aldershot Road and Connaught Road. The car park is not easily spotted and has an open red and white metal barrier at the entrance. If this car park is full, park along Connaught Road, opposite. Take care crossing back to the canal towpath.

2. Greywell Tunnel (grid reference SU 719513), to the west of Odiham. This is the westernmost limit of the towpath. The nearest car park is at the north-east edge of Odiham, near the Water Witch pub (grid reference SU 747517).

There are also car parks by the canal:

3. South-east of **Winchfield Hurst** (near the Barley Mow pub).

4. South of **Crookham Village** (near the George & Lobster pub).

On your bikes!

From the small car park by the canal in the centre of Fleet, follow the towpath south-west, keeping the water to your left. No instructions are needed as it is very straightforward to follow the canal. After about 9 miles and shortly after passing the extraordinary ruins of Odiham Castle (on your right), the towpath ends at the portal to Greywell Tunnel.

Station: Hook is the nearest station to the start in Greywell. There are stations all along the route.

TIC: Aldershot, 01252 320968.

Other nearby trails: You can follow the canal east from Fleet. There are woodland trails at The Look Out, Bracknell.

Useful publications & websites: OS Landranger Maps 186. GEOprojects produce a good map of the canal. Go to *www.geoprojects.net*. Try also *www.basingstoke-canal.co.uk*

Refreshments: Fox & Hounds pub, just west of Fleet. George & Lobster pub, Crookham Village. Barley Mow pub, Winchfield Hurst. Water Witch pub, Odiham. Jolly Miller pub and Swan pub in North Wanborough.

Ride 26 **Basingstoke Canal (2) from Fleet to the Canal Visitor Centre at Mytchett**

Category
Canal towpath.

Distance
9 miles each way.

This is the middle section of the Basingstoke Canal and despite its proximity to the built-up areas along the Blackwater Valley, it has a very green, woodland feel. It starts at the fascinating visitor centre at Mytchett (which also has a tearoom for when you get back after your ride), and heads south past Mytchett Lake and Greatbottom Flash. Pass high above the A331 dual carriageway running up the Blackwater Valley and continue across gorse- and heather-covered heathland to Fleet. You may wish to continue further west (see Ride 25, above) or indeed from the visitor centre you could just as easily head north then east towards Weybridge

(Ride 27, page 100). The Basingstoke Canal is held by many to be Britain's most beautiful waterway. From the rolling hills of North Hampshire to the dramatic flights of locks in Surrey, the tree-lined canal offers a variety of delights, from 200-year-old bridges and locks to traditionally painted narrow boats.

Starting points & parking

1. Canal Centre, Mytchett Place Road, **Mytchett**, south-east of the M3 Jct 4 (grid reference SU 893551).

2. Fleet – small car park at the traffic lights at the junction of the B3013 with the A323 just south of the centre of Fleet (grid reference SU 809537). This is at the junction of Reading Road South, Aldershot Road and Connaught Road. The car park is not easily spotted and has an open red and white metal barrier at the entrance. If this car park is full, park along Connaught road, opposite. Take care crossing back to the canal towpath.

On your bikes!

1. From the Mytchett Canal Visitor Centre cross the bridge over the canal and turn left, keeping the water to your left. Soon go past Mytchett Lake and Greatbottom Flash.

2. Cross the viaduct over the A331 and the Blackwater River. The quality of the towpath deteriorates then improves.

3. Pass through a landscape of heathland and gorse, and beneath two big black metal 'meccano' style bridges.

4. The suggested turnaround point is the centre of Fleet where there is a choice of pubs and cafés, but if you wish to carry on, the canal continues for a further 10 miles to the tunnel at Greywell (Ride 25).

Station: Ash Vale.

TIC: Aldershot, 01252 320968.

Other nearby trails: The canal can be followed further west (Ride 25) or further east (Ride 27).

Useful publications & websites: OS Landranger Map 186. GEOprojects produce a good map of the canal. Go to *www. geoprojects.net.* See also *www.basingstoke-canal.co.uk*

Refreshments: Canal Visitor Centre Tea Room in Mytchett. Lots of choice in Fleet.

Ride 27 Basingstoke Canal (3) from Mytchett Visitor Centre to Byfleet

27

Category
Canal towpath.

Distance
13 miles each way.

This is the third and final ride on the Basingstoke Canal, from the visitor centre at Mytchett to the canal's junction with the Wey Navigation near to Byfleet. The ride is predominantly on a wide stone and gravel track through beautiful broadleaf woodland, especially noticeable through the remarkable flight of locks at Deepcut where there are 14 locks in less than 2 miles. The best-quality towpath on the whole of the canal runs through Woking: wide and smooth with the vegetation cut well back away from the path – a real delight to ride. The end of the canal at its junction with the Wey Navigation is right underneath the M25, and as this is not an especially exciting place, you may prefer to continue north up towards Weybridge or south towards Pyrford for refreshments (See Ride 35, page 109).

Starting points & parking

1. Mytchett Canal Centre, Mytchett Place Road, Mytchett, off the B3411 between Frimley and Ash, south-east of M3 Jct 4 (grid reference SU 893551).

2. There are several Pay & Display car parks in **Woking** and **West Byfleet** close to the canal.

On your bikes!

1. From the Mytchett Canal Visitor Centre, cross the canal and turn right, keeping the canal to your right.

2. After $^3/_4$ mile at the B3012 (opposite the King's Head pub), turn right then left to rejoin the canal towpath. The railway line passes under the canal.

3. There may be a 1-mile diversion away from the canal east of the B3015 – follow signs on a track parallel with and to the north of the canal.

4. Rejoin the canal and follow through Brookwood, close to the railway line. The towpath quality improves dramatically at the western edge of Woking.

5. In central Woking you will need to cross Chobham Road using the traffic lights to regain the towpath on the other side.

6. The suggested end point is at the junction with the Wey Navigation beneath the M25. However, this is not a very exciting place and you may prefer to follow the Wey Navigation north to Weybridge for 2 miles to find refreshments, or south for 2 miles to the pub at Pyrford Lock (see Ride 35).

Station: Brookwood, Woking, West Byfleet.

TIC: Guildford, 01483 444333.

Other nearby trails: West on a continuation of the Basingstoke Canal or north-east along the Wey Navigation to Weybridge.

Useful publications & websites: OS Landranger Maps 186 and 187. GEOprojects produce a good map of the canal. Go to *www.geoprojects.net*. Also try *www. basingstoke-canal.co.uk*

Refreshments: Tearoom at Canal Visitor Centre at Mytchett. Lots of cafés and pubs just off the route through Woking.

Norbury Park Ride 28
Leatherhead

Norbury Park offers a short way-marked circuit in amongst woodland and farmland which seems a million miles from the busy roads in this densely populated part of Surrey. There is a good network of bridleways stretching to the south-east through Polesden Lacey and Ranmore Common along the North Downs towards Shere and Gomshall, so with an Ordnance Survey map you could easily devise your own off-road routes through the woodland. Norbury Park was the first area of countryside that Surrey County Council purchased in the 1930s to protect it from development. Lying within the Surrey Hills Area of Outstanding Natural Beauty and covering 1,300 acres, it comprises an attractive mix of woods, farms and grassland. Much of the park lies on chalk and flint with a clay cap on higher ground. These soil types support different woodland communities. Beech, yew, ash and cherry are classic chalk-area trees whereas clay supports oak and chestnut. Some of the yews are up to 2,000 years old.

Starting point & parking

Car park off the roundabout at the junction of the A246 and B2122 **south-west of Leatherhead,** signposted 'Bocketts Farm, Norbury Country Park' (grid reference TQ 152249).

On your bikes!

1. Exit the car park, turn sharp right on the tarmac lane leading directly away from the main road. After 200yds ignore a 'Byway' to the right. Continue straight ahead on the main track. Go gently downhill then at a crossroads with a wooden bench to the right continue straight ahead uphill, gently then more steeply.

2. At a fork of tracks by a wooden barrier and a 2-way 'Bridleway' signpost, bear left on the steeper of the two tracks. At the top of the hill at a second fork by a large triangle of grass and trees, with a wooden fence ahead, turn right, going past a timber yard.

3. After ³/₄ mile, at a fork on a tarmac descent not long after passing the viewpoint to the left, bear right on a track climbing to the right, following bike signs.

4. At the T junction at the end of Crabtree Lane car park, turn right uphill. With a flint and brick house to the left, bear right uphill around a wooden barrier.

5. Long, gentle descent. At a fork bear right alongside woodland. Follow this track past a red-brick farm (Roaring House Farm) then at the next crossroads turn left, signposted 'Fetcham, car park', and follow the outward route back to the start.

Category
Good-quality bridleways through country park.

Distance
4 mile circuit.

Station: Westhumble.

TIC: Guildford, 01483 444333.

Other nearby trails: Horton Country Park (Epsom), Wey Navigation (Weybridge).

Useful publications & websites: OS Landranger Map 187. Go to *www.surreywildlifetrust.co.uk,* click on 'Our places' then 'Norbury Park'.

Refreshments: The closest are in Leatherhead or Great Bookham.

Ride 29 Horton Park north-west of Epsom

29

Category
Cycle path through country park.

Distance
3-mile circuit.

This short circuit around Horton Country Park takes you past a mixture of woodland, farmland and through a golf course – as you are not crossing any greens you should be safe from flying golf balls! Part of the route uses the course of the old Horton Light Railway, a branch line that was used to supply coal to the hospital boiler house. In springtime some of the woods are covered with a carpet of bluebells, indicating that the woodlands have grown undisturbed for many years. There is also a circuit around Epsom Common starting from the car park located on the south side of the B280 (Christ Church Road), about 2 miles to the west of Epsom.

29

Starting point & parking

North-west of Epsom. From the centre of Epsom follow the B280 west towards the A243. Shortly after the start of Epsom Common on your left, turn right onto Horton Lane. The entrance to Horton Country Park is about ¹/₂ mile along on the left (grid reference 190618).

On your bikes!

1. Exit the car park and turn right. At a major track crossroads go straight ahead signposted 'Horseride, Chessington Countryside Walk' (the track to the left is the return route). Ignore a left turn. Shortly at a fork of tracks with low wooden posts to the right, bear right.

2. Gentle descent. At the T-junction by large concrete slabs, turn right. Go past a pond and between golf greens. At the crossroads of tracks at the top of a short rise, turn left. Bear right at a series of forks.

3. At the track T-junction with a narrow grass track ahead, turn left. At the crossroads of tracks by a red tile-hung house, turn right to return to the start.

Station: Epsom, Ewell or Chessington.

TIC: Guildford, 01483 444333.

Other nearby trails: Norbury Park (south-east of Leatherhead). The Wey Navigation and Thames Riverside Path from Weybridge.

Useful publications & websites: OS Landranger 187. *The Surrey Cycle Guide No. 3* that covers the ride is available from Epsom & Ewell Borough (01372 732000) or from *www.epsom-ewell.gov.uk/eebc* – follow links via 'Transport' to 'Cycling'.

Refreshments: Lots of choice in Epsom.

Kennet & Avon Canal through Newbury

Ride 30

On its way from Bath to Reading, National Cycle Network Route 4 diverges from the Kennet & Avon Canal towpath from Devizes through Hungerford to a few miles west of Newbury: there is an excellent network of quiet lanes which offers safe and attractive cycling. The towpath is rejoined 3 miles west of Newbury at Hamstead Park, giving the cyclist a fine entry into (or exit from) the centre of Newbury. The orange sandy path passes a series of pill boxes built as a line of defence during the Second World War and runs underneath the new Newbury A34 bypass. The path crosses Bridge Street in the centre of Newbury and continues eastwards alongside the canal to Thatcham. The next section (from Thatcham to Reading) is described in the next ride. Mountain bikes are recommended.

Starting points & parking

1. If arriving by bike, the route starts at the Bridge Street crossing of the canal in the heart of **Newbury** (grid reference SU 471671).

2. If arriving by car there are no car parks adjacent to the canal in the centre of town and it may be worth starting at **Thatcham** railway station (grid reference SU 528663). This is right on the towpath, and from here you can cycle west through Newbury to the end of the improved towpath at Hamstead Park. West of Hamstead Park, National Cycle Network Route 4 leaves the canal towpath and as a result the surface of the towpath is rougher and narrower.

Station: Newbury.

TIC: Newbury, 01635 30267.

Other nearby trails: The canal can be followed east into Reading. Sections of the Ridgeway offer good cycling in the summer months (mountain bikes only).

Useful publications & websites: OS Landranger Map 174. A good leaflet / map called *The Kennet & Avon Cycle Route* is available from *www.sustrans.org.uk*. This is also available as a download from: *www. waterscape.com/media/documents/20589*

Refreshments: Lots of choice in Newbury.

Category
Canal towpath.

Distance
7 miles each way.

Ride 31 Kennet & Avon Canal from Reading to Thatcham

Category
Canal towpath.

Distance
16 miles each way.

Forming part of National Cycle Network Route 4 between Bristol and London, the Kennet & Avon Canal towpath between Thatcham and Reading has been improved to a standard suitable for recreational cycling. Although the towpath is predominantly of stone and gravel, there is a 1-mile section that runs along the meadows by the canal, to the east of Aldermaston. There are several pubs along the way and a chance for tea and coffee at the British Waterways Visitor Centre at Aldermaston Wharf. It is in Reading that the canal links up with the Thames.

Starting points & parking

1. The centre of **Reading** by the Oracle Centre (grid reference SU 721733).
2. Sheffield Bottom picnic site **south of Theale** (grid reference SU 648705).
3. Tyle Mill, off the A4 towards **Sulhamstead** (grid reference SU 627691).
4. Aldermaston Wharf Visitor Centre (grid reference SU 603672).
5. The railway station at **Thatcham** (grid reference SU 528663).

On your bikes!

By bike from the centre of Reading. If
arriving by car it would be better to start at one of the alternative starting points listed above.

1. There are two cycle-route options to the south of Reading from the Oracle Centre. Either follow Fobney Street and signs for 'Green Park' and 'Majedski Stadium', soon joining the canal towpath on the west side of the canal, **OR** follow National Cycle Network Route 4 signs which link cyclepaths and quiet streets to the towpath running down the east side of the canal. Both link at the junction of the A33 and Rose Kiln Lane, to the south of Reading (near Whitley), then turn west towards Theale.

2. There is a short section near to Burghfield Mill where National Cycle Network Route 4 signs will direct you away from the canal and around the edge of a lake, close to the M4. You rejoin the towpath to the east of Theale (just east of where the M4 bridge crosses the canal).

Station: Thatcham, Midgham, Theale or Reading.

TIC: Reading, 0118 956 6226.

Other nearby trails: The Thames towpath can be followed east from Reading to Sonning. The Kennet & Avon Canal towpath can be followed through Newbury west to Hamstead Park.

Useful publications & websites: OS Landranger Maps 174 & 175. A good leaflet / map called *The Kennet & Avon Cycle Route* is available from *www.sustrans.org.uk*. This is also available as a download from: *www.waterscape.com/media/documents/20589*

Refreshments: Lots of choice in Reading. Teas and coffees at the visitor centre at Aldermaston Wharf. The Butt Inn, just south of Aldermaston Wharf and the Rowbarge Inn, just south of Woolhampton.

Reading Ride 32
along the Thames to Sonning

Maybe some time in the future there will be a path alongside the whole length of the River Thames, wide enough and of a good enough quality to cater for cyclists and walkers alike. Sadly, at present there are few stretches of the river west of London where it is possible to ride – this section in and near Reading is one of the exceptions. Reading is where the Kennet & Avon Canal, which starts in Bath, joins the Thames, linking Bristol (via the River Avon) to London (via the Thames). It is possible to cycle along the towpath of the canal into the centre of Reading and beyond towards Newbury. The town is at an important junction of the National Cycle Network: Route 4 runs through Reading on its way from London to Wales, and Route 5 heads north from Reading through the Chiltern Hills to Oxford. You will see one of the attractive Sustrans Millennium Mileposts at the point where Route 4 joins the Thames. Sonning is a fine little village with a good pub and tea shop.

Starting point & parking

Bridge Street (Oracle Centre) in the centre of **Reading**. If arriving by car it is better to park near the Thames Valley Business Park right by the river on the east side of Reading. The car park has a 'Wokingham Waterside Centre' sign and lies at the very northern end of the A3290, just off the roundabout that lies to the north of the A4 junction and beyond the railway bridge (grid reference SU 736740).

On your bikes!

East to Sonning

1. Exit the riverside car park and turn left on the shared-use pavement along Thames Valley Park Drive. After ½ mile turn left off the roundabout by the Thames Valley Park Security building onto the drive towards the David Lloyd fitness centre.

2. Pass to the left of the car park and around a metal field gate signposted 'Authorised vehicles only'. After ½ mile turn right alongside the river.

3. Follow the track by the river for 1 mile. The Lock Tea Gardens are just by Sonning Lock (no surprise!). For the Bull Inn, just **before** Sonning Bridge turn right and walk your bikes up past the church into the village.

Category
Riverside path.

Distance
4 miles each way.

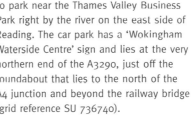

Ride 32   Reading along the Thames to Sonning

West to Caversham Bridge

From the boat club turn left alongside the river, with the Thames to your right. After $1/4$ mile, at the fork of rivers you have a choice:

(a) bear left up over the bridge signposted 'Wallingford National Cycle Network Route 5' and follow this for $1^1/2$ miles as far as the second bridge, with ornate balustrades and round-lamp streetlights (Caversham Bridge).

(b) stay on the path alongside the Kennet & Avon Canal and follow National Cycle Network Route 4 into the centre of Reading (or continue further west, joining Ride 31, page 104).

Station: Reading.

TIC: Reading, 0118 956 6226.

Other nearby trails: The Kennet & Avon Canal can be followed west from Reading towards Newbury.

Useful publications & websites: OS Landranger Map 175. A good leaflet called *Cycling in Reading* showing all the cycle routes and facilities in Reading is available from Reading Borough Council at *www.reading.gov.uk/cycling*. Another useful website is *www.readingcyclecampaign.org.uk*

Refreshments: Jolly Angler pub, Fisherman's Cottage pub, on the canal towpath near Reading centre. Lots of choice in Reading itself. The Bull Inn, Sonning. Lock Tea Gardens just west of Sonning.

Ride 33   **The Look Out in Bracknell Forest**

Category
Waymarked woodland trails.

Distance
Several circuits of between 3 and 10 miles.

This area of the Crown Estate comprises 2,600 acres of predominantly Scots Pine woodland. The current policy is to increase the amount of broadleaf trees where appropriate. Although owned and managed by the Crown Estate Commissioners, The Look Out has been set up in partnership with the Bracknell Forest Borough Council. From The Look Out, rides and tracks radiate through the forest. The ride suggested here is just one of many that could be devised along the wide gravel tracks that criss-cross the woodland. There is also a designated mountain bike area with tricky, testing singletrack, should you be looking for something more challenging. The Discovery Outpost at The Look Out is a hands-on science fun centre with over 70 exhibits.

Starting point & parking

The Look Out Visitor Centre is located in the woodland just to the **south of Bracknell**, about $3/4$ mile west of the roundabout at the junction of the B3430 and the A322 (grid reference SU 876661).

On your bikes!

1. With your back to the entrance of The Look Out Visitor Centre, go diagonally right towards Go Ape passing to the right of the coach park. Go through the gate.

2. Continue in the same direction on a broad track through pine trees. At the T-junction just before the tall Swinley Forest Post no. 1, turn sharp right signposted 'Pudding Hill'. After 600yds take the first left at a fork onto a similar broad stone track (no sign).

3. At a diagonal crossroads of tracks by Post no. 10, continue in the same direction uphill signposted 'MTB Trail' (red arrow), then very shortly at the next crossroads go straight ahead again, leaving the MTB Trail which goes off to the left.

4. After almost 1 mile at Lower Star Post no. 5 (under power lines), continue straight ahead gently downhill.

5. At a fork bear right, keeping the Ministry of Defence wire fence to your left. Stay close to the fence around a sharp right-hand then left-hand bend. At the next flag, with 'Gate 8' to your left, by yellow and black 'H' (hydrant) signs, turn right.

6. Emerge at Upper Star Post no. 6 and take the second left, signposted 'Caesar's Camp'. This can be explored on foot only.

7. At Post no. 8, turn right towards The Look Out alongside a wood and wire fence. Good downhill. At the T-junction shortly after passing a pond on the right, turn left.

8. Walk through the picnic area / café outdoor seating area to return to the car park.

Station: Bracknell.

TIC: At The Look Out, 01344 868196.

Other nearby trails: Windsor Great Park, Kennet & Avon Canal towpath through Reading, Basingstoke Canal between Frimley Green and Woking.

Useful publications & websites: OS Landranger 175. Much more useful is the map that can be purchased at the visitor centre or from the adjacent bike hire outlet. For general information about The Look Out, go to *www. bracknell-forest.gov.uk/lookout* and click on 'Outdoor activities'.

Refreshments: Café at the visitor centre.

33

Ride 34 Windsor Great Park

34

Category
Estate roads through magnificent parkland.

Distance
5-mile circuit.

Although there will be occasional vehicles within Windsor Great Park, it is a very cycle-friendly place and an amazing oasis of tranquility set in the heart of such a built-up area (the M3, M4, M25 and Heathrow are all less than 5 miles away). There is an estate village with a village shop, the fields are ploughed, seeded and harvested, there are woods and lakes, and a school. The place is free of the creeping urbanisation that blights so much of the area to the west of London. You are allowed on the tarmac roads (and through the big green gates operated by buttons!). Signs will tell you where you **cannot** go. Polo matches are frequently played here. Windsor Castle was established by William the Conqueror and it is the largest inhabited castle in the world. The enormous round tower has a view over 12 counties. Savill Garden is famous for its rhododendrons and the Valley Garden is noted for its heathers. Nearby is the 160-acre lake of Virginia Water.

Starting point & parking

Free car park by **Ranger's Gate / Ranger's Lodge** on the A322, about 3 miles south of Windsor (grid reference SU 954735).

On your bikes!

1. Use the toucan crossing to cross the busy A332 into the park via Rangers Gate. At a crossroads after ½ mile, go straight ahead signposted 'York Club'. Shortly at the next crossroads, go straight ahead again (same sign).

2. Climb past York Club to a pink castle on a left-hand bend at the top. Descend, passing a statue of Queen Elizabeth on a horse to your right.

3. At the fork at the bottom of the hill, bear right then go straight ahead at a crossroads by a red-brick house (or turn right along Duke's Lane as far as Prince Consort's Gate to see the magnificent trees).

4. At the T-junction after passing the Royal School, at the top of a climb, turn right (**not** sharp right to Cumberland Lodge) then at the next T-junction turn right (again **not** Cumberland).

5. Continue straight ahead past Cumberland Gate Lodge then at the end of the polo ground turn left at a 'Guards Polo Club' sign.

6. At the next crossroads turn left, 'No entry for gardens traffic'. Go past the Savill Garden, following signs for 'Bishopgate'

ALL CYCLES

PLEASE KEEP TO HARD ROADS

on a wide tarmac road, avoiding all 'No cycling' signs.

7. At the T-junction by Cumberland Gate turn right. Ignore left turns. Go past a large pink house, go straight ahead at a crossroads then pass through big gates operated by a button.

8. Go past Long Walk (with views down towards Windsor Castle) and through a second set of gates. Ignore a left turn then at the crossroads shortly after passing Russels Field Farm on the right, turn right signposted 'Rangers Gate exit' to return to the start.

Station: Windsor.

TIC: Windsor, 01753 743900.

Other nearby trails: The Thames Towpath and the Basingstoke Canal are nearby. Woodland tracks at Bracknell (The Look Out).

Useful publications & websites: OS Landranger Map 175. Maps of the park are available from the ticket office at the Savill Garden, just south of Bishop's Gate. Also try *www.theroyallandscape.co.uk* (for Savill Garden) or *www.thecrownestate.co.uk/ windsor_great_park*

Refreshments: Pub at Bishop's Gate. Café and restaurant at the Savill Garden.

Wey Navigation Ride **35** from Weybridge to Pyrford Lock

There are several traffic-free options for escaping from south-west London along the waterways: the Thames Towpath runs from Putney Bridge to Weybridge, the Basingstoke Canal starts south of Weybridge and runs south-west through Woking to Odiham in Hampshire. Connecting the two and taking a more southerly course, the Wey Navigation starts in Weybridge and heads through Byfleet towards Guildford and Godalming. South of Pyrford to Guildford the canal towpath is fairly rough, but the 5-mile stretch described here is in reasonable condition and offers a chance to enjoy a ride along a green corridor through this built-up area ending at a waterside pub at Pyrford Lock.

Starting points & parking

1. The riverside car park on the sharp bend on Thames Street / Walton Lane to the north of **Weybridge** High Street (grid reference TQ 076658). You can also get to this point by following the minor road or the Thames towpath for 1 mile west from Walton Bridge, where there is a much larger car park (grid reference TQ 094664).

2. Pyrford Lock, west of the A3 / M25 junction (grid reference TQ 054593).

On your bikes!

1. Exit the car park and bear right towards the Minnow pub. Immediately before the Old Crown pub turn right down Church Walk (by the public conveniences). Walk for 50yds.

2. At the end of the path turn right, cross the ornate metal bridge then at the T-junction turn left, signposted 'Flockton

Category
Canal towpath.

Distance
5 miles each way.

NB The Wey Navigation towpath can also be followed for 5 miles at its southern end between Guildford and Godalming (see Ride 8, page 78).

Ride **35** **Wey Navigation from Weybridge to Pyrford Lock**

House' and shortly turn right onto a wide gravel path alongside green railings. Dismount to cross a humpback metal bridge and turn left on the towpath.

3. At times narrow and rooty. After ³/₄ mile, at a grey-brick bridge at the T-junction with Addlestone Road, turn right signposted 'Addlestone / Chertsey Bike Route'. You may prefer to ride on the road parallel to the canal as a more comfortable option for ¹/₄ mile as far as the humpback bridge on your left, where the towpath changes sides.

4. You will occasionally need to cross roads as the towpath changes sides. Pass beneath the M25* following signs for Guildford and Godalming. It is suggested you continue for 2 miles beyond the canal junction as far as the Anchor pub at Pyrford Marina, then return to Weybridge. About 1 mile beyond Pyrford Marina the towpath becomes much rougher.

At the point where you pass under the M25 you have the option of turning right off the Wey Navigation and following the Basingstoke Canal for many miles through Woking, Aldershot and Fleet to Odiham.

Stations: West Byfleet and Brooklands.

TIC: Guildford, 01483 444333.

Other nearby trails: The Wey Navigation joins the Thames Towpath at Weybridge and this can be followed to Putney Bridge in London. It joins the Basingstoke Canal at West Byfleet.

Useful publications & websites: OS Landranger Maps 176 & 187. The Surrey Cycle Guides provide more detail: *www.surreycc. gov.uk* and put 'Surrey Cycle Guide' into the 'Search' box to find out how to order copies. The Wey Navigation is also covered by the Basingstoke Canal GEOproject map – go to *www.geoprojects.net*

Refreshments: Lots of choice in Weybridge. Minnow pub, Old Crown pub at the start. The Anchor at Pyrford Lock.

Thames Towpath Ride 36
between Putney Bridge and Weybridge

The Thames towpath is the best exit for cyclists from south-west London, with plenty of interest to see along this wonderful green and leafy corridor, including Hampton Court Palace. There is a striking contrast between the wide, untamed tidal stretch as far west as Teddington Lock and the highly managed pleasure-boat section which lies beyond. The towpath overlaps entirely with NCN Route 4 for the second half of the ride for the 11 miles from Teddington Lock through Kingston to Weybridge, and it is here that the quality of the towpath is at its very best. For the section between Putney Bridge and Teddington (a section where NCN 4 takes an alternative route across Richmond Park), the quality is variable and mountain bikes are recommended. There is one quite rough patch between Hammersmith Bridge and Chiswick Bridge.

Starting points & parking

1. Putney Bridge (grid reference TQ 252757).

2. Car park at **Ham Lands**, north of Ham, opposite Eel Pie Island (grid reference TQ 170732)

3. Car park at **Walton Bridge** (grid reference TQ 094664).

4. The south-west starting point is north of **Weybridge** at the small riverside car park on the sharp bend on Thames Street / Walton Lane (grid reference TQ 076658).

On your bikes!

Heading west from Putney Bridge

1. There is a short section between Hammersmith Bridge and Barnes railway bridge (along Lonsdale Road), where there is no towpath and it is suggested you walk along the pavement for about 600yds. The towpath is very narrow close to Chiswick Bridge.

2. In Kingston you should follow 'National Cycle Network 4' signs, turning left away from the river at a grey metal 'Meccano' bridge in the direction of 'Kingston Town Centre'. There is a safe waymarked route through the traffic on green painted cycle lanes signposted 'NCN 4' that will take you across Kingston Bridge.

3. After Hampton Court, cross the road at the toucan crossing, turn left across the bridge and then right at the end of the bridge to continue alongside the river towards Walton-on-Thames.

Station: Several railway stations along the route.

TIC: Richmond, 0208 940 9125.

Other nearby trails: This ride can be linked via the Wey Navigation to the Basingstoke Canal, forming a 50-mile route from Putney Bridge almost to Basingstoke in deepest Hampshire. The Tamsin Trail in Richmond Park.

Useful publications & websites: OS Landranger Map 176. Better to use street mapping. Try *www.tfl.gov.uk/cycling* and click on 'Routes, maps & guides'. The route is also covered by Sustrans' *Thames Valley Cycle Route* map (£5.99) available from *www.sustrans.org.uk*

Refreshments: All along the way.

Category
Riverside path.

Distance
Anything up to 23 miles each way.

NB Please note that the towpath is frequently busy with pedestrians, particularly on summer weekends, so please slow down and show consideration.

Ride 37 Tamsin Trail Richmond Park

37

Category
Cycle track around the park.

Distance
8 miles.

NB Several roads are crossed in the park, so take care if you are with young children.

Created by the generosity of an anonymous donor who wanted the trail named after his daughter, Tamsin, this 8-mile, purpose-built circuit of Richmond Park is one of the best things to have happened to recreational cycling in London. The trail runs along a fine gravel path with several gentle hills. The park lies on the sloping plateau above Richmond. It was enclosed by Charles I in 1637 with an 8-mile wall, enabling him to hunt for deer. From Pembroke Lodge, on the western edge of the park, the views on a clear day extend far into Berkshire. To the north of Pembroke Lodge is King Henry VIII's mound where it is possible to see the dome of St Paul's Cathedral.

Station: Richmond or Kingston.

TIC: Richmond, 0208 940 9125.

Other nearby trails: The Thames Towpath runs through Richmond. There is a very limited 4-mile network of cycle routes across Wimbledon Common. Signs will indicate where you can and cannot go. Visit the Wimbledon Common website: *www.wpcc.org. uk* and follow links via 'Sport' to 'Cycling' (at the bottom of the page).

Useful publications & websites: OS Landranger Map 176. Visit Richmond Park's website: *www.royalparks.org.uk*, choose 'Richmond Park' then 'Sport in the Park' then 'Cycling'.

Refreshments: There is a café at Pembroke Lodge on the west side of the park.

Starting point & parking

Any of the car parks near the gates / entrances into **Richmond Park**.

Ride 38 Slough Arm Grand Union Canal, east of Slough

38

Category
Canal towpath.

Distance
5 miles each way.

There are several 'arms' coming off the Grand Union Canal north-west of London: in addition to the one described here, others are to be found at Wendover, Aylesbury and Northampton. The Slough Arm runs from Slough via Langley and Iver to the Cowley Peachey Junction (south of Uxbridge). Built in 1883, the Slough Arm was, with the exception of the Manchester Ship Canal, the last canal to be built in Britain. It goes over several aqueducts and through a long cutting. To the west of Iver the water is surprisingly clear.

Starting points & parking

1. Cowley Peachey Junction lies 3 miles **south of Uxbridge** on the A408, just north of Yiewsley (grid reference TQ 056810).

2. The terminus is on the B416 Stoke Poges road to the **north of Slough railway station** (grid reference SU 979808).

Station: Yiewsley, Iver, Langley, Slough.

TIC: Windsor, 01753 743900.

Other nearby trails: The Grand Union Canal itself, Windsor Great Park.

Useful publications & websites: OS Landranger Map 176. The Nicholson *Guide to the Waterways (South)* is packed with detail about all the canals in England and Wales to the south of Birmingham. For a history of the canal go to www.sloughcanal.org.uk

Refreshments: Iver, Langley and Slough.

Grand Union Canal north of Denham Country Park   Ride 39

With the exception of a 5-mile section in London between Kensal Rise and Horsenden Hill (near Wembley), very little of the Grand Union Canal from Paddington right through to Uxbridge offers good recreational cycling: the towpath is too narrow, too rough, too overgrown or very slow with a succession of metal anti-motorbike barriers. To the north of Uxbridge things start to improve, and Denham Country Park is a good starting point for exploration further north. Having said this, mountain bikes or bikes with wide tyres are definitely recommended as there are still some short, rougher sections. The towpath is a green corridor past hundreds of brightly coloured narrowboats. The Batchworth Canal Visitor Centre or the café at the Aquadrome are good destinations, although you have two options for extending your trip: along the Ebury Way (a railway path) into Watford, or on a continuation of the towpath to the west of Watford, towards Hemel Hempstead.

Category
Canal towpath.

Distance
6 miles each way.

Ride **39** **Grand Union Canal, north of Denham Country Park**

Starting points & parking

1. Denham Country Park – just north of the M40, Jct 1. Follow the brown and white signs from the roundabouts at the motorway junction (grid ref TQ 047865).

2. Rickmansworth Aquadrome – it is a little complicated to describe how to get here! Take the A404 out of Rickmansworth towards Northwood and London. At the Moor Lane roundabout where 'A4145 / Watford Road' is signposted straight on and 'London (A404)' off to the right, complete a circuit of the roundabout and head back towards Rickmansworth – the turning for the Aquadrome is on your left on Harefield Road (grid reference TQ 057937).

On your bikes!

1. From the Denham Country Park Visitor Centre go back under the height barrier, turn left then right through the overflow car park, bearing left through the car park itself to pick up 'Grand Union Canal' signs. Follow the gravel path to the canal and turn left. Remember this point for your return (near Bridge 182).

2. Go past the tea gardens at the lock. About ½ mile after Bridge 180 and the Horse & Barge pub there is a rougher and narrower section to Bridge 179.

3. Go past the Coy Carp pub and Copper Mill Lock. The path is again a bit rougher either side of a concrete bridge with raised humps across it.

4. After 2 miles you will come to Batchworth Lock Visitor Centre, just beyond Rickmansworth Aquadrome. It is suggested you turn around here after visiting the centre and / or the café at the Aquadrome.

If you wish to extend your ride you can either stay on the Grand Union Canal towpath on its way towards Kings Langley and Hemel Hempstead, or follow the Ebury Way along the course of an old railway line into Watford.

Station: Rickmansworth or Denham.

TIC: Uxbridge, 01895 250706.

Other nearby trails: Slough Arm of the Grand Union Canal. North on the Grand Union Canal itself towards Hemel Hempstead.

Useful publications & websites: OS Landranger Map 176. *www.waterscape.com/ things-to-do/cycling* and click on 'Grand Union Canal' at the bottom of the web page.

Refreshments:
Café at Denham Country Park Visitor Centre
Horse & Barge pub, South Harefield
Coy Carp pub, Coppermill Lane, Harefield
Café at the Aquadrome, Rickmansworth.

40

Greenwich to Erith alongside the Thames   Ride 40

arlier in the book, Ride 36 explores the River Thames as it enters London from the west; this ride shows a very different face of the river as it approaches the final part of its journey to the sea. Starting in Greenwich, site of the Cutty Sark and the splendour of the Royal Naval College, the ride initially weaves its way through streets to emerge beneath the O2 Arena (what was originally the Millennium Dome). The silver shell structures of the Thames Barrier offer a memorable landmark. Beyond here there is a short, unavoidable section on road before rejoining the river near the Woolwich Ferry. East of here the character of the river is dominated by the shipping of sand and gravel. It is a wide commercial waterway, far removed from the pleasure boats and wooded banks of the Thames to the west of the city. There is plenty to see along the way, from metal sculptures to old wooden wharfs. The trail improves as it goes further east, becoming a wide, smooth path leading to Erith where you have several options (see below).

Starting points & parking

1. Greenwich – the Cutty Sark / the entrance for the Greenwich Foot Tunnel in Greenwich, east London (grid reference TQ 383779).

2. Erith train station, east along the Thames towards Dartford (grid reference TQ 512782).

On your bikes!

1. The route between Greenwich and the O2 Arena does not lie right by the river, so you will need to follow 'Thames Cycle Route / National Cycle Network Route 1' signs closely.

Category
Riverside path.

Distance
13 miles each way.

2. Pass around the peninsula beneath the outside of the O2 Arena.

3. Follow close to the river as far as the distinctive silver structures of the Thames Flood Barrier. At this point, you will once again need to leave the river on a well-signposted route along residential streets (and on a cyclepath alongside the busier Woolwich Road) to return to the river close to the Woolwich Ferry.

4. A 6-mile riverside section follows all the way to Erith. Here you may wish to turn around, catch a train back to Greenwich or carry on along National Cycle Network Route 1 on the banks of the River Darent and River Cray into Dartford.

Station: Greenwich, Woolwich, Erith.

TIC: Greenwich, 0870 608 2000.

Other nearby trails: Greenwich is at a crossroads of the National Cycle Network. The best nearby traffic-free section runs north from Limehouse Basin along the Regent's Canal (Grand Union Canal) and through Victoria Park to the Lee Navigation (see East of England, Ride 9, page 142).

Useful publications & websites: OS Landranger Map 177. A street map of London would be just as helpful or the Transport for London Cycle Guides: see *www.tfl.gov.uk/cycling*

Refreshments: Lots of choice in Greenwich, Woolwich and Erith. Otherwise you will need a street map to navigate your way from the river and back again.

Ride **41**   Thames through Oxford

Category
Riverside path.

Distance
4 miles each way.

Cycling and Oxford have gone together almost since the invention of the bicycle. This ride explores the towpath of the Thames from the Ring Road in the south, past all the Oxford University college boathouses, to the Perch pub in Binsey then to the north-east of the city centre. There are many architectural attractions along the way including the bridge at Iffley Lock and the folly at Folly Bridge. The southern half of this ride overlaps with the National Cycle Network, which continues south via a purpose-built cycletrack alongside the railway on its way towards Radley and Abingdon. It is also possible to cycle alongside the Oxford Canal up through north Oxford, although the towpath is much narrower and rougher than the Thames towpath.

Starting points & parking

1. By bike from the centre of the city. The Thames towpath can be joined at Folly Bridge on St Aldates in the **centre of Oxford**.

2. If arriving by car it would be better to start at the Redbridge Park & Ride car park just off the Ring Road at the **south of Oxford**, at the junction of the A4144 and the A423, to the east of the A34.

On your bikes!

Starting from the south.

1. Exit Redbridge Park & Ride car park via the entrance and turn right along the cyclepath (away from Oxford). Descend through the subway and at the first T-junction, turn left to go through a second subway. At the second T-junction (with metal barriers to your left), turn right and follow the cycle track parallel with the Ring Road.

2. Cross a bridge over a tributary of the Thames then just before the much larger bridge over the main course of the Thames, turn left downhill signposted 'National Cycle Network Route 5' then left along the towpath. (**Remember** this point for your return.)

3. Go past the lock, the Isis Tavern and past the college boathouses. At the crossroads by Folly Bridge, use the toucan crossing to go straight ahead onto a continuation of the towpath.

4. Walk your bike through Osney Lock. Descend off the towpath onto East Street by the Waterman's Arms pub and continue in the same direction parallel with the river. As the street swings round to the left, climb the steps up to the Botley Road.

5. Cross to the other side of the road to join a continuation of the towpath (now on the right side of the river). You may prefer to cross the road using the toucan crossings that lie to the east or west of the bridge.

6. Cross a hump-backed metal and wooden bridge and turn left, following the Thames Path. Follow this with water to both left and right. After 1/2 mile go straight ahead past the marina and turn left on the bridge across the river.

7. Go past the boatyard then follow the main wide stone track as it swings left away from the river to arrive at the Perch pub.

Station: Oxford.

TIC: Oxford, 01865 726871.

Other nearby trails: The Phoenix Trail from Thame to Princes Risborough. The Ridgeway is a long-distance bridleway / byway running from West Kennet to Goring on Thames that offers good riding for mountain bikes in the summer.

Useful publications & websites: OS Landranger Map 164. Cycling maps for Oxford can be viewed online and downloaded from the council website at *www.oxfordshire.gov. uk* – type 'Cycling Maps' into the 'search' box. Another useful website is *www.cyclox.org* (the Cycling Campaign for Oxford).

Refreshments:
Lots of choice in Oxford, most of it just off the route. Isis Tavern by the Thames, just north of the ring road. Head of the River pub at Folly Bridge. Waterman's Arms pub, East Street (south of the Botley Road). Perch Inn, Binsey.

NB This ride is also popular with walkers. Please ride with consideration for other users, let people know you are coming and thank them if they step aside for you. Where the path is narrow, show courtesy by pulling in and letting walkers pass.

Ride 42 Phoenix Trail
between Thame and Princes Risborough

42

Category
Railway path.

Distance
7 miles each way.

A section of the old railway line that used to link Princes Risborough to Oxford has been converted to recreational use and offers a fine, open ride across the Oxfordshire countryside with wide-ranging views to the steep wooded escarpment of the Chiltern Hills which lie to the south. Red Kites have been introduced to this area and you will see many of these majestic birds with their distinctive forked tails as they wheel high above. Some more unusual animals can also be seen along the trail: about halfway along, perched high up on poles, is a set of bizarre metal animal sculptures. This is one of those good 'conversational' rides where the path is wide and has a fine, smooth surface, allowing you to cycle side by side and put the world to rights. The ride is very popular on summer weekends, as is the Towersey Arms, the only pub along the route.

Starting point & parking
Thame Leisure / Sports Centre, on the west side of **Thame**, about 300yds east of the roundabout at the junction of the A418 and A329 (grid reference SP 696058).

NB There is no parking along Horsenden Lane at the Princes Risborough end of the Phoenix Trail. There is space for a few cars just off the B4009 immediately south of the old green metal railway bridge between Princes Risborough and Chinnor (grid reference SP 786036).

On your bikes!

1. From the Thame Leisure Centre car park, aim to pass between the white buildings of the leisure centre and the school. Go straight ahead at a mini-roundabout, then first left, keeping the leisure centre buildings close by on your right. Follow a tarmac path across the playing field to join the Phoenix Trail. Turn right. (Remember this point for the return trip.)

2. Follow the trail as it swings left (east). Go straight ahead at a crossroads of tracks signposted 'Towersey 2, Princes Risborough 7, National Cycle Network Route 57'.

3. Use the toucan crossing to cross the busy road by the industrial estate.

4. Go past a wooden 'Clam' sculpture. The Towersey Arms pub is shortly after this on your left. Go past animal sculptures on the top of tall poles.

5. The railway path itself finishes 2 miles after passing the animals, at the bridge over the busy B4009. You may wish to turn around here if you do not want to go into Princes Risborough.

6. (On to Princes Risborough.) There is a short, rough section then at the T-junction with tarmac by Glebe Cottage, turn right (remember this point for the return trip).

42

7. Go past the church. At the T-junction at the end of Horsenden Lane, turn left over the railway bridge and immediately left again following the National Cycle Network Route 57 signs into the centre of Princes Risborough. This will involve busier roads.

Exit from Princes Risborough

The waymarked Route 57 provides an alternative to the A4010 / B4444 from the centre of Princes Risborough to the start of the Phoenix Trail. The route is as follows: Market Square, Church Street, Stratton Road, Manor Park Avenue, Station Road, Picts Lane, Horsenden Lane.

Station: Princes Risborough.

TIC: Thame, 01844 212834.

Other nearby trails: Thames through Oxford, Wendover Woods, Grand Union Canal and the Ashridge Estate (see East of England, Ride 2, page 133, for this final ride).

Useful publications & websites: OS Landranger Map 165. For a leaflet go to *www. sustrans.org.uk* or *www.chilternsaonb.org* and search 'Phoenix Trail'.

Refreshments: Lots of choice in Thame and Princes Risborough.
Towersey Arms pub in Towersey, about 2 miles east of Thame.

43

There are very few Forestry Commission holdings of any size in the area immediately to the north and west of London. Wendover Woods are the one exception and are the only woodlands in the area with a waymarked trail aimed at recreational family cycling. There are some wonderful views as the car park and (excellent) café at the start of the ride are very close to the highest point of the Chilterns. The woodland is mainly broadleaf so there is a fantastic display of bluebells in the late spring, and a glorious riot of colour in the autumn as the trees start to lose their leaves. The only downside to this otherwise perfect combination is that with the car park / starting point at the top of the hill, the route starts off with a long descent and finishes with a long climb back up to the car park.

Starting point & parking

From Wendover (south-east of Aylesbury) follow the A4011 north towards Tring. After 3 miles take the first proper road to the right towards Buckland Common and Cholesbury. The entrance to the woodland is ³/₄ mile up this steep minor road on the right hand side. Climb on the road through the forest for about 1 mile to the car parks / information centre at the top of the hill (grid reference SP 889090).

On your bikes!

1. From the Wendover Woods car park continue past the café on the tarmac road towards the exit. After 200yds keep an eye out for a turning to the right by a tall wooden post with a purple arrow (Firecrest Trail). This is the start of the Family Cycle Route.

Category
Waymarked forestry routes.

Distance
6-mile circuit.

Ride 43 Wendover Woods, Chilterns, south-east of Aylesbury

2. Gentle descent with great views to the right. After 1/3 mile at a major track junction where the purple trail turns sharp right, **either** continue straight ahead for the main route **or** turn right for the shortcut route, avoiding one big hill.

3. After a further 2/3 mile, at a track crossroads, turn right (signs will tell you where you **can't** go) to continue downhill. At a second crossroads, with a wide stone forestry road at the bottom of a much steeper section, turn right uphill climbing steadily and steeply.

4. At a T-junction with 'Short Cut' signposted to the right, turn left for the main route (or right for the shortcut). At the next major track junction, turn right uphill then shortly at another T-junction turn left for the main route or right for a shortcut.

5. The track surface becomes rougher. After 1/3 mile, at a fork on the descent bear right. At a T-junction by wooden benches bear left. After a further 1/3 mile, immediately after a wooden barrier by a turning circle with a grass 'roundabout', bear left past wooden fitness equipment for the full route (or go straight ahead for shortcut).

6. Gentle descent. At a fork bear right on the upper track. At T-junction turn right sharply back on yourself uphill to return to the start.

Station: Wendover.

TIC: Wendover. 01296 696759.

Other nearby trails: The Grand Union Canal. The Ridgeway. Ashridge Estate.

Useful publications & websites: OS Landranger Map 165. Go to *www.forestry.gov. uk/WendoverWoods*

Refreshments: Excellent café at the start.

44

44

Milton Keynes to Winslow   Ride 44

This 9-mile section of the National Cycle Network connects the astonishing urban cycle network of Milton Keynes Redway to the small, attractive old town of Winslow via cyclepaths and quiet lanes across the gently undulating Buckinghamshire countryside. The ride starts from near the National Bowl at the distinctive silver star sculpture on the eastern edge of Furzton Lake, and follows the cyclepath that runs along Emerson Valley almost to the edge of town. A succession of Rights of Way have been improved with stone and gravel to create a route that travels almost due south-west to the edge of Winslow with its handsome red brick buildings and fine square. There are plenty of refreshments available at several cafés and pubs.

Starting points & parking

1. Furzton Lake, just off the A421 on the south-western edge of Milton Keynes (grid reference SP 851359).

2. Winslow, on the A413 Buckingham to Aylesbury road to the south-west of Milton Keynes (grid reference SP 771279).

On your bikes!

Start from Milton Keynes

1. Follow the cyclepath around the east side of Furzton Lake towards a tall silver star metal sculpture, soon picking up signs for 'National Cycle Network Route 51, Winslow'.

2. Turn left after passing a cricket pavilion on the left, following the path around the cricket pitch / playing field to your left. Shortly after crossing a small stream, turn right (all NCN 51 signs).

3. Follow the route along the valley for just over 1 mile. Immediately after passing under the second large concrete bridge, turn sharp left uphill by a tall metal Millennium signpost. Follow the cyclepath alongside V2 (Tattenhoe Street) under the subway then right alongside H8 (Standing Way).

4. Follow NCN 51 round to the left alongside Buckingham Road then after ¼ mile take care turning right onto the track (NCN 51) on the other side of the road.

5. Continue in the same direction at several crossroads over the next 3½ miles. The trail briefly joins the lane network. Follow signs for Swanbourne, then on a sharp left-

Category
Connecting cyclepaths and bridleways.

Distance
9 miles each way.

Ride **44** **Milton Keynes to Winslow**

hand bend after ²/₃ mile bear right onto a no-through-road by a 'Moco Farm' sign. Shortly, as the farm road swings right, bear left through a gate onto a track.

6. The track turns to tarmac. At a T-junction with a wider road, turn right on the shared-use pavement then shortly right again.

7. The route into Winslow town centre uses several roads and cyclepaths but it is well signposted. There are plenty of pubs, cafés and tearooms.

Station: Milton Keynes.

TIC: Destination Milton Keynes, 01908 677010.

Other nearby trails: Several trails in and around Milton Keynes.

Useful publications & websites: OS Landranger Maps 165 and 152. Better is the Milton Keynes Redway Map available as a download from *www.mkweb.co.uk/cycling*. See also *www.destinationmiltonkeynes.co.uk/family_cycling*

Refreshments: Lots of choice in Winslow.

Ride **45** **Milton Keynes to Leighton Buzzard on the Grand Union Canal**

Category
Canal towpath.

Distance
7¹/₂ miles each way.

The Grand Union Canal near Milton Keynes is featured twice in this book: Ride 48 on page 126 explores the canal north from the centre of the town along the Broadwalk as far as Cosgrove to the north-west; this ride heads due south from the southern edge of town to Leighton Buzzard. The towpath on the middle section between these two rides has a much poorer surface. By contrast, the recent improvements to the towpath south of Bletchley mean this is one of the best stretches for cycling on the whole canal between London to Birmingham. The excellent quality continues south beyond the centre of Leighton Buzzard for another 1¹/₂ miles to the pub near Grove Lock, then abruptly turns to grass.

Starting points & parking

1. Bletchley / Water Eaton – follow the A4146 south from the A5 towards Leighton Buzzard. At the first roundabout go straight ahead (Great Brickhill is to the left); at the second roundabout turn right and almost immediately, at the third roundabout, at the junction of Lomond Road and Stoke Road, turn right into the small car park next to the canal (grid reference SP 884318).

2. Leighton Buzzard – the canal runs right past Tesco in the town centre. The nearest car park is just west of the canal, off Old Road at the junction of Wing Road and New Road (grid reference SP 915240).

On your bikes!

Start from the southern edge of Milton Keynes

1. From the A4146 car park by Bridge 99 in Bletchley / Water Eaton, follow the towpath south with the canal to your right.

2. After 2¹/₂ miles go past the Grand Union pub at Three Locks.

3. After another 2¹/₂ miles, follow National Cycle Network Route 6 signs past the Globe Inn and Wyvern Shipping Boat Hire just north of Leighton Buzzard town centre.

4. The good-quality towpath continues beyond Leighton Buzzard for a further 1¹/₂ miles as far as the Grove Lock pub.

Station: Milton Keynes.

TIC: Destination Milton Keynes, 01908 677010.

Other nearby trails: There are several trails in and around Milton Keynes.

Useful publications & websites: OS Landranger Maps 152 and 165. Better is the Milton Keynes Redway map available as a download from *www.mkweb.co.uk/cycling*. See also the leaflet produced by Sustrans, available via *www.sustrans.org.uk* or *www. destinationmiltonkeynes.co.uk/family_cycling*

Refreshments: Lots of choice in Bletchley / Water Eaton. Grand Union pub, Three Locks. Globe Inn, just north of Leighton Buzzard. Lots of choice in Leighton Buzzard. Grove Lock pub, south of the A505.

Milton Keynes, Ride **46**
Willen Lake & Caldecotte Lake

It will come as a surprise to many people who are reluctant to dump their preconceived ideas that there is an excellent network of recreational cycle routes around Milton Keynes, including circuits of lakes, tree-lined canal towpaths and well-made paths across parkland. Other surprises include a Buddhist Pagoda and lots of adventure playgrounds. There are endless possibilities if you get hold of a *Redway Guide* (see **Useful publications** overleaf). The suggested ride below runs along the valley formed by the River Ouzel, linking Willen Lake and Caldecotte Lake, the two largest expanses of water in Milton Keynes. Willen Lake is also a major centre for watersports so you will probably see many brightly coloured sails of windsurfers and dinghies on the water. Near to Willen Lake is a Buddhist Pagoda and a maze, which are both well worth a visit. The ride takes you past woodland and along the willow trees lining the banks of the river. As you approach Caldecotte Lake you will see the windmill standing on its shores. A complete circuit of the lake, with the chance of refreshment at the Caldecotte Arms pub, points you back in the right direction for your return along the river back to the start at Willen Lake.

Starting point & parking

The car park on the western shore of **Willen Lake, Milton Keynes**. Follow signs

Category
Lakeside and riverside paths.

Distance
12 miles – approximately 3 miles for the circuit of Willen Lake, 3 miles for the circuit of Caldecotte Lake and 3 miles each way for the linking section along the Ouzel River.

Ride 46 Milton Keynes, Willen & and Caldecotte Lake

west from M1, Jct 14 or follow the A509 (H5) east from the A5 towards the M1. There are plenty of signs for Willen Lake (grid reference SP 873405).

On your bikes!

1. From the Willen Lake car park go to the path at the water's edge and turn right. Follow the lakeside path around the edge of the lake (with the water to your left), going past the Aerial Adventure playground.

2. At the T-junction where the main track continues around the edge of the lake, turn right following signs for 'Milton Keynes Village and the Ouzel Valley'. For the next 3 miles you are following signs for 'Riverside Walk, Walton Lake and Caldecotte'.

3. Keep the river on your left, do not cross bridges over it for 3 miles. At the T-junction with the road (Simpson Road), turn left then right through the metal height barrier bearing diagonally right through the car park to pick up signs for 'Caldecotte Lake'.

4. Complete a circuit of the lake – head towards the windmill, keeping the water on your left. Go past the Caldecotte Arms pub and the birdwatching point. Stay on the paths closest to the water's edge. At times this is a bit confusing but you'll soon find the right path!

5. On the return follow signs for 'Simpson' and 'Riverside Walk'. At the dam at the northern end of the lake bear right, away from the water, to join a wide cyclepath alongside the road.

6. Rejoin the outward route near the Simpson Road car park (mentioned in Instruction 4), cross the river on the road bridge then turn right to re-enter Ouzel Valley Park, following signs for 'Walton

Lake and Woughton on the Green'.

7. Keep the river to the right (do not cross it) and stay on the broad tarmac path, following signs for 'Riverside Walk, Woughton on the Green, Woolstones'. Continue in the same direction to join the lakeside path alongside Willen Lake, keeping the water to your left.

8. Follow signs for 'Willen Lake North' and 'Willen Village'. At the north end of the North Lake follow the shoreline round to the left past the Peace Pagoda to return to the start.

Station: Milton Keynes.

TIC: Destination Milton Keynes, 01908 677010.

Other nearby trails: The Grand Union Canal north of Milton Keynes and south to Leighton Buzzard. The Ouse Valley Trail runs west from Milton Keynes.

Useful publications & websites: OS Landranger Map 152. The indispensable publication for enjoying Milton Keynes by bike is the *Redway Guide*, available from *www.mkweb.co.uk/cycling*. See also *www.mkparks.co.uk* and *www. destinationmiltonkeynes.co.uk/family_cycling*

Refreshments:
Café at the Willen Watersports Centre. Lakeside pub, Willen South Lake. Caldecotte Arms pub on Caldecotte Lake.

Ouse Valley Trail Ride 47
Milton Keynes

For those who have not yet discovered the secret: Milton Keynes offers more miles of safe and enjoyable family cycling than any other town in the country! There is a vast network of traffic-free cycle tracks through parkland, around lakes, along canal towpaths and disused railways. It is also at a crossroads of the Sustrans National Cycle Network: Route 51 passes through Milton Keynes on its way from Oxford to Cambridge, whilst Route 6 runs south from Derby down to London. The ride described below starts on the western fringes of the town, at the old bridge over the River Great Ouse between Old Stratford and Stony Stratford, running alongside the river for 4 miles on a tarmac path. You pass through a narrow tunnel through the Iron Trunk Aqueduct carrying the Grand Union Canal over the River Ouse, then beneath the railway viaduct. At New Bradwell the route veers away from the river and joins the course of the dismantled railway through leafy cuttings as far as Newport Pagnell. With the aid of a *Redway Guide* (see **Useful publications** overleaf), it is easily possible to plan several days out exploring the network of traffic-free trails.

Starting points & parking

1. Old Stratford / Stony Stratford – from the roundabout at the junction of the A5, A508 and A422 to the north-west of Milton Keynes, take the exit towards Old Stratford and Stony Stratford, cross the bridge over the River Ouse then take the next right signposted 'Stony Stratford Centre' and park along this road (grid reference SP 782410).

2. Newport Pagnell – start from the car park at the junction of Marsh End Road,

Wolverton Road and High Street (grid reference SP 873437). Take Marsh End Road, signposted 'Ousedale Centre' then turn first right by traffic lights, between a car dealers and an off licence, signposted 'Milton Keynes Railway Walk'.

On your bikes!

Start from the western edge of Milton Keynes

1. From the bridge over the River Great Ouse on the road between Old Stratford and Stony Stratford, cross the road (take care) via the traffic island onto the path signposted 'Wildlife Conservation Area, Canal, New Bradwell'.

2. Stay close to the river (on your left). After almost 1 mile, go through a metal gate, turn left and then shortly, at an offset crossroads with a wide track / drive (there is a large red-brick house to your left), go straight ahead onto a continuation of the path. Go through a narrow tunnel beneath the Iron Trunk Aqueduct (carrying the Grand Union Canal). There are some steps down the other side.

3. Cross a wide wooden bridge over a side stream and turn left at the T-junction

Category
Riverside path and railway path.

Distance
7 miles each way.

125

Ride 47   Ouse Valley Trail, Milton Keynes

signposted 'Riverside Walk, New Bradwell' to pass beneath the massive brick railway bridge. After almost 1 mile, at a fork of tracks immediately after crossing a small bridge over a stream, bear right away from the river signposted 'National Cycle Network Route 6'.

4. Follow NCN 6 signs, running alongside a main road (V6), under two large, closely spaced concrete bridges then turn sharp left signposted 'Railway Walk, Newport Pagnell'.

5. Join the railway path (near Bradwell Windmill) and follow signs for 'Newport Pagnell'. Cross the Grand Union Canal after 1¹/₂ miles. Stay on the railway path for a further 2 miles. The trail ends at Sheppards Close in Newport Pagnell.

Station: Milton Keynes.

TIC: Destination Milton Keynes, 01908 677010.

Other nearby trails: There is a fantastic network of traffic-free paths throughout Milton Keynes. Try a circuit of Willen Lakes or a ride along the Grand Union Canal towpath.

Useful publications & websites: The indispensable publication for enjoying Milton Keynes by bike is the *Redway Guide*, available at *www.mkweb.co.uk/cycling*, See also *www.destinationmiltonkeynes.co.uk/ family_cycling*

Refreshments: Lots of choice in Old Stratford and Newport Pagnell. Pubs just off the route where it crosses the Grand Union Canal (follow the canal either north or south).

Ride 48   Grand Union Canal from Milton Keynes to Cosgrove

Category
Canal towpath.

Distance
11 miles each way.

This ride gives you a real idea of how much work has gone into the creation of the Redway in Milton Keynes. At one extreme, running four miles north from Woughton on the Green in the heart of town, you have the Broadwalk, one of the finest examples of landscaped, tree-lined, traffic-free cycle trails in the country. At the other end of the spectrum are stretches of the canal towpath lying outside the town boundaries where no improvement work has been undertaken and the rough surface means that your bones and bikes will get a good shaking. Luckily, these rough sections are a rarity. There is much to enjoy on this ride, from the aforementioned Broadwalk to the wide grass expanses of Great Linford

Park, the lovely old buildings in Great Linford itself, the rural vistas as the canal passes out into the countryside and the long mural of a freight train with its diverse load on the canalside wall in Wolverton. Cosgrove is a small, attractive village with two pubs and makes a convenient turn-around point. This being Milton Keynes there are plenty of options for varying your return journey, although it is recommended you carry a Redway map with you (see 'Useful publications & websites' opposite).

Starting point & parking

The car park on Newport Road, Woughton on the Green, on the **east side of Milton Keynes** (grid reference SP 877382).

On your bikes!

1. From the entrance to the car park in Woughton on the Green, turn left then right at the road hump onto the yellow gravel track on the other side.

2. Continue in the same direction through parkland, ignoring several left turns until arriving at a red-brick humpback bridge over the canal (Bridge 87). Turn right on the Broadwalk, keeping the canal to your left.

3. Continue north along the Broadwalk parallel with the canal for 3½ miles following signs for Woolstone, Newlands and Willen Park. Keep an eye out for the bridge numbers. At Bridge **78 B** (a new bridge with metal railings), the main wide path swings up and to the right, turning back on itself to cross this bridge over to the west side of the canal. Remember this point for the return trip.

4. Proceed north alongside the canal for ⅓ mile, then just before a red-brick bridge at a 4 way signpost turn left 'Linford Manor Park'. At a crossroads of paths go straight ahead, 'Playing fields', then cross the road onto High Street.

5. As the road swings left by the Nag's

Head pub turn right through gates into parkland. Pass between old houses, go past the church then a collection of large stones. Rejoin the canal towpath, which shortly changes sides.

6. Follow the canal over a variety of surfaces for a further 4½ miles to Cosgrove, passing the following landmarks: New Inn (Bridge 72), a long black and white mural with pictures of freight trains, the Galleon pub, the Trunk Viaduct over the River Ouse, the junction with the Buckingham Arm, and the Navigation Inn and Barley Mow pub at Cosgrove.

Station: Milton Keynes.

TIC: Destination Milton Keynes, 01908 677010.

Other nearby trails: Several other trails in the Milton Keynes area.

Useful publications & websites: OS Landranger Map 152. Far more useful is the Milton Keynes Redway Map, showing the vast network of cycle lanes in the area. See *www.mkweb.co.uk/cycling* and *www.destinationmiltonkeynes.co.uk/family_cycling*

Refreshments:
Nag's Head pub, Great Linford. New Inn (Bridge 72), Galleon pub, Old Wolverton. Barley Mow pub, Navigation Inn, Cosgrove.

East of England Trails

1 Grand Union Canal between Hemel Hempstead and Tring, Reservoir

2 Ashridge Estate, north-west of Hemel Hempstead

3 Nickey Line from Hemel Hempstead to Harpenden

4 Ebury Way from Rickmansworth to West Watford

5 Ayot Greenway from Wheathampstead, north of St Albans

6 Albanway from Hatfield to St Albans

7 Cole Green Way, west of Hertford

8 Lee Navigation (1): Hertford to Waltham Abbey

9 Lee Navigation (2): Islington to Waltham Abbey

10 Epping Forest, north of London

11 Flitch Way, west of Braintree

12 Valley Walk, Sudbury, north-west of Colchester

13 Colchester to Wivenhoe along the riverside path

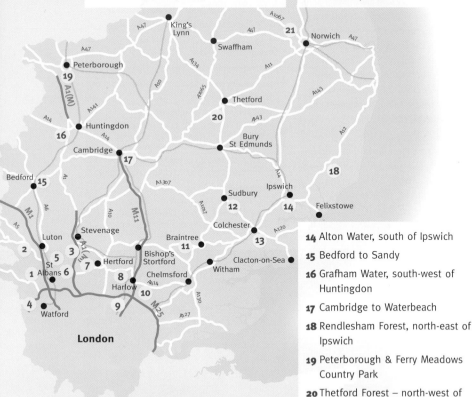

14 Alton Water, south of Ipswich

15 Bedford to Sandy

16 Grafham Water, south-west of Huntingdon

17 Cambridge to Waterbeach

18 Rendlesham Forest, north-east of Ipswich

19 Peterborough & Ferry Meadows Country Park

20 Thetford Forest – north-west of Cambridge

21 Marriott's Way, Norwich

03 East of England Mountain Biking

The East of England has several mountain biking options including Thetford Forest, the Suffolk Coast forests, Epping Forest and rides along the Icknield Way and Peddars Way. The latter is a long-distance trail that runs as a byway or bridleway for over 50 miles from Lackham, south-west of Thetford to the North Norfolk coast at Holme-next-the-Sea. Although maps show that there are plenty of bridleways and byways in Essex and Hertfordshire, these are predominantly very rough and very muddy in winter, and baked hard into bumpy corrugations in the summer.

There is no substitute for intimate local knowledge – try to explore every bridleway, byway, unclassified road, canal towpath and Forestry Commission track near to your home, sift out the good from the bad and link together the best off-road sections to form your own customised route(s). The best advice is to use the months from late spring to early autumn (May to October) to do the exploration, if possible after a spell of dry weather. In winter, the same track can take twice as long or even be impassable.

Note down on the map (or colour-code with highlighter pen) the quality of the trail and whether it is better done in one direction or the other – it is normally better to climb on tarmac and descend off-road so that gravity can help you through any muddy bits. Where there are no books or leaflets describing mountain bike rides, the staff in bike shops can often put you in contact with local riders or clubs who may have done some of this research already, saving you many hours of trial and error.

Bear in mind that everyone has a different view of what constitutes a good trail: hard or technical for some is easy for others, and a bit of mud for some is a quagmire for others!

20 Thetford Forest

Websites:

www.forestry.gov.uk and search 'Thetford Forest' or 'Rendlesham Forest'.

www.moredirt.co.uk and follow links from 'Trails & Tracks' to 'United Kingdom' to 'East of England'.

East of England Forestry

03

The East of England has a small, densely forested centre on the sandy soils around Thetford, and two reasonable-sized holdings (Tunstall and Rendlesham) to the north-east of Ipswich, near the Suffolk coast; but other than this the region is one of the least forested in the whole country.

In some forests and woods there are no waymarked routes, but you are free to explore the tracks. The relevant Ordnance Survey map is mentioned. It is highly recommended that you take a map for the larger woods as it is very easy to get lost.

4. West Harling Heath, east of Thetford (OS Explorer Map 230)

5. Swaffham Heath & Cockleycley Heath south-east of Swaffham (OS Explorer Map 236)

6. Coldharbour Wood & Shaker's Wood south of Swaffham (OS Explorer Maps 229 & 236)

7. Shouldham Warren / The Sincks, south of King's Lynn (OS Explorer Map 236)

8. Horsford Woods, north of Norwich (OS Explorer Map 238)

9. Swanton Great Wood, east of Fakenham (OS Explorer Map 251)

10. Woodlands between Holt and Sheringham (OS Explorer Map 252)

It is also worth contacting the following Forest District Office for further information:

East Anglia
Santon Downham, Brandon, Suffolk IP27 0TJ.
Tel: 01842 810271.
email: enquiries.eastanglia@forestry.gsi.gov.uk

The Forestry Commission's website, *www.forestry.gov.uk* is a good source of information. Click on 'Explore, Experience, Enjoy' then 'Cycling' and you can find out details of hundreds of waymarked trails throughout the UK. You can search by forest name or by the nearest town / city. The search will tell you the grade, length and waymarking details of the trails. Alternatively, by clicking on the map you can see the nearest forest to where you live.

Forests and woods with waymarked trails
There are two Forestry Commission holdings with waymarked trails in the East of England region:

1 **Rendlesham Forest**, north of Ipswich (Ride 18, page 154)

3 **Thetford Forest** (Ride 20, page 157)

The woodlands below correspond with the numbers on the map:

2. King's Forest & Mildenhall Woods, south-west of Thetford (OS Explorer Maps 226 & 229)

East of England National Cycle Network

Hull to Harwich (two maps)

369 miles. Highlights (in the southern half of the route) include King's Lynn, the North Norfolk Coast, Walsingham Abbey, the traffic-free Marriott's Way from Reepham to Norwich, Norwich Cathedral, Framlingham Castle, Orford Castle, Snape Maltings, Constable Country, Colchester's historic town centre and the traffic-free Wivenhoe Trail.

Traffic-free sections over 3 miles:

• Wivenhoe Trail from Wivenhoe to Colchester (NCN 1).

• Marriott's Way from Reepham to Norwich (NCN 1).

Sustrans

The Sustrans maps shown here cover various National Cycle Network routes within the region. Some of the maps may describe routes that continue into adjacent regions: these maps are mentioned in both chapters. The maps are not only useful for people wishing to ride the whole route over several days, they also show all the traffic-free sections that make good day rides.

Other good areas for lane cycling

East Anglia has hundreds of miles of quiet lanes with gentle gradients linking small villages. As the weather tends to be much drier than on the west side of the country you have a set of excellent conditions for enjoyable cycling for day rides or longer touring. The southern part of the region is fairly densely populated but there is a lot less traffic north of an imaginary line drawn from Luton to Colchester – ie **north Essex, Suffolk** and **Norfolk**. There are many attractive villages that would make good bases in Norfolk such as Castle Acre, Little Walsingham, Burnham Market, Reepham or Aylsham. Elsewhere, Thaxted in Essex or Lavenham, Framlingham and Beccles in Suffolk are all wonderful bases around which there is a delightful network of lanes to explore.

These maps are available from www.sustrans.org.uk or 0845 113 0065.

Ride 1 Grand Union Canal
between Hemel Hempstead & Tring Reservoir

Category
Canal towpath.

Distance
12 miles each way.

The Grand Union Canal connects London to Birmingham, but it would take a brave person to jump on their bike at one end and imagine a straightforward ride to the other. There is an enormous variety of surfaces you will encounter from very rough and rutted to fine, smooth gravel; parts may be overgrown with vegetation, other parts are very narrow and then there are barriers to keep out motorbikes. So it is best to pick and choose the best bits. Parts of this ride, through Berkhamsted, for example, are as good as it gets. However, even on a ride like this there are short, rougher sections, so be prepared for these. The ride runs alongside Tring Summit, the highpoint of the canal between London and the Midlands; to the north it drops down to Milton Keynes and to the south

towards London. You won't be stuck for refreshments on this ride as there are cafés at both ends and many pubs along the way, especially through Berkhamsted.

Starting points & parking

1. Tring Reservoirs – Startops car park, north of Tring, on the B489 in Marsworth just south-west of the White Lion pub (grid reference SP 920140).

2. Apsley Marina / Nash Mills, Hemel Hempstead – just off the A4251 to the east of Apsley railway station (grid reference TL 064050).

On your bikes!

1. From the Old Red Lion pub (by Nash Mills, at the southern edge of Hemel Hempstead) follow the canal towpath north-west towards Berkhamsted. Go past Apsley Marina.

2. Go past the Fishery Inn then after 1 mile, another marina and the Three Horseshoes pub.

3. The path improves through Berkhamsted as you pass several pubs and information boards about the history of the canal and the town itself.

4. The surface is good as far as Cow Roast Lock. After this the path becomes narrower and at times overgrown. This is the summit section of the canal.

5. The towpath improves again at Bulbourne as the canal starts its descent. It is suggested you go as far as Marsworth where there are two pubs and a café. There is also a car park here where you may prefer to start.

Station: Hemel Hempstead, Berkhamsted and Tring.

TIC: Hemel Hempstead, 01442 234222 or Tring, 01442 823347.

Other nearby trails: Nickey Line, Alban Way, Ashridge Estate, Wendover Woods.

Useful publications & websites: OS Landranger Maps 165 & 166. *www. waterscape.com/canals-and-rivers/grand-union-canal*

Refreshments:
Red Lion pub, Woody's Vegetarian Restaurant, Hemel Hempstead. Fishery Inn, Boxmoor. Three Horseshoes pub, Bourne End. Lots of choice in Berkhamsted. Grand Junction Arms pub, Bulbourne. Bluebell Café, White Lion pub, Anglers Retreat pub, Marsworth.

Ashridge Estate Ride 2
north-west of Hemel Hempstead

Comprising over 1,600 hectares of woodlands, commons, downland and farmland, the Ashridge Estate runs along the main ridge of the Chilterns from Berkhamsted to Ivinghoe Beacon. The main focal point of the estate is the granite monument erected in 1832 in honour of the 3rd Duke of Bridgewater, father of inland navigation, who was nicknamed 'the Canal Duke'. The ride starts from this mighty monument (which you can climb) and descends through broadleaf woodland on a series of bridleways marked with blue arrows. This is just one of many rides that could be devised in the estate. Be warned, however, that these are woodland tracks rather than specially-built cycle trails, so the going can become muddy in winter and after prolonged rain. Mountain bikes are recommended.

Starting point & parking

The **Ashridge Estate** car park by the visitor centre. From Berkhamsted follow the B4506 north for 3½ miles towards Ringshall and Dunstable, taking the second road to the left to arrive at the visitor centre (grid reference SP 970130).

On your bikes!

1. With your back to the café and facing the Bridgewater monument, turn left on a

Category
Bridleways and roads through Ashridge Estate.

Distance
5-mile circuit plus a 2-mile spur north from the monument towards Ivinghoe Beacon.

133

Ride 2   Ashridge Estate, north-west of Hemel Hempstead

broad tarmac path which soon becomes a wide track signposted with a blue arrow 'Bridleway'.

2. Ignore a first left signposted 'No horses, no bikes'. After 300yds of steep descent, at an obvious fork of tracks, bear left on the upper track. At a track T-junction by a telephone pole, turn left uphill.

3. Shortly go straight ahead past a house with a high surrounding hedge on your left. Continue in the same direction.

4. Long, gentle descent. At the B4506 go straight ahead (**take care**) onto the track opposite signposted 'Berkhamsted Common'. Continue descending on a slightly rougher track.

5. At a fork after ²/₃ mile bear right then at the crossroads, shortly after passing a house to the left, turn right uphill on a broad stone 'drive' (blue arrow).

6. At the next crossroads of tracks (with a red-brick barn 50yds ahead) turn right on a broad stone track (blue arrow). Shortly, at a 'Little Coldharbour Farm' sign, bear right away from the stone track onto a narrower track (blue arrow) and soon fork right again.

7. Follow the flat singletrack trail through woodland. At times there are roots and there will be mud after rain. At the junction with the B4506, go straight ahead onto the lane opposite signposted 'Aldbury, Tring'. Go past Base Camp on the right and a car parking area on the left. Just before '40mph' speed limit signs turn right onto a track signposted 'Bridgewater Monument'.

8. After 200yds, at a crossroads of tracks turn right then at the house with its high surrounding edge, turn left to rejoin the outward route, soon forking right. After a gentle descent, the last ¹/₄ mile back to the monument is steep and you may prefer to push.

Duncombe Terrace Route

There is also a 2-mile there-and-back ride on a broad stone track that heads due north from the Bridgewater monument through magnificent beechwood woodland as far as the Ivinghoe Beacon road, offering fine views west towards Wendover Woods.

Station: Tring.

TIC: Wendover, 01296 696759.

Other nearby trails: The Grand Union Canal runs close by. The Ridgeway / Icknield Way has some long bridleway sections which offer good riding on mountain bikes in the summer. There are waymarked forest trails in Wendover Woods between Wendover and Tring.

Useful publications & websites: OS Landranger Map 165. A free cycle map is available from the visitor centre or as a download at either *www.nationaltrust.org. uk* or *www.chilternsaonb.org* (put 'Ashridge Estate Cycle Map' into the 'Search' box).

Refreshments: There is a good café next to the visitor centre. Otherwise the nearest refreshments are either in the village of Aldbury or in Berkhamsted.

Nickey Line Ride 3
from Hemel Hempstead to Harpenden

The Nickey Line follows the course of the old railway gently uphill from Harpenden to Adeyfield Road in Hemel Hempstead (near the Town Hall). The name may have come from an abbreviation of 'funicular', referring to the steep gradients along the line, or from 'knickerbockers' either because the railway navvies wore such garments or because the line was considered half-size, being only single track. The Nickey Line was built in 1877 as a result of a proposal by businessmen of Hemel Hempstead to link the straw plait trade in the town with the hat-makers of Luton. It carried passengers until 1947 and freight until 1979.

Starting point & parking

From the centre of **Harpenden** take the A1081 Luton Road then turn left immediately after going under the railway bridge onto Park Hill. Park about 200yds along this road (grid reference TL 127150). The railway path is to your left.

On your bikes!

1. Join the railway path off Park Hill, Harpenden and turn right uphill. (Remember where you join the path for your return.) Climb gently then descend. At the roundabout after 1¹/₂ miles, cross the B487 and A5183 **with great care** following National Cycle Network Route 57 signs.

2. After ³/₄ mile at the fork bear left to avoid steps. At the road turn right then left.

3. After a further ³/₄ mile recross the B487 then shortly go through the tunnel under the M1.

4. After 2 miles the trail ends abruptly opposite Euro Car Parts on Eastman

Trading Estate on the edge of Hemel Hempstead. It is suggested you turn around at this point to return.

Station: Harpenden.

TIC: Hemel Hempstead, 01442 234222.

Other nearby trails: The Grand Union Canal passes through Hemel Hempstead.

Useful publications & websites: OS Landranger Map 166. The *Walking & cycling the Nickey Line* leaflet is available from TICs or go to *www.stalbans.gov.uk* then click on 'Transport and Streets' then 'Public Rights of Way' then 'Cycling'.

Refreshments: Lots of choice in Harpenden and Hemel Hempstead.

Category
Railway path.

Distance
8 miles each way.

NB There are four busy roads to cross – the B487 (twice), the A5183 (near Redbourn) and the A4147 (near Eastman Way Trading Estate).
Take great care.

Ride 4 Ebury Way
from Rickmansworth to West Watford

4

Category
Canal towpath and railway path.

Distance
3 miles each way.

This 3-mile railway path between Rickmansworth and West Watford is surprisingly green and leafy for such a built-up area. The trail crosses the Colne, Chess and Gade rivers and if you are lucky you may even see the flash of bright blue as a kingfisher flies low over the water. The path runs parallel with, then crosses, the Grand Union Canal so it would be easy to vary the there-and-back ride along the railway by returning via the canal towpath. Indeed, the Grand Union Canal could be followed for several miles in either direction, either south towards Uxbridge or north towards Hemel Hempstead and Berkhamsted. As the year progresses the dominant features of the ride change from birdsong in spring, to wildflowers and dragonflies in the summer, then berries on blackthorn, hawthorn and bramble in the autumn, offering important food sources for the resident thrushes and blackbirds but also migrants such as redwings and fieldfares.

Starting point & parking

The most convenient car park is at **Rickmansworth Aquadrome**, although it is

a little complicated to describe how to get there! Take the A404 out of Rickmansworth towards Northwood and London. At the Moor Lane roundabout where 'A4145 / Watford Road' is signposted straight on and 'London (A404)' off to the right, complete a circuit of the roundabout and head back towards Rickmansworth – the turning for the Aquadrome (Harefield Road) is on your left (grid reference TQ 057938).

On your bikes!

1. Exit the Aquadrome car park via the vehicle entrance, then shortly before the bridge turn left onto the canal towpath. Pass beneath the main road then immediately after the Batchworth Lock Visitor Centre bear left, cross a wooden bridge to the left and follow the path.

2. With a low 'drawbridge' to the right, turn left then shortly turn sharp right through metal posts / barrier and a car park to join the Ebury Way.

3. The Ebury Way, signposted as National Cycle Network Route 61, ends after 3 miles at the A4178 Wiggenhall Road, south of Watford (grid reference TQ 111953).

Station: Rickmansworth.

TIC: Hemel Hempstead, 01442 234222.

Other nearby trails: The Grand Union Canal.

Useful publications & websites: OS Landranger Map 176. An Ebury Way map can be downloaded from *www.watford.gov.uk* by typing 'Ebury Way' into the 'Search' box. See also *www.spokesgroup.com*, the website for the local cycle group in south-west Hertfordshire.

Refreshments: Café at Rickmansworth Aquadrome at the start of the ride.

Ayot Greenway from Wheathampstead
Ride 5

A short ride along the course of the old Luton, Dunstable & Welwyn Junction railway from Wheathampstead east to the minor road south of Welwyn, with some lovely wooded sections. Many men were employed building the line but the hardest workers would have been the navvies. A day's work for two of them would be to shovel 20 tons of rock and earth into 14 horse-drawn wagons. Although the work was hard, the pay, ranging between 15 and 22 shillings per week, was better than that of farm workers, so many men left the farms to work on the railway. It took two years to complete the stretch of the line between Luton and Hatfield, and the first excursion over the new section ran to London. The cheapest return fare from Luton to London was two shillings and sixpence (12.5p!).

Starting point & parking

Free car park near the Bull pub in **Wheathampstead** (grid reference TL 178142) on the B653 between Harpenden and Hatfield. (**NB** It is the car park beyond the Bull's own car park.)

On your bikes!

1. From the free car park return to the High Street by the Bull pub. Turn right to cross the bridge over the river, then after 50yds turn right onto Mount Road, following signs for 'Ayot Greenway, Welwyn Garden City, National Cycle Network Routes 12 / 57'.

2. Fine, wide, smooth gravel track. Pass through several bridle gates. At the T-junction turn left, 'Ayot Greenway' (remember this spot for the return leg).

3. Gentle climb. At a crossroads of tracks turn right, signposted 'Ayot Greenway'.

4. Lovely gentle climb through mature broadleaf woodland. The traffic-free section ends at its junction with Ayot St Peter Road, a minor road south of Welwyn (grid reference TL 221145).

> **Station:** Welwyn North or Harpenden.
>
> **TIC:** St Albans, 01727 864511.
>
> **Other nearby trails:** The Nickey Line, Cole Green Way and Albanway all lie nearby.
>
> **Useful publications & websites:** OS Landranger Map 166 or try *www.hertsdirect. org* (put 'Ayot Greenway' into the 'Search' box). *www.welhat.gov.uk/pedalpoint*
>
> **Refreshments:** In Wheathampstead or Welwyn, 1½ miles beyond the end of the trail on minor roads (you will need a map).

Category
Railway path.

Distance
3½ miles each way.

Ride 6 **Albanway from Hatfield to St Albans**

6

Category
Railway path

Distance
6½ miles each way.

It is well worth exploring this fine wooded railway trail between these two towns, forming part of Route 61 of the National Cycle Network. The route runs south-west from Old Hatfield to St Albans on a fine gravel path with a deep cutting at the St Albans end. There are short sections on quiet roads at the start and finish, and three other road crossings, but none are particularly busy. Opened in 1865 by the Hatfield & St Albans Railway Company, the line was absorbed by the Great Northern Railway in 1883. Passenger services continued until 1951 and freight lines until the late 1960s. In 1985 the line was given a new lease of life when it was converted to a cycleway / footpath. All that is left of Verulamium, once the most important Roman town in Britain, lies to the west of the present city of St Albans. There are the remains of a great amphitheatre and part of an underground heating system. Modern St Albans takes its name from Alban, the first Christian martyr in Britain. The mighty abbey was founded on the hill where he was beheaded.

Starting points & parking

1. Hatfield: from A1(M) Jct 4 take the A414 towards Hertford then after ¼ mile turn right at the roundabout onto Great North Road. As this swings right and becomes Longmead, bear left by a car dealership onto a continuation of Great North Road. Park at the top, beyond the Wrestlers pub and just before the 'No through road' sign. The cyclepath starts on your right just before the bridge (grid reference TL 232094).

2. St Albans: start from the crossroads of Leyland Avenue, Mentmore Road and Cottonmill Lane, just to the east of Abbey Station. To get here take Prospect Road from the A5183 near the station. After parking (no specific car park) take the track leading past Sopwell Youth Club then turn left under the railway arch (grid reference TL 150061).

On your bikes!

West from Hatfield

1. From the top of Great North Road turn right onto the cyclepath just before the bridge over the railway. After ¾ mile at a fork bear right to cross the road by Fiddlebridge Industrial Centre. At the road junction turn right then left opposite De Havilland Close.

2. Pass under the subway following National Cycle Network Route 61 signs. Turn right to cross the bridge over the A1 then left opposite The Galleria shopping mall to continue along the Albanway.

3. Move from town into the countryside, passing a small lake to your left.

4. Cross a road beyond a metal barrier, pass through a residential area and go past Body Limits Gymnasium.

5. After 1 mile pass under an enormous brick arch. After a further ¹/₂ mile at a T-junction just beyond a red-brick and concrete bridge, turn right signposted 'Abbey Station, City Centre, Harpenden'. The traffic-free trail shortly ends.

Station: Abbey Station, St Albans.

TIC: St Albans, 01727 864511.

Other nearby trails: The Ayot Greenway, Cole Greenway and Nickey Line all lie close by.

Useful publications & websites: OS Landranger Map 166. The Albanway leaflet is available from *www.hertsdirect.org* (put 'Albanway' in the 'Search' box. See also *www.welhat.gov.uk/pedalpoint*

Refreshments: Lots of choice in St Albans or Hatfield.

Cole Green Way Ride **7**
west of Hertford

This is the most rural of the four dismantled railways in Hertfordshire, passing through attractive woodland between the Rivers Lee and Mimram, linking Welwyn Garden City and Hertford. The trail follows the course of the old Hertford, Dunstable and Luton line. It was opened in 1858 by the Hertford & Welwyn Junction Railway and carried passengers up to 1951 and freight until 1962. It was acquired by Hertfordshire County Council in 1974 and converted to a walking and riding route.

Starting points & parking

1. In central **Hertford**, turn off the A414 by the Gates Ford dealers onto West Street, signposted 'Hertford Town FC'. On a sweeping left-hand bend about 300yds after the Black Horse pub, bear right signposted 'Cole Green Way, Welwyn Garden City' and park by the football ground (grid reference TL 321121).

2. The Cole Green Way car park near the Cowper Arms pub in **Cole Green**. Turn off the A414 following signs for 'Cole Green / Birch Green' then signs for 'Letty Green'.

Category
Railway path.

Distance
4 miles each way.

Ride 7 Cole Green Way, west of Hertford

The car park is just beyond the Cowper Arms pub on the left (grid ref TL 285112).

3. On the south-east edge of **Welwyn Garden City**. Follow the B195 towards Cole Green and Letty Green. At the start of the countryside at the edge of Welwyn Garden City, turn right off the B195 signposted 'QE2 Hospital'. Park on either Holwell Hyde Lane or Holwell Hyde (grid reference TL 265118).

On your bikes!

1. From the Hertford Football Club car park aim towards then pass beneath the large railway viaduct. After 200yds bear right at a National Cycle Network Route 61 sign, staying on the broad gravel track through woodland.

2. Go past a car park on the right. Exit here if you wish to visit the Cowper Arms pub.

3. Pass through the subway under the A414. Climb past the recently planted woodland on your right.

4. The traffic-free trail ends after a further mile at a T-junction with a road on the eastern edge of Welwyn Garden City (at the junction of Black Fan Road with Cole Green Lane). NCN 61 continues on a mixture of quiet streets and cyclepaths into Welwyn.

East from Hertford FC car park

A well-signposted route on quiet streets leads through Hertford town centre to the start of the Lee Navigation towpath near to Hartham Leisure Centre (Ride 8).

Station: Hertford.

TIC: Hertford, 01992 584322.

Other nearby trails: The Ayot Greenway, Albanway and Nickey Line are all nearby.

Useful publications & websites: OS Landranger Map 166. Go to *www.hertsdirect. org* and put 'Cole Green Way' into the 'Search' box. Also try *www.welhat.gov.uk/pedalpoint*

Refreshments: Lots of choice in Hertford. Cowper Arms pub at Cole Green.

Ride 8 Lee Navigation (1) from Hertford to Waltham Abbey

Category
Canal towpath.

Distance
14 miles each way.

Many of the best traffic-free cycling routes in and near London use the towpaths of the waterways that radiate from the capital – these also include the Grand Union Canal in the west of London, the Thames to the south-west and the Thames estuary east from Greenwich. The surface of the Lee Navigation towpath has been upgraded to a very high standard – if only all canal towpaths were as good! The whole Lee Valley (or **Lea** Valley,

both spellings are used, take your pick) has become one of the best areas for recreational cycling to the north of London. The ride described here follows the Lee Navigation from its northern terminus in Hertford eastwards through the attractive town of Ware before taking a more southerly course past Cheshunt to Waltham Abbey. This is only a suggested turnaround point: you may wish to do a much shorter ride going only as far as Ware or the pub

8

at Dobb's Weir, or perhaps you may wish to push on further right into London, joining the Thames near Limehouse Basin.

Starting points & parking

1. The long-stay car park near the swimming pool / leisure centre on Hartham Lane, **Hertford**. From the centre of Hertford follow signs for the B158 (Parliament Square roundabout, The Wash, Millbridge) past the library then turn right onto Hartham Lane past Hertford Brewery to the car park. The car park is free at the weekends (grid reference TL 325130).

2. Waltham Abbey – the best car parks for the canal towpath are signposted just to the north of the town, either at the Royal Gunpowder Mills (grid reference TL 377010) or a little way north along the B194 at Fishers Green (grid reference TL 376027).

On your bikes!

Starting from Hertford

1. From the Hartham Leisure Centre in Hertford follow 'National Cycle Network Route 61, Ware' signs on the cyclepath across the recreation ground, cross Bridge 69 over the canal by the lock keeper's cottage and turn left along the towpath of the Lee Navigation.

2. After 2 miles, at the road junction in Ware at the end of the towpath, bear right and use the traffic islands (**take care**) to cross the busy road straight ahead to rejoin the towpath.

3. Follow this excellent towpath for 5 miles to the Fish & Eels pub at Dobb's Weir. Beyond here the path quality varies: parts are excellent but there are also some short, rougher stretches.

4. After 1½ miles go past the Lee Valley Boat Centre and the Crown pub.

5. Continue for a further 6 miles to Waltham Abbey. You will know you are here as it is just after Waltham Town Lock, at Bridge 42. It is suggested you turn around at this point but you may wish to continue south towards London.

Station: Hertford, Waltham Abbey and several stations in between.

TIC: Hertford, 01992 584322.

Other nearby trails: The towpath alongside the Lee Navigation continues south to Limehouse Basin on the Thames (see next ride). The Cole Green Way is a railway path running west from Hertford to Welwyn Garden City. Epping Forest lies to the south-east of Waltham Abbey.

Useful publications & websites: OS Landranger Map 166. Go to *www.leevalleypark.org.uk*, follow links to 'Cycling' then click on 'London Docklands and the Lee Valley' under 'Cycle Routes'. A leaflet is available from *www. hertsdirect.org* (put 'Hertford & Ware activity map' in the 'Search' box.

Refreshments:
Lots of choice in Hertford. Lots of choice in Ware. Jolly Fisherman pub, Crown pub south of Ware. Rye House pub, Rye House. Fish & Eels pub, Dobb's Weir. Lots of choice in Waltham Abbey.

NB Care should be taken crossing the A1170 in Ware – use the cycle facility.

Ride 9 Lee Navigation (2) Islington to Waltham Abbey

9

Category
Canal towpath.

Distance
14 miles each way.

Linking Islington in central London with Waltham Abbey in Hertfordshire, the Lee Navigation is a green corridor offering one of the best escapes from city to country. At the southern end there are several canals: the Regents Canal which emerges from Islington Tunnel is part of the Grand Union Canal, leading to its junction with the Thames at Limehouse Basin; the Hertford Union Canal links Regents Canal with the Lee Navigation alongside Victoria Park – and then there is the Limehouse Cut. North of Hackney / Stratford and the Olympic Zone there is just the Lee Navigation, winding its way north past Hackney Marshes covered in hundreds of football pitches. The path is wide and there are no low bridges, by contrast with the route in London itself. To look at the map one would imagine seeing a succession of vast reservoirs up the valley. As it is, the towpath lies below the surrounding embankments for the reservoirs, and they remain hidden. There are lots of pubs and a couple of cafés along the way so you have plenty of reasons for taking this ride at a leisurely pace.

Starting points & parking

1. Waltham Abbey – the best car parks for the canal towpath are signposted just to the north of the town, either at the Royal Gunpowder Mills (Grid reference TL 377010) or a little way north along the B194 at Fishers Green (grid reference TL 376027). Another option is at Enfield Lock just south of the M25.

2. Islington, London – at the east end of the tunnel, at the junction of Noel Road, Danbury Street and Graham Street (grid reference TQ 316834).

On your bikes!

South from Waltham Abbey

1. From Waltham Abbey follow the towpath south, with the canal to your left. Pass under the M25, go past the Greyhound pub then Enfield Lock.

2. After 6 miles you will come to the Stonebridge Lock Café by the Lee Valley Canoe & Cycle Centre.

3. After a further 2 miles there is another café at the north end of Springfield Park.

NB In London along the Regents Canal, the towpath is narrow under the low bridges – ring your bell, slow down and be prepared to meet people and give way. This section is popular both with walkers and cyclists.

4. Go past the hundreds of football fields that cover Hackney Marsh.

5. About 12 miles south of Waltham Abbey, and just south of Hackney Wick, you will need to turn off the Lee Navigation onto the Hertford Union Canal to continue south to Limehouse Basin or west to Islington on Regents Canal. This point is by the Olympic site, marked by a 3-way sign. Turn right, signposted 'Hertford Union, Victoria Park'.

6. Pass alongside Victoria Park then at the T-junction* with Regents Canal you can:

(a) turn left for 1½ miles to Limehouse Basin and the Thames

(b) turn right for 2½ miles for Islington, as far as the tunnel (at the junction of Noel Road, Danbury Street and Graham Street).

Station: Several stations are close to the canal, enabling you to ride one way and catch the train back. Liverpool Street is the London terminal for the stations along the ride.

TIC: Hertford, 01992 584322.

Other nearby trails: Epping Forest and the Cole Green Way.

Useful publications & websites: OS Landranger Maps 166 & 177. More useful is a London street map or the London Docklands and Lee Valley map available from *www.leevalleypark.org.uk* – follow links to 'Cycling' then 'Cycle Routes'. Also visit *www.waterscape.com*, click on 'London' then click on the download for 'East End's canals'.

Refreshments: Pubs at regular intervals all the way along the towpath. Stonebridge Lock Café, Tottenham. Springfield Park Café, Upper Clapton.

* Remember this point for your return trip as it is easy to miss.

Epping Forest Ride 10
north of London

Although there is no specifically waymarked bike trail in Epping Forest, there is such a plethora of top-grade gravel tracks that it would be possible to make up any number of routes criss-crossing this ancient woodland, which is owned and managed by the Corporation of London. This ride starts from the King's Oak pub in the heart of the forest and wastes no time before diving into the wooded delights on a broad gravel track. There are some roads to be crossed during the course of the ride and great care should be taken on the crossings of the busier ones. As long as you are prepared to wait for a clear gap in the traffic, the roads should not be a deterrent to exploring Epping Forest's fine network of tracks. It is notoriously difficult to give woodland instructions so please do not get exasperated if you feel you are lost! The most important point is that you are outside cycling in beautiful woodland, you will never be that far from where you started and if you take a different route from the one described, it really doesn't matter! It is best to turn up with a map (or buy one from the excellent visitor centre at High Beach). There are plenty of good-quality gravel tracks in Epping Forest although these may become muddy in the depths of winter or after prolonged rain. There are several short hills, some of which are quite steep.

Category
Forest trail.

Distance
This is a suggested ride of 8 miles. There are many miles of tracks from which to make up your own routes.

Ride 10 Epping Forest, north of London

10

Starting point & parking

The King's Oak pub at **High Beach**, near the visitor centre in the middle of Epping Forest. This is located about 1 mile north-west of the Loughton / High Beach roundabout on the A104, the road running north from London towards the town of Epping (grid reference TQ 412980).

On your bikes!

NB Great care should be taken crossing the roads, particularly the A104 which is crossed twice. Allow yourself time to gauge the speed of the traffic and wait for a clear gap in both directions.

1. With your back to the Kings Oak pub by the High Beach Visitor Centre, turn right. At the T-junction (with a gravel parking strip opposite), turn right then left onto a track by a barrier and wooden posts. At a second road go straight across 'Emergency Access'. Ignore a left turn after 150yds.

2. At the busy A121 go straight ahead (**TAKE CARE**) then shortly at a T-junction of tracks turn right. At the next major track junction, with a tall wooden fence ahead and a metal barrier across access to the road to your right, turn left.

3. Cross a minor road (there is a 'Give Way' sign to the right). The next ¼ mile is noisy, running parallel with the B1393. Cross this road straight ahead. At a T-junction after 300yds (with silver birches to your left), turn right.

4. Go through car parks either side of the B172 and past a 'Jack's Hill' signboard. **Easy to miss:** after ½ mile, on a gentle descent, take the first broad track on the right. Descend then climb. Go through a car park and diagonally left across the busy A121 (**TAKE CARE**).

5. Follow another downhill stretch, climb up through a car park and cross the road past a pond. Go past a second pond then after ¼ mile, on a gentle descent shortly after a large grass clearing on the left, take the next right by a white post with a horseshoe sign.

6. Cross the busy A104 (**TAKE CARE**), go through a bridlegate then turn right on a minor road (this is a no-through-road, without traffic). At the T-junction, with a car park and tea hut to the right, turn left then right onto a broad track with 'Emergency access' barrier.

7. Lots of ups and downs. Ignore a right turn on a wide track by a small triangle of grass with trees in it. At the T-junction with the next road turn left to return to the Kings Oak pub / visitor centre.

Station: Chingford, Loughton, Epping.

TIC: At the High Beach Visitor Centre, 0208 508 0028.

Other nearby trails: The Lee Navigation runs to the west of Epping Forest.

Useful publications & websites: OS Landranger Maps 167 & 177. Better still are the larger-scale maps that can be purchased from the visitor centre at High Beach which show the trails in much greater detail. Also visit *www.cityoflondon.gov.uk* – put 'Epping Forest Cycle Map' in the 'Search' box.

Refreshments: King's Oak pub and café at the start. Several pubs (and odd tea wagons!) dotted around Epping Forest.

Flitch Way
west of Braintree
Ride **11**

This wide railway path has been improved over the years and offers an easy, flat ride through the gently undulating Essex countryside. The trail starts conveniently from the railway station car park at Braintree, soon passing the handsome old buildings of Rayne Station which is now a tearoom. A long footbridge over the new A120 takes you high above the traffic and back onto the wooded corridor leading westwards. There is one point (near the old Felsted station) where a bridge has been removed and you need to descend to the road before rejoining the path. Unfortunately the railway path does not continue into Great Dunmow so you can either turn around at the end of the traffic-free section (perhaps visiting the pub in Little Dunmow) or if you are happy to negotiate the traffic of Great Dunmow, to link with the western half of the Flitch Way (see below).

Starting point & parking

Braintree railway station (grid reference TL 762227).

On your bikes!

1. Follow through the overflow car park (furthest from the railway station) to the start of the Flitch Way. The surface is at first tarmac.

2. Cross a bridge over a road then after $1^1/_4$ miles there is a chance of refreshments at the old station at Rayne. Shortly, cross a long bridge over the new A120.

3. After $3^1/_4$ miles and shortly after a 'Felsted Station' signpost, descend to the road, cross to the pavement opposite, turn right then left up a flight of steps. At the tarmac turn left then right onto a

continuation of the railway path, passing above a travellers' site.

If you wish to visit the Flitch of Bacon pub at Little Dunmow, immediately after passing under the next bridge turn right, then at the lane turn left and follow this road (Brook Road) into Little Dunmow, turning left at the T-junction for the pub.

4. The railway path ends after a further $1^1/_2$ miles where National Cycle Network Route 16 is signposted off to the right. You can continue into Great Dunmow following NCN 16 signs although this will involve using busier roads.

Station: Braintree.

TIC: Braintree, 01376 550066.

Other nearby trails: South of Bishop's Stortford, the Stort Navigation runs towards London. Epping Forest has many miles of fine tracks.

Useful publications & websites: OS Landranger Map 167. www.essexcc.gov.uk and type 'Flitch Way leaflet' into the 'Search' box.

Refreshments: Lots of choice in Braintree. Tearoom at the old station at Rayne. Flitch of Bacon pub, Little Dunmow. Lots of choice in Great Dunmow, just beyond the western end of the ride.

Category
Railway path.

Distance
$7^1/_2$ miles each way.

NB There is a second 6-mile stretch of the Flitch Way to the west of Great Dunmow, although the surface is at times a lot rougher. It starts off the B1256 on the south-west edge of town (at grid reference TL 623216) and runs to Tilekiln Green, just east of M11, Jct 8.

Ride 12 Valley Walk
Sudbury, north-west of Colchester

Category
Railway path.

Distance
3 miles each way.

One of few dismantled railways in Suffolk that has been converted to recreational use, this one follows the delightful River Stour which forms the boundary between Suffolk and Essex for much of its length. The trail can be linked to a picnic site by the River Stour to the south-west of Rodbridge Corner by crossing the road bridge at the end of the trail to the other bank of the river. You might also choose to head east along the network of quiet Essex / Suffolk lanes to the village

pubs in Belchamp Otten, Belchamp St Paul and Pentlow.

Starting point & parking

The trail starts opposite the main entrance to the Leisure Pool in **Sudbury**, 15 miles north-west of Colchester. Look out for a 'Valley Walk' sign at the start of the trail. There is a large car park at the Leisure Pool (grid reference TL 877410).

Station: Sudbury (the route starts from the station).

TIC: Sudbury, 01787 881320.

Other nearby trails: The circuit of Alton Water is just south of Ipswich.

Useful publications & websites: OS Landranger Map 155. Go to *www.suffolk. gov.uk*, click on 'Transport and streets' then 'Cycling' then 'Cycle maps'.

Refreshments: Lots of choice in Sudbury. There are pubs in the villages a few miles along quiet lanes from the end of the railway path.

Ride 13 Colchester to Wivenhoe
along the riverside path

Category
Riverside path and cyclepaths through parkland.

Distance
5 miles each way.

This ride links Colchester to Wivenhoe Quay via a mixture of quiet streets, paths through parkland and (for the greater part of the ride) a traffic-free riverside path along the River Colne from the south-eastern edge of Colchester past the University of Essex to Wivenhoe railway station. It is well worth going beyond the station to explore the quay and pubs by the riverside in Wivenhoe.

For those of you looking for a totally traffic-free ride, it would be best to start at Wivenhoe station and turn around at the end of the cyclepath after 3 miles. However, if you are prepared to use some short sections on quiet streets you soon join another traffic-free stretch alongside the river and through parkland, arriving right in the heart of Colchester's historic city centre.

Colchester to Wivenhoe, along the riverside path · Ride **13**

Starting points & parking

1. Colchester – Leisure World / Ten Pin, just south of Cowdray Avenue, the A133 Colchester Bypass (grid ref TM 001260).

2. Wivenhoe – the railway station car park, 3 miles south-east of Colchester (grid reference TM 037216).

On your bikes!

1. Start at the Leisure World / Ten Pin Bowling car park. Follow the tarmac cyclepath (white line down the middle) directly away from the Ten Pin Bowling, soon passing a 'Wivenhoe Trail' sign. Cross a bridge and turn left, keeping close to the water on your left following 'Wivenhoe Trail' signs through the parkland.

2. Cross the busy road via a toucan crossing. Pass between allotments and past metal sculptures. Briefly join a road. Cross a bridge and turn left onto Hawkins Road through the industrial estate.

3. Immediately before the roundabout cross the road to join a cyclepath. Use the toucan crossing to cross this very busy road.

4. Follow the riverside path for 3 miles, passing the University of Essex up to your left. The trail passes through woodland with the railway to your left and the river to your right, and emerges at Wivenhoe station.

5. It is worth exploring the riverfront along Old Ferry Road and maybe taking refreshments at the Tudor Tea Rooms, the Station pub or the Rose & Crown pub in Wivenhoe.

Station: Colchester or Wivenhoe.

TIC: Colchester, 01206 282920.

Other nearby trails: The Flitch Way between Braintree and Little Dunmow.

Useful publications & websites: OS Landranger Map 168. There is also a Colchester Cycle Map available from Colchester Tourist Information Centre (01206 282 920) or go to *www.essexcc.gov.uk*, click on 'Cycling and walking' in the 'Travelling' section and go through to 'Leaflets' then 'Cycle Routes'.

Refreshments: Rose & Crown pub, Station pub, Tudor Tea Rooms, Wivenhoe. Lots of choice in the centre of Colchester.

Ride 14 Alton Water south of Ipswich

14

Category
Round-reservoir route.

Distance
8-mile circuit.

This fine reservoir circuit is being improved a little more each year, making the route safer and easier with each improvement. Alton Water is also popular with watersports, so on fine, breezy days you will catch sight of windsurfers racing each other across the lake with their bright sails skimming over the surface. Although this is a relatively easy and flat ride, you should be warned that there is a (short) hillier and rougher stretch on the north side of the lake between Birchwood car park and Lemons Bay. A map showing the route plus the surrounding lanes is available from the cycle hire centre. There is a cafe at the visitor centre and several pubs just near the route, so you could either follow the circuit close to the lake itself or make this part of a longer ride, exploring some of the beautiful and quiet lanes on the Shotley Peninsula.

Starting point & parking

The **Alton Water Visitor Centre**, off the B1080 between Stutton and Holbrook, 6 miles south of Ipswich and 4 miles east of the A12 at Capel St Mary (grid reference TM 156354).

On your bikes!

1. From the visitor centre keep the water to your right and follow the numbered waymarkers for the Alton Water Circuit clockwise around the lake.

2. After 3 miles, at the road turn right over the bridge then right again through the car park onto a gravel track, following the bike route signposts. Certain sections on the north side of the lake are a bit rough and there are some steeper climbs and descents.

3. Cross the dam and follow the lakeshore round to the right back to the start.

Station: Manningtree and Ipswich.

TIC: Ipswich, 01473 258070.

Other nearby trails: Rendlesham Forest lies to the east of Woodbridge.

Useful publications & websites: OS Landranger Map 169 or there is an A4 leaflet available from the visitor centre or Cycle Hire Centre, which shows the lanes in the immediate vicinity and the location of the pubs. You can download a copy of the Alton Water map from www.altoncyclehire.co.uk/images/altonmap2.jpg. See also www.anglianwaterleisure.co.uk

Refreshments:
Café at the visitor centre. Wheatsheaf pub, Tattingstone. Kings Head pub, Stutton. The Compasses pub, the Swan Inn, Holbrook.

15

Bedford to Sandy   Ride 15

Starting from the attractive setting of Bedford's Priory Country Park, with its marina, lakes, the River Great Ouse and a bike hire outlet, the course of the old railway whisks you east towards Sandy through a landscape of rich arable fields. Shortly after crossing the bridge over the A421 you have the option of following the direct route along the railway or taking a longer route alongside the River Great Ouse. Both join at the café at Danish Camp, a fine stopping point with lovely views out over the river. Another attraction along the way is the Dovecote at Willington. The railway path continues to the edge of Sandy, just west of the A1. The route into town from here uses a mixture of cyclepaths and residential roads so you may prefer to turn around at the end of the traffic-free section. Heading west from Priory Country Park there is an attractive riverside route right through the centre of Bedford.

Starting point & parking

Priory Country Park, to the east of **Bedford** town centre, signposted off the A428 Bedford to Cambridge road (grid reference TL 073494).

On your bikes!

East from Priory Country Park to Sandy

1. From the marina in Priory Country Park, follow signs for 'Willington', 'Sandy', 'National Cycle Network Route 51' and 'Danish Camp' along the course of the old railway. The cyclepath runs on a yellow gravel path parallel to the service road.

Category
Lakeside route and railway path.

Distance
(a) 7 miles from Priory Country Park east to the A1 near to Sandy.

(b) 3 miles from Priory Country Park west to the end of the riverside path, beyond Bedford County Hall.

Ride 15 Bedford to Sandy

15

NB There will be a short section on road if you wish to visit the pub and / or the Dovecote in Willington.

2. After 1½ miles, cross the bridge over the A421 dual carriageway. Shortly you have a choice to reach the café at Danish Camp, via the direct route or the riverside route. Both are attractive – why not try one on the outwards trip and the other on your return? If you wish to visit Willington Dovecote and the Crown pub in Willington, take the direct route.

3. Both routes rejoin at Danish Camp, Beyond here there is a short, narrow section of footpath where you will need to walk. Signs indicate the start and finish of this section.

4. If you are with children, it is suggested you turn around after a further 3 miles at the end of the traffic-free section immediately before the A1 dual carriageway

bridge. However, if you wish to go on into Sandy, there is a waymarked 1½-mile route mainly on cyclepaths and residential roads into the centre of town where there are plenty of refreshments.

West from Priory Country Park through Bedford

Following 'Town Centre' signs, there is an attractive riverside path running west from Priory Country Park into the centre of Bedford (by County Hall) along the south side of the river. Then, after crossing the main road bridge via a toucan crossing, it continues along the north side of the river for a further mile. You may wish to go and see the extraordinary Sikh Gurdwara Temple in Queens Park.

15

Station: Bedford.

TIC: Bedford, 01234 215226.

Other nearby trails: Grafham Water lies 15 miles to the north.

Useful publications & websites: OS Landranger Map 153. Cycle Map - Bedford and Kempston is available from *www. bedford.gov.uk* – follow links through

'Transport and streets' to 'Cycling' and 'Cycle Maps'. Also try *www.ccnb.org.uk* (Cycling Campaign for North Bedfordshire).

Refreshments:
Lots of choice in Bedford and Sandy. The Priory Marina pub in Priory Country Park (Bedford). The Crown pub at Willington. Café at the Danish Camp.

16

Grafham Water   Ride **16**
south-west of Huntingdon

One of the few traffic-free routes in Cambridgeshire, this well-signposted reservoir route on tracks and quiet roads is very popular, particularly during summer weekends. The trail uses stone and gravel paths with some gentle hills where the trail leaves the waterside. The reservoir was built in 1966 and holds 59,000 million litres of water. There is plenty of birdlife as well as attractive

Category
Round-reservoir route.

Distance
8-mile circuit.

Ride 16 Grafham Water, south-west of Huntingdon

woodland stretches. For what is meant to be a reservoir circuit it does spend very little time right by the water!

Starting point & parking

West Perry (just off the A1 between St Neots and Huntingdon). There are three main pay and display car parks – Mander Park, Plummer Park and Marlow Park. It is best to do the route anti-clockwise.

On your bikes!

The route is generally well signposted. On the road section through Perry, ignore left turns on Lymage Road and Chichester Way. About 400yds after passing the Wheatsheaf pub and soon after Duberley Close on your

left, turn left on to a waymarked track through Plummer Park.

Station: Huntingdon, 6 miles north-east of Grafham village.

TIC: St Neots, 01480 388788.

Other nearby trails: The country's most famous reservoir route, Rutland Water, lies 30 miles to the north. The Brampton Valley Way (Northampton to Market Harborough) lies 25 miles to the west.

Useful publications & websites: OS Landranger Map 153. The cycle hire centre has maps. For download go to *www.anglianwater. co.uk* and put 'Cycle Grafham Water' into the 'Search' box.

Refreshments: Cafés in Mander and Marlow Parks. Montagu Arms pub in Grafham and Wheatsheaf pub in West Perry.

Ride 17 **Cambridge to Waterbeach along the River Cam**

Category
Riverside path.

Distance
6 miles each way.

Oxford has the River Thames and Cambridge has the River Cam; both rivers offering wonderful rides along top-quality towpaths that go right into the heart of each city. If you are coming from outside Cambridge, there is a convenient car park at Waterbeach railway station that is connected by a cyclepath to the river. Follow the towpath along the banks of the willow-lined Cam for a chance of spotting the vivid turquoise of a kingfisher. The traffic-free path stops at Jesus Green but as bikes are such an integral part of life in Cambridge, it is possible to continue with confidence right into the heart of the city to see the magnificent colleges along Kings Parade.

Starting points & parking

1. **Waterbeach** railway station car park, off the A10 north of Cambridge (grid reference TL 500650).

2. The Jesus Green tennis courts near the River Cam just north of the centre of **Cambridge**, at the junction of Thompson's Lane and Park Parade (grid reference TL 448592).

On your bikes!

South from Waterbeach into Cambridge

1. Exit Waterbeach railway station car park onto the cyclepath parallel with the road leading away from the station. After ¼ mile bear right by the Bridge pub to join the river towpath and turn right (water to your left).

2. Follow the river towpath for 4 miles. At the end of the riverside route turn left onto the cyclepath / pavement on Water Street by the Penny Ferry pub. Bear left onto a continuation of Water Street.

3. Shortly turn left opposite the Green Dragon pub to cross a footbridge over the river, and turn right. This joins a quiet residential road for ¼ mile then becomes a traffic-free path once again alongside the river.

4. It is suggested you go as far as the tennis courts by the river on Jesus Green,

just beyond Jesus Green swimming pool. If you wish to continue into the heart of Cambridge, keep following National Cycle Network Route 11 signs along a series of quiet streets to emerge at Kings Parade.

Station: Waterbeach.

TIC: Cambridge, 08712 268 006.

Other nearby trails: Grafham Water.

Useful publications & websites: OS Landranger Map 154. You can either download a Cambridge Cycling Map or order a paper copy from *www.camcycle.org.uk/ resources/map*

Refreshments: The Bridge pub at Waterbeach. Lots of choice in Cambridge.

Ride 18 Rendlesham Forest north-east of Ipswich

Category
Forest trails.

Distance
6 or 10 miles.

There are two family cycle trails starting from Rendlesham Forest Centre. The short trail, waymarked yellow, is approximately 6 miles long with a shortcut allowing you to halve your ride. The long trail, waymarked green, is 10 miles in length. Both trails are off-road on sand, gravel and grass. The rides pass through mixed woodland and clumps of bright yellow gorse. For a section of the route you are right alongside the perimeter of a disused airfield with large round hangars. Rendlesham Forest was planted by the Forestry Commission between 1922 and the late 1930s. Before that the land was heathland. Two-thirds of the forest was prematurely felled by the Great Storm of 1987, when over one million trees were blown down. The forest has since been redesigned to take account of wildlife conservation, recreation and timber production. It now has greater diversity

with conifer and broadleaf woodland, open space, wetland and heathland. It lies within the Suffolk Coast and Heaths Area of Outstanding Natural Beauty.

Starting point & parking

Rendlesham Forest, north-east of Ipswich. Leave the A12 at Woodbridge. Follow the A1152 then the B1084 towards Butley. After 4 miles on the B1084, take the first road to the right (grid reference TM 355484).

Station: Market Wickham.

TIC: Woodbridge, 01394 382240.

Other nearby trails: Alton Water Reservoir is just south of Ipswich.

Useful publications & websites: OS Landranger Maps 156 & 169. A Rendlesham Forest leaflet is available by calling the forest centre (01394 450164). Try also *www.forestry. gov.uk/rendlesham*

Refreshments: None in the forest itself, the nearest are in Butley or Hollesley.

Peterborough & Ride 19
Ferry Meadows Country Park

This traffic-free ride on either side of the River Nene between Ferry Meadows Country Park and the centre of Peterborough is part of a much larger and more ambitious project known as the Peterborough Green Wheel. This is a network of cycleways, footpaths and bridleways that provides safe, continuous routes around the city and 'spokes' linking the Wheel to residential areas and the city centre. The Green Wheel celebrates over 2,000 years of Peterborough's social, cultural, economic and environmental history through a series of sculptures and colourful interpretation boards along the route. The ride described is just one suggestion; others might include a ride along the River Nene to the east of town or west from Farcet towards the A15 and A1.

Starting points & parking

1. The bridge over the River Nene by Asda in the **centre of Peterborough** (grid reference TL 192981).

2. If coming from outside Peterborough, it is better to park in **Ferry Meadows** (off the A605 Oundle Road on the west side of Peterborough) and cycle into town (grid reference TL 147974).

On your bikes!

Start from the centre of Peterborough

1. From the footbridge over the River Nene just south of the centre of Peterborough (by Asda and close to Railway World), turn right on Henry Penn Walk alongside the river (keeping the water to your left).

2. At the T-junction at the end of the tarmac turn right to cross the bridge, then left by the Boat House Inn. Follow the path around the edge of the rowing lake, keeping the water to your left.

3. At the T-junction by the main road at the end of the lake, turn left signposted 'Orton, Ferry Meadows'. Pass beneath the road bridge, over the green metal sluice gates, cross the railway line then turn right signposted 'Orton Meadows, Ferry Meadows, Lynch Wood'.

4. At the next T-junction turn right to cross the railway line then turn left and stay close to the railway line. Cross the road with care, then turn right on the tarmac path alongside the road to the visitor centre at Ferry Meadows.

5. For a full circuit of the lakes go past the visitor centre and at the first lake, bear left following the curve of the miniature

Category
Specially-built cyclepath.

Distance
7-mile circuit to Ferry Meadows Country Park.

Optional 3-mile circuit of lakes in the park.

railway line to your left. Pass to the left of the watersports centre then keep bearing right, staying on tarmac and keeping close to the lake to your right to return to the visitor centre.

6. To return to Peterborough along the south side of the River Nene, follow the tarmac path alongside the exit road from Ferry Meadows park then turn left just before the level crossing, signposted 'Station, Orton Mere, City Centre'.

7. Keep following the tarmac path as it crosses the railway line, then turn left parallel with the line signposted 'Orton Mere, City Centre'.

8. At the next junction, turn left then right signposted 'Woodston City Centre' to continue parallel with railway line.

9. Stay on the tarmac path as it swings right then left to recross the railway line

for a final time. Go past Railway World and take the next footbridge across the river (opposite new yellow-brick riverside houses) to return to Asda.

Station: Peterborough.

TIC: Peterborough, 01733 452336.

Other nearby trails: There are several sections of the Peterborough Green Wheel that offer traffic-free cycling, and more is being built each year. See details about the leaflet below.

Useful publications & websites: OS Landranger Map 142. The *Peterborough Cycle Map* (£1.50) is available from Peterborough Tourist Information Centre, 3-5 Minster Precincts, Peterborough PE1 1XS (01733 452336). Email: tic@peterborough.gov.uk. Also go to *www.travelchoice.org.uk* for information about cycling in Peterborough.

Refreshments: Lots of choice in Peterborough. Boat House Inn, near to the rowing lake. Café at the Ferry Meadows Country Park.

Thetford Forest Ride 20
north-west of Cambridge

Draw a line 10 miles around Thetford and you have some of the most consistently rideable offroad tracks in all of East Anglia: the soil has a sandy base and drains well and as the land is not good enough for farming, most of it is owned by the Forestry Commission and planted with pine trees. The forestry tracks around the plantations tend to have excellent all-year round surfaces and it is possible to devise any number of loops using these tracks. However, as is the case with all forestry land, it is almost impossible to give detailed route instructions when the only landmarks are trees and more trees, so the rides described are those that the Forestry Commission has already waymarked.

Starting points & parking

1. For Brandon Park Loop, start at **Mayday Farm car park**, 3 miles south of Brandon along the B1106 (grid reference TL 795834).

2. For High Lodge Loop and the red and black trails, start at **High Lodge Forest Centre**, on the Forest Drive, off the B1107 east of Brandon (grid reference TL 811852).

Station: Brandon.

TIC: Bury St Edmunds, 01284 764667.

Other nearby trails: The Peddars Way is a long-distance bridleway that runs north from Thetford to the Norfolk coast, offering good cycling for mountain bikes in the summer months.

Useful publications & websites: OS Landranger Maps 143 & 144. Much better is the Forestry Commission *Thetford Forest Park Cycling Guide and Map*, available from the Forest Centre. Also try *www.forestry.gov.uk/thetfordforestpark*

Refreshments: At High Lodge Forest Centre.

Category
Forest trails.

Distance
High Lodge Loop
– Green –
6.3 miles (Easy)

Brandon Park
Loop – Blue –
8.1 miles (Easy)

Red Route –
11 miles (Age 12+)

Black Route –
10 miles (Age 15+)

NB If you decide to link rides either side of the B1106, take great care at the crossing points as traffic travels fast along this road.

21

Ride 21 Marriott's Way from Norwich to Reepham

Category
Railway path.

Distance
15 miles each way.

Escape from the heart of Norwich into the countryside on one of the longest disused railways in the country. The route is signposted as the Wensum Valley Walk from the centre of Norwich, and becomes the Marriott's Way near to Drayton. If you do not live in Norwich itself, Reepham is a better place to start. The woodlands of Mileplain Plantation are a real delight: a deep cutting planted with sweet chestnut trees, especially attractive during the changing autumn colours. The whole route is studded with a wide variety of broadleaf trees – oak, ash, hawthorn, silver birch and sycamore. The clear, gently-flowing waters of the River Wensum are crossed three times on fine old metal bridges with wooden planking. Between Lenwade and Reepham you have the option of the full route following the Themelthorpe Loop, or taking a shortcut that saves 4 miles.

NB The railway path can be followed east from Reepham to Aylsham where it is possible to link to the Weavers Way as far as North Walsham. However, the surface is much rougher, there are several road sections and also a crossing of the busy A140 to the east of Aylsham.

Starting points & parking

1. On the north-west side of the centre of **Norwich,** at the roundabout by the River Wensum at the junction of Barn Road and St Crispins Road (grid reference TG 226094).

2. Drayton – the trail crosses the A1067 between Drayton and Taverham (grid reference TG 176139).

3. Reepham – access to the railway path is 1 mile south of the crossroads in the centre of Reepham along the minor road towards Whitewell at the old Whitewell Station (grid reference TG 091217).

On your bikes!

Route instructions from south to north (Norwich to Reepham)

1. From the Barn Road / St Crispins Road roundabout in the centre of Norwich, join

MARRIOTT'S WAY **21**
This former railway line is not a public right of way.
Residents and Visitors to Norfolk are permitted to use it at their own risk as a footpath, cycleway and bridleway.

Please respect wildlife, keep dogs under control and take your litter home.

No vehicular access. No shooting. No camping.

NORFOLK COUNTY COUNCIL

the track alongside the river signposted 'Wensum Valley Walk'.

2. Follow National Cycle Network Route 1 signs along a tarmac then gravel path for 5 miles, crossing one road and continuing in the same direction (take either fork after road crossing – they join up).

3. Shortly after a triangular-shaped metal bridge over the river, the railway path peters out. Descend to the left then at the T-junction with the road turn right then left onto Station Road, signposted 'No through traffic'. At the T-junction at the end of Station Road, turn right then left through a gap in the wooden fence signposted 'Marriott's Way' to descend to a continuation of the railway path.

4. Over the next 4 miles go straight ahead at several crossroads, following signs for Reepham.

5. At the T-junction with road, turn right signposted 'Reepham' then after 150yds turn left on a broad gravel track. Go through the car park to rejoin the course of the railway.

6. Cross the river. The industrial estate begins to the left. Go straight ahead at several crossroads.

7. About 3 miles after passing the industrial estate and immediately after passing the old Whitewell Station, turn right*. You may wish to turn around here or if you want refreshments in Reepham, follow the minor road uphill and past the school to the crossroads in the centre of the town.

or continue straight ahead on the Themelthorpe Loop on a much longer (traffic-free) course into Reepham.

Station: Norwich.

TIC: Norwich, 01603 727927.

Other nearby trails: The Peddars Way lies 25 miles to the west and runs for 50 miles from near Thetford to the Norfolk coast at Holme-next-the-Sea. Best ridden on mountain bikes in the summer months.

Useful publications & websites:
OS Landranger Maps 133 & 134. For the most up-to-date cycling information visit *www.norfolk.gov.uk*, then 'Transport & Streets' and 'Cycling'. For background detail go to *www.countrysideaccess.norfolk.gov.uk/long-distance.aspx* and click on 'Marriotts Way'.

Refreshments: Lots of choice in Reepham and Norwich, and just off the route in Drayton and Lenwade.

East Midlands Trails

1 Pitsford Reservoir

2 Brampton Valley Way

3 Market Harborough Arm: Grand Union Canal

4 Rutland Water

5 Leicester & Watermead Park

6 Ashby Woulds Moira Heritage Trail

7 Etwall to Derby

8 Cloud Trail, Derby

9 Derby to Elvaston Castle Country Park

10 Nutbrook Trail, Long Eaton

11 Shipley Country Park

12 River Trent through Nottingham

13 Southwell Trail

14 Newark to Cotham

15 Tissington Trail

16 Carsington Water

17 High Peak Trail

18 Monsal Trail

19 Five Pits Trail

20 Silverhill Trail

21 Pleasley Trails

22 Sherwood Pines Forest

23 Clumber Park

24 Worksop to Sherwood

25 Routes through Lincoln

26 Sett Valley Trail

27 Longdendale Trail

28 Upper Derwent Valley

29 Chesterfield Canal

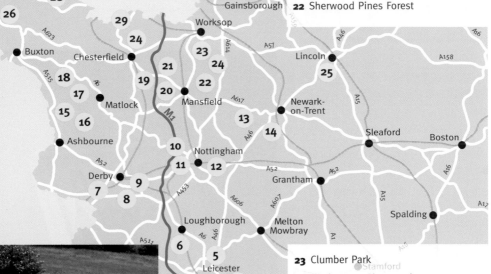

Ride 1 Pitsford Reservoir

04 East Midlands Mountain Biking

Mountain biking in the East Midlands is fairly limited to the bridleways and byways in Derbyshire, many of which are fairly challenging as they lie within the hilly and dramatic Peak District. Most of the best tracks (and many of the more popular railway trails) are located in a 10-mile radius around Bakewell. There are several guides covering these trails, available from good bookshops and the larger Tourist Information Centres. A few bridleway and byway sections of the Viking Way through Lincolnshire, and longer sections of the Midshires Way through Leicestershire, can be ridden legally.

There is no substitute for intimate local knowledge – try to explore every bridleway, byway, unclassified road, canal towpath and Forestry Commission track near to home, sift out the good from the bad and link together the best off-road sections to form your own customised route(s). The best advice is to use the months from late spring to early autumn (May to October) to do the exploration, if possible after a spell of dry weather. The same track in winter can take twice as long or even be impassable.

Note down on the map (or colour-code with highlighter pen) the quality of the trail and whether it is better done in one direction or the other – it is normally better to climb on tarmac and descend off-road so that gravity can help you through any muddy bits. Where there are no books or leaflets describing mountain bike rides, the staff in bike shops can often put you in contact with local riders or clubs who may have done some of this research already, saving you many hours of trial and error.

Bear in mind that everyone has a different view of what constitutes a good trail: hard or technical for some is easy for others and a bit of mud for some is a quagmire for others!

Websites:

www.forestry.gov.uk and search 'Sherwood Pines Forest Park' for a singletrack trail near to Mansfield.

www.moredirt.co.uk and follow links from 'Trails & Tracks' to 'United Kingdom' to 'East Midlands'.

Ride 28 Upper Derwent Valley

East Midlands Forestry

The Midlands are the least forested area of Great Britain. With the exception of Sherwood Forest and the woodlands to the east of Mansfield, there is very little woodland at all in the region. In some forests and woods there are no waymarked routes, but you are free to explore the tracks. The relevant Ordnance Survey map is mentioned. It is highly recommended that you take a map for the larger woods as it is very easy to get lost.

Forests and woods with waymarked trails

There is just one Forestry Commission holding with a waymarked trail in the East Midlands region:

5 **Sherwood Pines Forest**, north-east of Mansfield (Ride 22, page 190)

The woodlands listed right correspond with the numbers on the map:

1. Harry's Park Wood & Souther Wood, south-east of Corby (OS Explorer Map 224)

2. Fineshade Wood & Wakerley Great Wood, south-west of Stamford (OS Explorer Map 234)

3. Twyford Wood & Morkery Wood, south of Grantham (OS Explorer Map 247)

4. Temple Wood & Bourne Wood, north of Peterborough (OS Explorer Map 248)

6. Stapleford Wood, north-east of Newark-on-Trent (OS Explorer Map 271)

7. Chamber's Farm Wood, east of Lincoln (OS Explorer Map 273)

8. Ostler's Plantation, east of Woodhall Spa, east of Lincoln (OS Explorer Map 273)

9. Willingham Forest & Willingham Woods, east of Market Rasen (OS Explorer Map 282)

10. Laughton Woods, south-west of Scunthorpe (OS Explorer Map 280)

The Forestry Commission's website, *www. forestry.gov.uk* is a good source of information. Click on 'Explore, Experience, Enjoy' then 'Cycling' and you can find out details of hundreds of waymarked trails throughout the UK. You can search by forest name or by the nearest town / city. The search will tell you the grade, length and waymarking details of the trails. Alternatively, by clicking on the map you can see the nearest forest to where you live.

5 Sherwood Pines

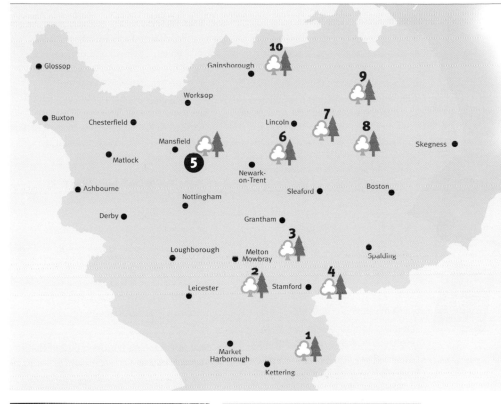

It is also worth contacting the following
Forest District Offices for further information:

Sherwood & Lincolnshire
Edwinstowe
Mansfield
Nottinghamshire NG21 9JL
Tel: 01623 822447
Email: enquiries.sherwood@forestry.gsi.gov.uk

Northants
Top Lodge
Fineshade
Corby
Northants NN17 3BB
Tel: 01780 444920
Email: enquiries.northants@forestry.gsi.gov.uk

East Midlands National Cycle Network

West Midlands Cycle Route

163 miles from Oxford to Derby via Birmingham. Highlights include the ancient city of Oxford, Blenheim Palace at Woodstock, North Oxfordshire villages, Stratford-upon-Avon, the Rea Valley Route into Central Birmingham, Lichfield Cathedral and the traffic-free routes through Derby.

Traffic-free sections over 3 miles long:

- Stratford-upon-Avon Greenway from Stratford to Long Marston (NCN 5).
- Rea Valley Route – King's Norton to Cannon Hill Park (Birmingham) (NCN 5).
- Birmingham Canal between Birmingham and Wolverhampton (NCN 5).
- Etwall to Mickleover (Derby) (NCN 5).

South Midlands Cycle Route

148 miles from Oxford to Derby via Leicester. Highlights include the ancient city of Oxford, the largely traffic-free route from Winslow through Milton Keynes to Wolverton, the Brampton Valley Way railway path between Northampton and Market Harborough, the Grand Union Canal towpath, the traffic-free route through Leicester, and the railway path from Worthington into Derby.

Traffic-free sections over 3 miles long:

- Route through Milton Keynes (NCN 51).
- Brampton Valley Way from Northampton to Market Harborough (NCN 6).
- Market Harborough to Foxton along the Grand Union Canal (NCN 6).
- Route through Leicester to Birstall (NCN 6).
- Cloud Trail from Derby to Worthington (NCN 6).

Derby to York

154 miles from Derby to York via Nottingham, Sheffield and Doncaster. Highlights include Elvaston Castle Country Park (Derby), Bestwood Country Park (Nottingham), Newstead Abbey, the traffic-free route through Sherwood Forest and Clumber Park, Rother Valley Country Park, the Old Moor Wetland Centre and the historic city of York.

Traffic-free sections over 3 miles long:

- Derby to Elvaston Country Park alongside the Derwent (NCN 6).
- Blidworth to Worksop through Sherwood Forest and Clumber Park (NCN 6).
- The Elsecar Greenway from Hoyland to the Old Moor Wetland Centre (NCN 62 & 67).
- Harlington to Bentley along the Trans-Pennine Trail (NCN 62).
- Riccall to York (NCN 65).

Hull to Fakenham (northern part of Hull to Harwich Route)

206 miles from Hull to Fakenham via Market Rasen, Lincoln, Boston, Wisbech and King's Lynn. Highlights include the Lincolnshire Wolds, Lincoln Cathedral and Castle, Boston's St Botolph Church (the Boston Stump) and the fine buildings of King's Lynn.

Traffic-free sections over 3 miles long:
None

Leicester

Sustrans

The Sustrans maps shown on the far left cover various National Cycle Network routes within the region. Some of the maps may describe routes that continue into adjacent regions; these maps are mentioned in both chapters. The maps are not only useful for people wishing to ride the whole route over several days, they also show all the traffic-free sections that make good day rides.

Other good areas for lane cycling

There is a huge variety of terrain within this region, from the very steep and challenging lanes of the Peak District in the west to the fens of Lincolnshire – one of Britain's flattest counties – in the east. If neither of these extremes appeals to you then the gently rolling countryside of Leicestershire and Northamptonshire, with their plethora of attractive stone villages, may be the solution. The best network of lanes in the Peak District is in the southern half of the National Park, south of Buxton.

Derby

Market Harborough

Lincoln

165

Ride 1 Brixworth Country Park / Pitsford Reservoir north of Northampton

Category
Lakeside path.

Distance
7-mile circuit of the reservoir.

This cycle trail around Pitsford Water is a model of its kind, keeping you close to the water for the whole circuit, on well-maintained paths and avoiding time spent on roads, which is so often the failing of circuits around reservoirs. The lake is popular with swans, anglers and windsurfers, and if the wind is blowing strongly you may well witness some pretty amazing acrobatics by top-class windsurfers whizzing over the surface of the lake and turning on a sixpence! Anglian Water, in conjunction with Northamptonshire County Council, has been successful in gaining a grant from the Millennium Fund to provide 'Access for All' at Pitsford Water. Brixworth Country Park is being developed to include special gardens and ponds, tracks suitable for disabled access and a link to the Brampton Valley Way. It is intended that the project will provide an opportunity for everyone to experience the wonderful countryside around Pitsford Water.

Starting point & parking

The visitor centre at **Pitsford Water** in Brixworth Country Park, off the A508, about 6 miles north of Northampton (grid reference SP 753695).

On your bikes!

From the visitor centre, head downhill towards the masts of the dinghies. At the main track around the reservoir you can turn right or left, as the circuit is signposted in both directions and there is no obvious advantage one way or the other. The dam is at the western end of the circuit, close to the visitor centre; at the eastern end, the cycle trail uses the causeway across the water.

Station: Northampton or Kettering.

TIC: Northampton, 01604 838800.

Other nearby trails: The Brampton Valley Way between Northampton (Chapel Brampton) and Market Harborough. The Market Harborough Arm of the Grand Union Canal.

Useful publications & websites: OS Landranger Maps 141 & 152. Much more useful is the map you can get from Pitsford Water Cycle Hire (01604 881777) near the visitor centre. Try *www.anglianwater.co.uk*, click on 'Leisure' then 'What to do' then 'Cycling' then 'Pitsford Water Park'.

Refreshments: Café at the visitor centre.

Brampton Valley Way
from Market Harborough to Northampton

The Brampton Valley Way is the longest dismantled railway path in the region, connecting Market Harborough with the outskirts of Northampton and forming part of National Cycle Network Route 6, which, when complete, will run all the way from London to Keswick in the Lake District. It is a wide, well-maintained trail with few barriers, making it a perfect 'conversational' ride: a chance to catch up with friends while getting some exercise. The trail includes two tunnels where you will need lights. There are some old steam locomotives and rolling stock at Chapel Brampton. The railway line was closed in 1981 and was purchased by Northamptonshire County Council in 1987. It opened for recreational use as the Brampton Valley Way in 1993. It is named after the tributary of the River Nene – the Brampton Arm – the valley of which it follows for much of its length.

Starting points & parking

1. Market Harborough: from the traffic lights in the centre of town, follow the A508 Northampton Road for ¹/₂ mile. The Bell Inn is on your left. The cycle path starts at the back of the pub (grid reference SP 737867).

2. Northampton: from the centre of town follow the A508 / A5199 north towards Leicester for 4 miles. Shortly after the end of the built-up area and the start of the countryside, turn right on Brampton Lane, signposted 'Boughton', then right again into the car park (grid reference SP 737653).

On your bikes!

Start from Market Harborough

1. It is not hard to follow the course of this railway line south from Market Harborough as it is almost all intact. There are several road crossings.

2. It is suggested you only go as far as the Windhover pub on the A5199, just beyond the old Pitsford & Brampton railway station. Beyond here the trail soon becomes much rougher.

> **Station:** Market Harborough.
>
> **TIC:** Market Harborough, 01858 828282.
>
> **Other nearby trails:** Rutland Water lies 15 miles to the north-east. Brixworth Country Park (Pitsford Water). The Grand Union Canal to the north of Market Harborough.
>
> **Useful publications & websites:** OS Landranger Maps 141 & 152. *www. northamptonshire.gov.uk* or *www.leics.gov.uk* and search 'Brampton Valley Way'.
>
> **Refreshments:** Waterloo Farm tearoom about 2 miles south of Market Harborough. Windhover pub at the southern end of the route on the A5199 to the south of Chapel Brampton.

Category
Railway path.

Distance
14 miles each way.

Ride 3 **Market Harborough Arm of Grand Union Canal**

3

Category
Canal towpath.

Distance
6 miles each way.

Forming part of National Cycle Network Route 6, this canal offers a fine ride with good views, refreshments at the pub or café at Foxton Locks, and a chance to visit the museum there. The winding course of the canal is explained by the canal builders' aim to hug the contours and thus avoid the need to build any locks. As the height they followed is at about 300ft there are some fine views out into the surrounding countryside. The banks are crowded with wildflowers and hawthorn blossom in the late spring and early summer. It is suggested you turn around at Debdale Wharf Bridge: at this point the towpath becomes a lot rougher. The ten locks at Foxton opened in 1814. They raise the canal by 75ft and take an average of 45 minutes to negotiate, using 25,000 gallons of water per passage. The locks linked together the Leicestershire & Northamptonshire Union Canal and the (Old) Grand Union Canal. Following a takeover by the Grand Junction Canal, a lift was opened in 1900 to compete against the railways for traffic. It was part of a scheme to widen the route from the Derbyshire coalfields to London. The locks were refurbished for night traffic in 1909 but in 1911 the lift was mothballed to save money and the machinery was sold for scrap in 1928.

Starting point & parking

Northern edge of Market Harborough
From the centre of Market Harborough follow signs for 'Melton Mowbray B6047' and 'St Lukes Hospital'. After passing a garage and then the Police Headquarters, turn left immediately before the Union Inn Hotel signposted 'Union Wharf South' (grid reference SP 727879).

On your bikes!

1. The canal towpath starts near the Union Inn Hotel on the B6047 Melton Mowbray road. From the hotel follow signs for 'Union Wharf South'.

2. Follow the canal towpath for 6 miles, passing through Foxton. It is suggested that you go as far as Debdale Wharf (about 1 mile beyond Foxton Locks). After this the towpath becomes grassy and rougher.

> **Station:** Market Harborough.
>
> **TIC:** Market Harborough, 01858 828282.
>
> **Other nearby trails:** The Brampton Valley Way runs between Market Harborough and Northampton.
>
> **Useful publications & websites:** OS Landranger Map 141. Go to *www.waterscape.com* and search 'Cycling' and 'Market Harborough' or *www.leics.gov.uk* search 'Cycle trails' then choose 'Grand Union'.
>
> **Refreshments:** Lots of choice in Market Harborough. Café and Locks Inn at Foxton.

Rutland Water Ride 4
east of Leicester

Britain's favourite reservoir route offers a superb day out around the largest man-made lake in Western Europe, covering an area of 3,100 acres. The ride uses a good, all-year-round track with some tarmac sections and links Egleton (near Oakham), Manton, Edith Weston, Whitwell and Upper Hambleton. The visitor centres all have something of interest: there are tropical butterflies, exotic insects and fish at the Empingham Leisure Centre, the Normanton Church and Water Museum at Normanton Leisure Centre and the Drought Garden at Barnsdale Leisure Area. There are three short sections on public roads: the section along the lane which leads from the A606 near Oakham to Hambleton Peninsula is fairly quiet, likewise the lane to Egleton. There is a busier 1-mile section east of Manton but much of this is either on a parallel cyclepath or on a designated cycle lane.

Starting point & parking

Located along the eastern half of the lake and listed clockwise from the north, there are Pay & Display car parks at Barnsdale, Whitwell, Empingham and Normanton Visitor Centres. Rutland Water lies between Oakham (A606 / A6003) and Stamford (A1).

On your bikes!

The route is well signposted. The route is best ridden anti-clockwise to minimise right turns. It is just after turning off the cyclepath alongside the A606 (east of Oakham) that you have the choice of adding another 7 miles to your trip by completing a circuit of the Hambleton Peninsula.

Station: Oakham.

TIC: Oakham, 01572 653027.

Other nearby trails: The Brampton Valley Way between Market Harborough and Northampton lies 16 miles to the south-west.

Useful publications & websites: OS Landranger Map 141. The cycle hire outlets also have maps. Also try *www.anglianwater. co.uk/leisure/what-to-do/cycling*

Refreshments: Cafés at the visitor centres. Horse & Jockey pub in Manton at the south-west corner of the lake.

Category
Round-reservoir route.

Distance
17 miles for the circuit plus 7 miles for the Hambleton Peninsula.

NB For people looking for a shorter ride, the best bit of the circuit runs from Whitwell Centre on the north shore via the dam at the east end of the lake to the Normanton Centre at the south-east corner of the lake (or vice versa).

Ride 5 Leicester to Watermead Park

Category
Riverside path.

Distance
4 miles each way.

The River Soar offers a largely traffic-free corridor from the landscaped gardens of Abbey Park in the centre of Leicester, past the National Space Centre (there is a rocket inside!) to Watermead Country Park in the north, where there is a chance of exploring a whole network of trails around the watercourses and lakes, including a climb up a hill to see the sculpture of a mammoth.

Starting points & parking

1. Watermead Park, north of Leicester, near the junction of the A46 and A607 (grid reference SK 608114).

2. St Margaret's Pasture car park near the Sports Centre, just off St Margaret's Way, near Abbey Park in the **centre of Leicester** (grid reference SK 584054).

NB There is also a 3-mile ride south from the centre of Leicester on a railway path known as the Great Central Way.

On your bikes!

North from Leicester city centre to Watermead Park

1. From the car park by the sports centre in Abbey Park, follow the tarmac path around the perimeter of the five-a-side football pitch to cross the concrete bridge over the River Soar then turn right (north), soon arriving at the large ornate building housing the tearooms.

2. Follow signs for Watermead Park and Riverside Way, with the river to your right. Cross Abbey Park Road via a toucan crossing. Go past the National Space Centre. At the next road (Thurcaston Road) turn right to cross the bridge then turn left to rejoin the riverside path, with the river now to your left.

3. Continue alongside the river / canal and into Watermead Country Park. There are many trails around the lakes, which may seem confusing, but the area is bounded on three sides by residential housing or dual carriageways so you can't get too lost! There is a sculpture of a mammoth at the top of a small hill which is worth climbing up to see.

Station: Leicester.

TIC: Leicester, 09062 941113.

Other nearby trails: Rutland Water lies 20 miles to the east. The Brampton Valley Way (Market Harborough to Northampton) lies 16 miles south-east.

Useful publications & websites: OS Landranger Map 140. Visit the following websites: *www.leicesterspokes.org.uk* or the council's own website *www.leicester.gov.uk* and follow links through 'Transport & Streets' to 'Cycling'.

Refreshments: Gazebo Café in the Abbey Grounds. White Horse pub, Birstall.

Ashby Woulds Heritage Trail Ride 6
north-west of Leicester

The signboards along this short railway path ride to the north-east of Measham offer a clear explanation not only of the area's industrial history, but also of the huge efforts needed to restore nature's balance after more than 150 years of dumping mining and industrial waste without thinking through the long-term environmental consequences. As a result of these huge efforts, lakes, grassland and woodland have been created where before there were stagnant hazardous pools and a moonscape of spoils. Within a generation, the area will be covered by mature trees and a visitor would never know what was previously there! In addition to the 7-mile there and back ride along the railway path there are three different circuits of between 1 and 2 miles in what is now called Donisthorpe Woodland. The ride described also visits Moira Furnace and the Conkers Centre, set in the heart of the new National Forest.

Starting point & parking

The library car park in the centre of **Measham**, just off the M42 / A42 to the north-east of Junction 11, about 9 miles south-east of Burton-upon-Trent (grid reference SK 332119).

On your bikes!

1. From the car park by the library in the centre of Measham, follow the 'Ashby Would Heritage Trail' signposts.

2. After ³/₄ mile turn left to join the pavement alongside the road that passes beneath the A42, then shortly, at the next Heritage Trail signpost, turn right to rejoin the railway path.

3. Follow the trail into Donisthorpe Woodland. After about 300yds of gentle descent, turn right off the railway path by a National Cycle Network Route 63 signpost onto a similar wide gravel path following signs for 'Spring Cottage via Moira'. At the T-junction with the canal turn left.

4. Go past Moira Furnace then cross the road onto a continuation of the canal towpath.

5. Go through the Conkers Waterside car park and bear left* onto a gravel path, then turn left to cross the railway line.

* Or to visit the main Conkers Visitor Centre, continue straight ahead through the tunnel – the visitor centre is a few hundred yards along this trail.

6. At the junction with the railway path turn left to return to Measham (or right to visit the Navigation Inn on the B5004).

7. Rejoin the outward route and follow back to the start.

Category
Railway path and canal towpath.

Distance
3¹/₂ miles each way.

Ride **6** **Ashby Woulds Heritage Trail, north-west of Leicester**

6

Station: Burton-upon-Trent.

TIC: Ashby-de-la-Zouch, 01530 411767.

Other nearby trails: The Derby to Worthington Path (the Cloud Trail) lies 9 miles to the north-east.

There are also rides in the Donisthorpe Woodland Park:
Green route – Woodland Park Circular – 1.5 miles

Purple route – Hill Street Circular – 1.1 miles
Orange route – Moira Road Circular – 1 mile

Useful publications & websites: OS Landranger Map 128. Go to *www.leics.gov.uk/ ashby_cycle_info.pdf*

Refreshments: Lots of choice in Measham. The Navigation Inn on the B5004 at the northern end of the trail. Cafés at the two Conkers Visitor Centres.

Ride **7** **Mickleover to Etwall railway path west of Derby**

7

Category
Railway path.

Distance
5 miles each way.

A fine flat ride through lush countryside to the west of Derby along the course of an old railway that used to link Derby to Hilton. One curiosity is that the bridges all have names such as Egginton Junction Bridge, Hargate Bridge and unsurprisingly for one that is painted bright pink, 'The Pink Bridge'.

Starting point & parking

The trail lies to the **west of Derby**. Heading north on the B5020 from Mickleover towards Kirk Langley, the start of the railway path lies to the left just after passing a residential road called Whistlestop Close. The trail is signposted 'Burton, Ashbourne' and 'National Cycle Network Routes 54 / 68' (grid reference SK 309359).

On your bikes!

1. Follow the railway path south-west for 3¹/₂ miles. At the subway beneath the A516 and a cast-iron Millennium signpost you can:

(a) continue on the railway path (following signs for Burton) for a further 1¹/₂ miles to its end at the A5132 to the east of Hilton.

(b) pass beneath the subway then bear right up onto the bridge over the railway path to follow Sutton Lane into Etwall. At the T-junction at the end of Sutton Lane, turn right for pubs or the café in the Post Office.

Station: Hatton.

TIC: Derby, 01332 255802.

Other nearby trails: Derby to Worthington (Cloud Trail). Derby to Elvaston Castle.

Useful publications & websites: OS Landranger Map 128. For the latest information about cycling in Derby and cycle leaflets covering the city, call the Cycle Derby Team (01332 715054) or visit their website: *www.cyclederby.co.uk*

Refreshments: Spread Eagle pub, Hawk & Buckle pub, Post Office café in Etwall.

Derby to Worthington on the Cloud Trail

Ride **8**

This route out of Derby was one of the first built by Sustrans, the driving force behind the National Cycle Network. The route has many of the best features of a Sustrans project – it starts from the very heart of the city, uses an attractive riverside path, a canal towpath and a disused railway on its way from the urban centre into the heart of the countryside. As the route becomes more rural in character you will come across some beautifully painted Millennium Mileposts and some very fine stone sculptures. This ride follows the same course as the Derby to Elvaston Castle Country Park route at the start before turning south away from the River Derwent and eventually reaching the village of Worthington, which has a curious red-brick octagonal lock-up and a pub. There is also the option of visiting the vast quarry that lies just to the north-east of Worthington.

Starting points & parking

1. Riverside Gardens in the **centre of Derby**, near the Council House, the bus station and the Eagle Centre Market (grid reference SK 356364).

2. If coming from outside Derby it is best to start (and park) at the south end of the trail in **Worthington**, a village about 7 miles west of Loughborough (grid reference SK 406210). The nearest motorway junction is M1, Jct 23. From the crossroads in Worthington by St Matthew's Church follow Breedon Lane downhill, signposted 'Cloud Trail', then shortly turn first right and follow this to the car park.

On your bikes!

1. The ride starts in the Riverside Gardens in the centre of Derby (near the bus station and the Council House). Follow signs for the Riverside Path and stay close to the river for 2 miles.

Category
Railway path.

Distance
13 miles each way.

173

Ride **8** **Derby to Worthington on the Cloud Trail**

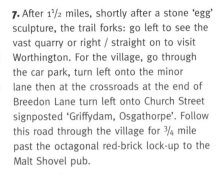

2. Go past Pride Park, the stadium for Derby County Football Club, pass beneath a low black bridge (with attached pipe) then take the **second** of two closely spaced paths to the right by a brightly painted cast-iron Millennium signpost. Turn right on National Cycle Network Route 6.

3. Keep following signs for Swarkestone, Melbourne and National Cycle Network Route 6, crossing several roads.

4. Pass beneath the A50, cross a bridge over the Trent & Mersey Canal then turn left onto the towpath signposted 'Melbourne'.

5. After 1¹/₂ miles, just before the large metal bridge over the canal, bear right and join the railway path, soon crossing the River Trent.

6. After 4 miles the path veers right and runs parallel with the A42. Cross the bridge over the dual carriageway then bear left to rejoin the railway path.

7. After 1¹/₂ miles, shortly after a stone 'egg' sculpture, the trail forks: go left to see the vast quarry or right / straight on to visit Worthington. For the village, go through the car park, turn left onto the minor lane then at the crossroads at the end of Breedon Lane turn left onto Church Street signposted 'Griffydam, Osgathorpe'. Follow this road through the village for ³/₄ mile past the octagonal red-brick lock-up to the Malt Shovel pub.

Station: Derby.

TIC: Derby, 01332 255802.

Other nearby trails: Derby to Elvaston Castle Country Park. Mickleover to Etwall railway path.

Useful publications & websites: OS Landranger Maps 128 & 129. For the latest information about cycling in Derby and cycle leaflets covering the city, visit *www. cyclederby.co.uk*

Refreshments:
Lots of choice in Derby. Lots of choice in Melbourne (1 mile off the route). Bulls Head pub, Wilson. The Malt Shovel pub, Worthington (³/₄ mile on quiet roads beyond the end of the trail).

Derby to Elvaston Castle Country Park

Ride **9**

A fine escape from the heart of Derby via a top-quality track alongside the River Derwent to Elvaston Castle Country Park, passing Pride Park stadium, home of Derby County Football Club. Elvaston Castle is an imposing stone and brick-built house dating from the early 19th century. It is situated in 200 acres of beautiful parkland containing many rare trees planted over 150 years ago. There is an adventure playground, an ornamental garden, a topiary and an Old English garden with herbaceous borders and a rose garden. The gardens are free and open all year round.

Starting points & parking

1. Riverside Gardens in the centre of Derby, near the Council House, the bus station and the Eagle Centre Market (grid reference SK 356364).

2. If arriving by car it would be better to start at **Elvaston Castle Country Park** (grid reference SK 413328). Turn off the A6005 Derby to Long Eaton road in Borrowash onto the B5010 towards Elvaston. The entrance to the park is 1¹/2 miles along on the right. (The B5010 can also be approached from the A6 Derby to Loughborough Road). From the castle head north to join the riverside path.

On your bikes!

1. From the corner of Bass's Recreation Ground / Riverside Gardens in the centre of Derby, follow the riverside path. (An alternative option at the start is to follow National Cycle Network Route 6 on the north side of the river; shortly after passing the Derby Telegraph buildings, cross to the south side of the river via a footbridge with white railings.)

2. **Easy to miss:** after 4¹/2 miles, at the weir where the pylons carry the power lines across to the other side of the river, turn right, heading away from the riverside path.

3. At a T-junction after ³/4 mile turn left, signposted 'Elvaston Castle'. After a further ¹/4 mile, at the T-junction with tarmac, turn left to visit Elvaston Castle (remember this point for the return trip).

Station: Derby.

TIC: Derby, 01332 255802.

Other nearby trails: The trail links with the Derby to Worthington Trail (the Cloud Trail). The Nutbrook Trail runs from Long Eaton to Shipley Country Park. The Mickleover to Etwall railway path lies to the west of Derby.

Useful publications & websites: OS Landranger Maps 128 & 129. For the latest information about cycling in Derby and cycle leaflets covering the city, visit *www.cyclederby.co.uk*

Refreshments: Tea rooms at Elvaston Castle.

Category
Riverside path and tracks in country park.

Distance
5¹/2 miles each way.

Ride 10 Nutbrook Trail
Shipley Country Park to Long Eaton

10

Category
Railway path,
canal towpath
and specially-built
cycle path.

Distance
6 miles each way.

Shipley Country Park has many
fine tracks within its 600 acres of
landscaped parkland – should you
not feel up to a 16-mile there-and-back ride
to Long Eaton there are plenty of shorter
options within the park itself (see Ride 11,
page 178). Once you have negotiated your
way up and down the hill to the south
of the country park, you find yourself
on a railway path that runs along the
course of the old Stanton Branch Line for
5 miles down to the Erewash Canal, linking
Eastwood with the River Trent at Trentlock,
south of Long Eaton. You pass many fine
red-brick buildings along the banks of the
canal before the trail drops you somewhat
abruptly at Asda supermarket in the middle
of Long Eaton.

Starting points & parking

1. Midland Street, **Long Eaton** (near the
junction of the A6005 and the B6540,
south-west of Nottingham). Parking near
to the Town Hall and Asda superstore
(grid reference SK 492338). Follow signs
for 'National Cycle Network Route 67' and
'Shipley Country Park' .

2. Shipley Country Park (Heanor), off the
A608 / A6007 to the west of Nottingham
(grid reference SK 431452).

On your bikes!

1. From the information board in the car
park in Shipley Country Park, take the
gravel track signposted 'Public bridleway,
Osborne Pond'. At a crossroads of tracks,
go straight ahead to join the track running
just inside the strip of woodland.

2. The track turns to tarmac. At the
crossroads with a lane (with Lakeside
Business Centre to your right), turn right
downhill, following signs for 'Nutbrook
Trail', 'Long Eaton' and 'National Cycle
Network Route 67'. Continue in the same
direction, staying on the tarmac path, at
one point jinking left then right. Climb
then descend.

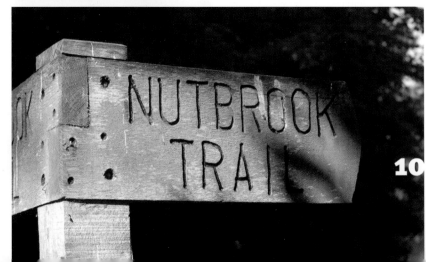

3. At the T-junction at the bottom of the descent turn right then shortly take the first tarmac track to the left opposite a red-brick house. Follow the tarmac path for 5 miles, at one point turning sharp right then sharp left.

4. At the canal turn right (remember this point for the return route).

5. Easy to miss: after almost 3 miles, by Dockholme Lock, turn left by a 'Nutbrook Trail' signpost onto a broad gravel path running parallel with the towpath.

6. Follow the trail past a tall red-brick chimney as it swings left away from the canal, passing through a barrier then turning right onto a tarmac path. The trail ends near Asda and the Town Hall in the centre of Long Eaton.

Station: Long Eaton.

TIC: Nottingham, 0115 915 5330.

Other nearby trails: There are more trails in Shipley Country Park.

Useful publications & websites: OS Landranger Map 129. Go to *www.derbyshire. gov.uk* and put 'Nutbrook Trail' into the search box. You can download a map from the bottom of the Nutbrook Trail page.

Refreshments: Long Eaton, Sandiacre, Kirk Hallam, Shipley Country Park.

Ride 11 **Shipley Country Park west of Nottingham**

Category
Estate roads and tracks.

Distance
There are many possible rides using the map.

A country park near to Nottingham with several miles of quiet estate roads and good-quality tracks around lakes and through woodland. Buy a map from the visitor centre and explore the park at your leisure. The routes in the park can easily be linked to the Nutbrook Trail to Long Eaton. Mentioned in the Domesday Book, Shipley was developed during the 18th century as a farming and coal mining area by the influential Miller Mundy family. Fine lodges and cottages dating from this period can still be seen around the park. Following restoration of the old coal mine sites, former railway lines have become walkways and cyclepaths, and reclaimed colliery spoils are now woodlands and wildflower meadows.

Starting point & parking

The visitor centre at the entrance to **Shipley Park**, 1 mile south of Heanor (A6007) and west of M1, Jct 26 (grid reference SK 431452).

On your bikes!

As mentioned above, either pick up a map from the visitor centre or download one from the website below and make up your own routes: there are too many tracks on the ground to be able to describe an individual circuit.

Station: Heanor.

TIC: Nottingham, 01159 155330.

Other nearby trails: The Nutbrook Trail goes south to Long Eaton. There are two trails starting from Derby, 6 miles to the south-west.

Useful publications & websites: OS Landranger Map 129. A better map is available at the visitor centre or go to *www.derbyshire.gov.uk* and type 'Shipley Country Park' in the 'Search' box. Click on 'Shipley Country Park Visitor Centre' and at the bottom of the linked page you can download a map of the park.

Refreshments: Café at the visitor centre.

The River Trent through Nottingham

Ride **12**

Follow the River Trent for 12 miles on an almost entirely traffic-free ride, passing close to the centre of Nottingham on a journey north-east from Trent Lock (south of Long Eaton) to the National Watersports Centre at Holme Pierrepont. The first few miles have a more rural aspect, passing alongside a series of lakes in the Attenborough Nature Reserve. From Clifton Bridge through to the Nottingham Forest Football Club, the route is much more urban. Beyond the football club and rowing clubs, the trail opens up again on its way towards the National Watersports Centre where you may well see kayakers battling with water rushing over weirs, or rowers out practising on the rowing lake.

Starting points & parking

1. Trent Lock, south-west of Nottingham (grid reference SK 489313).

2. Trent Bridge, **Nottingham city centre** (grid reference SK 581383).

3. National Watersports Centre, north-east of Nottingham (grid reference SK 681389).

On your bikes!

South to north, from Trent Lock to the National Watersports Centre

1. From the free car park at Trent Lock, make your way towards the River Trent past the 'Steamboat Inn' signpost. Cross the footbridge over the Erewash Canal towards the Lock House Tea Rooms and turn right alongside the River Trent (with the water to your right).

2. Follow the wide gravel path past Nottingham Yacht Club, then past a series of lakes on your left. At a junction of tracks shortly after a wooden swing gate, turn right following signs for 'Riverside Path, Beeston Marina, Nottingham'. (Remember this point for the return trip).

3. Go past the Beeston Marina Boathouse Café then immediately after Beeston Locks cross the canal via a wooden bridge (No. 20) and continue straight ahead to rejoin the River Trent path (ie do not turn left along the Beeston Canal).

4. Go past Grove Farm sports ground onto a quiet road, then on a left-hand bend just before a large road bridge turn right off

Category
Riverside path.

Distance
12 miles each way.

179

Ride 12 The River Trent through Nottingham

tarmac following signs for 'Trent Valley Way'.

5. After ¹/₂ mile the path bears left away from the river to join a shared-use pavement alongside the busy Queens Drive (take good note of this junction for your return trip as it is easy to miss). Rejoin the riverside path beyond the ornate red-brick bridge.

6. Go past parkland and the war cemetery on your left. Shortly after passing under an ornate blue metal bridge (Trent Bridge), turn sharp left back on yourself to cross the bridge via the pavement and join the riverside path on the south side of the river, running past Nottingham Forest Football Club and a series of rowing clubs.

7. Follow for a further 2 miles until you arrive at the National Watersports Centre. It is suggested you turn around at this point, following 'Trent Valley Way' and 'Riverside Path to Beeston Marina / Trent Lock' signs back to the start.

Station: Nottingham.

TIC: Nottingham, 08444 77567.

Other nearby trails: Nutbrook Trail from Long Eaton. Shipley Country Park. See also *www.thebigwheel.org.uk* for a route around Nottingham.

Useful publications & websites: OS Landranger Map 129. There are also two good cycling maps (north and south) produced by Nottingham City Council covering the city. See *www.nottinghamcity.gov.uk* or *www.nottinghamshire.gov.uk* and search 'Cycling'.

Refreshments: Lots of choice all the way along.

Southwell Trail Ride **13**
east of Mansfield

You are in Robin Hood Country here with Sherwood Forest just a few miles to the west. It would seem to stretch belief that Robin Hood had much to do with the course of the dismantled railway used in this ride, but nevertheless the map shows the Robin Hood Way following the railway path between Southwell and Farnsfield. Although the ride starts from the northern edge of Southwell, it is well worth exploring the centre of this fine old village, especially its magnificent minster. The ride itself is a very pleasant outing through wooded cuttings and rich arable country glimpsed between the hedgerows. Bilsthorpe lies on the eastern edges of what was the great Nottinghamshire coal mining area, almost all of which has disappeared in the last 30 years. The lovely cream-coloured Southwell Minster with its slender towers and spires dates from 1108. There is a magnificent stone carving called 'The Leaves of Southwell' in the Chapter House. Charles I gave himself up to the Scots Commissioners in the 17th-century Saracens Head in 1646.

Starting points & parking

1. Southwell. The car park next to the Newcastle Arms pub, Station Road, Southwell (grid reference SK 707545). The one-way system makes this hard to describe! You are aiming to head north-east out of Southwell on Station Road towards Hockerton and Caunton. Station Road is at the crossroads formed by Lower Kirklington Road, Newark Road and Burgage.

2. Bilsthorpe. The end of Forest Link (a new housing estate), signposted 'Picnic Site' at the southern end of Bilsthorpe. Proceeding south from Bilsthorpe along the Kirklington Road, turn off the roundabout onto Forest Link (grid reference SK 650602).

Station: Fiskerton Station, east of Southwell.

TIC: Newark, 01636 655765.

Other nearby trails: There is a waymarked forest trail in Sherwood Pines Forest.

Useful publications & websites: OS Landranger Map 120. Go to *www.nottinghamshire.gov.uk*, put 'Southwell Trail' in the search box and follow links through 'Our Local Nature Reserves'.

Refreshments: The Newcastle Arms pub at the start of the trail in Southwell. Lots of choice in Southwell itself.

Category
Railway path.

Distance
6 miles each way.

181

Ride 14 Newark to Cotham railway path

14

Category
Railway path.

Distance
5 miles each way.

Waymarked as National Cycle Network Route 64, which connects Lincoln to Market Harborough, this short section of railway path runs south from the centre of Newark towards the Vale of Belvoir. The Newark to Bottesford railway was open to passenger traffic between 1878 and 1955. The local gypsum industry helped to keep the line open for freight traffic until the 1980s.

Starting point & parking

Newark Northgate railway station (grid reference SK 805545). The railway station car park is very expensive – it is best to park elsewhere if starting from Newark.

On your bikes!

The route starts from the railway station car park and follows close to the existing railway line before joining the course of the dismantled railway. Follow for 5 miles until reaching the road at Cotham (grid reference SK 799471). You may choose to follow the lane network beyond Cotham to pubs in the villages to the south-west (you will need OS Landranger Map 129).

Station: Newark.

TIC: Newark, 01636 655765.

Other nearby trails: Southwell Trail. Sherwood Pines Forest. Routes through Lincoln.

Useful publications & websites: OS Landranger Maps 121, 129 & 130. See also *www.nottinghamshire.gov.uk/ newarkcycleguide.pdf*

Refreshments: Lots of choice in Newark.

Tissington Trail Ride 15
Peak District

Together with the High Peak Trail, this is one of the most famous railway paths in the Peak District If not the whole country. Passing through neat pastures bounded by drystone walls and the dramatic limestone scenery of the Derbyshire Dales, including several rock cuttings, it climbs gently up from Ashbourne to Parsley Hay setting you up for a fantastic descent. If you ever need to persuade a non-cyclist of the joys of cycling, drop them at the top and pick them up at the bottom! If you are at the other end of the spectrum in terms of fitness and experience, there are now waymarked routes along lanes through the villages of Tissington, Bradbourne and Hopton linking the Tissington Trail, Carsington Water and the High Peak Trail offering a tough, full-day challenge.

Starting points & parking

1. The trail starts from the far end of the Leisure Centre car park on the west side of **Ashbourne**, near the Station Hotel / Beresford Arms Hotel (grid reference SK 177463).

2. Bike Hire Centre at Mapleton Lane in Ashbourne (grid reference SK 177469).

3. On the minor road east of **Thorpe** (grid reference SK 166503).

4. On the A515 near **Alsop** (grid reference SK 157549).

5. Car parks on the B5054 east of **Hartington** (grid reference SK 151611).

6. There is a large Pay & Display car park and cycle hire centre at **Parsley Hay** (grid reference SK 147637).

Station: Matlock, Buxton or Uttoxeter.

TIC: Ashbourne, 01335 343666.

Other nearby trails: High Peak Trail, Carsington Water, and the Monsal, Manifold and Churnett Valley Trails are all nearby.

Useful publications & websites: OS Landranger Map 119. A leaflet is available from the Peak District National Park Office (01629 816200) or download from *www.peakdistrict.gov.uk/hptisstrails.pdf*

Refreshments: Lots of choice in Ashbourne. Soft drinks and sweets at the cycle hire / visitor centres. The Dog & Partridge pub in Thorpe and the Waterloo Inn in Biggin are just off the route. Coffees and teas at Basset Wood Farm, Tissington.

Category
Railway path.

Distance
13 miles each way.

NB There is a steady drop of almost 700ft (215m) from Parsley Hay to Ashbourne. For this reason it is worth starting at Ashbourne when you are fresh, riding uphill towards Parsley Hay, leaving you with a downhill on the way back.

Ride 16 Carsington Water north-east of Ashbourne

16

Category
Round-reservoir route.

Distance
8 miles.

Built in 1992, Carsington Water has established itself as a major focus for recreational cycling, offering a circuit around the lake which is demanding enough to give young children a real sense of achievement when they complete the ride. There are two crossings of the B5035 and about 1 mile is spent on a minor road, but as the latter runs parallel with the main road, very few vehicles have any reason to use it. This lane detour to the lovely stone-built village of Hopton enables you to enjoy a stopping point at the pub about three-quarters of the way around the circuit.

Starting points & parking

Pay & Display car park at the **Carsington Water Visitor Centre**, 5 miles north-east of Ashbourne. Turn off the B5035 Wirksworth to Ashbourne road at the Knockerdown pub (grid reference SK 240515).

NB Care should be taken on the two crossings of the B5035. There is a 1-mile section on minor lanes through Hopton. There are several short, steep hills on the far side of the lake from the visitor centre so don't think of this as a flat ride around the lakeside!

On your bikes!

1. With your back to the visitor centre entrance turn left, then at the corner of the building continue straight ahead on the broad gravel track.

2. Follow this obvious track with the water to your left, crossing the dam wall, following the frequent signposts.

3. The route becomes hillier! At the main road (B5035) **TAKE CARE** crossing onto the minor lane opposite. Follow the waymarks through the villages of Hopton and Carsington, passing the Miners Arms pub.

4. At the second crossing of the B5035 **TAKE CARE** as you go straight ahead towards the car park, then bear right at the fork and follow this track for 2 miles back to the start.

Station: Belper or Cromford.

TIC: Ashbourne, 01335 343666.

Other nearby trails: The High Peak Trail, Tissington Trail and Manifold Trail are all close by.

Useful publications & websites: OS Landranger Map 119. Better is the free map available from the visitor centre (01629 540696). Visit *www.carsingtonwater.com* or Severn Trent Water's website at *www.stwater.co.uk*. Put 'Carsington Water' in the 'Search' box. The 'Carsington Anglers Guide' offers the best map.

Refreshments: Café at the visitor centre. Miners Arms pub between Hopton and Carsington on the far side of the lake.

High Peak Trail
west of Matlock
Ride **17**

One of the best known and most popular routes in the country, offering a superb challenge in the heart of the Peak District from High Peak Junction (south of Matlock) via Middleton Top and Parsley Hay to Sparklow. The trail runs through the limestone scenery of the White Peak and links with the Tissington Trail in the north at Parsley Hay, 10 miles south-east of Buxton. If you start at the northern end of the trail, remember it is all downhill on the outward leg. The 33-mile Cromford & High Peak Railway was one of the earliest railways in the country, built between 1825-30. In the early days, horses were used to haul wagons along the rails.

Starting points & parking

1. There is a large Pay & Display car park and cycle hire centre at **Parsley Hay**, just off the A515 about 10 miles south-east of Buxton (grid reference SK 147637).

2. Car park at **Friden**, near the junction of the A515 and A5012 (grid reference SK 172607).

3. **Middleton Top Visitor Centre**, south-west of Matlock on the B5035 towards Ashbourne (grid reference SK 276552).

4. High Peak Junction, on the A6 south of Matlock (grid reference SK 315561). This last option is not recommended unless you are super-fit.

Station: Matlock, Buxton or Uttoxeter.

TIC: Buxton, 01298 25106. Matlock, 01629 55082.

Other nearby trails: Tissington Trail, Carsington Water, and the Monsal, Manifold and Churnett Valley Trails are all nearby.

Useful publications & websites: OS Landranger Map 119. A leaflet is available from the Peak District National Park Office (01629 816200). Try www.derbyshire-peakdistrict.co.uk/thehighpeaktrail.htm or for a map go to www.peakdistrict.gov.uk/hptisstrails.pdf

Refreshments: Soft drinks and sweets at the cycle hire / visitor centres. Royal Oak pub at Hurdlow (north of Parsley Hay). Rising Sun pub just off the route in Middleton.

Category
Railway path.

Distance
18 miles each way. The flattest section runs for 12 miles between Middleton Top, Parsley Hay and Sparklow.

NB Unless you are experienced and fit, it is suggested you go no further east than the Middleton Top Visitor Centre (ie do not go down to High Peak Junction in the valley) as there are two very steep sections needing very good brakes on the way down and very strong legs on the way back up.

185

Ride **18** **Monsal Trail**
Bakewell, Peak District

18

Category
Railway path.

Distance
4 miles each way.

Although the Monsal Trail runs for 9 miles from Bakewell towards Buxton, only a 4-mile section – from Bakewell north-west as far as Little Longstone – is open to cyclists. It is nevertheless well worth riding this fine trail through beautiful countryside in the southern Peak District. The ride starts with a short section on a no-through-road with almost no traffic. You may wish to stop at the second-hand bookshop along the way where there is also a café. You will need to use quiet lanes to get to the pubs at Little Longstone and Great Longstone. In 1863 the railway link between Rowsley (north of Matlock) and Manchester was completed, and the Midland Railway achieved its own London to Manchester mainline route. Coal was unloaded at Bakewell Station and delivered to remote areas, while milk churns from surrounding farms were sent to London. Closure of the Peak section occurred in 1968. After 12 years of negotiation, the Peak National Park finally persuaded the rail authorities to allow them to turn it into a recreational trail.

Starting point & parking

From the centre of **Bakewell** take the A619 towards Chesterfield. Immediately after crossing the bridge over the River Wye, turn first right onto Station Road, then right again onto Coombs Road – there is a car park on the right (grid reference SK 224686). To get to the railway path, turn right out of the car park for ³/₄ mile along this minor, no-through-road then turn left steeply uphill just before the railway bridge.

Station: Buxton.

TIC: Bakewell, 01629 816558.

Other nearby trails: The High Peak and Tissington Trails can both be accessed 6 miles west of Bakewell at Parsley Hay.

Useful publications & websites: OS Landranger Map 119. A leaflet is available from the Peak District National Park Office (01629 816200) or visit *www.peakdistrict.gov. uk/monsal-trail-leaflet.pdf*

Refreshments: Lots of choice in Bakewell. The Crispin pub, Great Longstone and the Pack Horse Inn, Little Longstone.

Five Pits Trail Ride 19
south-east of Chesterfield

The trail follows the course of the railway that used to serve the collieries between Grassmoor and Tibshelf Ponds, passing through rolling countryside with fine views. There are several hills, which may come as a surprise to anyone expecting railway paths to be flat! One is near the start and another near to Tibshelf. The railways used in this ride were opened in 1892 to serve the expanding coalfield and operated initially by the Midland Railway Company's mineral line and later by the Great Central Railway Company. The railway served the five pits of Tibshelf, Pilsley, Holmewood, Williamthorpe and Grassmoor. By 1971 the collieries it served had closed, causing the closure of the railway. Pilsley coal received royal patronage when Queen Mary (wife of George V) chose to burn nothing but 'Pilsley Brights' on her drawing-room fire at Buckingham Palace.

Starting point & parking

The **Grassmoor Country Park** car park between Temple Normanton and Grassmoor, south-east of Chesterfield. Take the A617 Mansfield Road out of Chesterfield for 4 miles. Turn off south onto the B6245, then take the B6039, following signs for 'Temple Normanton' and 'Holmewood'. Turn second right. The car park is ³/₄ mile along this road on your right (grid reference SK 413673).

On your bikes!

1. Follow 'Five Pits Trail' signs from the car park, fork left under the bridge and continue up a steady climb.

2. At the next fork of tracks, just after passing beneath power lines, bear right*, passing to the right of a 'No swimming' sign, then to the right of a small lake.

* If you bear left here there is an alternative route via Holmewood, although this is quite complicated and you will need the 'Five Pits Trail' map.

3. Continue heading south following signs for 'Five Pits' and 'Tibshelf', crossing roads as necessary. There is a steep climb after passing Locko Wood on your left.

4. Drop down into, then climb up out of, the valley formed by Westwood Brook. At the brow of the hill by the church and the Wheatsheaf pub in Tibshelf, cross the road using the pelican crossing.

Category
Railway path.

Distance
6 miles each way.

Ride **19** **Five Pits Trail, south-east of Chesterfield**

5. Keep bearing left. The route ends after ³/₄ mile at the junction with the Silverhill Trail, just beyond Tibshelf Ponds. Here you have a choice of (a) retracing your steps, (b) turning right for 1.3 miles to the end of the Silverhill Trail, (c) turning left for Teversal Visitor Centre and links to Brierley Forest Park and the Teversal Trail.

Station: Alfreton, south of the route.

TIC: Chesterfield, 01246 345777.

Other nearby trails: The Teversal Trail lies just to the east, linked by the Silverhill Trail. Chesterfield Canal starts in the centre of Chesterfield. Clumber Park has several trails. Sherwood Pines Forest. Rother Valley Country Park (see Yorkshire chapter, Ride 1, page 278).

Useful publications & websites: OS Landranger Map 120. *The Five Pits Trail* map is available from *www.derbyshire.gov.uk* – search for 'Five Pits Trail'.

Refreshments: The Wheatsheaf pub, Tibshelf.

Ride **20** **Silverhill Trail
west of Teversal (near Mansfield)**

Category
Railway path.

Distance
4 miles each way.

This trail links two long-established trails, namely the Teversal Trail which runs south from Pleasley to Skegby, and the Five Pits Trail which runs from Grassmoor Country Park south to Tibshelf. The surface is wide and smooth as you pass beneath the M1 and descend gently at the western end of the trail to

20

the bridleway connecting Stonebroom to Blackwell. This means a climb on the way back, but you are likely to have the wind on your backs giving you some help. You may also wish to explore the spur that leads to Brierley Forest Park, lying just to the south of the trail, or perhaps link to the Five Pits Trail near Tibshelf Ponds.

Starting point & parking

Teversal Visitor Centre, just off the B6014 between Sutton and Tibshelf, west of Mansfield (grid reference SK 479614).

On your bikes!

1. From the Teversal Visitor Centre, head past the old mining artefacts to the barrier to gain access to the trail. Turn left then

shortly left again following 'Silverhill Trail' and 'Tibshelf' signs.

2. The ride passes beneath the M1 then a high red-brick bridge and descends to finish at the bridleway that connects Blackwell to Stonebroom (at grid reference SK 427589). Retrace your steps.

Station: Alfreton or Mansfield.

TIC: Chesterfield, 01246 345777.

Other nearby trails: Five Pits Trail and Teversal Trail.

Useful publications & websites: OS Landranger Map 120. For an overview map go to *www.derbyshire.gov.uk/leisure/countryside*, click on 'Trails and greenways' then 'Cycle Derbyshire Map'. Alternatively, go to *www.teversaltrails.com/visitorscentre.htm*

Refreshments: At the Teversal Visitor Centre.

21

Teversal Trail / Pleasley Trails Ride 21
north-west of Mansfield

The Pleasley Trails are three separate railway paths lying between Pleasley, Skegby and Teversal. They are linked together to form a circular route. Deep cuttings show the exposed limestone rock of the area. The Pleasley Trails network runs along the track beds of the Great Northern Railway and the Midland Railway. The sections explored in this ride were built between 1866 and 1900, and closed between 1965 and 1982.

Starting points & parking

1. Pleasley Pit Country Park, Pit Lane, **Pleasley**, just off the A617 / B6417 / B6407

roundabout about 3 miles north-west of Mansfield (grid reference SK 502645).

2. The Teversal Trail car park in **Skegby**, on Buttery Lane, just off the B6014 Mansfield to Tibshelf Road, signposted 'Manor Estate' (grid reference SK 495614).

Category
Railway path.

Distance
5-mile circuit.

189

Ride **21**   **Teversal Trail / Pleasley Trails, north-west of Mansfield**

3. Teversal Visitor Centre, just off the B6014 between Sutton and Tibshelf, west of Mansfield (grid reference SK 479614).

On your bikes!

1. Exit the Pleasley Pit Country Park car park back towards the main road, then turn, right opposite the start of the low wall on the left and a red-brick house with white columns (number 4) through a wooden barrier onto the railway path. The path turns right parallel with the road.

2. Pass through several rock cuttings. There is one steep descent with loose gravel where you should take care. About 2¹/₂ miles after leaving Pleasley you will arrive at the car park at Skegby. Retrace your steps for 300yds then at the fork of tracks, bear left signposted 'Silverhill Trail'.

3. After 1 mile, you will arrive at a track junction close to the Teversal Visitor Centre (well worth a visit).

4. There are several junctions and several signs near here. Follow 'Teversal Track'

signs back towards Pleasley. After almost 1¹/₂ miles, at the junction with a lane, turn right then left to drop back down onto the railway path.

5. After about ¹/₂ mile, at a T-junction of tracks just after an information board and the junction with the Rowsley Trail, turn right to return to the Pleasley Pit Country Park car park.

Station: Alfreton, to the south-west.

TIC: Chesterfield, 01246 345777.

Other nearby trails: The Silverhill Trail runs between the Pleasley / Teversal Trail and the Five Pits Trail. Sherwood Pines Forest lies 7 miles to the east.

Useful publications & websites: OS Landranger Map 120. For an overview map go to *www.derbyshire.gov.uk/leisure/countryside*, click on 'Trails and greenways' then 'Cycle Derbyshire Map'. Alternatively go to *www. teversaltrails.com/visitorscentre.htm*

Refreshments: Carnarvon Arms, Fackley, just off the route, near Teversal.

Ride **22**   **Sherwood Pines Forest north-east of Mansfield**

There are three well-signposted trails through the forest. The easier trails are wide and well-maintained so these are good rides for cycling in a group. There is also a much tougher mountain bike trail (red grade) adjoining the family route if you want a harder challenge. Sherwood Pines Forest forms part of the largest single tract of woodlands in the East Midlands. Most of the forest was

planted in the 1920s and 1930s in the early days of the Forestry Commission. Much of the timber here has supplied local businesses, particularly as pit wood for the mining industry. In some parts of the forest the heathland vegetation, once so common in Sherwood, still exists. These areas are now being kept as heathland as part of the conservation plan. There is a Robin Hood exhibition at the visitor centre.

Sherwood Pines Forest, north-east of Mansfield Ride **22**

Starting point & parking

Sherwood Pines car park, off the B6030, 5 miles north-east of Mansfield (grid reference SK 611638).

On your bikes!

Make your way from the car park towards the visitor centre and you will come across the markers that indicate the course of the trails. The rides are very well waymarked.

> **Station:** Fiskerton Station, south-east of Southwell.
>
> **TIC:** Ollerton, 01623 824545.
>
> **Other nearby trails:** The Southwell Trail, which runs from Southwell to Bilsthorpe, lies 5 miles to the south-east. Clumber Park lies 6 miles to the north.
>
> **Useful publications & websites:** OS Landranger Map 120. Forest Enterprise also produce a leaflet which is available at the visitor centre. Visit *www.forestry.gov.uk* and search 'Sherwood Pines Forest'. You should be able to find the *Sherwood Pines Mountain Bike Trails* map as a download.
>
> **Refreshments:** Café at the visitor centre.

Category
Forest trail.

Distance
Family route
(green – easy):
3 miles.

Adventure route
(blue – moderate):
6 miles.

Kitchener's Trail
(red – hard):
8 miles.

Bike Park
(extreme).

Clumber Park Ride **23**
south-east of Worksop

Clumber Park has become one of the most popular destinations for recreational family cycling in the country, ranking alongside Rutland Water and the Peak District railway trails. This is due to the superb infrastructure of bike hire with all sorts of bikes and trailers available, the excellent mix of quiet estate roads, broad gravel tracks through woodlands, waymarked circuits and the beautiful setting with the lake, famous old stone bridge and chapel. There is an excellent visitor centre and café, and plenty of places to choose for a picnic or barbecue in the thousands of acres of parkland. It is also on National Cycle Network Route 6, which runs north from Derby to York, and if you arrive by bike there is no entry fee to pay to get into the park! For a small charge it is a very

Category
Estate roads and cyclepaths.

Distance
A variety of routes and distances are possible from 5 to 10 miles.

Ride 23 Clumber Park, south-east of Worksop

good idea to buy the large colour map of Clumber Park showing all the tracks. There is a charge to enter the park by car.

Starting point & parking

Clumber Park lies south-east of Worksop (east of M1, Jct 30). There are five entrances to the park – off the A57 from the north, off the B6034 to the west and off the A614 to the east. The main car park is near the chapel, restaurant and shops (grid reference SK 626747).

NB There is some light traffic on the estate roads. The park is busier in high season.

On your bikes!

There are four suggested routes on the Clumber Cycle Route Guide and these link up with the numbered waymarks through the park:

Lakeside – 5 miles
Southern Explorer – 7 miles
Northern Fringe – 8 miles
Borders – 10 miles

Station: Worksop.

TIC: Worksop, 01909 501148.

Other nearby trails: There are waymarked trails in Sherwood Pines Forest, 6 miles to the south. National Cycle Network Route 6 from Worksop to Sherwood Pines Forest.

Useful publications & website: OS Landranger Map 120. Much better is the map produced by the park which can be purchased from the Information Centre and also from the cycle hire centre (01909 476592). Or visit *www.nationaltrust.org.uk* and search 'Clumber Park'.

Refreshments: Café and restaurant, in the park.

Ride 24 **Worksop to Sherwood Pines Forest on National Cycle Network Route 6**

Category
Railway paths and forest tracks.

Distance
13 miles each way.

In the middle of the forest just to the north of Clumber Park there is an extraordinary metal Millennium National Cycle Network sign with 'Dover 504 miles' in one direction and 'Inverness 786 miles' in the other. Feeling fit? This ride explores a 13-mile traffic-free section of National Cycle Network Route 6 from near Worksop Golf Course down through Clumber Park and Sherwood Forest to the waymarked blue route around Sherwood Pines Forest Park.

Starting point & parking

Car park on the minor road about 3 miles **south of Worksop** between Manton Lodge and Truman Lodge (grid reference SK 611762). This is accessed by turning east off the B6034 Worksop to Edwinstowe road.

On your bikes!

1. Cross to the south side of the road and follow the track opposite towards Clumber, turning right after 300yds at a metal Millennium signpost, a cycling information board and a bench. Shortly, at a T-junction with a Clumber Park estate road, turn left then after 200yds first right onto the road beyond the barrier.

2. After almost 1 mile at a T-junction with another road turn right then left (beyond another barrier). Continue straight ahead at a crossroads, bear right to cross the bridge then right again signposted 'South Lodge, National Cycle Network Route 6 (NCN 6)'.

3. After a further mile, and about 50yds before ornate gates, turn left off tarmac and follow NCN 6 signs to join a wide, smooth red gravel track.

4. At the crossroads with the busy B6034 go straight ahead, then after $^1/_2$ mile turn left by a Millennium signpost to cross the A616 (take great care).

5. Keep following NCN 6 signs, crossing roads as necessary, on a variety of different surfaces. There are two more busy road crossings, the first (A6076) without a pelican crossing and the second (B6030) by the Dog & Duck pub, which does have a pelican crossing.

6. Go past the winding machinery of the old colliery and through Vicars Water Country Park. Join the blue waymarked trail in Sherwood Pines Forest Park. It is suggested you do a circuit of the forest, stop for refreshments at the café, and return to Vicar's Water Country Park to rejoin NCN 6 and head back to Worksop.

Station: Worksop.

TIC: Worksop, 01909 501148.

Other nearby trails: Clumber Park and Sherwood Pines Forest.

Useful publications & websites: OS Landranger Map 120. The route is shown on Sustrans Derby to York map. Go to *www. sustrans.org.uk*

Refreshments: Cafés at Clumber Park and Sherwood Pines Forest Park.

NB There are two busy roads to cross (the B6034 and A616) where there are no pelican crossings, so great care should be taken.

Routes through Lincoln from Harby to Woodhall Spa   Ride 25

This very long traffic-free path offers a full day out for the very fit, a total of 50 miles from Harby through Lincoln – all the way to Woodhall Spa and back! For those with more modest ambitions the ride can easily be broken down into shorter sections – for example, Harby to Lincoln, Lincoln to Dardney and Dardney to Martin Dales (Woodhall Spa). The 1$^1/_2$-mile linking route through the centre of Lincoln is (at the time of writing) not suitable for young children. There are various artworks along

Ride **25** **Routes through Lincoln from Harby to Woodhall Spa**

Category
Railway path and riverside path.

Distance
7 miles each way from Harby to Lincoln.

17 miles each way from Lincoln to Woodhall Spa.

the course of the ride including paintings, metal sheep and wooden carvings, including one of a mermaid. There is a real sense of space as you glide alongside the River Witham. The numerous information boards will give you fascinating details of local history. The Heritage Centre at Bardney in the old railway station is well located for refreshments.

Starting points & parking

1. Harby, off the A57 to the south of Saxilby. The trail starts about ¹/₂ mile north of Harby. There is no designated car park (grid reference SK 881715).

2. Skellingthorpe, off the A57 to the south-east of Saxilby. Park at the community centre on Lincoln Road (grid reference SK 927717).

3. Lincoln city centre: best to start from Titanic Bridge to the south-east of the city centre (grid reference SK 981712).

4. The old railway station at **Bardney** (grid reference TF 193692).

5. Martin Dales, about 1¹/₂ miles west of **Woodhall Spa** (grid reference TF 177622).

On your bikes!

East from Harby towards Lincoln

1. Join the railway path about ¹/₂ mile north of Harby and head east.

2. After 5 miles cross the Fossdyke and railway via the footpath on the A46 road bridge, descend and pass through the

subway to join the river near the Pyewipe Inn.

3. You may wish to turn around at the end of the traffic-free section at the western edge of Lincoln city centre.

4. (Continuing east.) Follow 'City Centre' signs on a variety of pavements and cyclepaths, crossing roads as necessary, aiming to stay close to the river and rejoin the traffic-free section and the start of the Water Rail Way at the end of Waterside South.

5. Follow the obvious route for 9 miles to Bardney.

6. East of Bardney you have a choice of a rough track for approximately 1 mile or a longer route via roads to rejoin the railway path near the River Witham.

7. The traffic-free trail ends after a further 7 miles at the old station at Martin Dales to the west of Woodhall Spa.

Station: Lincoln.

TIC: Lincoln, 01522 873213.

Other nearby trails: The Newark to Cotham Railway Path.

Useful publications & websites: OS Landranger Map 121. Or go to *www.woodhallspa.org/ leisure_waterrailway.html*, *www.lincolnshire. gov.uk* and search 'Cycling routes'.

Refreshments: Bottle & Glass pub in Harby. Pyewipe Inn, 2 miles west of Lincoln. Lots of choice in Lincoln. Nags Head pub. Café at the Heritage Centre, Bardney. Riverside Inn, Southrey. Kings Arms pub, Martin Dales.

26

Sett Valley Trail Ride **26**
Hayfield, south-east of Manchester

A short section of railway path on the western edge of the Peak District, with fine views east towards Kinder Scout. It is worth visiting the New Mills Heritage Centre and the Torrs Riverside Park in New Mills. Hayfield sits peacefully in the narrow valley of the River Sett, surrounded by some of the wildest hills in the Dark Peak. Things were much different in its industrial past, when cotton and paper mills, calico printing and a dye works made it a busy and anything but quiet place. In 1868, the railway came to Hayfield and was soon busy with both passengers and goods, servicing all the mills in the valley. Passenger trains ran regularly to Manchester, and shortly after the First World War it was quite common for 4,000 to 5,000 people to use the Sett Valley Line on a summer Sunday to visit the countryside. Business gradually diminished and the line closed in 1970.

Starting point & parking

Sett Valley Visitor Centre in **Hayfield**. Turn off the A624 Glossop to Chapel-en-le-Frith road on to the A6015 to New Mills, then first right on to Station Road (grid reference SK 035869).

On your bikes!

Follow the trail towards New Mills. The trail ends at St Georges Road where a sign indicates that there is no cycling beyond this point. If you wish to go further you will either need to dismount and push your bikes through Riverside Park to The Torrs waterfalls (this will involve some steps), or go by road into New Mills: turn right on St Georges Road, right again at the T-junction at the bottom, cross the river then turn left into New Mills.

Category
Railway path.

Distance
3 miles each way.

NB *You will need to go on-road if you wish to visit New Mills.*

Station: New Mills.

TIC: Glossop, 01457 855920.

Other nearby trails: The Middlewood Way from Marple to Macclesfield lies west of New Mills. The Longdendale Trail starts at Hadfield, north of Glossop.

Useful publications & websites: OS Landranger Map 110. A leaflet is available from Hayfield Countryside Centre, Hayfield, Derbyshire (01663 746222). Or go to *www.derbyshire.gov.uk* and search 'Sett Valley Trail'.

Refreshments: Hot drinks at the visitor centre. Lots of choice in New Mills (this will involve a short road section).

26

Ride 27 **Longdendale Trail east of Manchester**

27

Category
Railway path.

Distance
6½ miles
each way.

*NB There is a
330ft (100m) climb
from Padfield to
the Woodhead
Tunnel.*

Forming part of the Trans Pennine Trail, the route runs along the side of Longdendale following the course of the old railway from Hadfield to the Woodhead Tunnel (A628), past a string of reservoirs lying at the bottom of the valley. The scenery is spectacular, if a little spoiled by the line of pylons that runs parallel with the trail. The railway through Longdendale provided the first railway link between Manchester and Sheffield. The first passenger train ran in 1845. The Woodhead Tunnel was one of the great achievements of the early years of the railway age. After 136 years of operation the line was finally closed in 1981. The five reservoirs of Bottoms, Valehouse, Rhodeswood, Torside and Woodhead were completed in 1877 and formed the largest artificial expanse of water in the world at the time.

Starting point & parking

Hadfield / Padfield are well signposted off the A57 Manchester to Glossop Road. Climb through the centre of Hadfield following 'Longdendale Trail' signs, then just before the railway bridge over the road there is a car park to the left at the start of the trail (grid reference SK 025962).

Station: Hadfield.

TIC: Glossop, 01457 855920.

Other nearby trails: The next traffic-free section of the Trans Pennine Trail to the east is the Upper Don Trail, which runs from Dunford Bridge towards Penistone (see Yorkshire chapter, Ride 4, page 282). The Sett Valley Trail runs between New Mills and Hayfield (south of Glossop on the A624). There is a trail around the edge of the Derwent Valley Reservoirs.

Useful publications & websites: OS Landranger Map 110. Go to *www.derbyshireuk.net/longdendale_trail.html*. The three maps covering the whole of the Trans Pennine Trail are available from *www.transpenninetrail.org.uk*

Refreshments: Only in Hadfield.

Upper Derwent Valley Reservoirs Ride **28**
between Manchester & Sheffield

A magnificent ride amid the beauty of woodland, lakes and moorland alongside the reservoirs in the Upper Derwent Valley. Various routes are possible from the Ladybower Reservoir and Fairholmes Visitor Centre – circuits of one, two or three of the reservoirs. The easiest ride is the there-and-back ride along the west side of Derwent and Howden Reservoirs, starting from the visitor centre. Other rides use a mixture of tarmac, fine stone tracks and slightly rougher tracks on the east side of the reservoirs. There are several short climbs. It is also possible to do a 6-mile there-and-back ride on a track along the south side of Ladybower Reservoir by following the cyclepath along the A6013 Bamford Road and crossing the dam.

Starting point & parking

Turn off the A57 Sheffield to Glossop road on the west side of the viaduct over **Ladybower Reservoir**. The visitor centre lies 2¹/₂ miles up this road (grid reference SK 173894).

On your bikes!

Described below is a full clockwise circuit of all three lakes, starting from the visitor centre. The tracks on the east side of the reservoirs are only appropriate for mountain bikes. An easier there-and-back ride follows the tarmac road on the west side of Derwent Reservoir to its end alongside the northern arm of the Howden Reservoir.

1. From Fairholmes Visitor Centre, turn right (north) on the tarmac lane alongside Derwent Reservoir, keeping the water to your right. Follow this for 5 miles to the end of the tarmac.

2. Follow the track down to cross the river via the bridge at Slippery Stones and keep following signs for 'Cycle Trail', soon heading south back down the valley. After a further 4¹/₂ miles, at a T-junction shortly after rejoining tarmac at the southern end of Derwent Reservoir, you have the option of turning sharp right to return to the visitor centre or continuing straight ahead for the full circuit.

Category
Round-reservoir route.

Distance
(a) 16 miles for the circuit of all three reservoirs.
(b) 5 miles each way from the visitor centre alongside Derwent and Howden Reservoirs to the end of the tarmac road.

NB The road from the A57 to the visitor centre carries a reasonable amount of traffic at the height of the season, but the cars are probably carrying other cyclists to get to the start.

3. (Full circuit.) The tarmac turns to track after 1 mile and follows the east side of Ladybower Reservoir. At the T-junction with the busy A57, turn right on the shared-use pavement then right again to return to the visitor centre. The final 2½ miles will be busier with traffic, especially in the high season.

Station: Hope Station is south of Ladybower Reservoir.

TIC: Glossop, 01457 855920.

Other nearby trails: The Longdendale Trail is just north of Glossop.

Useful publications & websites: OS Landranger Map 110. Also try *www.peakdistrict.gov.uk/ cycle-routes-in-the-upper-derwent-valley.pdf*

Refreshments: Hot drinks, cakes and sweets available at the visitor centre.

Ride **29** **Chesterfield Canal & the railway path to Rother Valley Country Park**

Category
Canal towpath and railway path.

Distance
9 miles each way.

At the Tapton Lock Visitor Centre about 1 mile north of the start of the ride in Chesterfield, you will come across a sign which indicates that following the canal south will lead to Chesterfield, whereas following it north will lead to Istanbul! The Chesterfield Canal towpath is part of the Southern Link of the Trans Pennine Trail and the Trans Pennine Trail itself is part of the much larger European Long Distance Footpath system, which extends right down as far as Turkey! A bold and imaginative product of the early years of the Industrial Revolution, the prime purpose of the Chesterfield Canal was to take Derbyshire's coal to new markets. The original surveys were done by the famous canal engineer James Brindley, although he did not live to see its opening in 1777. For its time it was a magnificent piece of engineering with the country's longest tunnel (at the time) at Norwood, and one of the earliest examples of a large staircase of locks at Thorpe Salvin. The route of the Chesterfield Canal follows the River Rother valley out of the town and Tapton Lock is the first of five carrying the canal down to Staveley. The lock was constructed in 1777 and it is a typical narrow lock, 72ft long and 7ft wide. It fell into disuse

and was restored in the late 1980s. Each lock gate weighs approximately 1 ton and was manufactured from solid oak at the Rochdale Canal Workshops.

Starting point & parking

Tapton Lock Visitor Centre about 1 mile **north of the centre of Chesterfield**. Park on the no-through-road signposted 'Tapton Lock' off the 'Tesco' roundabout at the junction of the A61 and the A619 (grid reference SK 389729).

On your bikes!

From the Tapton Lock Visitor Centre head north, keeping the canal to your right. The canal ends after almost 4 miles on the western edge of Staveley (grid reference

SK 430746) but it is possible to continue north to the Rother Valley Country Park following Trans Pennine Trail signs along the Staveley to Beighton railway path.

Station: Chesterfield.

TIC: Chesterfield, 01246 345777.

Other nearby trails: Five Pits, Silverhill and Teversal Trails to the south-east of Chesterfield.

Useful publications & websites: OS Landranger Maps 119 & 120. Various leaflets about the canal can be obtained from the Tapton Lock Visitor Centre. Also try *www. transpenninetrail.org.uk* or *www.waterscape. com/canals-and-rivers/chesterfield-canal*

Refreshments: Lots of choice in Chesterfield and Staveley. Limited refreshments at the Tapton Lock Visitor Centre.

West Midlands Trails

**Ride 20
Churnet Valley Trail**

05 West Midlands Mountain Biking

The best mountain biking in the West Midlands is in Cannock Chase (see Ride 13, page 220) and the Shropshire hills. Church Stretton would be a good base to explore three areas: the tracks on the Long Mynd; the area west towards the border with Wales; and the tracks on Wenlock Edge and Brown Clee Hill to the east. The area to the south and west of Bishop's Castle also offers a good number of bridleways and byways. Most of the best riding near to Ludlow uses the forestry holdings to the south-west, mentioned in 'Shropshire Woodlands' (Ride 5, page 209).

There is no substitute for intimate local knowledge – try to explore every bridleway, byway, unclassified road, canal towpath and Forestry Commission track near to home, sift out the good from the bad and link together the best off-road sections to form your own customised route(s). The best advice is to use the months from late spring to early autumn (May to October) to do the exploration, if possible after a spell of dry weather. The same track in winter can take twice as long or even be impassable.

Note down on the map (or colour-code with highlighter pen) the quality of the trail and whether it is better done in one direction or the other – it is normally better to climb on tarmac and descend off-road so that gravity can help you through any muddy bits. Where there are no books or leaflets describing mountain bike rides, the staff in bike shops can often put you in contact with local riders or clubs who may have done some of this research already, saving you many hours of trial and error.

Bear in mind that everyone has a different view of what constitutes a good trail: hard or technical for some is easy for others, and a bit of mud for some is a quagmire for others!

Websites:

www.forestry.gov.uk/marches has a list of several centres in Shropshire where there are waymarked forest trails – for example, Hopton or Eastridge (see also Ride 5).

www.chasetrails.co.uk for trails in Cannock Chase (see also Ride 13).

www.moredirt.co.uk and follow links from 'Trails & Tracks' to 'United Kingdom' to 'West Midlands'.

www.shropshirecycling.co.uk click on 'Advanced Route Search' (on the left-hand side), put a tick in the 'Mountain biking' box and press the 'Search' button.

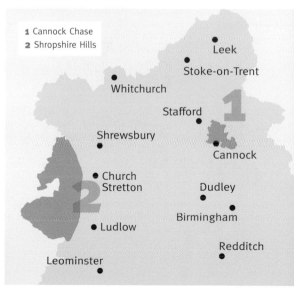

1 Cannock Chase
2 Shropshire Hills

Leek
Stoke-on-Trent
Whitchurch
Stafford
Shrewsbury
Cannock
Church Stretton
Dudley
Birmingham
Ludlow
Redditch
Leominster

1 Cannock Chase

West Midlands Forestry

With the exception of Cannock Chase and the woodlands of Shropshire, the West Midlands have few forestry holdings of any size. By good fortune, almost all of these larger holdings have some form of waymarked trails in them. The main entry under 'Shropshire Woodlands' (Ride 5, page 209) brings together all the forest trails in the county.

Forests and woods with waymarked trails

There are nine Forestry Commission holdings with waymarked trails in the West Midlands region:

2 Wapley Hill, south-east of Knighton

3 Shobdon Hill Wood, south of Wigmore, north-west of Leominster

4 Mere Hill Wood, south of Wigmore, north-west of Leominster

5 Mortimer Woods, south-west of Ludlow

6 Hopton Titterhill, north-east of Knighton

7 Bury Ditches, south of Bishop's Castle, west of Craven Arms

8 Eastridge Wood, Snailbeach, south-west of Shrewsbury

9 Wyre Forest, west of Kidderminster (Ride 3, page 206)

11 Cannock Chase, north of Birmingham (Ride 13, page 220)

In some forests and woods there are no waymarked routes, but you are free to explore the tracks. The relevant Ordnance Survey map is mentioned. It is highly recommended that you take a map for the larger woods as it is very easy to get lost.

The woodlands below correspond with the numbers on the map:

1. Haugh Wood, east of Hereford (OS Explorer Map 189)

10. Haughmond Hill, east of Shrewsbury (OS Explorer Map 241)

> **It is also worth contacting the following Forest District Office for further information:**
>
> **West Midlands**
> Lady Hill, Birches Valley, Rugeley, Staffordshire WS15 2UQ. Tel: 01889 586593
> Email: enquiries.westmids@forestry.gsi.gov.uk

The Forestry Commission's website, *www.forestry.gov.uk* is a good source of information. Click on 'Explore, Experience, Enjoy' then 'Cycling' and you can find out details of hundreds of waymarked trails throughout the UK. You can search by forest name or by the nearest town / city. The search will tell you the grade, length and waymarking details of the trails. Alternatively, by clicking on the map, you can see the nearest forest to where you live.

West Midlands National Cycle Network

The West Midlands Cycle Route

163 miles from Oxford to Derby via Birmingham. Highlights include the ancient city of Oxford, Blenheim Palace at Woodstock, North Oxfordshire villages, Stratford-upon-Avon, the Rea Valley Route into Central Birmingham, Lichfield Cathedral and the traffic-free routes through Derby.

Traffic-free sections over 3 miles long:

• Stratford-upon-Avon Greenway from Stratford to Long Marston (NCN 5).

• Rea Valley Route – King's Norton to Cannon Hill Park (Birmingham) (NCN 5).

• Birmingham Canal between Birmingham and Wolverhampton (NCN 5).

• Etwall to Mickleover (Derby) (NCN 5).

Sustrans

The Sustrans map shown here covers various National Cycle Network routes within the region. This map also describes routes that continue into the East Midlands and so is mentioned in both chapters. The map is not only useful for people wishing to ride the whole route over several days; it also shows all the traffic-free sections that make good day rides.

Other good areas for lane cycling

There is a major contrast within this region: the eastern half is flatter with almost all the big conurbations – Stoke, Wolverhampton, Birmingham and Coventry – and most of the people, whereas the western half, with the exception of Telford and Shrewsbury, is almost exclusively rural with all the hills. It is in Herefordshire and Shropshire, in the western half, that you will find the best network of quiet lanes and myriad attractive towns and villages that are good bases from which to explore the area: try Ludlow, Church Stretton, Tenbury Wells, Bishop's Castle, Hay-on-Wye or Upton upon Severn. The other areas worth exploring are in the far north of Staffordshire, up into the Peak District National Park and the south of Warwickshire, where it borders with the northern Cotswolds.

A map for this route is available from www.sustrans.org.uk or 0845 113 0065.

Stoke

Kidderminster

Ride 1 **Stratford Greenway**
south-west of Stratford-upon-Avon

1

Category
Railway path.

Distance
5 miles each way.

Finding the start of the trail will be your hardest task when you choose to explore this railway path, running south-west from Shakespeare's Stratford and crossing the River Avon on a fine metal bridge. The trail soon runs past the racecourse and a bike hire centre, operating out of an old railway carriage. It is an easy, wide, flat trail that forms part of National Cycle Network Route 5 from Oxford to Birmingham. Renowned as the birthplace of Shakespeare, the well-preserved market town of Stratford-upon-Avon is a showcase of Tudor architecture, its broad streets lined with half-timbered houses.

Starting points & parking

1. Stratford-upon-Avon. It is very hard to give detailed instructions to get to the car park at the start, on the southern edge of town. Follow signs for A4390 and Shipston-on-Stour to get to the roundabout where the trail starts (grid reference SP 196540).

2. If coming from outside Stratford, it may be better to start from the **Milcote car park** about halfway along the trail on the minor road between Welford-on-Avon and Clifford Chambers (grid reference SP 171515).

NB *There is a short section on a quiet road if you wish to visit the pub at Long Marston.*

On your bikes!

The trail ends after 5 miles at the industrial estate in Long Marston, but you will need to leave before the end if you wish to go to the pub in Long Marston: on your outward journey from Stratford, cross the road at Milcote car park, then at a house called Railway Cottage, by a line of telegraph poles, turn right signposted 'Village shop and post office'. At the T-junction at the end of Wyre Lane, turn right for 200yds for the Masons Arms pub.

Station: Stratford.

TIC: Stratford, 0870 160 7930.

Other nearby trails: The Stratford Greenway is part of Sustrans National Cycle Network Route 5 from Oxford to Birmingham. It uses short traffic-free sections along the Stratford-upon-Avon Canal towpath to the north of Stratford and also in the Arrow Valley Park through Redditch.

Useful publications & websites: OS Landranger Map 151. Go to *www. warwickshire.gov.uk* and search 'Stratford Greenway'.

Refreshments: Café in railway carriage near the start. Café in railway carriage about halfway along (just after road crossing and second car park). Masons Arms pub, Long Marston (just off the route).

Worcester – the River Severn, the Worcester & Birmingham Canal & the racecourse

Two short rides and one longer one start from the main bridge over the River Severn in the centre of Worcester, exploring the banks of the mighty Severn, Worcester racecourse and a section of the Worcester & Birmingham Canal. Do not try to do a circuit of the racecourse when there is a race meeting going on!

Starting point & parking

The Worcestershire Cricket Club car park at the west end of **Worcester Bridge** (the main bridge over the River Severn in the centre of town). Follow signs for Hereford and Leominster from the centre of Worcester and turn immediately left into the car park after crossing the bridge (grid reference SO 847547).

There are several other car parks close to Worcester racecourse or to Diglis Basin that are also alternative starting points.

On your bikes!

Race course

1. WITH CARE cross the road onto the north side of the bridge and continue with the river to your right. After ¹/₂ mile, cross to the other side of the river via the Sabrina footbridge.

2. Turn sharp left on the road and complete a circuit of the racecourse on the tarmac path that runs outside the perimeter of the track.

3. At the end of the Pay & Display car park on your left (at the south-east corner of the racecourse) turn right across the track, towards the footbridge over the river.

4. Recross the river, turn left and follow back to the bridge.

River Severn

Stay on the south side of the main road and follow the River Severn south for 1.3 miles, keeping the water to your left to the point where the traffic-free path turns away from the river to join Weir Road by Lower Wick Swimming Pool.

Worcester & Birmingham Canal

1. Stay on the south side of the main road. Cross the bridge, walking your bike along the pavement then turn right and follow the riverside path (with the river to your right) as far as the Diglis Basin. Cross the lock gates at the junction of the canal with the River Severn and turn left to link with the Worcester & Birmingham Canal towpath.

2. Cross Diglis Basin on the footbridges between the two marinas and turn left to rejoin the canal towpath as it heads north-east out of town.

Category
Riverside path, canal towpath, round race course track.

Distance
Race course circuit: 2.2 miles.

South along the Severn: 1.3 miles each way.

The Worcester & Birmingham Canal to Tibberton: 7 miles each way.

3. After almost 1 mile at Bridge 5A, the towpath crosses sides then after a further mile (at Bridge 13) it crosses back.

4. After 3½ miles, pass beneath the M5 then after a further ½ mile it is suggested you turn around at the Bridge pub at Tibberton. Soon after this the towpath surface deteriorates (grid reference SO 906581).

Station: Worcester.

TIC: Worcester, 01905 726311.

Other nearby trails: The Staffordshire & Worcestershire Canal north of Stourport.

Useful publications & websites: OS Landranger Map 150 or there is an excellent *Worcester Walking and Cycling Map* available from *www.worcestershire.gov.uk/choose* – click on 'Cycling' then 'Cycling maps'.

Refreshments: Lots of choice in Worcester. Bridge Inn at Tibberton at the northern end of the canal towpath ride.

Ride 3   Wyre Forest west of Kidderminster

Category
Woodland trails.

Distance
Green route:
3½-mile circuit.

Blue route:
5-mile circuit.

With its attractive visitor centre, good café, Go Ape and climbing equipment for young children, Wyre Forest is a popular destination for families. There are two waymarked cycle routes through the woodland, both involving some climbing with occasional views north-east down into the Severn Valley. Just 6,000 acres survives of a wood that once stretched along the Severn Valley from Worcester to Bridgnorth. It is one of the largest remaining ancient woodlands in Britain. Much of the area is designated as a Site of Special Scientific Interest (SSSI) and many rare species of flora and fauna can be found here.

Starting point & parking

Wyre Forest Visitor Centre off the A456 about 6 miles west of Kidderminster (grid reference SO 750740).

On your bikes!

1. Facing the entrance to the visitor centre, bear right downhill towards – then past – Go Ape.

2. Descend then climb. At the T-junction turn right following blue and green signs.

3. More downhill. After almost 1 mile, at the next junction you can **either** turn right (green route) for a short route back to the start **or** continue straight ahead for the longer route.

4. (Long route). At the next wooden signpost turn right signposted 'Bewdley,

Family Mountain Bike Route' (Button Oak and the mountain bike area are straight ahead).

5. Good views left. At the crossroads of tracks by a 4-way signpost turn right, 'Callow Hill Visitor Centre, Family Mountain Bike Route'. Shortly at a T-junction turn left, following a blue and white arrow.

6. Gentle climb on broad stone track with some wet / muddy sections. At a T-junction turn left downhill, 'Visitor Centre 1 mile'.

7. Climb for ¾ mile, steeply then more gradually. Following blue and green bike signs, turn right then shortly left onto a narrower track back to the visitor centre.

Station: Bewdley.

TIC: Bewdley, 01299 404740.

Other nearby trails: The Staffordshire & Worcestershire Canal from Stourport to Kidderminster.

Useful publications & websites: OS Landranger Map 138 or go to *www. worcestershire.gov.uk* and search 'Cycling maps'. Scroll down to *Wyre Forest Walking & Cycling Map*.

Refreshments: Café at the visitor centre.

Ride 4 **Staffordshire & Worcestershire Canal Stourport**

4

Category
Canal towpath.

Distance
5 miles each way.

A fine stretch of towpath at the southern end of the Staffordshire & Worcestershire Canal just to the north of its junction with the River Severn, linking the two Worcestershire towns of Stourport and Kidderminster. At Caldon Lock you pass a red sandstone cutting, giving an indication of the area's ancient geology. The 46-mile-long canal was designed by James Brindley as part of the 'Grand Cross' scheme to link the rivers Mersey, Trent, Severn and Thames.

It was opened from Stourport to Great Haywood in 1772. It meets the River Severn at an impressive series of basins at what once was the hamlet of Lower Mitton – on the canal's arrival it took the name of Stourport. This was later extended to include reference to both rivers, as Stourport-on-Severn. The canal was an immediate commercial success, and remained prosperous for longer than most waterways. The carriage of Cannock coal became a staple, and trade continued on some stretches until well into the 1960s.

Starting point & parking

York Street in **Stourport-on-Severn**, just east of the A451 (Bridge Street / High Street) and north of the River Severn (grid reference SO 812712).

On your bikes!

The good-quality towpath can be followed for almost 5 miles from the heart of Stourport north into the centre of Kidderminster. The surface quality deteriorates almost 1 mile after passing through the subway under the Ringway, past the church.

Station: Kidderminster.

TIC: Bewdley, 01299 404740.

Other nearby trails: Wyre Forest.

Useful publications & websites: OS Landranger Map 138. Visit *www.canaljunction. com/canal/staffs_worcs.htm* or *www. waterscape.com* – click on 'Canals & rivers' then scroll down through the 'Complete list of canals & rivers' to 'Staffordshire & Worcestershire Canal' and click on 'Cycling'.

Refreshments: Lots of choice in Stourport and Kidderminster.

Shropshire Woodlands Ride 5
(7 routes)

There are several short waymarked woodland trails in the beautiful unspoilt Welsh Border country, also known as The Marches. It is best to get hold of the leaflets mentioned in 'Useful publications' and use these in conjunction with the appropriate Ordnance Survey Landranger maps.

Snailbeach / Eastridge Woods, south-west of Shrewsbury

OS Landranger Map 126 (grid reference SJ 373023). A 4-mile circuit of Eastridge Woods with several climbs, starting from the village of Snailbeach, just off the A488 about 12 miles south-west of Shrewsbury. Short sections of quiet lanes are used near to Snailbeach to access the woodlands. The forest trails lie to the north and east of the village.

Bury Ditches, south of Bishop's Castle

OS Landranger Map 137 (grid reference SO 334839). A hilly woodland circuit around an Iron Age Fort 5 miles to the south of Bishop's Castle, which itself lies about 20 miles south of Shrewsbury on the A488. Follow the B4385 south-east out of Bishop's Castle towards Lydbury North. After 2 miles right onto the minor road to Lower Down and Bury Ditches.

Hopton Titterhill, north-east of Knighton

OS Landranger Map 137 (grid reference SO 348778). Hopton Mountain Bike Trail offers the freedom to explore some 860 acres of woodland. Select your route by visiting the numbered marker posts located at the track and path junctions. To get the most out of the woodland, it is essential to obtain the leaflet produced by the West Midlands Forest District (see **Useful publications & websites**). The car park is about 12 miles west of Ludlow and 1 mile west of the hamlet of Hopton Castle, near the junction of the B4367 and B4385.

Mortimer Woods, south-west of Ludlow

OS Landranger Map 137 (grid reference SO 500720 and SO 474732). Woodland trail running from near Overton, towards High Vinnalls car park and picnic area. Start from either the car park on the B4361 about 4 miles south of Ludlow, just beyond Overton (grid reference SO 500720)

Category
Woodland trails.

Distance
Various distances.

Ride 5   Shropshire Woodlands (7 routes)

OR High Vinnalls car park on the minor road between Ludlow and Wigmore (grid reference SO 474732).

Wapley Hill, east of Presteigne

OS Landranger Map 137 (grid reference SO 360622). 3-mile circuit to the base of Wapley Hill Fort. This lies just off the B4632 about 4 miles east of Presteigne.

Shobdon Hill Wood, south of Wigmore (A4110)

OS Landranger Map 137 (grid reference SO 397634 or SO 407643). 4-mile linear route from Uphampton to Covenhope. Located west of Mortimer Cross, at the junction of the A4110 and the B4632.

Mere Hill Wood, south of Wigmore (A4110)

OS Landranger Map 137 (grid reference SO 407643 or SO 425624). 3-mile linear route from Covenhope to the summit of Mere Hill and down to Aymestrey. Located north of Mortimer Cross – at the junction of the A4110 and the B4632.

TICs: Shrewsbury, 01743 281200. Ludlow, 01584 875053.

Useful publications & websites: OS Landranger Maps 126 & 137. For the most up-to-date information about cycling in Shropshire visit *www.shropshirecycling. co.uk*. Alternatively, visit *www. wheelywonderfulcycling.co.uk*

The Forestry Commission website is also excellent: go to *www.forestry.gov.uk/marches* and search for the woodland of your choice.

For Hopton Titterhill map, obtain leaflet from West Midlands Forest District, Birches Valley, Rugeley, Staffordshire WS15 2UQ (01889 586593).

Ride 6   **Worcester & Birmingham Canal in Birmingham**

Category
Canal towpath.

Distance
6 miles each way.

A short section of the Worcester & Birmingham Canal towpath is used by National Cycle Network Route 5, the long-distance trail that runs from Reading to Birmingham. The surface of the towpath is excellent but, as this is also a popular walking route, please show consideration to other users and be prepared to take your time. The ride starts from the exciting bustle of Gas Street Basin in the centre of Birmingham and ends 6 miles to the south at King's Norton Tunnel, one of the longest of its kind in

the country. On its way south it passes the tall, ornate, red-brick clocktower of Birmingham University, and Cadbury World at Bournville.

Starting points & parking

1. Gas Street Basin in the **centre of Birmingham** (grid reference SP 060086).

2. The towpath ends at **King's Norton Tunnel** (also known as Wast Hill Tunnel), which is located near the junction of Shannon Road and Primrose Hill in the Hawkesley / Walker's Heath area (grid reference SP 048780).

On your bikes!

From the Gas Street Basin in the centre of Birmingham, follow signs for the Worcester & Birmingham Canal for 6 miles as far as King's Norton tunnel. Please walk your bike at the start if the towpath is busy with pedestrians.

Station: Birmingham / King's Norton.

TIC: Birmingham, 0870 2250127.

Other nearby trails: The Birmingham Canal to Wolverhampton. Rea Valley Route. Sutton Park.

Useful publications & websites: OS Landranger Map 139. *The Birmingham Cycling & Walking Map* is available from *www.birmingham.gov.uk/transportation*. Click on 'Cycling' then 'Cycling and Walking Map'. See also *www.cyclingwestmidlands.org.uk*

Refreshments: Lots of choice in the centre of Birmingham.

NB You will need to walk your bike through the Edgbaston Tunnel and be aware of any other users, as the towpath is narrow between the railings and the tunnel wall.

Ride 7 **Rea Valley Route Birmingham**

Category
Riverside path through parkland.

Distance
6 miles each way.

Forming part of the National Cycle Network through Birmingham, the Rea Valley Route follows the River Rea (at times more like a stream) through the delights of Cannon Hill Park where there are always fantastic displays of flowers, shrubs and rare ornamental trees. Beyond Cannon Hill Park the ride follows a tarmac path alongside the river through Stirchley and onto a short section of the Worcester & Birmingham Canal. It ends at King's Norton Park where there is a playground

for children. To the north of Cannon Hill Park the National Cycle Network Route uses traffic-calmed streets and specially-built cyclist contraflow lanes to take you right into Centenary Square. The River Rea is 15 miles long and rises south-west of Birmingham in Waseley Country Park, flowing north-east across the city to join the River Tame near to Spaghetti Junction. Although a small river, it has been called the 'Mother of Birmingham' as it has played a vital role in the development of the city, particularly in the Digbeth area where there was a small settlement hundreds of years ago. Over 20 mills once flourished along the Rea Valley, many of them built for corn grinding but during the Industrial Revolution they provided water power for Birmingham's industries.

Starting points & parking

1. Cannon Hill Park, **central Birmingham**. The car park lies off the A441 (Pershore Road), just to the south of Edgbaston Cricket Ground (grid reference SP 070840).

2. Middlemore Road, **Northfield**, just east of Northfield railway station (grid reference SP 026790).

On your bikes!

1. From the lodge at the north end of Cannon Hill Park follow the cycle track through the park and signs for National Cycle Network Route 5 or Rea Valley Route. Continue in the same direction with the river close by to your right.

2. The tarmac path swings right to cross the river via a brick and metal bridge. Shortly, the track joins Kitchener Road. Turn first left onto Cecil Road then at the T junction, turn left then right onto a continuation of the riverside path.

3. Follow the Rea Valley Route and signs for 'Stirchley, King's Norton'. At the next busy road (Cartland Road), go straight ahead via a toucan crossing onto a continuation of the riverside path.

4. At the T-junction with the trading estate road, turn right to cross bridge then immediately left. At the crossroads with Fordhouse Lane use the toucan crossing to go straight ahead, signposted 'King's Norton, Northfield'.

5. At the end of the cyclepath by a tall wooden signpost, turn left on the quiet estate road (Dacer Close) then shortly first left. Follow Rea Valley Route signs to join the Worcester & Birmingham Canal towpath. Turn left along the towpath.

6. At the second bridge over the canal you will need to cross to the towpath on the other side. **Easy to miss:** immediately after passing a red-brick bridge with a '72' plaque on it, turn right by a large red-brick house away from the towpath signposted 'Rea Valley Route, King's Norton'. Cross the playing fields then cross Pershore Road.

7. The ride crosses Westhill Road, Popes Lane and Wychall Lane, and ends on Middlemore Road just east of Northfield railway station.

Station: Birmingham.

TIC: Birmingham, 0870 225 0127.

Other nearby trails: The Birmingham & Worcester Canal. The Birmingham Canal to Wolverhampton. Sutton Park. The Kingswinford Railway Walk.

Useful publications & websites: OS Landranger Map 139. *The Birmingham Cycling & Walking Map* is available from *www.birmingham.gov.uk/transportation*. Click on 'Cycling' then 'Cycling and Walking Map'. See also *www.cyclingwestmidlands.org.uk*

Refreshments: Café in Cannon Hill Park.

Ride **8** **Birmingham & Fazeley Canal**
Birmingham

Category
Canal towpath.

Distance
8 miles each way.

It may seem bizarre to recommend a ride that has as one of its most dramatic features a worm's eye view of Spaghetti Junction – the famous junction of roads on the M6 motorway – but sure enough, the Birmingham & Fazeley Canal passes right beneath the great tangle of roads as you ride along the towpath from the soaring, dramatic buildings in the heart of Birmingham eastwards into the countryside. The ride starts in the heart of Birmingham's canal system and quickly drops down a flight of locks, passing factories and out to the countryside.

Starting points & parking

1. National Indoor Arena and the Gas Street Basin in the centre of Birmingham (grid reference SP 060086).

2. Curdworth, just west of the junction of the M42 with the M6 Toll Road (grid reference SP 177930).

On your bikes!

1. Follow the signs for Birmingham & Fazeley Canal from the National Indoor Arena on Gas Street Basin in the centre of Birmingham. You are advised to walk down past the steep flight of locks at the start of the canal.

2. After 1$\frac{1}{2}$ miles, at the junction with the Birmingham & Warwick Canal and the Tame Valley Canal, keep following signs for Minworth and Tamworth, passing under the famous Spaghetti Junction at Junction 6 of the M6 motorway.

3. The canal towpath is in good condition for 5 miles beyond Spaghetti Junction as far as Curdworth, just beyond Wiggins Hill Bridge.

Station: Birmingham New Street.

TIC: Birmingham, 0870 225 0127.

Other nearby trails: Rea Valley Cycle Route. Birmingham & Worcester Canal. Main Line Canal to Wolverhampton. Sutton Park.

Useful publications & websites: OS Landranger Map 139. The *Birmingham Cycling & Walking Map* is available from *www.birmingham.gov.uk/transportation*. Click on 'Cycling' then 'Cycling and Walking Map'. See also *www.cyclingwestmidlands.org.uk*

Refreshments: Lots of choice in the centre of Birmingham.

Kingswinford Railway Walk
south-west of Wolverhampton

Ride **9**

Despite its proximity to the conurbation of Wolverhampton, this ride along the disused railway of the Kingswinford line has a very fine, wooded, countryside feel to it. The trail is in reasonable condition between Tettenhall and Wombourne. Along its whole length the trail runs parallel with the Staffordshire & Worcestershire Canal. Indeed you have the option of extending your ride northwards by following the canal towpath for a few miles before turning around. Although the old railway line continues south of Wombourne, it soon becomes very muddy and / or rough.

Starting points & parking

1. Wombourne. Turn off the A449 Wolverhampton to Kidderminster road at the roundabout near Wombourne (at the junction with the A463), signposted 'Kingswinford Railway Walk'. Follow signs for Trysull onto Billy Buns Lane then, just before a brown and cream coloured railway bridge, turn right onto a track signposted 'Kingswinford Railway Walk' (grid reference SJ 870940).

2. Aldersley Stadium, 2 miles north-west of Wolverhampton city centre between the A41 and the A449 (grid reference SJ 897007).

On your bikes!

North from Wombourne

1. From the car park turn right onto the railway path. Continue for 3 miles to Castlecroft and a further 3 miles to Aldersley Stadium.

2. At Aldersley Leisure Village (Hugh Porter Way) you can either retrace your steps or link to the Staffordshire & Worcestershire Canal towpath. To get to the canal, turn right downhill towards the car parking area then, opposite the visitor centre, turn left on a wide tarmac path by a yellow metal barrier signposted 'National Cycle Network Route 81'.

3. Follow the perimeter of the 5-a-side football pitch (on your right) to join the canal. Here you can:

(a) Turn left on the Staffordshire & Worcestershire Canal for 3 miles as far as the A449 at Coven Heath

Category
Railway path.

Distance
8 miles each way.

Ride 9 Kingswinford Railway Walk, south-west of Wolverhampton

(b) Turn right on the Staffordshire & Worcestershire Canal as an alternative return route back to Wombourne

(c) Cross the bridge over the canal onto the towpath of the Birmingham Main Line Canal alongside Wolverhampton Locks to go into the centre of Wolverhampton (and on towards Birmingham)

South from Wombourne

The railway path soon deteriorates and is only fit for mountain bikes and mud lovers! It can be followed south then east for 3½ miles towards Pensnett as far as a set of wooden steps by a car crusher's yard.

> **Station:** Wolverhampton.
>
> **TIC:** Wolverhampton, 01902 556110.
>
> **Other nearby trails:** The Birmingham to Wolverhampton Canal runs from the centre of Birmingham to the centre of Wolverhampton.
>
> **Useful publications & websites:** OS Landranger Map 139. Visit *http://wmcycling. webs.com/southstaffsrailwaytrail.htm* or go to *www.dudley.gov.uk* and put 'Cycling' in the 'Search' box. See also *www. cyclingwestmidlands.org.uk*
>
> **Refreshments:** Tea shop at Wombourne station. Pubs just off the route.

Ride 10 **Birmingham & Black Country Canal Cycleway**

Category
Canal towpath.

Distance
14 miles each way.

Although it is often stated that Birmingham has more miles of canals than Venice (there are over 130 miles of canals in Birmingham and the Black Country), this does not translate, unfortunately, into a fine network of broad, smooth, gravel towpaths – some are considerably better than others. The hub of the canal network in Birmingham lies around Digbeth Basin and Gas Street

Basin. To the north-west, the canal from Birmingham to Wolverhampton – known simply as the Birmingham Canal or the Main Line – is largely good quality. This is a trip past the sinews of a muscular, industrial city with metal foundries and hot-metal smells. By 1769, the engineer James Brindley had completed the first of Birmingham's canals from Wednesbury to Newhall, then to a wharf beyond Gas Street

Basin. By 1772 the Old Main Line extended to Wolverhampton. The canal created rapid growth in industry – coal and building supplies were brought in and manufactured goods carried out. In the next half-century the canal system spread rapidly, and expanding trade brought great congestion. In the 1820s, Thomas Telford constructed a straight canal, the New Main Line, running parallel at a lower level to the Old Main Line. Despite advances in canal planning, the Galton Valley cutting was still dug out by men using picks, shovels and wheelbarrows.

Starting point & parking

The National Indoor Arena on Gas Street Basin in the centre of **Birmingham** (grid reference SP 060086).

On your bikes!

From the centre of Birmingham to Wolverhampton

With your back to the National Indoor Arena, turn right with the water to your left. There are occasionally paths on both sides of the canal. Keep an eye out for the signs indicating where you change sides. The path can be followed for up to 14 miles to Wolverhampton, including the long and dark Coseley Tunnel!

Stations: Wolverhampton, Tipton, Birmingham New Street.

TIC: Birmingham, 0870 225 0127.

Other nearby trails: The Kingswinford Railway Walk runs south from Wolverhampton through Wombourne to Pensnett.

Useful publications & websites: OS Landranger Map 139. *The Birmingham Cycling & Walking Map* is available from *www. birmingham.gov.uk/transportation*. Click on 'Cycling' then 'Cycling and Walking Map'. Also useful is the *Wolverhampton Bike Map* from *www.wolverhampton.gov.uk/cycling* or for a more general overview of the region go to *www.cyclingwestmidlands.org.uk*

Refreshments: All along the way.

Ride 11 Sutton Park north of Birmingham

11

Category
Country park trails.

Distance
A 4-mile circuit.

A 4-mile circuit is described but there are several miles of quiet roads and broad gravel tracks in Sutton Park. Use the map available from the visitor centre to plan other routes. Sutton Park is one of those parks on the edge of a large city, not unlike Richmond Park in London, where you often have to remind yourself that you are less than a couple of miles from a huge conurbation where millions of people are living and working. Sutton Park offers a sense of wide open spaces, with grassland, woodland and a plethora of tracks to explore. There is no specifically waymarked cycle trail – this is just one of many that you could easily devise yourself. The best way of exploring the park is by buying the map from the visitor centre and giving yourself plenty of time to explore – the map will tell you the areas where cycling is not allowed.

Starting point & parking

Sutton Park Visitor Centre, off the A5127 on the west side of Sutton Coldfield, north of Birmingham (grid reference SK 115961).

On your bikes!

1. With your back to the visitor centre, turn right towards the children's playground and the Sutton Coldfield entrance, then take the first road to the left. Shortly, take the next road to the right beyond a metal barrier.

2. Climb through broadleaf woodland, crossing the railway. Just after a metal barrier but before the cattle grid, turn left on tarmac to continue uphill. Bear right* at the car park to descend to the lake.

For refreshments in Blackroot Bistro bear left.

3. Follow the tarmac path to the end of the lake and turn right onto a broad gravel track along the dam wall. At the T-junction at the end of the dam turn right, then shortly bear left and climb steeply to a bench at the top.

4. At the crossroads with tarmac by the square granite 'Jamboree' stone, go straight ahead then after 20yds at the next crossroads (with a wide stone track ahead) turn left on tarmac.

5. Go past a barrier and past a car park on your right. At a tarmac crossroads turn left through a barrier and follow this downhill all the way back to the visitor centre, ignoring turns to left and right.

Station: Sutton Coldfield.

TIC: Birmingham, 0870 225 0127.

Other nearby trails: The Birmingham & Black Country Canal Cycleway links the city centres of Birmingham and Wolverhampton. The Kingswinford Railway Walk runs from Wombourne (west of Dudley) to Aldersley Stadium, north of Wolverhampton. There are several waymarked trails in Cannock Chase.

Useful publications & websites: OS Landranger Map 139. *The Birmingham Cycling & Walking Map* is available from *www. birmingham.gov.uk/transportation.* Click on 'Cycling' then 'Cycling and Walking Map'. See also *www.cyclingwestmidlands.org.uk*

Refreshments: Café at Blackroot Bistro.

Silkin Way Ride **12**
Telford

The route, starting in the heart of the New Town of Telford, uses a dismantled railway for much of its course, passing through deep rock cuttings and thickly wooded stretches. The River Severn is reached at Coalport where there is a pub on the other side of the lovely bridge over the river. This is the area where the Industrial Revolution started. The iron bridge over the River Severn in the village of Ironbridge was a major step on the route which saw Great Britain rise to industrial pre-eminence throughout the world in the late 18th century and most of the 19th century. The iron wheel used as the motif for the Silkin Way is an indication of the area's industrial past.

Starting points & parking

1. Town Park (follow brown and white signs) in the centre of **Telford**, which lies about 1 mile south-east of M54, Jct 5 (grid reference SJ 700082).

2. The China Museum, **Coalport**, on the road alongside the River Severn, parallel with the A442 to the south of Telford and to the south of M54, Jct 4 (grid reference SJ 698024).

On your bikes!

The route is signposted with an iron wheel logo

1. From the Town Park car park in the centre of Telford, go into the park through the green metal gates, continue straight ahead along a road with humps and a white painted cycle lane (pass to the left of the Wonderland theme park).

2. Exit the park, ignore the car parks to the left and take the next left downhill by a black metal barrier and a wooden 'Silkin Way' signpost, then shortly right. Shortly, at a fork of tracks, bear right downhill to join the railway path. Take good care to remember this point for the return trip.

3. Pass beneath several bridges, following signs for 'National Cycle Network Route 55, The Gorge and Blists Hill'.

4. About 3 miles after leaving Town Park, the course of Silkin Way runs on the pavement alongside the main road, crossing the approach road to Blists Hill Victorian Town (there is a good café here, just before the entrance). Continue past Blists Hill and follow the pavement as it bears left away from the road.

Category
Railway path.

Distance
5 miles each way.

Ride **12** **Silkin Way, Telford**

5. Follow the trail past the Brewery Inn and onto a continuation of the path, then bear right to arrive at the end of the path at Coalport Bridge and the Woodbridge Inn.

6. If you wish to visit Ironbridge, cross the bridge over the River Severn and turn sharp right* signposted 'Severn Valley Way', and follow this for 2 miles.

For Bridgnorth cross the bridge and turn left after the Woodbridge Inn.

Station: Telford or Wellington.

TIC: Telford, 01952 238008.

Other nearby trails: There are several waymarked forest trails in Cannock Chase to the north of Cannock.

Useful publications & websites: OS Landranger Map 127. *The Walking & Cycling Map of Telford & Wrekin* is available from www.telford.gov.uk (search 'Cycling maps').

Refreshments: Lots of choice in Telford. Hot Metal Café near entrance to Blists Hill. Brewery Inn, Woodbridge Inn at Coalport.

Ride **13** **Cannock Chase north of Birmingham (2 routes)**

Category
Forest trails.

Distance
1. Up to 19 miles of easy routes. Green signs.

2. 7 miles. 'Follow the Dog' technical trail. Red signs.

Cannock Chase is the largest Forestry Commission holding in the West Midlands. In character it is far from the dense blocks of conifers that cloak hillsides in Wales and Scotland. There are many open, sandy spaces, a pleasant mixture of broadleaf and coniferous trees, and more importantly from the cyclist's point of view, a large network of bridleways – many of which are well-drained, broad, stone-based tracks where it is possible to cycle all year round. Cannock Chase is the remnant of a vast royal hunting forest (chase). At 17,000 acres it is the smallest mainland Area of Outstanding Natural Beauty in Britain. Much of Cannock Chase is recognised by English Nature as a Site of Special Scientific Interest.

Starting point & parking

At the **Birches Valley Visitor Centre**, 2 miles west of Rugeley (grid reference SK 019171).

Follow the A51 north (towards Stone / Stafford) from the roundabout with the A460 in the centre of Rugeley, then shortly turn left towards Slitting Mill and the Birches Valley Visitor Centre on the edge of Cannock Chase. All routes start from Swinnertons Cycles at the visitor centre.

On your bikes!

1. Leisure Routes. Green waymarkers.

1 - 19 miles. The Leisure Routes are a series of loops on wide forest tracks. The shortest route is just 1 mile long. Build up your route to 19 miles taking in the Fairoak Valley and the heathland of Sherbrook Valley. These routes are marked with green discs starting at number 100 and are suitable for groups of all ages, tandems, trailer bikes and buggies.

2. 'Follow the Dog' Technical Route. Red waymarkers. 7 miles.

Built by the volunteer group, Chase Trails, this intermediate-grade singletrack route is designed for skill and not speed. The route winds through the trees in Fairoak Valley and is marked with red discs.

For more information on Chase Trails, visit *www.chasetrails.co.uk*

Station: Rugeley.

TIC: Stafford, 01785 619619.

Other nearby trails: The Stafford to Newport Greenway is a dismantled railway running west from Stafford.

Useful publications & websites: OS Landranger Maps 127 & 128. *The Cannock Chase Cycling Map* can be purchased from the visitor centre or visit either *www.cannockchaseaonb.org.uk* or *www.staffordshire.gov.uk* and type 'Cycle Maps' in the search box at the top of the page. Also see *www.forestry.gov.uk* and follow links through 'England' to 'Explore, Experience, Enjoy' and 'Cycling and mountain biking'.

Refreshments: At Birches Valley and Marquis Drive Visitor Centres. The White House Motel & Restaurant is on the minor road to Penkridge about 2 miles west of Birches Valley Visitor Centre.

Ride 14 Stafford to Newport Greenway

Category
Railway path.

Distance
4 miles each way.

A short ride on a wide, well-maintained railway path to the west of Stafford, best seen in late spring / early summer when the wildflowers are at their most colourful. The line was built in 1849 by the Shropshire Union Railway and ran from Stafford to Newport and Wellington and beyond, being an important link between the Midlands and Wales. The line was used for 115 years until 1964, when the last steam engine plied its way along the line carrying a wreath to mourn its passing.

Starting points & parking

1. Stafford. Take the A518 out of Stafford towards Telford. Cross the railway and at the roundabout turn right, signposted 'Castlefields'. Follow Martin Drive straight ahead at two roundabouts on to the narrow lane signposted 'No Through Road'. There is a car park along to the left (grid reference SJ 908234).

2. There is also a car park at the western end of the trail, **north of Haughton** (grid reference SJ 862213).

On your bikes!

Exit the car park, turn left along the narrow lane then about 200yds after passing under power lines, keep an eye out for the start of the railway path to your right. Follow the trail for 4 miles to the point where the surface quality suddenly deteriorates, shortly after the Haughton car park and picnic tables.

At the time of writing there are plans to continue the section open to cyclists beyond the present finish towards Newport.

Station: Stafford.

TIC: Stafford, 01785 619619.

Other nearby trails: The Silkin Way runs south of Telford. There are trails in Cannock Chase to the south-east of Stafford.

Useful publications & websites: OS Landranger Map 127. *Cycling in Stafford Borough* leaflet available from Stafford TIC or visit *www.staffordshire.gov.uk/tourism* or for a Stafford cycling map go to *www.staffordshire. gov.uk* and put 'Cycling maps' into the 'Search' box.

Refreshments: The Red Lion pub, Derrington.

Salt Line Ride 15
north-west of Stoke

The Salt Line consists of two short, well-maintained stretches of dismantled railway between Ettiley Heath (west of Sandbach) and Alsager, connected in the middle (Hassall Green) by a short section on quiet roads. The trail passes through attractive woodland and ends close to a good family pub in Alsager at the eastern end of the ride. The railway was built by the North Staffordshire Railway Company in 1858 with the primary function of carrying minerals to and from Stoke-on-Trent. The Trent & Mersey Canal proved vital in the construction of the line as many of the bulky materials were transported by narrowboat. The line began as goods only, expanded to take passengers, then reverted to goods only between 1930 and 1970 when it finally closed. The old course of the railway is rich in species of flowers, birds and butterflies.

Starting point & parking

Hassall Green, north-east of Crewe. Turn off the A533 about 2½ miles south of Sandbach (M6, Jct 17) opposite the New Inn pub onto New Inn Lane, signposted 'Hassall Green, Wheelock'. Go under the motorway and take the first right into the car park (grid reference SJ 775583).

On your bikes!

East

1. Follow the trail eastwards away from the car park, passing under the M6. At the second road (the B5078) turn right, walking your bikes along the pavement, to go to the Wilbraham Arms pub or ...

2. At the end of the trail, at the B5078, if you go straight ahead uphill on Cherry Lane then straight ahead again for ¾ mile, at the crossroads by the New Horse Shoe pub signposted 'Rode Heath' you will come to the improved towpath of the Trent & Mersey Canal, which can be followed south into Stoke.

West

Exit the car park and turn left on the road. Pass under the M6. You can either take the bumpy Trent & Mersey Canal towpath for 1 mile west to Wheelock or follow the road through Hassall Green and turn left towards Malkin's Bank, joining the traffic-free path parallel with the towpath that links to the railway path to Ettiley Heath. The trail ends at the B5079 roundabout (grid reference SJ 741604).

Category
Railway path.

Distance
5 miles each way.

NB *Care should be taken crossing the A534 near Wheelock, especially westbound where the visibility is less good.*

Ride 15 Salt Line, north-west of Stoke

Station: Alsager.

TIC: Stoke, 01782 236000.

Other nearby trails: The Trent & Mersey Canal can be followed into Stoke from Alsager. The Biddulph Valley Trail is 5 miles east of Alsager. Rudyard Lake is 9 miles to the east.

Useful publications & websites: OS Landranger Map 118. Go to *www.welcometocongleton.com*, click on 'Attractions / Cycling' then 'Search for Cycle Routes in South East Cheshire'. Alternatively

go to *www.cheshireeast.gov.uk* and follow links from 'Transport & Travel' to 'Cycling and Cycle Lanes' to 'Cycle routes in Cheshire' then 'Traffic Free Routes' for a list of downloadable leaflets about several routes.

Refreshments: The Lockside Café and Romping Donkey pub in Hassall Green are both about $1/2$ mile from the start. The Wilbraham Arms pub is located at the eastern end of the trail, about 200yds along the B5078 towards Alsager.

Ride 16 **Trent & Mersey Canal north and south from Stoke**

Category
Canal towpath.

Distance
11 miles each way north from Stoke to Alsager.

5 miles each way south from Stoke to Barlaston.

This ride largely follows the course of the Trent & Mersey Canal between Stoke and Barlaston to the south, and between Stoke and Alsager to the north. On the northern ride, the canal passes through the Harecastle Tunnel, one of the longest of its kind in the country, so you have to divert for 3 miles via lanes and parkland tracks to link the towpath either side of the tunnel. The ride starts right in the heart of Stoke, near to the railway station, and runs north past the industrial sinews of the city before following the green corridor that runs parallel with the

A500 up to Kidsgrove. Here the trail joins National Cycle Network Route 5 through to Alsager. To the south, the canal is followed to the Plume of Feathers pub in Barlaston.

Starting points & parking

1. Stoke: Glebe Street in the city centre, just south of the railway station, between Queensway (A500) and the Leek Road (A52) (grid reference SJ 880454).

2. Rode Heath (Alsager) at the junction of the A50 and A533 to the north-west of Stoke (grid reference SJ 809569).

3. Barlaston (Plume of Feathers pub), just east of the A34 between Stone and Stoke (grid reference SJ 888384).

On your bikes!

South

Follow the canal south from the centre of Stoke, keeping the water to your left. The towpath can be followed for 5 miles as far as the Plume of Feathers pub in Barlaston.

North

1. Follow the canal north from the centre of Stoke, keeping the water to your right. Follow for 1¹/₂ miles, then shortly after the marina cross to the east side for about ¹/₂ mile.

2. Go past Westport Lake (to your left) then after almost 1¹/₂ miles, at the start of Harecastle Tunnel, bear up to the left on the broad stone track. Climb to the road and at the T-junction turn left then left again at the roundabout, using the pavement / cyclepath and changing sides as necessary.

3. After ¹/₂ mile, at the tall Bathpool Park sign, turn right through the car park to join a wide tarmac path, passing under the railway then alongside Bath Pool and a toddlers' playground.

4. At the T-junction shortly after passing a car park on the right, turn left downhill then at a second T-junction turn right. Just before a modern brick church on the right, turn left uphill onto a track signposted 'Harecastle Tunnel'. Follow this round to the right to rejoin the towpath.

5. The good-quality towpath continues as far as Rode Heath, to the north of Alsager. After this the surface quality deteriorates. It is possible to link with the Salt Line at the B5078 to the north-west of Alsager and continue to Wheelock.

Station: Stoke, Kidsgrove.

TIC: Stoke, 01782 236000.

Other nearby trails: The Biddulph Valley Trail runs from the north-east edge of Stoke to Congleton. The Salt Line Way goes west from Alsager towards Elworth (Sandbach).

Useful publications & websites: OS Landranger Map 118. Much more useful is the *Stoke-on-Trent Cycling Map & Guide.* See *www.stoke.gov.uk/cycling*

Refreshments: Bluebell pub, Canal Tavern, Red Bull pub, Kidsgrove.

Ride 17 Caldon Canal east from Stoke

Category
Canal towpath.

Distance
7 miles each way.

Stoke has four potential traffic-free exits to the north of the city: the Trent & Mersey Canal, National Cycle Network Route 5 through Burslem to Kidsgrove, the Biddulph Valley Trail to Congleton and this ride, the towpath of the Caldon Canal, which starts from the fascinating Etruria Industrial Museum. Here you can learn about Stoke's industrial past and the history of the Potteries. Opened in 1779 the Caldon Canal runs for 18 miles from Stoke to Froghall in Staffordshire. It passes through the heart of Stoke and out into the countryside.

Starting points & parking

1. Etruria Industrial Museum, Lower Bedford Street at the junction of the Caldon Canal with the Trent & Mersey Canal to the west of the centre of **Stoke** (grid reference SJ 873469).

2. The eastern finish point is in **Stockton Brook,** where the canal passes under the A53 close to the Sportsman pub (grid reference SJ 917520).

On your bikes!

1. From the museum, head towards the arched metal footbridge over the canal by a red and white 'Dispensary and House of Recovery' information board. Follow the tarmac path, keeping the water to your left.

2. Follow the tarmac or paved towpath for 7 miles as far as Bridge 25 at Stockton Brook (the Sportsman pub is up on the main road). You can either retrace your route or ...

Link to the Biddulph Valley Way

A. From Stockton Brook return back towards Stoke. Turn left immediately before Bridge 18. Climb to the road, cross with care to the pavement on the other side, turn right over the bridge then on the sharp right-hand bend, bear left onto the no-through-road.

B. Continue straight ahead at the end of the road as this becomes a wide tarmac cyclepath. At the T-junction with the road by the Foxley pub, turn left. Go through a set of traffic lights and under a bridge. Go through a second set of traffic lights and around a sharp right-hand bend, then immediately after crossing the bridge, turn right onto the tarmac path signposted 'Brindley Ford 3, National Cycle Network Route 55'.

Station: Stoke.

TIC: Stoke, 01782 236 000.

Other nearby trails: The Trent & Mersey Canal. The Biddulph Valley Trail runs from the north-east edge of Stoke to Congleton. The Salt Line Way goes west from Alsager towards Elworth (Sandbach).

Useful publications & websites: OS Landranger Map 118. Much more useful is the *Stoke-on-Trent Cycling Map & Guide.* See www.stoke.gov.uk/cycling

Refreshments: Café at the Etruria Industrial Museum.

Biddulph Valley Trail
Congleton to Stoke

Ride **18**

The ralsed track bed of the old Biddulph Valley Line provides fine views towards the Peak District. The ride passes through woodland and beneath a magnificent viaduct near Congleton on its way south to Biddulph and on to Holden Lane Pools on the north-east outskirts of Stoke. The Biddulph Valley Line was opened in 1859 and as Congleton's main arterial link with the Potteries, it provided the town's economic lifeblood with the movement of freight of every description from straw to war weapons. It lasted 109 years and the final train ran in 1968. In 1980, Congleton Borough Council bought the line from British Rail and the line was put into service once again to provide recreation for local people, and a refuge for wildlife

Starting points & parking

1. Congleton: the track / lane to the right of the Brunswick Wharf Depot opposite Brook Street Garage and petrol station, ¹/₂ mile out of Congleton on the A54 Buxton Road (grid reference SJ 865634).

2. Biddulph: leave the A527 Congleton to Stoke road at the traffic lights at the southern end of Biddulph, turning on to Newpool Road, signposted 'Mow Cop / Brown Lees'. The trail starts beneath the railway bridge after 200yds (grid reference SJ 878568).

3. Stoke: the trail starts from the Holden Lane Pools car park on the south side of the A53 Leek Road, about 3 miles north east of the city centre (grid reference SJ 893501). From the car park descend past the lake then turn left at the T-junction to pass through the subway under the A53.

Station: Congleton.

TIC: Congleton, 01260 271095.

Other nearby trails: The Trent & Mersey Canal towpath can be followed from the centre of Stoke north to Alsager. Rudyard Lake lies 4 miles to the east. There is a possible link to the Caldon Canal (see the previous ride for details).

Useful publications & websites: OS Landranger Map 118. Much more useful for Stoke is the *Stoke-on-Trent Cycling Map & Guide*. See *www.stoke.gov.uk/cycling*

Refreshments: In Congleton or Biddulph.

Category
Railway path.

Distance
10¹/₂ miles each way.

Ride 19 Rudyard Lake near Leek

19

Category
Railway path.

Distance
$4^1/2$ miles
each way.

A delightful ride alongside Rudyard Lake with colourful yachts and dinghies set against a background of steep wooded slopes. The ride starts on the western edge of Leek and runs along the east side of Rudyard Lake. The surface becomes rougher for the final mile to Rushton Spencer (off the A523 south of Macclesfield). The young Kiplings spent their courting days here and were so enamoured of the place that they named their first son, Rudyard, after the area.

Rudyard Lake is a feeder reservoir for the Caldon Canal. It was a very popular Victorian resort with hundreds of holiday-makers arriving by train during the season.

Starting points & parking

1. Leek: turn off the A523 Macclesfield road on to the road next to the Dyers Arms pub. The tarmac lane becomes a track. Join the railway path at the bridge (grid reference SJ 973567). There is also a signed on-road route from the centre of Leek (Stanley Street / Strangman Street) to the start of the trail, but the signing is a bit hit and miss.

2. The southern end of **Rudyard Lake** – turn off the A523 Leek to Macclesfield road, about 2 miles north-west of Leek onto the B5331, signposted 'Rudyard Lake'. Just after going under a railway bridge turn left into the car park (grid reference SJ 956578).

3. Car park near the Knot Inn at **Rushton Spencer**, just off the A523, about 8 miles south of Macclesfield (grid reference SJ 936625).

On your bikes!

North from the lake car park

Follow the broad track alongside the eastern side of Rudyard Lake, running parallel with the miniature railway line. At the end of the railway line follow the road / track as far as the Ryecroft Gate – Congleton road. You may wish to turn around here, or if the track is not too wet, to continue on the railway path under the road as far as the Knot Inn in Rushton Spencer.

South from the lake car park

The trail runs for $1^1/2$ miles to the outskirts of Leek. There is a sporadically signposted

route from the end of the trail into the centre of town (North Street, Spring Gardens, Langford Street, Waterloo Street, Wellington Street and Strangman Street).

Station: Congleton.

TIC: Congleton, 01260 271095.

Other nearby trails: The Biddulph Valley Trail lies 5 miles to the west. The Manifold Way starts at Waterhouses, on the A523, about 8 miles south-east of Leek.

Useful publications & websites: OS Landranger Map 118. Go to *www.waterscape. com/canals-and-rivers/rudyard-lake*

Refreshments: Café at the southern end of the lake. Knot Inn pub in Rushton Spencer.

Ride 20 Churnet Valley Trail west of Ashbourne

20

Category
Railway path.

Distance
4¹/₂ miles
each way.

The Churnet Valley Trail is a railway path through woodland at the south-west edge of the Peak District, running from Oakamoor, east of Stoke on Trent to Denstone. Look high above the valley for the dramatic Gothic-style castle in Alton village to the south of the trail, built by Pugin, the 19th-century architect famous for his work on the House of Commons. You will probably be aware of music drifting over from Alton Towers Theme Park, which lies in parkland to the north of the valley. The eastern end of the path is a riot of wildflowers in late spring and as you approach Oakamoor, keep an eye out for the tall sandstone cliffs to your right.

Starting points & parking

1. The car park in **Oakamoor** is just off the B5417 at the bottom of the hill, just to the west of the bridge over the River Churnet. Turn off the B4517 past the Admiral's House, signposted 'Ramblers Retreat', to the end of the overflow car park. The trail starts on the left about 30yds after the end of the tarmac (grid reference SK 054444).

2. The village hall car park, on the B5032 in **Denstone**, 5 miles north of Uttoxeter. From the car park, go past Frances Close and just before the telephone box turn left through a wide wooden gate on to the railway path (grid reference SK 099410).

Station: Uttoxeter.

TIC: Ashbourne, 01335 343666.

Other nearby trails: The Tissington Trail starts in Ashbourne, 8 miles to the north-west of Denstone. The Manifold Trail starts at Waterhouses, 6 miles north-east of Oakamoor.

Useful publications & websites: OS Landranger Map 119 or 128. Go to *www.staffordshire.gov.uk* and search 'Cycle maps'.

Refreshments: The Tavern pub, Denstone. The Admiral's House, Oakamoor.

Manifold Trail Ride 21
north-west of Ashbourne

The Manifold Trail is one of the most popular trails in the Peak District. The scenic railway path follows the course of two rivers, the Manifold and the Hamps, from Waterhouses (west of Ashbourne) via Wettonmill to Hulme End. The River Manifold appear and disappears; during the drier months it takes an underground course, leaving just the dry, stony river bed and tree-lined banks. High above the wooded hillsides are accessible caves. The Manifold Trail dips in the middle, at the junction of the Rivers Hamps and Manifold, so there is a gentle climb from this point (Weags Bridge) north to Hulme End or south to Waterhouses. The Leek & Manifold Valley Light Railway was opened in 1904, closed In 1934 and was converted to recreational use in 1937. It was a narrow-gauge railway designed by E.R. Calthrop, who had tested and proved his ideas on the Barsi Light Railway in India.

Starting points & parking

1. Hulme End, 12 miles south-west of Bakewell. Turn off the B5054 just to the west of the Manifold Inn (grid reference SK 103594).

2. Waterhouses, 9 miles north-west of Ashbourne. Turn off the A523 Ashbourne to Leek road at Ye Olde Crown Hotel in Waterhouses, signposted 'Cauldon Lowe, Manifold Track'. Go under the bridge and immediately left into the car park (grid reference SK 085501). To get to the start of the trail go to the far end of the car park and follow the waymarks.

Station: Uttoxeter, 10 miles to the south.

TIC: Ashbourne, 01335 343666.

Other nearby trails: The Tissington Trail lies 4 miles to the east of Hulme End along the B5054. The Churnet Valley Trail from Oakamoor to Denstone lies 6 miles south of Waterhouses.

Useful publications & websites: OS Landranger Map 119. A leaflet Is available from the Peak District National Park Office (01629 816200) or visit their website, *www.peakdistrict.gov. uk/cycle*

Refreshments: The Manifold Inn at Hulme End. Various tea shops and refreshment vans along the way. Ye Olde Crown Hotel at Waterhouses.

Category
Railway path.

Distance
8 miles each way.

NB *There is one busy road (the A523) to cross at Waterhouses. The trail uses a short section of quiet lane for about 1 1/2 miles.*

North-West Trails

North-West Mountain Biking

There is some mountain biking in Lancashire but the majority of the best trails in the North-West are in Cumbria. Within Lancashire try Salter Fell in the Forest of Bowland, or the Mary Townley Loop north of Rochdale. These and other routes are promoted in a mountain biking booklet produced by Lancashire County Council. For more information go to *www.lancashire.gov.uk/cycling*. As for Cumbria, there are books and leaflets too numerous to mention describing rides in this beautiful area. These can be obtained in good bookshops, from local Tourist Information Centres or by trawling the Internet.

The best rides are those which do not overlap with very popular walking trails in the heart of the Central Fells – ie, it is better to go to the fringes of the National Park: north of Keswick around the back of Skiddaw; south of Penrith on Askham Fell; between the valleys of Longsleddale and Troutbeck north-east of Windermere; or

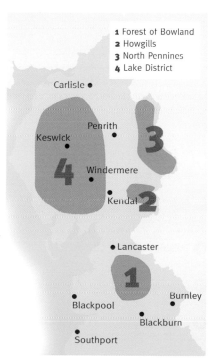

1 Forest of Bowland
2 Howgills
3 North Pennines
4 Lake District

Carlisle

Penrith
Keswick
3
4
Windermere
Kendal 2

Lancaster

1

Burnley
Blackpool
Blackburn
Southport

4 The Lake District

between the Duddon Valley and Coniston Water in the south-west corner of the National Park.

There are also some 'expedition' style crossings of the Pennines on bridleways to the north-east of Appleby in Westmorland and, strange though it may seem, part of the Yorkshire Dales National Park is located in Cumbria. There are many tracks around Sedbergh in the Howgills that offer tough but exhilarating mountain biking.

Websites:
www.forestry.gov.uk and search 'Grizedale', or 'Gisburn'.

www.forestry.gov.uk/alturatrail for Whinlatter.

www.moredirt.co.uk and follow links from 'Trails & Tracks' to 'United Kingdom' to 'Cumbria & Lancashire' or 'North West'.

www.cyclingcumbria.co.uk and click on 'Mountain Biking'.

www.lancashire.gov.uk/environment/maps/cycling.asp and click on 'Mountain biking'.

North-West Forestry

The North-West divides into two as far as forestry is concerned. The southern half is one of the least forested areas of the country, with only two forestry holdings: at Delamere, to the east of Chester, and Gisburn, to the north of Burnley. By contrast, Cumbria and the Lake District are considerably more forested with visitor centres and waymarked trails at Grizedale and Whinlatter, and several more holdings where cycling is possible. Although parts of Kielder Forest lie within the North-West, all the routes there are covered in the North-East chapter, from pages 304 to 327.

7 Whinlatter Forest

Forests and woods with waymarked trails

There are four Forestry Commission holdings with waymarked trails in the North-West region:

❶ **Delamere**, east of Chester (Ride 2, page 239)

❷ **Gisburn**, north of Burnley (Ride 23, page 262)

❹ **Grizedale**, in the heart of the Lake District (Ride 27, page 266)

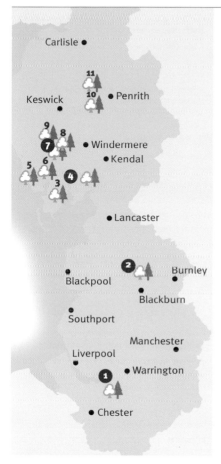

7 **Whinlatter Forest,** in the north-west of the Lake District (Ride 31, page 270)

In some forests and woods there are no waymarked routes, but you are free to explore the tracks. The relevant Ordnance Survey map is mentioned. It is highly recommended that you take a map for the larger woods as it is very easy to get lost.

The woodlands below correspond with the numbers on the map:

3. Broughton Moor & Hardknott Forest, west of Coniston Water (OS Explorer Map OL 6)

5. Miterdale & Dlengdale Forest, cast of Sellafield, West Cumbria (OS Explorer Map OL 6)

6. Ennerdale Forest, east of Ennerdale Water, Lake District (OS Explorer Map OL 6)

8. Dodd Wood, north of Keswick, Lake District (OS Explorer Map OL 4)

9. Setmurthy Common, east of Cockermouth, Lake District (OS Explorer Map OL 4)

10. High Stand Plantation, south-east of Carlisle (OS Explorer Map OL 5)

11. Kershope Forest, north-east of Carlisle (OS Explorer Map 315)

The Forestry Commission's website, *www. forestry.gov.uk,* is a good source of information. Click on 'Explore, Experience, Enjoy' then 'Cycling' and you can find out details of hundreds of waymarked trails throughout the UK. You can search by forest name or by the nearest town / city. The search will tell you the grade, length and waymarking details of the trails. Alternatively, by clicking on the map you can see the nearest forest to where you live.

It is also worth contacting the following Forest District Office for further information:

North-West England
Grizedale, Hawkshead, Ambleside, Cumbria LA22 0QJ.
Tel: 01229 860373
Email: enquiries.nwefd@forestry.gsi.gov.uk

North-West National Cycle Network

Maps for these routes are available from www.sustrans. org.uk or 0845 113 0065.

C2C / Sea to Sea Cycle Route

140 miles from Whitehaven or Workington on the West Cumbrian coast, over the Pennines to Sunderland or Tynemouth on the North Sea coast. Highlights include: the route through the Lake District; the delightful wooded, riverside railway path to the east of Keswick; the crossing of the Pennines with a highpoint of 2,000ft between Nenthead and Allenheads; the long, gentle, almost entirely traffic-free descent for the final 35 miles to Sunderland or Tynemouth.

Traffic-free sections over 3 miles long (only the first two are in the North-West):

- Whitehaven to Rowrah (NCN 71).
- Keswick to Threlkeld (NCN 71).
- The Waskerley Way from Rookhope to Consett (NCN 7).
- Consett to Sunderland railway path (NCN 7).
- The Derwent Valley Walk from Consett to Newcastle (NCN 14).
- Newcastle to Tynemouth along Hadrian's Way (NCN 72).

Hadrian's Cycleway

174 miles from Ravenglass on the West Cumbrian coast to South Shields on the North Sea Coast, following a course parallel to Hadrian's Wall from Bowness-on-Solway (west of Carlisle), to Wallsend, on the River Tyne between Newcastle and Tynemouth. Highlights include: the traffic-free trails along the Cumbrian Coast; easy, flat riding along the Solway Coast with views to Scotland; Carlisle's historic centre; links to Hadrian's Wall near Haltwhistle; rolling Northumberland countryside; Hexham Abbey; the largely traffic-free route alongside the Tyne to the coast.

Traffic-free sections over 3 miles long:

- Seascale past Sellafield to Beckermet (NCN 72).
- Lowca through Workington to St Helens (NCN 72).
- From Prudhoe east to South Shields is almost all traffic-free (NCN 72).

Walney to Wear

153 miles from Barrow-in-Furness in south-west Cumbria to Sunderland, crossing the Pennines between Kirkby Stephen and Barnard Castle, passing the famous Tan Hill Inn, the highest inn in England. Highlights include: the route through the Lake District National Park; Cartmel Priory; the Lune Gorge at the foot of the Howgills; the route up over the Pennines; Bowes Castle; the city of Durham with its magnificent castle and cathedral; the National Glass Centre and marina in Sunderland.

Traffic-free sections over 3 miles long:

- Bishop Auckland to Durham.
- Doxford Park to the marina in Sunderland is almost all traffic-free.

Trans Pennine Trail (west): Irish Sea to Yorkshire

215 miles from Southport to Hull via Liverpool, Manchester, Barnsley, Doncaster and Selby. Highlights in this section include: the sculpture at the start point on the Irish Sea in Southport; the deep stone cuttings along the Liverpool Loop Line; wide views of the Mersey from Pickering's Pasture; Sale and Chorlton Water Parks in south Manchester; the Longdendale Trail climbing from Hadfield to the Woodhead Tunnel alongside the string of reservoirs in the valley below.

Traffic-free sections over 3 miles long:

• Cheshire Lines Path from Ainsdale near Southport to Maghull in north Liverpool (NCN 62).

• Liverpool Loop Line from Aintree to Halewood (NCN 62).

• St Helens Canal from Spike Island to Sankey Bridges (NCN 62).

• Thelwall to Altrincham along the railway path (NCN 62).

• River Mersey through south Manchester (NCN 62).

• The Longdendale Trail from Hadfield to the Woodhead Tunnel (NCN 62).

Pennine Cycleway: South Pennines & the Dales

124 miles from Holmfirth in the South Pennines, through the Yorkshire Dales, to Appleby in Westmorland in the Eden Valley. Highlights include: the beautiful and challenging lanes through the South Pennines between Holmfirth and Burnley; the canal towpath between Burnley and Colne; the Yorkshire Dales, particularly the lanes through Kingsdale and Dentdale; the handsome town of Appleby in Westmorland.

Traffic-free sections over 3 miles long:

• Burnley to Barnoldswick along the Leeds & Liverpool Canal (NCN 68).

Sustrans

The Sustrans maps shown here cover various National Cycle Network routes within the region. Some of the maps may describe routes that continue into adjacent regions: these maps are mentioned in both chapters. The maps are not only useful for people wishing to ride the whole route over several days, they also show all the traffic-free sections that make good day rides.

Other good areas for lane cycling

There is a good lane network with plenty of easy cycling in the far south-west of Cheshire, bordering on Wales to the west and Shropshire to the south. Tarporley, Bunbury and Beeston are attractive villages in the area. Moving north from here there is a great swathe of the region dominated by the vast cities and suburbs of Liverpool and Manchester, densely populated as far north as Blackpool and Burnley; traffic is generally heavy. Beyond here there is an attractive web of lanes around the fringes of the Forest of Bowland with the fine settlements at Chipping, Dunsop Bridge and Slaidburn. It is north of here, however, that there is the most fantastic of cycling opportunities, from the Lune Valley north to the Eden Valley, and of course the Lake District and Cumbria. The best lane cycling here lies outside of the Central Fells where many of the roads tend to be busy, especially at weekends and during school holidays. For easier Cumbrian cycling try the area south and west of Carlisle along the Solway Firth, with fine views of both Scottish and English hills.

A map for this route is available from www. sustrans.org. uk or 0845 113 0065.

Ride 1 **Whitegate Way east of Chester**

1

Category
Railway path.

Distance
6 miles each way.

There aren't many cycle trails in the country that end at a salt mine, as the Whitegate Trail does just to the north of Winsford. The railway path, is predominantly wooded through the cuttings with views across to arable farmland and pasture on the more open sections. As with so many of these railway paths, the Whitegate Way is at its best either in late spring / early summer when the young leaves are a fresh green and the verges and woodland are full of bright wildflowers, or in late autumn when the leaves are changing colour and the path is carpeted with all shades of yellow and red. The Whitegate Line was opened in 1870 to transport salt from the mines along the west bank of the River Weaver. The line closed in 1966. The old railway is now managed for maximum benefit of wildlife as well as providing an attractive environment for people to enjoy. Trees are coppiced in a traditional form of woodland management whereby the trees are cut down to ground level every 6-8 years. This encourages tremendous re-growth and provides useful timber for poles and logs.

Starting point & parking

The car park for the Whitegate Way is at **Marton Green,** to the north of the A54 between Kelsall and Winsford (about 10 miles west of M6, Jct 18). Turn onto Clay Lane, opposite a lane signposted 'Budworth'. After 1 mile, just before a railway bridge, bear right downhill signposted 'Whitegate Way' for the car park (grid reference SJ 615680).

On your bikes!

The route follows the course of the old railway so it is impossible to get lost. From the car park you can:

• **Head east** (turn right) for 3 miles until you reach the T-junction with the road by the salt mines.

• **Head west** (turn left) for 3 miles until you come to a huge railway bridge over the trail by Ravensclough Manor House in Cuddington. If you wish to visit the pub in Cuddington you will need to follow the lane for $^1/_2$ mile then at the T-junction at the end of Waste Lane, turn right uphill for another $^1/_2$ mile.

Station: Cuddington.

TIC: Nantwich, 01270 610983.

Other nearby trails: Delamere Forest Trails.

Useful publications & websites: OS Landranger Maps 117 & 118. For the most up-to-date information about this trail and other cycle routes in the county (including maps to download), go to *www.cheshire.gov. uk/cycling*, click on 'Cycle Routes in Cheshire' then on 'Traffic Free Routes'. Also try *www. discovercheshire.co.uk*, click on 'Cycling', click on the map, tick the 'Traffic Free' box and click on the green balloon by Winsford.

Refreshments: None on route. White Barn pub in Cuddington at the crossroads with the A49 at the top of a climb.

Delamere Forest Ride 2
east of Chester (2 routes)

There are very few Forestry Commission holdings of any size in this part of the North-West – you would need to go to Cumbria (or Wales) for that – but whilst Delamere Forest Park is not particularly large, it does have two waymarked cycle routes which are ideal for family cycling: broad gravel tracks with a few gentle hills but nothing to really worry about. There is also a mountain bike skills area in the north-west corner of the forest. Starting from the visitor centre, the ride crosses and recrosses the railway line, passing through mixed broadleaf and conifer woodland, with a fine display of wildflowers in the spring and early summer. Delamere Forest was once the royal hunting preserve of the Earls of Chester – the visitor centre has displays of Delamere's history. The forest is noted for kestrels, sparrowhawks, foxes and badgers.

Starting point & parking

Delamere Forest Visitor Centre, Linmere, **Delamere**, just off the B5152, 6 miles south of M56, Jct 12 (grid reference SJ 548704).

On your bikes!

From the car park by the Delamere Forest Visitor Centre, return towards the public road and take the first left over a bridge with a 'Forest Trails' and a 'No entry for cars' signpost. After almost 1 mile you will come to an obvious crossroads of tracks where you have a choice:

• **Hunger Hill Trail,** 4 miles, blue arrows, to the right.

• **White Moor Trail,** 7 miles, white arrows, to the left.

Station: Delamere.

TIC: Chester, 01244 402111.

Other nearby trails: The Whitegate Way starts 3 miles to the east.

Useful publications & websites: OS Landranger Map 117. A leaflet called *Delamere Forest Guide Map* (£2) can be purchased from the Delamere Visitor Centre (01606 889792). Also try *www.forestry.gov.uk/delamerehome* and click on 'Cycling'.

Refreshments: At the visitor centre. There is also a café at the old station just by the main road.

Category
Forestry trails.

Distance
Hunger Hill Trail – 4 miles.

White Moor Trail – 7 miles.

NB A minor road needs to be crossed twice. The traffic can be travelling quite fast on this road so take care.

Ride 3 Chester to Hawarden Bridge via the railway path or via the River Dee

3

Category
Railway path or riverside path.

Distance
(a) Railway path: 7 miles each way.

(b) Riverside path: 7 miles each way.

Chester is one of the chosen cities for the Cycling Demonstration Towns Project, and more traffic-free routes are being built each year. See *www.cyclechester.com* for up-to-date details. Chester is a most attractive town full of half-timbered buildings ringed by medieval walls with fragments dating back to Saxon and even Roman times. Opposite the centre is the site of the Roman amphitheatre and Roman archaeological finds, as well as displays on local history, can be seen at the Grosvenor Museum. There is a cyclepath along the towpath of the Shropshire Union Canal that links the centre of town to the railway path. The latter is an attractive open ride taking you from the north side of Chester out into the Wirral's rich arable farmlands, planted with potatoes, maize and cereal crops. The Mickle Trafford to Dee Marsh railway line once carried steel to and from the steelworks on the banks of the Dee at Hawarden Bridge. Away in the distance are the Clwyd Hills. At Hawarden Bridge you may wish to try the alternative return route to Chester by following the excellent trail alongside the River Dee (Regional Route 89) back into the centre of town.

Starting points & parking

1. Anywhere along the **canal in the centre of town** (head north to Bridge 128B then join the railway path).

2. Kingsway shopping centre on the **north-east side of Chester**, just west of M53, Jct 12 (grid reference SJ 419681).

3. Hawarden Bridge station on the north side of the River Dee to the north of Connah's Quay, west of Chester (grid reference SJ 312695).

On your bikes!

1. From the Kingsway shopping centre, take the tarmac path across the park following National Cycle Network Route 5 signs past metal sculptures. At the railway path turn right.

2. After 7 miles you will arrive at Hawarden Bridge. Either retrace your steps or, for an alternative route back to Chester, follow the path on the raised embankment alongside the River Dee (Regional Route 89).

3. (River Dee option.) After 7 miles, once you are back in the centre of Chester, leave the river after it turns a sharp right-hand bend, cross the A548 and join the Shropshire Union Canal towpath near Tower Road / South View Road.

4. Leave the canal towpath by Bridge 128B at the 'National Cycle Network Route 5' sign and turn right up the ramp to rejoin the railway path. Turn right on the railway path to return to Kingsway (or left for Hawarden Bridge).

3

Station: Chester, Hawarden Bridge.

TIC: Chester, 01244 402111.

Other nearby trails: Shropshire Union Canal from Waverton to Ellesmere Port. Delamere Forest Park.

Useful publications & websites: OS Landranger Map 117. Go to *www.sustrans.org.uk* and put

'*Chester to Connah's Quay leaflet*' in the 'Search' box. For other information about bike routes and maps to download go to *www.cyclechester.com*. For other routes in the county go to *www.cheshire.gov.uk/cycling* or *www.discovercheshire.co.uk*.

Refreshments: Lots of choice in Chester.

4

Shropshire Union Canal Ride 4
through Chester

The towpath of the Shropshire Union Canal has an improved surface all the way from Waverton (south of Chester) to its junction with the Manchester Ship Canal at Ellesmere Port, some 12 miles to the north. Starting in a rich, arable landscape, the scenery turns from rural to urban, passing expensive riverside properties then running right through the heart of Chester between some atmospheric red sandstone cuttings where the towpath narrows. Emerge from town and move once again out into the countryside, passing under the junction of the M53 and M56 to arrive at journey's end at the National Waterways Museum at Ellesmere Port, with wide views north across the Mersey.

Starting points & parking

1. Waverton, south-east of Chester (grid reference SJ 454643).

2. The National Waterways Museum in **Ellesmere Port,** near M53, Jct 9 (grid reference SJ 406772).

On your bikes!

It is not hard to follow the canal. The surface and width of the towpath varies and you will occasionally need to change sides, but this presents no difficulties.

Station: Chester.

TIC: Chester, 01244 402111.

Other nearby trails: Chester to Hawarden Bridge.

Useful publications & websites: OS Landranger Map 117. For information about bike routes in Chester go to *www.cyclechester.com*. For other routes in the county go to *www.cheshire.gov.uk/cycling* or *www.discovercheshire.co.uk*

Refreshments: Cheshire Cat pub (1 mile west of Waverton). Lots of choice in Chester. Café at the National Waterways Museum, Ellesmere Port.

Category
Canal towpath.

Distance
12 miles each way.

Ride 5 Wirral Way (Hooton to West Kirby) on the Wirral Peninsula

Category
Railway path.

Distance
12 miles each way.

From Hooton station the path runs through broadleaf woodland, banks of wildflowers and, as you proceed north, you will enjoy views across the Dee Estuary to Wales. On the outskirts of Neston you will pass through an amazing rock cutting, where you feel as though Indiana Jones might suddenly swing across the path on a hanging creeper! Pick marks can still be seen in the sandstone where it was gouged out by hand. Wirral Country Park is based on the former 12-mile Hooton to West Kirby Branch Line Railway. The line opened in 1866 and ran for 90 years carrying freight and passengers, and for a further six years carrying just freight. The dismantled railway became Britain's first country park in the late 1960s. The most important remaining feature of railway days is the station at Hadlow Way, Willaston, which still looks as it might have done in the 1950s.

Starting point & parking

1. Hooton railway station car park (Park and Ride car park), to the north-west of Ellesmere Port and just west of the M53, Jct 5. Follow the A41 towards Chester then turn first right onto the B5133 to get to the station (grid reference SJ 350783).

2. The visitor centre, at the end of the minor road through **Thurstaston**, off the A540 between Heswall and West Kirby (grid reference SJ 237836).

On your bikes!

1. Exit the Hooton station car park, cross the railway line via the road bridge then turn immediately left to descend to the Wirral Way, at first running parallel with the railway line on a narrow track.

2. After almost 2 miles, go past Hadlow Road station.

3. Pass through an underpass beneath the A540 then through amazing rock cuttings. At the road junction continue straight ahead on Station Road. Continue in the same direction, rejoining the traffic-free path after $1/3$ mile.

4. At the junction with the next road, with black and white timbered houses ahead, turn right then left at the 'Wirral Way' signpost.

5. Views of the Dee Estuary open up to the left. At the T-junction with a road, turn right along Riverbank Road / Davenport Road (quiet residential roads with new houses). After $1/2$ mile bear right to rejoin the railway path.

6. After 2 miles go past Thurstaston Visitor Centre (refreshments).

7. The Wirral Way ends after almost 3 miles at the busy A540 in West Kirby (opposite Orrysdale Road).

Link to the North Wirral Coastal Park

A. Proceed along Orrysdale Road, continuing straight ahead at a crossroads. After ¹/₂ mile, as the road turns sharp right, bear left to pass to the left of green metal railings onto a tarmac cyclepath.

B. At the T-junction with the road by Hoylake railway station, turn left on Station Road. At the roundabout go straight ahead onto The Kings Gap. At the coast turn right. The wide promenade starts after ¹/₂ mile by the Lifeboat Station.

Station: Hooton or West Kirby.

TIC: Birkenhead, 0151 647 6780.

Other nearby trails: North Wirral Coastal Park runs from Hoylake to the Seacombe Ferry Terminal. There are waymarked trails in Delamere Forest. The Whitegate Way runs from Cuddington to Winsford.

Useful publications & websites: OS Landranger Maps 108 & 117. Go to *www.discovercheshire.co.uk*, click on 'Cycling', click on the map, tick the 'Traffic Free' box and click on the green balloon to the left of 'Liverpool'. Or go to *www.visitwirral.com*, click on 'Attractions & Activities' then 'Activities' then 'South West Cycle Route Map'. Also try *www.cheshire.gov.uk/cycling* for other routes in Cheshire.

Refreshments: Coach & Horses pub, Neston. Lots of choice just off the route in Heswall. Refreshments at Thurstaston Visitor Centre. Lots of choice in West Kirby.

North Wirral Coastal Park Ride 6
west of Liverpool

Enjoy this open, breezy ride from the Seacombe ferry terminal through New Brighton to Hoylake at the north-west tip of the Wirral Peninsula. It starts with wonderful views across the Mersey, with the famous ferry plying its trade between Seacombe and the Royal Liver Buildings. Further north on the other side of the Mersey is the Port of Liverpool, with hundreds of cranes loading and unloading containers. After passing through the Victorian resort of New Brighton, the path runs alongside a golf course under big open skies with the vast expanse of Liverpool Bay to the north, and banks of wind turbines generating clean energy. The trail known as the North Wirral Coastal Park ends at Hoylake, but if you want to extend the ride it is possible to link up with the Wirral Way in West Kirby by using roads through Hoylake for about 2 miles.

Category
Coastal promenade.

Distance
8 miles each way.

Ride 6 North Wirral Coastal Park, west of Liverpool

Starting points & parking

1. The Seacombe Ferry Terminal on the west side of the Mersey, **Birkenhead** (grid reference SJ 326909).

2. The Lifeboat Station in **Hoylake** (grid reference SJ 214895).

On your bikes!

1. From the Seacombe Ferry Terminal follow the broad (traffic-free) road north with the River Mersey to your right.

2. The route goes through New Brighton, turning west and running along the cycleway on the pavement, then continues in the same direction with the golf course to your left.

3. Follow this traffic-free route for 5 miles. It stops at the Lifeboat Station in Hoylake.

Station: New Brighton.

TIC: Liverpool, 0151 233 2008.

Other nearby trails: The Wirral Way. The Otterspool Promenade on the other side of the Mersey.

Useful publications & websites: OS Landranger Map 108. Go to *www.visitwirral. com*, click on 'Attractions & Activities' then 'Activities' then 'North East Cycle Route Map'. Or go to *www.wirral.gov.uk* then 'Transport and Streets' then 'Walking and Cycling' then click on 'Wirral Cycle Map Download'. Also visit *www.letstravelwise.org* – click on 'Cycling' then 'Cycle Maps'.

Refreshments: Lots of choice in New Brighton and Hoylake.

Ride 7 Cheshire Lines Path north of Liverpool

Category
Railway path.

Distance
7 miles each way.

Cycle from the outskirts of Liverpool to the coast south of Southport, following the old Cheshire Lines railway across the West Lancashire Moss. This is the first (most westerly) railway path section of the Trans Pennine Trail, soon followed to the east by the Liverpool Loop Line. Moss is an old Lancashire word meaning marsh, and like much of this part of the West Lancashire Plain, this former marshland was drained in the 19th century to produce richly fertile farmland. The area is renowned for its potatoes, green vegetables, flowers and market gardening. The pinewoods close to the Liverpool – Southport railway line are one of the last sanctuaries of the red squirrel. Although the trail is called the Cheshire Lines, it is actually in Lancashire. The railway was opened in 1884 by the Cheshire Lines Committee to link their railway at Aintree with Southport. It was mainly used by express trains from Manchester to Southport on holiday weekends. The railway closed to passengers in 1952.

7

Starting points & parking

1. Maghull, off the A59 to the north of the M57, Jct 7. The railway path starts from the B5422 (Sefton Lane) to the west of Maghull, just west of the Sefton Drive turning and opposite Old Racecourse Road (grid reference SD 364017).

2. Moor Lane / Plex Moss Lane, a minor road off the A565 to the **south-east of Ainsdale**, between Formby and Southport (grid reference SD 325102).

Station: Maghull or Ainsdale.

TIC: Southport, 01704 533333.

Other nearby trails: Liverpool Loop Line.

Useful publications & websites: OS Landranger Map 108. A series of seven cycling leaflets showing traffic-free routes, recommended routes, waymarked routes in the Merseyside area is available from *www.letstravelwise.org*. Click on 'Cycling' then 'Cycle Maps'. Also try *www.transpenninetrail.org.uk* and click on the map between Southport and Liverpool.

Refreshments: Lots of choice in Maghull and Ainsdale.

8

Liverpool Loop Line Ride 8
(Halewood & Aintree)

The railway path runs along wooded embankments and between sandstone cuttings around the eastern edge of Liverpool, from Halewood (south-west of M62, Jct 6) through Knotty Ash and Walton to the A59 just south of Aintree station. There are extensive views as far as the Pennine foothills. Opened in 1879, the Liverpool Loop Line was planned to provide a direct route to the Lancashire coast from Cheshire and Warrington, bypassing central Liverpool. The line was used for 90 years and has since been converted to recreational use, forming part of the Trans Pennine Trail which crosses the country from Southport to Hull. Halewood Triangle was once a busy railway junction. Now the trains have gone the area has been developed into an attractive country park, served by a visitor centre.

Category
Railway path.

Distance
10 miles each way

Ride 8   Liverpool Loop Line (Halewood & Aintree)

8

Starting points & parking

1. Halewood Triangle Country Park (Okell Drive), south-west of M62, Jct 6 (grid reference SJ 439862). The railway line runs along the north-east edge of the park.

2. Walton Hall Park, north Liverpool, west of M57, Jct 4/5 (grid reference SJ 375952). The trail runs just to the east of the park.

3. The trail (signposted as the Trans Pennine Trail) can be picked up from **Aintree railway station**. Access to the start of the traffic-free railway path is from Greenwich Road, near to its junction with Melling Avenue, to the south-east of Aintree station (grid reference SJ 369975).

Station: Halewood, Broad Green, Rice Lane or Aintree.

TIC: Liverpool, 0151 233 2008.

Other nearby trails: The Cheshire Lines Path starts 5 miles north of Walton (the northern end of the Liverpool Loop Line).

Useful publications & websites: OS Landranger Map 108. A series of seven cycling leaflets showing traffic-free routes, recommended routes, waymarked routes and the National Cycle Network in the Merseyside area is available from *www.letstravelwise.org*. Click on 'Cycling' then 'Cycle Maps'. Also try *www.transpenninetrail.org.uk* and click on the map between Southport and Liverpool.

Refreshments: At the Halewood Visitor Centre. Café and pubs in West Derby (Mill Lane). Pubs in Rice Lane.

Ride 9   Otterspool Promenade Liverpool

9

Category
Promenade alongside the Mersey.

Distance
5 miles each way.

The regeneration of Albert Dock has been the driving force behind the improvement along the whole length of the River Mersey, from Cressington and Otterspool to the Royal Liver Buildings. A broad, top-grade promenade now sweeps alongside the river for 5 miles with wide, open views across the water to the Wirral. The path is popular with walkers, joggers and cyclists, but is wide enough to accommodate all three without trouble. Albert Dock houses the Beatles Museum amongst others, and offers a model of what can be done in terms of inner-city regeneration. If you want to enjoy the quintessential Liverpool experience, why not take the ferry across the Mersey?

Opened in 1846 as England's gateway to the New World, Albert Dock is the largest group of Grade 1 listed buildings in Great Britain. It fell into disuse but has now been revamped into a quayside complex featuring watersports and museums. Alongside Animation World, The Beatles Story, the Tate Gallery and the Maritime Museum are a number of speciality shops and restaurants.

Starting points & parking

1. The **Liver Buildings**, in the centre of Liverpool (grid reference SJ 338905).

2. The south end of the Otterspool Promenade. Turn off the A561 just west of **Cressington railway station** down Riversdale Road, following signs for 'Liverpool Cricket Club' (this is a large red-brick building with green and white timbers). There is a car park at the end. Descend to the riverside promenade and turn right by a large orange bull sculpture (grid reference SJ 385851).

On your bikes!

It is hard to lose something as large as the River Mersey! Stay close to the water and you won't go far wrong. There are one or two short diversions away from the promenade but you soon return to the water's edge. From the Royal Liver Buildings you could easily catch a ferry to

Seacombe on the other side, then continue north along the traffic-free promenade that runs to New Brighton and around the coastline of the Wirral to Hoylake.

Station: Liverpool.

TIC: Liverpool, 0151 233 2008.

Other nearby trails: On the other side of the Mersey there is a cyclepath from the Seacombe Ferry Terminal to New Brighton and on to the North Wirral Coastal Park. On this side of the Mersey are the Liverpool Loop Line (Halewood), the Cheshire Lines Path (Maghull – Ainsdale) and Saint Helen's Canal (Widnes).

Useful publications & websites: OS Landranger Map 108. A series of seven cycling leaflets showing traffic-free routes, recommended routes, waymarked routes and the National Cycle Network in the Merseyside area is available from *www.letstravelwise.org*. Click on 'Cycling' then 'Cycle Maps'. Also try *www.transpenninetrail.org.uk* and click on the map just south of Liverpool.

Refreshments: Lots of choice in Albert Dock.

St Helen's Canal, Widnes (east of Liverpool) Ride 10

Several rides in this book use sections of the Trans Pennine Trail, the path that crosses the country from Southport on the West Coast to Hull and the North Sea Coast, officially opened at the end of 2000. This ride along St Helen's Canal is surprisingly green, quiet and secluded for a setting so much in the heart of the industrial area between Liverpool and Manchester. Do not be surprised to see herons and even kingfishers along this stretch of water.

There are several interpretation boards and metal cut-outs of wildfowl. The pub at Fiddler's Ferry offers a welcome refreshment stop and is a good turnaround point for an 8-mile ride. If you want to extend the ride, you can easily follow the Trans Pennine Trail signposts through Warrington on a mixture of tracks and quiet streets to join the railway path from Warrington to Lymm. Spike Island and the surrounding area was the birthplace of the British chemical industry, and the Catalyst Museum explains

Category
Canal towpath.

Distance
5^1/$_2$ miles each way.

Ride **10**   **St Helen's Canal, Widnes (east of Liverpool)**

the industry's history with photographs, slide shows and working machines. Since 1975 the area has been transformed into a green space and haven for wildlife.

Starting point & parking

The Catalyst Museum car park in **Widnes**, just north of the Runcorn – Widnes Bridge (grid reference SJ 513842). Follow the brown and white signs from the A562 / A533 / A557.

On your bikes!

1. From the corner of the Catalyst Museum car park by the path leading to the museum entrance, bear left towards the locks. Cross the narrow bridge and turn left alongside the canal.

2. After 4 miles you will go past the Ferry Tavern.

3. The towpath ends after a further 1¹/₂ miles. It is possible to continue eastwards on the Trans Pennine Trail by following signposts through the southern

edge of Warrington on quiet roads and sections alongside the River Mersey and the Manchester Ship Canal. Then join the next long traffic-free section which runs along a railway path from Warrington through Lymm to the outskirts of Altrincham.

Station: Warrington.

TIC: Warrington, 01925 428585.

Other nearby trails: This route is part of the Trans Pennine Trail. To the east, the next traffic-free section is the railway path from Warrington to Altrincham. There are three more traffic-free routes just to the west: the Otterspool Promenade in Liverpool, the Cheshire Lines Path and the Liverpool Loop Line.

Useful publications & websites: OS Landranger Map 108. A series of seven cycling leaflets showing traffic-free routes, recommended routes, waymarked routes and the National Cycle Network in the Merseyside area is available from *www.letstravelwise.org*. Click on 'Cycling' then 'Cycle Maps'. Also try *www.transpenninetrail.org.uk* and click on the map south-east of Liverpool.

Refreshments: Ferry Tavern at Fiddler's Ferry.

Warrington to Altrincham Railway Path

Ride 11

There is a signboard at the western end of this trail, at the bottom of the approach ramp on the outskirts of Warrington, that places this short ride within a much wider context: not only is Warrington to Altrincham part of the Trans Pennine Trail stretching from coast to coast, but the Trans Pennine Trail itself is part of the European Long Distance Footpath system, which links such far-flung destinations as Geneva, Istanbul, St Petersburg and Riga. Finding the car park and the start of the ride on the west side of Altrincham will probably represent the hardest part of the day. Once on the trail it is impossible to get lost as you travel through open countryside and woodland with verges full of wildflowers in the late spring and early summer. This is a good ride for conversation – no hills, a wide track and good visibility – so you can put the world to rights while keeping yourself fit. It would be easy to extend this ride westwards by following the Trans Pennine Trail signs through Warrington to join St Helen's Canal to Widnes.

Starting points & parking

1. Altrincham (grid reference SJ 751889). From the M6 or the M56 follow the A556 north towards Altrincham. Go past the left turn to Dunham Massey (B5160) then after $^{1}/_{2}$ mile, on a sharp right-hand bend, take the second of two closely-spaced left turns onto Highgate Road. This becomes Gorsey Lane. At the T-junction (mini-roundabout), turn left onto Oldfield Road, which becomes Seamons Road. Cross the bridge over the canal via traffic lights, then 150yds after passing the Bay Malton pub turn left into the car park. Beware the height barrier.

2. Bradshaw Lane, off the B5157 Thelwall New Road, on the south-east edge of **Warrington,** close to the Latchford Locks on the Manchester Ship Canal (grid reference SJ 638871).

On your bikes!

The route is well signposted and easy to follow. If you are travelling from east to west, the M6 is about 6 miles along the trail (three-quarters of the total distance from Altrincham to Warrington).

Station: Warrington or Altrincham.

TIC: Altrincham, 0161 912 5931.

Other nearby trails: This is part of the Trans Pennine Trail. To the west is St Helen's Canal; to the east, the next traffic-free section is the Mersey River through South Manchester.

Useful publications & websites: OS Landranger Map 109. Visit *www. transpenninetrail.org.uk*. Ten (free) maps covering the whole of Greater Manchester are available from the relevant District Cycling Officers or can be downloaded from the website. Go to *www.cyclegm.org* for contact details. The eastern half of this route is on Map 9 – Trafford.

Refreshments: Bay Malton pub, west of Altrincham. Star pub at Lymm.

Category
Railway path.

Distance
$7^{1}/_{2}$ miles each way.

NB The trail can become muddy in winter and after prolonged rain. It is best ridden in summer after a dry spell.

Ride 12 Tatton Park north-west of Knutsford

12

Category
Estate roads and tracks.

Distance
There are 8 miles of quiet estate roads within Tatton Park and just as many tracks.

NB *There is traffic on the estate roads but it is travelling slowly and signs tell motorists to be aware of cyclists. There is more traffic during summer weekends, so plan accordingly.*

There is a charge to enter this country estate by car (although it is free if you turn up on your bikes), so there is very little traffic on the estate roads within the park. As a result it is a fine place to cycle, exploring the attractive parkland which has been a refuge for deer for hundreds of years. You can buy a family ticket for combined admission to all the attractions. The Old Hall displays 500 years of history; Home Farm explains how the wealth of Tatton Hall was derived from agriculture, and at the Stables the vital role of the horse on a country estate is brought to life; the Mansion juxtaposes majestic staterooms and the life of the servant 'below stairs'. You are free to explore all the roads and the tracks around the estate unless marked 'Private'. For example, there is a track running down the east side of Tatton Mere and another one around the western perimeter of the park. Pick up a map from the entrance gates or the visitor centre.

Starting point & parking

Tatton Park (grid reference SJ 744816). Follow signs off the A556, which runs between Junction 7/8 of the M56 and Junction 19 of the M6 between Altrincham and Knutsford. There is a charge to enter the park by car.

Station: Knutsford.

TIC: Knutsford, 01565 632611.

Other nearby trails: The Middlewood Way from Marple to Macclesfield lies 8 miles to the east. Warrington to Altrincham along the Trans Pennine Trail.

Useful publications & websites: OS Landranger Maps 109 & 118. The park also produces a map, available at the entrance gates and from the visitor centre. See also *www.tattonpark.org.uk* and either click on 'Park' then 'Visitor Activities' then 'Cycling' or put 'Park Map' in the 'Search' box.

Refreshments: Restaurants and refreshments near the mansion.

Middlewood Way
Manchester

Along stretch of dismantled railway, much of it in woodland, running from Marple to the south-east of Manchester, via Higher Poynton and Bollington to Macclesfield, on the edge of the Peak District. There are good views in both directions and plenty of carved wooden sculptures of animals. Can you manage the two zig-zag sections of path? During the Industrial Revolution, many local industries flourished in this area, especially silk, coal, cotton and stone. Rail and canal links with Stockport were built so that products could be moved more easily. The Macclesfield, Bollington & Marple Railway was opened in 1869 and was in use until 1970. In the early 1980s work was carried out to reopen the routes for recreational use, and the Middlewood Way was opened in 1985.

Starting points & parking

1. Tesco supermarket petrol station just off the roundabout at the start of the A523 dual carriageway to the north of **Macclesfield** (grid reference SJ 919741).

2. Adlington Road car park by the viaduct in **Bollington**, 3 miles north-east of Macclesfield, by the Dog & Partridge pub, signposted 'Middlewood Way' (grid reference SJ 931782).

3. Poynton Coppice and Higher Poynton, **east of Poynton** and the A523 (grid reference SJ 945834).

4. Marple. Turn off the A626 Stockport to Glossop road in Marple, opposite the Rose Hill Post Office (close to the Railway pub) onto Railway Road, signposted 'Middlewood Way / Station car park'. Look for a sign for the start of the Middlewood

Way to the left of the recycling site (grid reference SJ 949888).

Stations: Marple, Middlewood and Macclesfield.

TIC: Macclesfield, 01625 504114.

Other nearby trails: The Sett Valley Trail runs between New Mills and Hayfield, to the south-east of Marple. Rudyard Lake lies 10 miles south of Macclesfield. The Biddulph Valley Line starts from Congleton, 10 miles south-west of Macclesfield.

Useful publications & websites:
OS Landranger Maps 109 & 118. For information about this trail and all other cycle routes in Cheshire (including maps to download), go to *www.cheshire.gov.uk/cycling*. Click on 'Cycle Routes in Cheshire' then 'Traffic Free Routes' then 'Middlewood Way' to download a map.

Ten (free) maps covering the whole of Greater Manchester are available from the relevant District Cycling Officers or can be downloaded from the website. Go to *www.cyclegm.org* for contact details. The Middlewood Way is on Map 7 – Stockport.

Refreshments: Lots of choice in Marple, Bollington and Macclesfield.

Category
Railway path.

Distance
10 miles each way.

NB The 7 miles of trail south from Marple to the Bollington Viaduct can get muddy in the winter or after prolonged rain.

251

Ride 14 **Mersey River through south Manchester**

Category
Riverside paths.

Distance
West from the visitor centre 1 mile each way.

East from the visitor centre 2½ miles each way.

Forming part of the Trans Pennine Trail, this route alongside the River Mersey through Sale Water Park and around Chorlton Water Park is one of many that could be devised in the area. Enjoy the open green spaces alongside the River Mersey with its profusion of wildflowers and birdlife. Occupying the site of the old Barlow Hall Farm, 170-acre Chorlton Water Park is now one of the most popular sites in the Mersey Valley. Like Sale Water Park a kilometre downstream, the lake at Chorlton was excavated in the early 1970s to provide gravel for the M60 motorway. Since then the area has been developed to cater for all kinds of recreational activities in a countryside setting. During the winter months the lake is visited by large numbers of ducks including Pochard, Tufted Duck and Goldeneye.

Starting point & parking

Mersey Valley Visitor Centre (signposted as 'Trafford Water Sports Centre') off the M60, Jct 6 (grid reference SJ 807925).

On your bikes!

With your back to the entrance to the visitor centre, go straight ahead on the narrow path running parallel with the road. Continue in the same direction to join the River Mersey by a sluice control building (remember this point for your return). At this point you have a choice:

• **West**. Turn left on the track alongside the river. Follow this for 1 mile as far as the railway line and the next bridge over the river. From this point you can return on the higher or lower track. There is also a track on the other side of the river, but

it is rougher. Return to the sluice control building.

• **East**. Turn right along the river then cross the bridge over the river (by Jackson's Boat Inn) and turn right. After 1 mile, opposite a metal bridge with anti-climbing barbs, go through the barrier and turn left down to Chorlton Water Park. Complete a circuit of the lake, return to this point on the River Mersey then go back to the visitor centre.

Station: Sale or East Didsbury.

TIC: Manchester, 0871 222 8223.

Other nearby trails: The Middlewood Way runs from Marple (east of Stockport) to Macclesfield. The Trans Pennine Trail continues west from Altrincham to Warrington.

Useful publications & websites: OS Landranger Map 109. Maps showing the trails through the water park are available from the visitor centre (0161 905 1100). Go to *www.transpenninetrail.org.uk*

Ten (free) maps covering the whole of Greater Manchester are available from the relevant District Cycling Officers or can be downloaded from the website. Go to *www.cyclegm.org* for contact details. This route is on Map 9 – Trafford.

Refreshments: Café adjacent to the visitor centre. Jackson's Boat Inn at Jackson's Bridge.

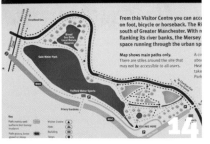

explore and discover

Fallowfield Loop Line south Manchester   Ride 15

Forming part of the National Cycle Network, this popular green corridor through urban Manchester lies on the course of the old Fallowfield Line and skirts to the south of the city centre. In contrast to many of Manchester's trails, the surface is tarmac, meaning it is popular with commuters and can be ridden all year round without fear of getting muddy. There is a short section on a quiet street in Fallowfield. The Fallowfield Loop was previously part of the old Manchester Central Station Railway, built in the 1890s and closed in 1988. The line had lain derelict for many years until the late 1990s, when a group of cyclists started campaigning for its conversion to a traffic free greenway across south Manchester.

Starting points & parking

1. West start point. The A6010 Wilbraham Road, between Chorlton-cum-Hardy and Whalley Range, to the **south of Manchester** city centre. The trail starts on the south side of Wilbraham Road, almost opposite Morrisons supermarket and Buckingham Road (grid reference SJ 820940).

2. East start point. Fairfield railway station on Booth Road to the south of Droylsden and to the east of Manchester city centre, just off the A635 Ashton Old Road (grid reference SJ 904972). Follow Fallowfield Loop signs past the golf club entrance.

Station: Fairfield.

TIC: Manchester, 0871 222 8223.

Other nearby trails: River Mersey through south Manchester from Sale Water Park.

Useful publications & websites: OS Landranger Map 109. Ten (free) maps covering the whole of Greater Manchester are available from the relevant District Cycling Officers or can be downloaded from the website. Go to *www.cyclegm.org* for contact details. This route is on Map 8 – Manchester. See also *www.cycle-routes.org/fallowfieldloopline*

Refreshments: Lots of choice just off the trail.

Category
Railway path.

Distance
7 miles each way.

Ride 16 Salford Looplines west Manchester

16

Category
Railway path.

Distance
4$\frac{1}{2}$ miles each way from Monton to Little Hulton.

1$\frac{1}{2}$ miles each way on the spur from Roe Green to Ellenbrook.

The old railway line skirts Worsley Wood as it heads north-west from Monton Church and divides after 1$\frac{1}{2}$ miles into two separate trails: the lower arm, called the Tyldesley Loopline, goes to Ellenbrook; the upper arm, the Roe Green Loopline, to Little Hulton. The Looplines have become a valuable wildlife corridor, encouraging the free movement of plants and animals into the heart of the urban area. A variety of trees and shrubs have been planted to enhance the area for wildlife. The old railways were some of the earliest to be converted to cyclepaths in the North-West region.

Starting point & parking

Monton Green, south-east of M60, Jct 13 to the west of Manchester. Street parking by Monton Church on Stableford Avenue just north of the roundabout (grid reference SJ 765996).

On your bikes!

1. At the roundabout by Monton Church, turn right along the pavement of the B5229 (Parrin Lane) for 30yds then turn right up the tarmac ramp past a 'Monton Green' signboard onto the railway path.

2. Follow the wide track for 1$\frac{1}{2}$ miles. At the fork at Roe Green Junction you can bear left for 1$\frac{1}{2}$ miles to Ellenbrook, or bear right for 3 miles to the trail end at the M61 north of Little Hulton.

Station: Patricroft or Walkden.

TIC: Manchester, 0871 222 8223.

Other nearby trails: Irwell Sculpture Trail south of Radcliffe. River Mersey through South Manchester (Sale Water Park).

Useful publications & websites: OS Landranger Map 109. Ten (free) maps covering the whole of Greater Manchester are available from the relevant District Cycling Officers or can be downloaded from the website. Go to *www.cyclegm.org* for contact details. This route is on Map 10 – Salford. See also *www.visitsalford.info/montontrail.htm*

Refreshments: Pubs, cafés at Monton Green. Red Lion pub, Ellenbrook.

Irwell Sculpture Trail
south-west of Bury
Ride 17

The River Irwell rises high in the moors above Bacup and heads south through Bury before joining the Manchester Ship Canal. This ride follows part of the Irwell Sculpture Trail through woodland south down the Irwell Valley, passing an enormous stone monolith in the woods. The trail turns from tarmac to good-quality track to something a lot rougher, so mountain bikes are recommended. The Irwell Sculpture Trail is the largest public art scheme in the United Kingdom, featuring works commissioned by regional, national and international artists. It follows a 30-mile footpath stretching from Salford Quays through Bury into Rossendale and up to the Pennines above Bacup.

Starting point & parking

Asda supermarket, off the A665 Pilkington Way in **Radcliffe**, north-west of M60, Jct 17, north-west of Manchester. Street parking along Sion Street, a no-through-road heading west from Asda (grid reference SD 782069).

On your bikes!

1. Climb up from Asda / Sion Street on the tarmac path past metal sculptures leading to the blue metal bridge over the River Irwell.

2. Follow National Cycle Network Route 6 signs on the tarmac path past the great stone monolith. Tarmac turns to a good sandy track then a rougher track after a further mile.

3. Cross the bridge over the M60 and turn left steeply downhill.

4. At the T-junction with tarmac turn left, then after 200yds turn right towards the recycling centre (**not** through the barrier towards Prestwick Clough). Just before the recycling centre, bear left and follow this rough track to its end at the A6044 at Rainsough (grid reference SD 807021). Retrace your steps.

Station: Kearsley.

TIC: Bury, 0161 253 5111.

Other nearby trails: Salford Loop Line.

Useful publications & websites: OS Landranger Map 109. Ten (free) maps covering the whole of Greater Manchester are available from the relevant District Cycling Officers or can be downloaded from the website. Go to *www.cyclegm.org* for contact details. This route is on Map 3 – Bury. For details about the sculptures go to *www.irwellsculpturetrail. co.uk*

Refreshments: Asda café at the start.

Category
Railway path.

Distance
4$\frac{1}{2}$ miles each way.

Ride 18 Blackpool Promenade

Category
Seafront
promenade.

Distance
9 miles each way.

Blackpool is famous for its illuminations, its tower and its fairground rides. It also boasts a wonderful unbroken stretch of traffic-free promenade open to cyclists, running north from North Pier all the way to the lighthouse at Fleetwood, offering close-up views of the extraordinary variety of bright and brash sculptures along the route of the illuminations. Out to the north-west there are views towards the Isle of Walney and the Furness Peninsula in Cumbria. There are also sections of traffic-free promenade to the south but these are shorter and are linked by sections on road.

Starting points & parking

1. The cenotaph on the seafront in the centre of **Blackpool**, just to the north of North Pier, near the junction of The Promenade with Talbot Square (grid reference SD 304365).

2. The Lower Lighthouse, near North Euston Hotel, at the junction of Bold Street and The Esplanade in **Fleetwood**, to the north of Blackpool (grid reference SD 340485).

On your bikes!

It is impossible to get lost as you head north with the sea to your left. To the south of Blackpool's South Pier there are also some traffic-free coastal sections between South Pier and the windmill in Lytham St Annes, but they are linked by several sections on road, some of which are busy.

Station: Blackpool.

TIC: Blackpool, 01253 478222.

Other nearby trails: Routes through Preston.

Useful publications & websites: OS Landranger Map 102. Go to *www.visitblackpool.com*, click on 'Things To Do' then 'Activities' then 'Cycling' and you can download maps showing cycle routes around Blackpool.

Refreshments: Lots of choice all along the way. More closer to the centre of Blackpool and in Fleetwood itself.

Preston Riverside Ride 19
& Cuerden Valley Park

Preston is at the meeting point of the National Cycle Network: the Lancaster Canal forms part of Route 62 running west to Fylde, Route 6 passes through Preston on its way from Keswick to Manchester, and Route 55 goes south from Avenham Park to Wigan. Two rides are described here, both starting from the centre of Preston. One is a cigar-shaped loop along the north and south banks of the River Ribble on its way through the city. The other heads south to Cuerden Valley Park via a railway path, specially-built cyclepaths and a riverside route alongside the River Lostock down to Whittle-le-Woods, where it is possible to link to the Liverpool & Leeds Canal towpath south to Wigan.

Starting points & parking

1. Avenham Park in the centre of **Preston** (grid reference SD 537286).

2. Cuerden Valley Park car park off the A6 in Whittle-le-Woods to the south of Preston. The car park is signposted along Factory Lane, opposite Whittle Brook Pharmacy near to the church and the primary school (grid reference SD 575217).

On your bikes!

1. From Avenham Park turn right (west) alongside the River Ribble on a wide tarmac path, keeping the water to your left. Pass beneath a metal railway bridge (disused) and a stone-arched railway bridge (still in use).

2. The path joins a quiet residential road. Cross the next river bridge (with a sharp left turn after the bridge) towards the Bridge Inn, then turn left again at the end of the bridge onto Riverside Road.

3. Continue in the same direction under the active and disused railway bridges. At the footbridge turn right for the Cuerden Valley route, left for a shortcut back to the start or continue ahead for the Riverside Loop.

Riverside Loop

The path bears right away from the river. At the T-junction with a lane turn left then at a crossroads of streets go straight ahead. At the T-junction with the A6 turn left onto the shared-use pavement, cross the bridge over the river and turn left again onto Ashworth Grove. Stay close to the river to return to Avenham Park.

Category
Riverside paths and railway paths.

Distance
4-mile riverside loop in Preston.

6 miles each way on the Cuerden Valley Park ride.

4. (Cuerden Valley option.) Follow the tree-lined tarmac path south away from the river. Keep following signs for 'Cuerden Valley' and 'National Cycle Network Route 55'. There is a 1½-mile middle section on shared-use pavements and quiet streets, crossing two busy roads via a traffic island then traffic lights to arrive at the start of Cuerden Valley Park.

5. Follow the waymarked cycle route along the valley through the park to the first car park on the B5256. Turn right then left onto a continuation of the traffic-free path to Lower Kem Mill car park / Factory Lane / the A6 at Whittle-le-Woods. Retrace your steps.

Station: Preston.

TIC: Preston, 01772 253 731.

Other nearby trails: Leeds & Liverpool Canal between Preston and Wigan.

Useful publications & websites: OS Landranger Map 102. A leaflet called *Preston & South Ribble Cycle Network* is available from TICs. For Lancashire cycling maps and leaflets, visit *www.lancashire.gov.uk*, put 'Cycling' in the 'Search' box, click on 'Cycling in Lancashire – FAQs', access the 'Cycling in Lancashire Mini Site' link on the right-hand side of the page and then click the 'Maps & Leaflets' option on the left-hand side. Choose 'Preston & South Ribble'.

Refreshments: Lots of choice on the north side of Avenham Park in Preston city centre.

20

Ride **20**   # Leeds & Liverpool Canal between Preston & Wigan

Category
Canal towpath.

Distance
14 miles each way.

The long Trans Pennine Canal linking the industrial hubs of Liverpool and Leeds took 46 years to complete (1770 – 1816). Water supply was always a problem and the canal had to be closed for months on end during dry summers. Use of the canal for freight declined throughout the 20th century, with the hard winter of 1962-63 finishing off many traders. There are several sections which offer good cycling on improved towpaths. This stretch between Wigan and Whittle-le-Woods (south of Preston) connects two good lengths of towpath with a rougher middle stretch.

Starting points & parking

1. The canal towpath just to the east of **Whittle-le-Woods** (south of Preston), off the minor road between the A6 and the A674 (grid reference SD 588209).

2. The Orwell pub at Wigan Pier on the canal in the centre of **Wigan** (grid reference SD 577053).

On your bikes!

Start from the north, from Whittle-le-Woods:

1. Follow the branch of the canal to the main Leeds & Liverpool Canal and turn right.

20

2. After 1 mile go past the Botany Bay retail centre. The towpath surface is rougher for ¹/₂ mile then turns to tarmac at Bridge 78.

3. The surface is good for 3 miles to Bridge 71. Beyond here, mountain bikes are recommended.

4. Go past the Bridge pub. About 2¹/₂ miles after passing the Crawford Arms pub, at Wigan Top Lock, the canal turns right down a flight of locks.

5. The towpath improves. Go past a turn to Haigh Hall Country Park. There are a couple of road crossings as you make your way into the centre of Wigan and past the Orwell pub at Wigan Pier.

6. The good-quality towpath continues past the JJB Stadium as far as Bridge 49, about 1 mile east of the M6.

Station: Chorley, Adlington or Wigan.

TIC: Wigan, 01942 825 677.

Other nearby trails: Canal and riverside routes in Preston and Blackburn.

Useful publications & websites: OS Landranger Maps 102 & 108. For Lancashire cycling maps and leaflets visit *www.lancashire.gov.uk*, put 'Cycling' in the 'Search' box, click on 'Cycling in Lancashire – FAQs', access the 'Cycling in Lancashire Mini Site' link on the right-hand side of the page and then click the 'Maps & Leaflets' option on the left-hand side. Ten (free) maps covering the whole of Greater Manchester are available from the relevant District Cycling Officers or can be downloaded from the website. Go to *www.cyclegm.org* for contact details. Half of this route (south of Adlington) is on Map 1 – Wigan.

Refreshments: Café at Botany Bay retail centre. Fredericks Ice Cream Factory at Bridge 73. Bridge pub, Adlington. Crawford Arms pub, Red Rock Lane, Haigh. Lots of choice in Wigan.

21

Blackburn to Baxenden via the Leeds & Liverpool Canal & the Hyndburn Greenway   Ride **21**

The improved towpath of the Leeds & Liverpool Canal can be followed north-east from Feniscowles through Blackburn out into the countryside at Rishton. Here you have the option of taking an old railway path into Great Harwood, or turning south towards Accrington and joining the lovely wooded climb up the Woodnock Greenway to Baxenden. Opened in 1816, the 127-mile-long Leeds & Liverpool Canal was originally built for Bradford merchants to reach the north-west port of Liverpool, and it runs through or near some of the most significant industrial towns of the North: Liverpool, Wigan, Preston, Blackburn, Burnley, Bradford and Leeds. The canal played a major part in the development of East Lancashire, with mills springing up along its banks in much the same way as industry today congregates around motorway junctions. An early

Category
Canal towpath and railway path.

Distance
14 miles each way.

Ride 21   Blackburn to Baxenden via the Leeds & Liverpool Canal & the Hyndburn Greenway

21

use of bicycles on the canal was for the bargeman's mate to cycle ahead of the boat to set up the locks ready for the boat to go through.

Starting points & parking

1. Feniscowles, at the south-west edge of Blackburn, just off the A6062 Livesey Branch Road near its junction with the A674 Preston Old Road (grid reference SD 648253).

2. Great Harwood, north-east of Blackburn, is linked to the canal via a cyclepath that starts on the south side of the town at the junction of Alan Ramsbottam Way with Meadow Street (grid reference SD 739319).

3. The Globe Centre, Scaitliffe Street (grid reference SD 758284) in the middle of **Accrington** is close to the start of the Woodnock Greenway, climbing to Baxenden.

On your bikes!

East from Feniscowles

1. The towpath of the Leeds & Liverpool Canal is easy to follow. The good-quality surface starts at Bridge 93B in Feniscowles (to the south-west of Blackburn) and continues eastwards for 9 miles.

2. At Bridge 108 (grid reference SD 728309) you can leave the canal towpath on the short spur via the railway path to Great Harwood.

3. For Accrington, stay on the canal towpath, crossing over the M65, then at Bridge 109 (at grid reference SD 734294), south-east of Rishton, leave the towpath and follow 'Hyndburn Greenway' and 'Accrington' signs. The route uses streets through the village of Church and then the cyclepath on the south side of the railway to the Globe Centre in Accrington.

4. To join the Woodnock Greenway, keep following 'Hyndburn Greenway' signs across the causeway between the tall red metal pillars, then climb steadily for 2 miles on the railway path up through woodland to its end at a small lake popular with anglers.

Station: Blackburn.

TIC: Blackburn, 01254 688053.

Useful publications & websites: OS Landranger Map 103. For Lancashire cycling maps and leaflets visit *www.lancashire.gov.uk*, put 'Cycling' in the 'Search' box, click on 'Cycling in Lancashire – FAQs', access the 'Cycling in Lancashire Mini Site' link on the right-hand side of the page and then click the 'Maps & Leaflets' option on the left-hand side.

Refreshments: The Navigation Inn (Bridge 96A) and the Moorings pub (Bridge 99), both in Blackburn. Lots of choice in Great Harwood and Accrington.

Leeds & Liverpool Canal Ride 22
from Burnley to Barnoldswick

Three canals were built to cross the Pennines between Liverpool and Hull: the Huddersfield Narrow Canal and the Rochdale Canal took more direct lines whereas the Leeds & Liverpool – used in this route between Burnley and Barnoldswick – made the most of the gap created by the tributaries of the Rivers Aire and Calder, reaching its highest point just north of Colne. The towpath runs through the rich industrial heritage of Burnley's old mills, lining the canal. At its northern end the canal winds through lush green rolling pastures past clumps of woodland.

Starting points & parking

1. The picnic site by the Lock Stop Café just off the B6252 at the north end of **Barnoldswick** (grid reference SD 888482).

2. Barrowford Locks, north of **Nelson** (grid reference SD 863399).

3. The Pay & Display car park in the centre of **Burnley**, opposite the bus station and next to the Tesco petrol station (grid reference SD 845325).

On your bikes!

1. (Starting from the centre of Burnley.) Climb from the car park near Tesco up to the canal towpath and turn left (ie keep the canal to your right).

2. After 6 miles the canal climbs past Barrowford Locks, then after a further 1¹/₂ miles goes through Foulridge Tunnel.

3. To avoid the tunnel, climb up from the canal to join a minor lane, turn right then left through a narrow gate onto a stone track. Continue in the same direction at the road junction. At the end of Reedymoor Lane turn right (take care – this is a busier

road), then at the Hole in the Wall pub turn left downhill to rejoin the canal towpath.

4. You need to cross sides by Ouzledale Foundry on the east side of Barnoldswick.

5. It is suggested going as far as the Lock Stop Café. The good-quality towpath continues for a further mile to Bridge 159.

Category
Canal towpath.

Distance
15 miles each way.

Stations: Colne, Nelson, Brierfield and Burnley.

TIC: Burnley, 01282 664421.

Other nearby trails: The Leeds & Liverpool Canal through Blackburn. The Calder Valley Cycleway from Todmorden to Sowerby Bridge. Gisburn Forest, 10 miles north of Clitheroe.

Useful publications & websites: OS Landranger Map 103. For Lancashire cycling maps and leaflets visit *www.lancashire.gov.uk*, put 'Cycling' in the 'Search' box, click on 'Cycling in Lancashire – FAQs', access the 'Cycling in Lancashire Mini Site' link on the right-hand side of the page and then click the 'Maps & Leaflets' option on the left-hand side.

Refreshments: Hole in the Wall pub, Foulridge. Anchor Inn, Salterforth. Lock Stop Café to the north of Barnoldswick near Bridge 157 and the Greenber Field Locks is open Easter to mid-October.

Ride 23 Gisburn Forest north of Clitheroe

23

Category
Waymarked forest trails.

Distance
Bottoms Beck Purple Trail (easy) 6 miles.
'The 8' Red Trail (hard) 11 miles.

There are two waymarked trails in this small and remote forestry holding to the north of Clitheroe. The easier one (waymarked with purple arrows) has the following description on the signboard at the start: 'A trail for younger and novice riders. Includes forest roads, a mellow green-grade beck-side trail and some funky blue singletrack'. The trail crosses Stocks Reservoir, passes some remote stone farm buildings, crosses a bridge over the river at about the halfway point then, towards the end of the ride, on the singletrack section, runs over some raised planking with twists and turns and berms. Gisburn is the only Forestry Commission holding worth mentioning between Manchester and the Lake District; indeed, Gisburn Forest and Delamere Forest near to Chester are the only holdings south of Cumbria in the North-West region.

Starting point & parking

Cocklet Hill car park, on the minor road which crosses the B6478 Slaidburn to Long Preston road, 4 miles north-east of Slaidburn and 10 miles **north of Clitheroe** (grid reference SD 745551).

On your bikes!

The trails start by the signboard in the car park. You can either follow the purple arrows for the easier trail or the red arrows for the longer, harder trail.

Station: Long Preston.

TIC: Clitheroe, 01200 425566.

Other nearby trails: The River Lune Cycleways start in Lancaster.

Useful publications & websites: OS Landranger Map 103. Go to *www.forestry.gov. uk* and search 'Gisburn'. There is a trail leaflet to download.

Refreshments: None on the route. The nearest are in Slaidburn (café and pub).

The Promenade along Morecambe Bay

Ride 24

This breezy ride along Morecambe's seafront gives wide views across to the Lake District. In 1999, the Eric Morecambe statue on Morecambe's Central Promenade was unveiled by the Queen. It has since become an iconic visitor attraction. West of here, the Stone Jetty has been a major Morecambe landmark for 150 years. It has recently been lengthened and refurbished with art installations and a café. It offers uninterrupted views of the fells of the Lake District across Morecambe Bay.

Starting points & parking

1. At the V V V Health & Leisure Centre off the A5105 between **Hest Bank** and Morecambe (grid reference SD 462659).

2. At the junction of Woborrow Road and Knowlys Road, west of the A589 towards St Patrick's Chapel in **Lower Heysham** (grid reference SD 414616). Turn off the A589 at the Strawberry Gardens pub onto Knowlys Road and park about 300yds along here on the right.

On your bikes!

From the north

Simply follow the wide promenade south-west with the sea out to your right. After

4½ miles the traffic-free path ends as it swings left up and away from the coast to Woborrow Road in Heysham.

Station: Morecambe.

TIC: Morecambe, 01524 582808.

Other nearby trails: Lune Cycleways. Carnforth to Lancaster along the Lancaster Canal.

Useful publications & websites: OS Landranger Map 97. For Lancashire cycling maps and leaflets visit *www.lancashire.gov.uk*, put 'Cycling' in the 'Search' box, click on 'Cycling in Lancashire – FAQs', access the 'Cycling in Lancashire Mini Site' link on the right-hand side of the page and then click the 'Maps & Leaflets' option on the left-hand side.

Refreshments: Lots of choice in the centre of Morecambe.

Category

Seaside promenade.

Distance

5 miles each way.

NB It is easy to follow a waymarked link on a pavement cyclepath and a short stretch of quiet residential road to join the Lancaster Canal towpath, and turn left for Carnforth or right for Lancaster. There is also the option of following a railway path from central Morecambe to the Millennium Bridge over the River Lune into Lancaster.

Ride 25　Lune Cycleways
from Caton to Lancaster & Glasson Dock

Category
Railway paths and riverside paths.

Distance
11 miles each way.

The Lune Cycleways are two traffic-free rides running down the valley of the River Lune, linked by a short section on quiet roads in Lancaster. The northern trail heads south from Caton, following the River Lune and the wide bend in the river known as the Crook o' Lune through to Lancaster to link with the second trail, continuing south to the marina and the docks at Glasson with wide views over the estuary. The path to the north follows the course of the old Lancaster to Wennington railway, opened in 1850 and passing beneath the remarkable Lune Aqueduct carrying the Lancaster Canal. To the south the trail runs along the old Lancaster to Glasson Dock Railway, which ran for 60 years from 1887 to 1947.

Starting points & parking

1. Bull Beck car park, off the A683 about 4 miles north-east of Lancaster, between **Caton** and Claughton (grid reference SD 541649).

2. Lancaster city centre, on the southern side of the new Millennium Bridge (grid reference SD 473622).

3. Glasson Dock car park at the southern end of the bike path (grid reference SD 446561).

On your bikes!

1. Exit the Bull Beck car park and **WITH GREAT CARE** cross the busy A683 to the railway path opposite, and turn left.

2. Follow the trail for 4 miles into the heart of Lancaster. Pass to the left of the skateboard park and aim for the subway about 20yds to the left of the riverside path (blue and white bike sign).

3. Bear right towards the Millennium Bridge but do NOT cross the river. Turn left and follow signs for Glasson and National Cycle Network 6, staying as close as possible to the river along St George's Quay / New Quay Road. After less than 1 mile this becomes the traffic-free path to Glasson Dock.

Station: Lancaster.

TIC: Lancaster, 01524 32878.

Other nearby trails: Lancaster Canal from Carnforth to Lancaster. Morecambe Promenade. Gisburn Forest, north of Clitheroe.

Useful publications & websites: OS Landranger Maps 97 & 102. For Lancashire cycling maps and leaflets visit *www.lancashire.gov.uk*, put 'Cycling' in the 'Search' box, click on 'Cycling in Lancashire – FAQs', access the 'Cycling in Lancashire Mini Site' link on the right-hand side of the page and then click the 'Maps & Leaflets' option on the left-hand side.

Refreshments: Lots of choice in Lancaster. Pubs and cafés in Glasson Dock.

Carnforth to Lancaster Ride 26
along the Lancaster Canal

The Lancaster Canal used to run as far north as Kendal, but several sections between Carnforth and Kendal were lost when the M6 was built. This ride is all on improved towpath, much of it tarmac, running south from Carnforth through Lancaster with magnificent views across Morecambe Bay to the fells of the Lake District. At one point you cross a mighty viaduct over the River Lune, enabling you to join up with the railway path that runs below, alongside the river. The canal was built between 1792 and 1799, linking Preston in the south with Tewitfield (near Carnforth) in the north. The route was extended to Kendal in 1819 and the arm to Glasson Dock (near Lancaster) was added in 1826, creating a direct link with the sea. Remarkably, the canal was not connected to the national network until 2002 when the Ribble Link was opened, connecting via the tidal River Ribble to the Leeds & Liverpool Canal via the Rufford Branch.

Starting points & parking

1. Carnforth. Turn off the B6254 Over Kellet road by the Shovel Inn near the centre of Carnforth onto North Road. Park on this road beyond Redmayne Drive, which is on the right after about 400yds (grid reference SD 503706).

2. Parking on Aldcliffe Road on the southern edge of **Lancaster** (grid reference SD 469603).

On your bikes!

1. Carnforth – go down Redmayne Drive then shortly turn right onto Yealand Grove (a no-through-road), following bike signs. At the bridge over the canal, turn right then left to gain access to the towpath.

2. Follow the towpath for 11 miles, crossing from one side to the other at the White Cross pub in the centre of Lancaster for about ½ mile before recrossing.

3. The good-quality surface ends where the canal crosses the A588 Ashton Road, south of Lancaster, about 2 miles south of the town centre.

Category
Canal towpath.

Distance
11 miles each way.

Station: Carnforth or Lancaster.

TIC: Lancaster, 01524 32878.

Other nearby trails: Lune Valley Cycleways (Glasson Dock to Caton), Gisburn Forest. Morecambe Promenade.

Useful publications & websites: OS Landranger Map 97. For Lancashire cycling maps and leaflets visit *www.lancashire.gov.uk*, put 'Cycling' in the 'Search' box, click on 'Cycling in Lancashire – FAQs', access the 'Cycling in Lancashire Mini Site' link on the right-hand side of the page and then click the 'Maps & Leaflets' option on the left-hand side.

Refreshments: Canal Turn pub, Carnforth. Royal Hotel (2 miles south of Carnforth). Packet Boat pub (Bolton-le-Sands). White Cross pub, Water Witch pub, Lancaster.

Ride 27   Grizedale Forest
south-west of Ambleside, Lake District (6 routes)

Category
Forest trails.

Distance
Between 2 and 14 miles.

The main forestry area in the Lake District with several waymarked trails. Pick up a leaflet describing all the trails from the visitor centre and explore the woodland with all its amazing sculptures.

Starting point & parking

The Grizedale Visitor Centre is located on a minor road 4 miles south-west of Hawkshead and 10 miles south of Ambleside (grid reference SD 335944).

Route name	Distance	Grade	Waymarks
Goosey Foot Tarn	2 miles	Moderate	Blue
Grizedale Tarn	4$^{1}/_{2}$ miles	Moderate	Black
Moor Top	7 miles	Moderate	Purple
Hawkshead Moor	10$^{1}/_{2}$ miles	Demanding	Green
Silurian Way	14 miles	Demanding	Orange

Starting point for Goosey Foot Tarn

Moor Top car park, on the road towards Hawkshead (grid reference SD 343965).

Recommended ride direction: anti-clockwise

Starting point for Grizedale Tarn

Bogle Crag car park, on the road towards Satterthwaite (grid reference SD 338933).

Recommended ride direction: clockwise

Starting point for Moor Top

Grizedale Visitor Centre.

Starting point for Hawkshead Moor

Grizedale Visitor Centre, Moor Top car park (on the Hawkshead road) or High Cross car park (on the B5285 west of Hawkshead).

Recommended ride direction: clockwise

Starting point for Silurian Way

Grizedale Visitor Centre.

Recommended ride direction: clockwise

North Face Trail

There is also a 10-mile waymarked singletrack route (white arrows / red background), which is for experienced mountain bikers only.

Station: Windermere.

TIC: Windermere, 015394 46499.

Other nearby trails: Whinlatter Forest, west of Keswick, also has waymarked mountain bike trails.

Useful publications & websites: OS Landranger Map 97. Go to *www.forestry.gov. uk/grizedalehome* then click on 'Activities' then 'Cycling'.

Refreshments: Café at the visitor centre. Pub in Satterthwaite.

28

Whitehaven to Workington & Camerton

Ride **28**

The west coast of Cumbria forms a total contrast to the rest of the county. This is where there was once a great deal of heavy industry based around the high-grade deposits of iron ore. Now most of the heavy industry has gone and many of the tramways and old railways have been converted to recreational use. The ride starts with a scenic coastal section alongside the railway past red sandstone cliffs north from Whitehaven. It then climbs through Distington, drops down into Workington then climbs once again up to Camerton to the end of the traffic-free path, with fine views of the Lakeland fells.

Starting points & parking

1. Whitehaven near Tesco and the railway station (grid reference NX 975186).

2. The centre of **Workington** near the bus station (grid reference NY 004288).

3. Camerton, to the north-east of Workington (grid reference NY 037313).

On your bikes!

1. From the north end of Whitehaven's marina, follow 'National Cycle Network Route 72' signs up past the Tesco petrol station, turn left then immediately left again onto a road which becomes a track parallel to the railway line beneath the red sandstone cliffs.

2. Join Bank Yard Road then at the T-junction turn left uphill towards Lowca, then first right onto Stamford Hill. Keep following 'NCN 72' signs, rejoining the traffic-free trail by a garden nursery.

3. Descend to Workington and continue in the same direction through the town centre and over the bridge across the River Derwent, then gently up towards Camerton (following 'C2C' signs). The traffic-free trail ends just above the village.

Station: Whitehaven or Workington.

TIC: Whitehaven, 01946 598914.

Other nearby trails: Whitehaven to Rowrah. Ennerdale Water.

Useful publications & websites: OS Landranger Map 89. Sustrans Sea to Sea (C2C) map shows this and other traffic-free trails in Cumbria and Durham. Visit *www. sustrans.org.uk.* Or try *www.cyclingcumbria. co.uk*, click on 'Routes' then 'Routes in Keswick & the Western Lake District' then select 'Workington to Camerton' or 'Workington to Whitehaven'.

Refreshments: Lots of choice in Workington and Whitehaven. Pubs in each of the villages just off the trail.

Category
Railway path.

Distance
12 miles each way.

Ride 29 **Whitehaven to Rowrah West Cumbria**

29

Category
Railway path.

Distance
9 miles each way.

This is one of the starting options for the Sustrans C2C Route, the long-distance trail which crosses the Pennines and reaches the East Coast at Sunderland (or Tynemouth). The trail climbs slowly away from the Cumbrian coast at Whitehaven via Moor Row, Cleator Moor and Rowrah towards the western fells of the Lake District. If you are feeling fit you can easily link this ride via Kirkland and Croasdale to the trail alongside Ennerdale Water, taking you right into the heart of the fells. The Whitehaven to Rowrah line was built in the 1850s and passes through an area dotted with old mines and quarries, which formed the basis of West Cumbria's rapid growth through the second half of the 19th century. By 1900 the population of Cleator Moor had grown to 10,000. The villages and towns remain but the mines and quarries that created them have largely gone, leaving only old mine buildings and spoil heaps.

Starting point & parking

Whitehaven Harbour (grid reference NX 971181) or **Rowrah** (grid reference NY 055185). There are several car parks in Whitehaven and also in Rowrah.

On your bikes!

From the harbour, head south on the (busy) B5345 towards St Bees, keeping your eyes out for 'C2C' or National Cycle Network Route 71 signs on the somewhat complicated exit from town. Remember the route for your return. The route is soon waymarked with blue metal train signposts and becomes much easier to follow. Keep following signs for Rowrah. After climbing 600ft over 9 miles, the traffic-free path ends on the minor lane just south of Lamplugh Primary School (grid reference NY 063178).

Station: Corkickle on the south side of Whitehaven.

TIC: Whitehaven, 01946 598914.

Other nearby trails: Whitehaven to Workington, Ennerdale Water.

Useful publications & websites: OS Landranger Map 89. Go to *www.cyclingcumbria.co.uk*, click on 'Routes' then 'Routes in Keswick & the Western Lake District' then select 'Whitehaven Harbour to Cleator Moor' and 'Cleator Moor to Sheriff's Gate'. Alternatively, the route is shown on the Sustrans C2C map: go to *www.sustrans.org.uk*

Refreshments: Lots of choice in Whitehaven. Pubs in Cleator Moor and Rowrah.

30

Ennerdale Water Ride 30
on the west side of the Lake District

Although this is not a waymarked forestry trail as such, it nevertheless offers an attractive ride through woodland on wide stone forest roads with dramatic views over Ennerdale Water and up into the surrounding fells. Unlike most non-waymarked forest routes, it is very hard to get lost. You can either go for a there-and-back ride or form a circuit: cross the River Liza via a ford just below the Black Sail Hut Youth Hostel and follow the river on the south side as far as the eastern end of Ennerdale Water, where you recross to rejoin the outward trail. Mountain bikes are recommended.

Starting point & parking

The car park at the end of the minor road leading east then south-east from Kirkland and Croasdale, 10 miles **east of Whitehaven** (grid reference NY 110152).

On your bikes!

1. Turn left out of the car park. After just over 1 mile you come to the end of the lake. Continue up the valley, keeping the river to your right, ignoring a bridge (this is the return route).

2. Go past Low Gillerthwaite Field Centre then at Ennerdale Youth Hostel take the right-hand fork to continue along the valley, crossing a cattle grid.

3. After 1¹/₄ miles, at the next fork ('Pillar' is signposted to the right), stay on the upper, left-hand track.

4. Follow for 2 miles then at two tall green wooden 'plank' signposts, with a bridlegate and field gate ahead, bear right downhill to cross the river via the ford. (If the river is high, retrace your outward route.)

5. At a fork after 1¹/₂ miles, shortly after crossing a bridge over a side stream, bear right on the lower track.

6. Do NOT cross the bridge over the main river but stay on the left-hand side. Follow for 2¹/₂ miles then, with the lake in sight, follow the forest road round to the right to cross to the other side of the valley. Turn left at the T-junction to rejoin the outward route back to the car park.

Station: Whitehaven.

TIC: Whitehaven, 01946 598914.

Other nearby trails: Whitehaven to Rowrah, Whitehaven to Workington.

Useful publications & websites: OS Landranger Map 89. Go to *www.visitcumbria.com/wc/ennerdal.htm*

Refreshments: None on the route. The nearest is at Ennerdale Bridge.

Category
Woodland trail.

Distance
6 miles each way.

NB *There is a 500ft climb from the start to the highpoint near to Black Sail Hut Youth Hostel. The ford should be avoided if the river is high – retrace your steps on the same side of the valley.*

Ride 31 Whinlatter Forest Park west of Keswick

31

Category
Forest trail.

Distance
Quercus Trail
Blue Grade
(Moderate)
5 miles.

Altura Trail
Red Grade
(Hard)
12 miles.

There are two waymarked mountain bike routes on the steep woodland slopes of this spectacularly set Forestry Commission holding west of Keswick. If you are looking for easier forest trails, you can make up your own routes by using the wide forest roads in conjunction with the map you can buy from the visitor centre. This allows you to make sense of the waymarkers on the ground and choose the sequence of posts to visit. You could also try Grizedale Forest, south of Hawkshead, where the gradients are less severe. Open daily, the visitor centre uses films, computers and a unique working model to depict the life of a working forest. Information about activities in the forest and the work of the Education Service can be obtained from the visitor centre staff,

who will be happy to help you plan your day in the forest.

Starting point & parking

The Whinlatter Visitor Centre on the B5292 between Keswick and Cockermouth (grid reference NY 208244).

Station: Workington.

TIC: Keswick, 01768 772645.

Other nearby trails: Keswick Railway Path, Whitehaven to Workington, Ennerdale Water.

Useful publications & websites: OS Landranger Map 89. A leaflet can be purchased from Whinlatter Forest Park visitor centre. For more details of the trails go to *www.forestry.gov.uk*, search 'Whinlatter' and click on 'Whinlatter Mountain Bike Trails'.

Refreshments: Café at the visitor centre.

32

Keswick Railway Path Ride 32
Lake District

A short, delightful trail starting from the old railway station, Keswick Railway Path (near the Leisure Pool) crosses and re-crosses the scenic River Greta on its way towards Threlkeld. Here you have several options to vary your return route to Keswick by following quiet, attractive lanes – for example, via Castlerigg Stone Circle. As this is the Lake District you should be aware that these lane options will involve several steep hills. If you are searching for tougher off-road challenges, there are spectacular tracks to the north of Skiddaw or along the Old Coach Road over Matterdale Common, east of Keswick. The latter is an option on the C2C (Sea to Sea), Sustrans' most popular long-distance route on the National Cycle Network.

Starting point & parking

At the old railway station in **Keswick**, near the Leisure Pool (grid reference NY 273237). Keswick is in the northern half of the Lake District, west of M6, Jct 40.

Station: Nowhere nearby. Penrith or Workington are both 16 miles away.

TIC: Keswick, 01768 772645.

Other nearby trails: There are plenty of forest roads to explore in nearby Whinlatter Forest.

Useful publications & websites: OS Landranger Map 90. Go to *www.visitcumbria.com/kes/kesfoot.htm*

Refreshments: Lots of choice in Keswick. Pubs in Threlkeld.

Category
Railway path.

Distance
4 miles each way.

Yorkshire Trails

1 Rother Valley Country Park

2 Sheffield to Rotherham via the Five Weirs Walk

3 Wharncliffe Woods,

4 Upper Don Trail from Penistone

5 Dove Valley Trail

6 Trans Pennine Trail: Old Moor Wetlands Centre to Sprotbrough

7 Barnsley Canal

8 Spen Valley Greenway

9 Calder Valley Cycleway

10 Leeds & Liverpool Canal: Aire Valley, west of Leeds

11 Aire & Calder Navigation Towpath,

12 Harland Way, south-east of Harrogate

13 York to Riccall Cycle Path

14 York north to Overton

15 Hudson Way: Beverley to Market Weighton

16 Hull to Hornsea Trail

17 Hull to South Holderness

18 Dalby Forest

19 Scarborough to Whitby Railway Path

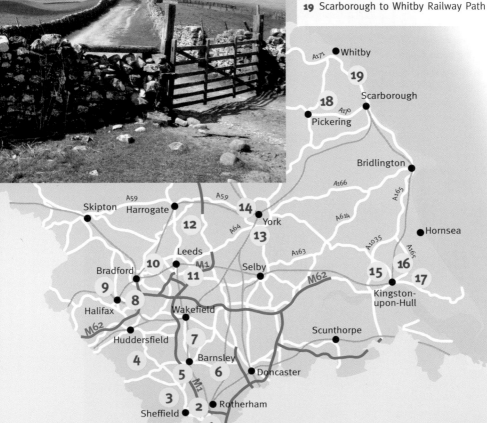

Yorkshire Mountain Biking

The region offers the aficionado some of the finest mountain biking in England, with a plethora of excellent well-drained tracks in the Yorkshire Dales and the North York Moors. There are scores of possibilities in the Yorkshire Dales right from the far north in upper Swaledale and Arkengarthdale, down through the centrally located Wensleydale (Bainbridge or Aysgarth would be good bases) to the southern tracks around Settle, Horton in Ribblesdale, Malham and Grassington. Although lying outside the National Park boundary, the hill country west from Ripon towards Nidderdale and around Pateley Bridge also offers a vast range of possibilities.

The North York Moors – although less well provided than the Yorkshire Dales with bridleways and byways – have as compensation great swathes of forestry, a drier climate and sandier soils, which tend to drain better. There are some fine ridge rides such as Rudland Rigg to the north of Kirkbymoorside and the Cleveland Way to the north of Sutton Bank Visitor Centre. Even the there-and-back ride along the Scarborough to Whitby railway path is more of a mountain bike challenge than a Sunday afternoon pootle.

Further south, well away from the two National Parks, Hebden Bridge and Todmorden would make good bases for exploring the Central Pennines to the north-west of Huddersfield.

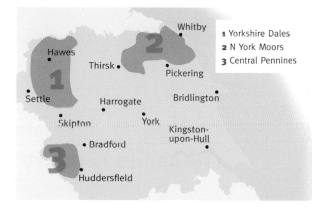

1 Yorkshire Dales
2 N York Moors
3 Central Pennines

1 Yorkshire Dales

2 North York Moors

Websites:

www.forestry.gov.uk/england-cycling and click on 'Dalby Forest' for several trails. Try also searching 'Stainburn Forest' (north of Leeds) for three short waymarked trails.

www.moredirt.co.uk and follow links from 'Trails & Tracks' to 'United Kingdom' to 'Yorkshire & Humberside'.

www.yorkshire.com/inspire/outdoors/cycling and go to 'Adventure'.

Guidebooks:

Yorkshire Dales Mountain Biking: North
Yorkshire Dales Mountain Biking: South
Both books are by Nick Cotton and feature 24 rides of varying lengths and difficulty through the beautiful scenery of the Yorkshire Dales National Park. The **North** book focuses on rides from the Howgills and Dentdale in the west to Swaledale and Arkengarthdale in the east, while the **South** book covers the area from Ingleton in the west through to Pateley Bridge and Nidderdale in the east.

Go to *www.v-graphics.co.uk* for more details of both publications.

Yorkshire Forestry

Yorkshire

07

With the exception of Wharncliffe Woods to the north-west of Sheffield, all of Yorkshire's Forestry Commission's best holdings for cycling are located to the north-east of the county, in or near the North York Moors National Park, with several large holdings to the north of Pickering. The relevant Ordnance Survey map is mentioned. It is highly recommended that you take a map for the larger woods as it is very easy to get lost. Local bike shops and the Forestry Commission website *(www.forestry.gov.uk)* may point you towards the best spots.

Forests and woods with waymarked trails

These are shown with a corresponding ride number and page reference. There are two Forestry Commission holdings with waymarked trails in the Yorkshire region:

1 **Wharncliffe Woods**, north-west of Sheffield (Ride 3, page 281)

9 **Dalby Forest**, north of Pickering in the North York Moors (Ride 18, page 301)

9 Dalby Forest

In some forests and woods there are no waymarked routes, but you are free to explore the tracks. The relevant Ordnance Survey map is mentioned. It is highly recommended that you take a map for the larger woods as it is very easy to get lost.

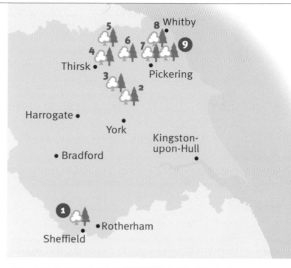

The woodlands below correspond with the numbers on the map:

2. Yearsley Moor, north-east of Easingwold (OS Explorer Map 299)

3. Woodlands along A170 east of Thirsk (Scawton & Wass Moor) (OS Explorer Map OL 26)

4. Over Silton Moor, east of Northallerton (OS Explorer Map OL 26)

5. Arncliffe Wood, north-east of Northallerton (OS Explorer Map OL 26)

6. Boltby Forest, north-east of Thirsk (OS Explorer Map OL 26)

7. Langdale, Broxa, Wykeham, Sneaton High Moor & Harwood Dale, north-east of Pickering (OS Explorer Map OL 27)

8. Cropton Forest, north of Pickering (OS Explorer Map OL 27)

It is also worth contacting the following Forest District Office for further information:

North York Moors
Outgang Road, Pickering
North Yorkshire YO18 7EL
Tel: 01751 472771
Email: enquiries.northyorkmoors@forestry.gsi.gov.uk

9 Dalby Forest

The Forestry Commission's website, *www.forestry.gov.uk,* is a good source of information. Click on 'Explore, Experience, Enjoy' then 'Cycling' and you can find out details of hundreds of waymarked trails throughout the UK. You can search by forest name or by the nearest town / city. The search will tell you the grade, length and waymarking details of the trails. Alternatively, by clicking on the map you can see the nearest forest to where you live.

Yorkshire National Cycle Network

Derby to York

154 miles from Derby to York via Nottingham, Sheffield and Doncaster. Highlights include Elvaston Castle Country Park (Derby), Bestwood Country Park (Nottingham), Newstead Abbey, the traffic-free route through Sherwood Forest and Clumber Park, Rother Valley Country Park, the Old Moor Wetland Centre and the historic city of York.

Traffic-free sections over 3 miles long:

- Derby to Elvaston Castle Country Park alongside the Derwent (NCN 6).

- Blidworth to Worksop through Sherwood Forest and Clumber Park (NCN 6).

- The Elsecar Greenway from Hoyland to the Old Moor Wetland Centre (NCN 62 & 67).

- Harlington to Bentley along the Trans Pennine Trail (NCN 62).

- Riccall to York (NCN 65).

Maps for these routes are available from www.sustrans. org.uk or 0845 113 0065.

Yorkshire Moors & Coast

Day rides and cycle touring in and around the North York Moors National Park including sections of the North Sea Cycle Route, White Rose Cycle Route, Walney to Wear & Whitby Cycle Route and the Moor to Sea Cycle Route.

Traffic-free sections over 3 miles long:

- Scarborough to Whitby Railway Path (NCN 1).

Yorkshire Wolds, York & Hull

Day rides and cycle touring in and around the Yorkshire Wolds including sections of the North Sea Cycle Route, White Rose Cycle Route and the Trans Pennine Trail.

Traffic-free sections over 3 miles long:

- South Holderness Rail Trail from Hull to Ottringham.

- Hull to Hornsea Rail Trail (NCN 65).

- Hudson Way: Beverley to Market Weighton.

- York to Riccall Railway Path (NCN 65).

- York to Overton Railway Path (NCN 65).

Trans Pennine Trail: Derbyshire & Yorkshire

215 miles from Southport to Hull via Liverpool, Manchester, Barnsley, Doncaster and Selby. Highlights in this section include the Chesterfield Canal, Rother Valley Country Park, Wharncliffe Woods, and the Aire & Calder Navigation into Leeds.

Traffic-free sections over 3 miles long:

- Chesterfield Canal north of Chesterfield (NCN 67).

- Staveley to Beighton Railway Path (NCN 67).

- Sheffield to Rotherham along the River Don (NCN 6).

- Grenoside to Penistone along the Upper Don Trail (NCN 67).

- Silkstone Common to Bolton upon Dearne along the Dove Valley Trail (NCN 62).

- Harlington to Sprotbrough along the River Dearne and the River Don (NCN 62).

- Royston to Walton along the Barnsley Canal north of Barnsley (NCN 67).

- The Aire & Calder Navigation from Woodlesford into Leeds (NCN 67).

Trans Pennine Trail:
Yorkshire to the North Sea

215 miles from Southport to Hull via Liverpool, Manchester, Barnsley, Doncaster and Selby. Highlights in this section include Cusworth Country Park (Doncaster), lanes across the Vale of York, the historic town of York, views over the River Humber, the North Sea at Hornsea.

Traffic-free sections over 3 miles long:

- Sprotbrough to Bentley (NCN 62).
- Riccall to York (NCN 65).
- The Hornsea Rail Trail from Hull to Hornsea (NCN 65).

Other good areas for lane cycling

Much of the southern half of Yorkshire is dominated by the huge conurbations of Sheffield / Rotherham and Leeds / Bradford with several other large towns such as Huddersfield, Wakefield, Barnsley and Doncaster: lots of traffic and few roads free of it. In the northern half there is an amazing choice; from the steep challenges of the Yorkshire Dales and the North York Moors to the easier, rolling countryside of the Yorkshire Wolds and the almost flat Vale of York and Holderness.

A map for this route is available from www.sustrans.org.uk *or 0845 113 0065.*

Sustrans

The Sustrans maps shown here cover various National Cycle Network routes within the region. Some of the maps may describe routes that continue into adjacent regions: these maps are mentioned in both chapters. The maps are not only useful for people wishing to ride the whole route over several days, they also show all the traffic-free sections that make good day rides.

Ride **1** **Rother Valley Country Park
south to Staveley**

Category
Reservoir circuit
within a country
park; railway path.

Distance
3-mile circuit of
the lake.

6 miles each way
from Beighton to
Staveley.

With its craft centre, exhibitions, café, plentiful wildfowl plus a variety of rides and walks, Rother Valley Country Park is an ideal place to spend the day. At the centre of the park stands an historic complex of buildings based around Bedgreave Mill, now the visitor centre. Bedgreave New Mill was built near the site of earlier mills and dates from the late 1700s. A 3-mile circuit of the two lakes may be all the cycling that you want to do, but if you are interested in a longer challenge there is a dismantled railway on the western side of the lakes that runs 6 miles south from Beighton to Staveley through a mixture of wooded cuttings and open stretches, with views out into the surrounding countryside. The ride forms part of the southern link of the Trans Pennine Trail from Barnsley through Sheffield to Chesterfield.

Starting point & parking

The **Rother Valley Country Park** Visitor Centre, 6 miles south-east of Sheffield (grid reference SK 454827). The closest motorway is M1, Jct 31.

On your bikes!

The route may be signposted as the Trans Pennine Trail, Route 6 or Route 67.

1. From the Rother Valley Country Park Visitor Centre, make your way to the lakeside and turn right (ie keep the water to your left). Pass between the two lakes and continue alongside the water.

2. You can either complete a circuit of the lake for a 3-mile ride **OR** for a link to the Trans Pennine Trail, when you reach a point opposite the Sailing Club (on the other side of the water), turn right by a metal 'National Cycle Network Route 67' sign (NCN 67) and a Rother Valley Country Park information board to pass under a railway bridge, soon turning left and following 'NCN 67' signs towards Killamarsh.

3. After almost 3 miles pass around a barrier, descend beneath power lines then bear left uphill signposted 'Chesterfield 7^1/$_2$', soon passing under the A616 road bridge.

4. At a fork of tracks after 2 miles you can either turn around or, for a 4-mile extension to the route along the

Chesterfield Canal, bear right by a low wooden post marked 'Doorstep Ride', 'Trans Pennine Trail'. Go as far as Tapton Lock Visitor Centre then turn around.

Station: Kiveton Bridge, 2 miles east of the park.

TIC: Sheffield, 0114 221 1900.

Other nearby trails: At the southern end of the Staveley to Beighton railway path you can easily link to the Chesterfield Canal.

Useful publications & websites: OS Landranger Map 120. The Trans Pennine Trail Map 2 (Central) (£4.95) shows this trail and several other traffic-free routes in the area. Go to *www.transpenninetrail.org.uk* or for the country park's website visit *www.rvcp.co.uk*.

Refreshments: Café at the visitor centre.

Rotherham to Sheffield   Ride 2
via the Five Weirs Walk

The trail runs along the course of the River Don and the Sheffield & Keadby Canal, between the centres of Rotherham and Sheffield for almost 7 miles. The route follows National Cycle Network Route 6, which also forms a spur off the main east-west Trans Pennine Trail from Hull to Southport, so you may see a mixture of signs. This route becomes more enjoyable as you do it a second and third time, as there are many turns to look out for.

Starting points & parking

1. Rotherham. The trail starts south from Rotherham Central railway station (grid reference SK 426930).

2. Sheffield. The riverside path starts on Leveson Road, off Attercliffe Road (A6178) to the north-east of the city centre where the railway bridge crosses the road and the river (grid reference SK 368883).

3. If coming from outside Sheffield or Rotherham, the best place to park is at the **Meadowhall Shopping Centre**, off the M1, Jct 34 (grid reference SK 397910).

On your bikes!

1. Exit Rotherham Central railway station and turn sharp right, keeping the river to your left. Follow Trans Pennine Trail signs. At the Law Courts follow cycle route signs for Meadowhall and Sheffield. Cross a busy

Category
Riverside path.

Distance
7 miles each way.

road onto Don Street opposite.

2. A cantilevered riverside section leads to a short overgrown stretch. With the railway line and CF Booth scrap metal merchant to the right, turn left across the bridge, follow the main track for 200yds then turn right by a 'Sheffield Bike Route' sign.

3. Follow the river / canal for 2 miles, crossing sides as necessary. Immediately after passing under a huge metal double-decker bridge, turn right following signs for the Five Weirs Walk.

4. Keep following signs for Sheffield City Centre, Five Weirs Walk and National Cycle Network Routes 6 & 67 past Meadowhall Shopping Centre and frequently alongside the River Don, on a mixture of shared pavements and riverside cyclepaths, to the end of the traffic-free section at the bridge near the junction of Leveson Street with

Attercliffe Road (A6178), to the north-east of the city centre.

Stations: Sheffield or Rotherham.

TICs: Sheffield, 0114 221 1900. Rotherham, 01709 835904.

Other nearby trails: There are trails in Wharncliffe Woods to the north-west of Sheffield. Rother Valley Country Park and the Staveley to Beighton Railway Path lie to the south-east.

Useful publications & websites: OS Landranger Map 111. More useful is the *Sheffield Cycle Map* which can be downloaded (also available in paper form) from *www.sheffield.gov.uk/roads-and-transport* and follow links to 'Cycling' and 'Cycle maps'. Scroll down to 'Downloads'. For Rotherham go to *www.rotherham.gov.uk/graphics* and search 'Cycling map'.

Refreshments: The nearest to the route are at Meadowhall Shopping Centre.

NB The Sheffield & Tinsley Canal runs parallel with this trail for much of its length. Although passable by bike, it is often very narrow and the surface is a lot rougher and occasionally overgrown.

Wharncliffe Woods Ride 3
north-west of Sheffield

There are few large Forestry Commission woodlands in the area and even fewer with waymarked trails, so Wharncliffe Wood – lying just north of Sheffield – is something of an exception. There are two trails waymarked: one described as difficult using narrow, twisting tracks; the other uses the broad forestry roads but also involves a long climb back to the start, as is inevitable with any ride that starts on top of a hill. If you are looking for a longer ride it would be quite feasible to drop down the hillside towards the bottom of the valley of the River Don on forestry tracks, and head north along the railway path that leads north and west to Penistone and Dunford Bridge all off-road and traffic-free. Further afield, to the west of Sheffield, there are some superb traffic-free trails in the Upper Derwent Valley. The Wharncliffe and Grenoside area has been extensively used by man since the Iron Age, first as a base for hunting groups then later as a source of querns or hand mills for grinding grain. This gave rise to the original name 'Querncliff'. In the medieval period, parts of the chase were enclosed as a deer park and in more recent times, much mining and quarrying has taken place for coal, ganister and fire clay in Wharncliffe, and building stone in Grenoside.

Starting point & parking

There is a car park in the woods at the top of the hill off the minor road that leads north from **Grenoside** to Wortley, about 5 miles north-west of Sheffield (grid reference SK 325950).

On your bikes!

1. From the car park go through the metal barrier and continue downhill following black and green bike route waymarks. Ignore a left turn, take the next turning to the right.

2. Ignore the next left turning, continue on to a T-junction (grid reference SK 307947), turn left* and carry on downhill.

* or for a longer route, turn right here to explore the lower part of the forest. You will need OS Landranger Map 110 to help find your way.

3. Ignore another left turn. At a major crossroads of tracks go straight ahead, then shortly follow the main track round to the left.

4. Long climb. At the T-junction turn right onto the steepest climb of the day to return to the car park / start.

Category
Waymarked forestry route.

Distance
3-mile circuit (or longer options on woodland tracks if you take a map with you). There is also a longer 10-mile Red Grade route for experienced riders (see *www.wharncliffe.info*).

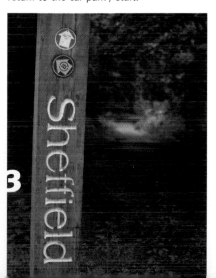

281

Ride 3 Wharncliffe Woods, north-west of Sheffield

3

Station: Sheffield.

TIC: Sheffield, 0114 221 1900.

Other nearby trails: Traffic-free sections of the Trans Pennine Trail run from Worsbrough Mill Country Park (on the A61 south of Barnsley) to Silkstone Common in the west (Dove Valley Trail) and to Bolton upon Dearne in the east (Barnsley to Old Moor Wetland Centre). The Five Weirs Walk links the centre of Sheffield

via the River Don to the centre of Rotherham. There are trails in Rother Valley Country Park to the south-east of Sheffield.

Useful publications & websites: OS Landranger Map 110. Visit *www.wharncliffe. info* or *www.mtbbritain.co.uk/wharncliffe_ woods.html*

Refreshments: In Grenoside.

Ride 4 The Upper Don Trail from Penistone east to Wharncliffe Woods or west to Dunford Bridge

4

Category
Railway path and woodland trail.

Distance
Penistone to Dunford Bridge – 6 miles each way.

Penistone to Wortley (A616) – 4¹/₂ miles each way.

The Trans Pennine Trail crosses the Pennines between Longdendale and Dunford Bridge, passing above the Woodhead Tunnels which used to carry the railway line. From Dunford Bridge down to the end of the ride at the River Don, south of Thurgoland, there is a drop of 500ft over almost 11 miles. Take into account the likelihood of the wind blowing from the west and you soon see that it is normally a lot quicker heading east downhill with the wind behind you than heading west uphill into the wind. Penistone is an attractive stone-built town with plenty of choices of refreshment. Heading west from here, the views are of dry-stone walls and sheep-grazed moorland in the Upper Don Valley. To the east of Penistone the trail is increasingly wooded as it drops height, passing through the Thurgoland Tunnel. The ride could easily be linked either to the Dove Valley Trail, by following the Trans Pennine Trail signs from Oxspring to Silkstone Common, or Wharncliffe Woods, by joining the forestry track just south of the A616.

Starting points & parking

1. Dunford Bridge, on a minor road off the B6106 about 6 miles west of Penistone (grid reference SE 159024).

2. Penistone, about 7 miles west of Barnsley on the A628 (west of M1, Jct 37). Follow signs for the free car park in Penistone, just west of the main part of the village, near to the market (grid reference SE 245034).

3. West of Wortley at the Equine Centre (grid reference SK 299994).

4. Wharncliffe Woods, north of Grenoside (grid reference SK 326950).

On your bikes!

The route is well signposted as the Trans Pennine Trail or the Upper Don Trail. From the free car park in Penistone, join the railway path and either:

1. Turn left (west) for Dunford Bridge (6 miles, gentle 300ft / 90m climb). Or

The Upper Don Trail from Penistone east to Wharncliffe Woods or west to Dunford Bridge

Ride 4

2. Turn right (east) towards Wharncliffe and Sheffield as far as the A616 (4¹/₂ miles, gentle 200ft / 60m descent). After 3 miles you will pass through the long, lit tunnel at Thurgoland, which has the most amazing echo!

Trans Pennine Trail south to Grenoside via Wharncliffe Woods

A wide, stone-based forestry track continues south from the A616 through Wharncliffe Woods for a further 5¹/₂ miles. This is a tough rollercoaster route with several short, steep climbs and one long final climb (450ft / 140m) up to the car park in Grenoside. There are also mountain bike trails in the woods (see *www.wharncliffe.info*).

Station: Penistone.

TICs: Sheffield, 0114 221 1900. Holmfirth, 01484 222444.

Other nearby trails: Waymarked trails in Wharncliffe Woods. Dove Valley Trail and the Trans Pennine Trail from Barnsley to the Old Moor Wetland Centre.

Useful publications & websites: OS Landranger Map 110. *The Trans Pennine Trail Map 1: Irish Sea – Yorkshire* (£4.95), shows this trail and several other traffic-free routes in the area. Available from *www.transpenninetrail.org.uk*

Refreshments: Lots of choice in Penistone. Pub just off the route in Oxspring.

Ride 5 Dove Valley Trail south-west of Barnsley

5

Category
Railway path.

Distance
10 miles each way.

Passing through the rolling countryside to the south of Barnsley, it is gratifying to see the enormous efforts that have been made to transform the ugly spoil heaps and wastelands of the coal-mining industry into green, wooded areas. There is a real case of nature being actively encouraged to heal over scars – and one wonders whether any present inhabitant would recognise the place in 50 years' time, when the trees have had a chance to mature and the hard edges of the massive earth-moving exercises have been softened by the growth of grass and wildflowers. The Worsbrough Bank Railway was opened in 1880 to allow large amounts of Lancashire-bound coal traffic to bypass the serious bottleneck of Barnsley. The Bank included 2^1/$_2$ miles of 1 in 40 gradient – one of the steepest gradients in the country and a severe obstacle to heavily-laden westbound coal trains. In 1952 the line was electrified, one of the first such schemes in Britain. The 142-minute journey from Wath to Dunford Bridge was whittled down to 66 minutes! The track was closed in 1981.

Starting points & parking

1. Worsbrough Mill Country Park, 3 miles north of M1 / Jct 36, along the A61 towards Barnsley. The Trans Pennine Trail crosses the A61 about 200yds north of the exit to the car park (grid reference SE 353034). There is also a small car park right on the trail itself, on the minor road west of Worsbrough towards the M1 and Hood Green (grid reference SE 344037).

2. Old Moor Wetland Centre, near the junction of the A6195 and A633 to the south-east of Barnsley (grid reference SE 423022).

On your bikes!

The route is signposted as 'Trans Pennine Trail' or 'Dove Valley Trail'. Exit Worsbrough Country Park car park and turn left along the main A61 (push your bike along the pavement for 200yds).

Route west to Silkstone Common

1. Follow 'Trans Pennine Trail West' signs, climbing gently for 4^1/$_2$ miles, crossing the M1 after 1^1/$_2$ miles. The trail runs along the

bed of the old railway as far as Silkstone Common, then on a narrower path on the top of the embankment through woodland.

2. It is suggested you turn around when you come to a T-junction with a wider, rougher stone track by a gate and a wooden seat (grid reference SE 283036). Following the Trans Pennine Trail west from here involves steep gradients, roads and some rougher tracks to link to the Upper Don Trail in Oxspring.

Route east to the Old Moor Wetland Centre

1. Follow 'Trans Pennine Trail East' signs, soon crossing the busy A61 via a toucan crossing. After 1½ miles pass beneath a railway viaduct, then keep bearing right to cross two bridges over the A633.

2. A track from Barnsley joins from the left (remember this point for your return).

3. Go past Wombwell Football Club ground. Cross into the Old Moor Wetland Reserve (there is a good café here, just off the route). Turn around here, or for a longer ride continue east to Sprotbrough.

Station: Silkstone or Wombwell.

TIC: Barnsley, 01226 206757.

Other nearby trails: The Dove Valley Trail is part of the Trans Pennine Trail that runs from Southport to Hull. To the west the trail goes on to Penistone; to the east to Doncaster, with spurs south towards Wharncliffe Woods (Sheffield) and north-west into Barnsley.

Useful publications & websites: OS Landranger Maps 110 & 111. *The Trans Pennine Trail Map 2: Derbyshire & Yorkshire* (£4.95) shows this and several other traffic-free routes in the area – available from *www. transpenninetrail.org.uk*. For a wider overview of cycling in Yorkshire, go to *www.yorkshire. com/inspire/outdoors/cycling*

Refreshments: In Silkstone, Worsbrough and Wombwell. Café at the Old Moor Wetland Visitor Centre.

NB You will probably prefer to use the pavement for 200yds from the car park at Worsbrough Mill to the point where the Trans Pennine Trail crosses the A61. Heading east, care should be taken crossing the B6100 in Worsbrough, close to the start of the ride. You should also be aware that there is a gentle 280ft (85m) descent from Silkstone Common east to the Old Moor Wetland Centre.

Ride 6 The Trans Pennine Trail from the Old Moor Wetland Centre to Sprotbrough

Category
Railway path, riverside path and newly-built cyclepath.

Distance
10 miles each way.

Continuing east along the Trans Pennine Trail from the Old Moor Wetland Centre, this ride is dominated by two rivers, the Dearne and the Don. Year by year, the trail is being improved and realigned closer to the two rivers, offering an ever more attractive route through a land reinvented and remodelled after decades of heavy industry. The ruins of Conisbrough Castle, dating back to Norman times, can be seen on the horizon from the trail. The wooded section alongside the Don from Sprotbrough to the enormous viaduct over the river is one of the loveliest on the whole of the coast-to-coast trail. The Boat Inn at Sprotbrough offers a welcome opportunity of refreshment.

Starting points & parking

1. Old Moor Wetland Centre, near the junction of the A6195 and A633 to the south-east of Barnsley (grid reference SE 423022).

2. Sprotbrough, west of Doncaster: small public car park near to the Boat Inn by the River Don on the south side of the village (grid reference SE 537015).

On your bikes!

Old Moor Wetland Centre east to Sprotbrough

1. Follow 'Trans Pennine Trail East' signs, past the lakes of the Old Moor Wetland Centre. After 1^1/$_2$ miles, at the road junction go straight ahead onto a continuation of the path.

2. After almost 1 mile, at the next road turn right to pass under the railway bridge, then immediately left signposted 'National Cycle Network Route 62'.

3. Cross a footbridge over the River Dearne, then after ¼ mile, at a crossroads of tracks, turn right. Join the road, bear left then take the first road right, signposted 'Sprotbrough 4'. Go past the Harlington Inn and as the road swings left, turn right onto Mill Lane (no-through-road) to the river. Turn left along the embankment.

4. Cross a road onto a continuation of the trail, cross a bridge over the River Dearne, climb and go past the old Earth Centre.

5. Drop down to the River Don alongside a huge brick viaduct. Turn left alongside the river for almost 2 miles to the Boat Inn at Sprotbrough.

This traffic-free section of the Trans Pennine Trail can be followed further east then north as far as Bentley, where it ends abruptly. There are also signposted links into Doncaster.

Station: Doncaster.

TIC: Doncaster, 01302 734309.

Other nearby trails: The route is part of the Trans Pennine Trail that continues west to Barnsley or along the Dove Trail and Upper Don Trail.

Useful publications & websites: OS Landranger Map 111. *The Trans Pennine Trail Map 3: Yorkshire – North Sea* (£4.95) shows this trail and several other traffic-free routes in the area – available from *www.transpenninetrail.org.uk*

Refreshments: Café at the Old Moor Wetland Visitor Centre. Harlington Inn, Harlington. Boat Inn, Sprotbrough.

Ride 7 Barnsley Canal

Category
Canal towpath.

Distance
5 miles each way.

The Trans Pennine Trail uses an attractive 4½-mile section of the disused Barnsley Canal between Wakefield and Barnsley, passing some atmospheric rock cuttings between Walton and Royston. The Barnsley Canal ran from the Aire and Calder Navigation, east of Wakefield, to Barugh, via Barnsley. It was 16 miles long with 20 locks, and had a junction near Barnsley with the Dearne & Dove Canal. The canal closed in 1953 following many problems with mining subsidence. The Barnsley, Dearne & Dove Canals Trust is seeking to re-open the canal.

Starting points & parking

1. The northern end of the trail starts just east of the New Inn on Shay Lane (B6378) in **Walton**, south-east of Wakefield (grid reference SE 357173). A footpath signposted 'Trans Pennine Trail' soon leads to the start of the canal towpath.

2. The southern end of the trail lies about 3 miles **north-east of Barnsley** on the minor road between Carlton and Shafton (grid reference SE 373102).

On your bikes!

The hardest part of the day will be finding the start of the canal. Once you have done this it can be followed for 5 miles between Walton and Royston.

1. (North to south.) The footpath joins the start of the canal towpath. Go past a golf course and clubhouse. At a fork of tracks, ignore the right turn to Anglers Country Park (unless you wish to divert off the trail for refreshments).

2. Go past Haw Park and Cold Hiendley Reservoir. Cross a road to rejoin the towpath (grid reference SE 366143).

3. After ¾ mile, at the top of a short, steep climb, turn sharp left then at the road turn right, cross the bridge over the railway and turn immediately left, signposted 'Royston, Barnsley'.

4. Cross Midland Road (B6428) in Royston, follow the canal for a further mile to its end at Shaw Lane, the minor road between Carlton and Shafton (grid reference SE 373102). Retrace your steps.

Station: Wakefield or Barnsley.

TIC: Barnsley, 01226 206757.

Other nearby trails: The Trans Pennine Trail to the south of Barnsley.

Useful publications & websites: OS Landranger Map 110. Also try *www.penninewaterways.co.uk/barnsley* or *www.transpenninetrail.org.uk*

Refreshments: New Inn, Walton. Café at Anglers Country Park about 1 mile east of the route.

Spen Valley Greenway Ride 8

A quick look at a map of the area would give you no indication of this wonderful hidden green corridor running along the course of an old railway line. It is one of those self-contained rides, floating above the urban areas and heavy industry that lie to either side. There is also a fine sense of humour evident along the course of the route, with seats shaped like bicycles, a chair made of old digger parts and 'road' signs with a whole series of prose poems, such as:

verges grassing
flowers blooming
buds appearing
blossom opening

The ride travels gently downhill from Oakenshaw past a golf course, alongside verges of willowherb, elderflower, clover and campion, seemingly over the top of Cleckheaton, Liversedge and Heckmondwike, and finishes at the riverside path along the River Calder.

Starting points

1. The junction of Green Lane with Wyke Lane to the west of **Oakenshaw** (grid reference SE 170278). Best to park in Oakenshaw and cycle up to this point.

2. Huddersfield Road (A644), 1 mile **south-west of Dewsbury** town centre (grid reference SE 231206).

On your bikes!

The hardest part will be finding your way to access the trail, whether starting from home or arriving by car. It is worth downloading the Sustrans map of the path to find out all the access points (see **Useful publications & websites**, right).

The traffic-free trail runs for 7 miles from the edge of a trading estate located north-west from Oakenshaw (grid reference SE 168287), south-east past Cleckheaton, Liversedge and Heckmondwike, to the edge of Dewsbury at the junction with the Calder & Hebble Navigation.

Station: Bradford or Dewsbury.

TIC: Bradford 01274 433678.

Other nearby trails: Calder Valley Cycleway from Todmorden to Sowerby Bridge and Brighouse.

Useful publications & websites: OS Landranger Map 104. You can download a map from *www.sustrans.org.uk*. Enter 'Spen Valley Greenway' into the search engine on the website.

Refreshments: You will need to descend from the path to access the facilities in Cleckheaton, Liversedge and Heckmondwike.

Category
Railway path.

Distance
7 miles each way.

NB There are plans to build a continuous traffic-free trail all the way west to Brighouse to link with the Calder Valley Greenway, which continues to Todmorden.

Ride 9 Calder Valley Cycleway: Todmorden – Hebden Bridge – Sowerby Bridge – Brighouse

9

Category
Canal towpath.

Distance
17 miles each way.

The Calder Valley Cycleway runs along the towpath of the Rochdale Canal alongside the River Calder from Todmorden through Sowerby Bridge to Brighouse. Attractive broadleaf woodlands rise up on the steep hillsides to the south of the valley, and many old mills can be seen on the north side. There are several cobbled sections where the river is connected to the canal, and care should be taken riding across these as they can sometimes be slippery with algae. Mountain bikes are recommended as the surface is stone rather than fine gravel or tarmac. The towpath is also popular with Canada geese and white geese. The Rochdale Canal is one of three canals that cross the Pennines. It was opened in 1804 and ran successfully for over a hundred years until competition from railway, then road, led to its demise as a commercial operation. It has been restored over the last 30 years.

Starting points & parking

1. Todmorden. The canal is accessed from between the Tourist Information Centre and the Golden Lion pub in Fielden Square on the A6033 Rochdale Road (grid reference SD 937240). There are several free car parks in Todmorden.

2. Hebden Bridge. Signs from near the Co-op on the main street through town indicate the way to the Calder Valley Cycleway alongside the canal (grid reference SD 987271).

3. Sowerby Bridge. The trail starts from the car park off Tuel Lane (close to The Wharf pub) in the centre of the town (grid reference SE 059236).

4. Brighouse. The A643 bridge (Owler Ings Road) over the canal in the centre of Brighouse (grid reference SE 145227). There are several car parks nearby.

On your bikes!

1. Todmorden. You can either access the canal towpath as described above or by following NCN Route 66 signs from the back of Market Square (near the bus station), parallel with the railway line that runs to Hebden Bridge, crossing the A646 with care and soon joining the canal.

2. Follow the canal towpath through Hebden Bridge and Mytholmroyd (take care crossing the busy A646, where the canal switches to the north side of the road). Go past the picnic tables by the distinctive tall wooden sculpture of Branwell Brontë, through a long tunnel to the car park on Tuel Lane in Sowerby Bridge.

3. To continue along the canal (the Calder & Hebble Navigation) towards Elland and

Brighouse for 6¹/₂ miles, go to the end of the car park, turn right, descend on Tuel Lane and cross with care onto the canal towpath on the other side of the main road.

4. After 2¹/₂ miles go past the canal junction at Salterhebble Locks.

5. After a further mile, the towpath crosses sides. Shortly cross the canal at the next road bridge, turn left onto Gas Works Lane then **easy to miss:** keep an eye out for an alleyway between the houses to the left to regain the towpath. Short rough section.

6. The towpath briefly crosses to the north side at Brook Foot Lock before switching back. The final canal crossing comes at Ganny Lock and the towpath ends shortly after Owler Ings Road (the A643) in the centre of Brighouse.

Station: Todmorden, Hebden Bridge, Sowerby Bridge and Brighouse.

TIC: Todmorden, 01706 818181. Hebden Bridge, 01422 843831.

Other nearby trails: The Rochdale Canal can be followed south from Todmorden all the way into Manchester. There is a real sense of adventure to climb up to the summit section – at 600ft, the highest canal in England. The Spen Valley Greenway lies to the east of Brighouse.

Useful publications & websites: OS Landranger Maps 103 & 104. *The Calder Valley Cycleway* leaflet is available from TICs. Also visit *www.calderdale.gov.uk*, click on 'Transport and streets' then 'Cycling' then 'Routes and facilities' to get to 'Calder Valley Cycleway'.

Refreshments: Lots of choice in Todmorden, Hebden Bridge, Sowerby Bridge and Brighouse.

NB There are plans to continue the trail east to join up with the network of traffic-free trails in Huddersfield and the Spen Valley Greenway between Dewsbury and Bradford.

Ride **10**   **Leeds & Liverpool Canal
along the Aire Valley, west of Leeds**

10

Category
Canal towpath.

Distance
21 miles each way.

Running west from Granary Wharf in the centre of Leeds to Shipley, Bingley and Silsden, this ride uses the improved towpath of the oldest surviving Trans Pennine waterway, exploring this green corridor west along Airedale. The canal climbs up to run along the side of the valley formed by the River Aire, with wide views across to the wooded hillside to the south. For what would appear to be a built-up urban corridor, the ride has a remarkably green and rural feel about it. The Leeds & Liverpool Canal was opened between Bingley and Shipley in 1777 and barges were soon carrying coal, chemicals, limestone and wool between Lancashire and Yorkshire. Nowadays leisure craft and anglers are the main users of the canal, although the canal corridor retains its rich industrial heritage.

Starting points & parking

1. Granary Wharf in the centre of **Leeds**, just west of the railway station (grid reference SE 293331).

2. Saltaire railway station, west of Leeds (grid reference SE 139380).

3. South-east of **Silsden**, at the start of the improved towpath (grid reference SE 051441). To get here by car and bike, turn off the A629 onto the A6034 about 3 miles north-west of Keighley. After ¹/₂ mile take the first right onto Belton Road then park near the T-junction with Hainsworth Road. Get on your bikes and turn right along Hainsworth Road to its end, turning left at the end by the farm up onto the towpath (join it by climbing the stone steps).

On your bikes!

The towpath is signposted as 'National Cycle Network Route 69' or the 'Airedale Greenway' between Silsden and Leeds. The path crosses sides frequently. The surface varies from tarmac to smooth stone and gravel to occasionally short, rougher stone sections, where water may gather in large puddles after rain. There are several minor roads to cross.

Station: Leeds, Saltaire or Silsden & Steeton.

TIC: Leeds, 0113 242 5242.

Other nearby trails: The Aire & Calder Navigation runs south-east from Leeds city centre. To the west, the next section of the Leeds & Liverpool Canal where the towpath has been improved is just south of West Marton, 8 miles west of Skipton.

Useful publications & websites: OS Landranger Map 104. *The Leeds Cycling Map* can be viewed online at *www.leeds.gov.uk*. Just type 'Cycling Map' into the search box at the top of the page. Also visit *www. leedscyclists.org.uk*

Refreshments: Lots of choice in Leeds and just off the route all the way along (especially near Shipley and Bingley). It would help to carry a street map of the area.

Aire & Calder Navigation Towpath south-east from Leeds Ride 11

An attractive, open section of canal towpath signposted as the Trans Pennine Trail, starting from the Royal Armouries Museum on Clarence Road in the gleaming new centre of Leeds and running past Thwaite's Mill Industrial Museum, south-east to Mickletown. Just before Thwaite's Mill you pass a curious stone circle with sculptures of the sun carved into the rocks. The surface of the trail varies from tarmac to fine stone-based track with the odd rougher section. The route is briefly diverted away from the canal onto roads about 1 mile east of the Armouries Museum.

Starting points & parking

1. Royal Armouries Museum on the south-east edge of the centre of **Leeds** on Clarence Road, just off the A61 Wakefield Road (grid reference SE 310330).

2. Mickletown, off the A639, about 8 miles to the south-east of Leeds (grid reference SE 394274).

On your bikes!

The route is signposted as the Trans Pennine Trail for almost 9 miles from the centre of Leeds to Station Road in Mickletown.

1. From the Royal Armouries Museum, follow the Aire & Calder Navigation south-east out of Leeds with the water to your left. The towpath soon narrows.

2. After 1 mile the trail turns right away

Category
Canal towpath.

Distance
9 miles each way.

from the canal onto Goodman Road. Turn left onto National Road then at the next roundabout, turn left again onto Old Mill Lane. Pass to the left of industrial units and cross a wooden bridge over the canal to rejoin the towpath, following signs for Methley.

3. Go past the stone circle with sun carvings then, at a Thwaite Mill sign, turn sharp right to cross the bridge then left on a continuation of the riverside path. After ¼ mile climb steep steps to cross the bridge and return to the north side of the canal.

4. Follow the towpath for 5½ miles, changing sides as necessary, passing Woodlesford Lock and some large oil storage tanks.

5. The Trans Pennine Trail turns away from the towpath at a 3-way sign by a

large stone and heads south-west on a mixture of roads and traffic-free paths to Wakefield.

Station: Leeds or Woodlesford.

TIC: Leeds, 0113 242 5242.

Other nearby trails: The Leeds & Liverpool Canal runs north-west from Leeds city centre. The Trans Pennine Trail spur continues south towards Wakefield and Barnsley, on a mixture of traffic-free paths and quiet roads / streets.

Useful publications & websites: OS Landranger Map 104. *Trans Pennine Trail Map 2 – Derbyshire & Yorkshire* shows this and several other trails in the area. Go to *www. transpenninetrail.org.uk*. The *Leeds Cycling Map* can be viewed online at *www.leeds.gov. uk*. Just type 'Cycling Map' into the search box at the top of the page. Also visit *www. leedscyclists.org.uk*

Refreshments: At either end of the ride.

Harland Way
south-east of Harrogate

Ride 12

Follow the railway path from Wetherby through gentle countryside to the village of Spofforth, with its medieval castle. Wetherby is an historic market town overlooking the River Wharfe, with a handsome stone bridge downstream from the ancient weir which once powered the town's corn mill. The town was an important staging post on the Great North Road to Scotland; one of the staging inns, The Angel, was known as 'Halfway House' because it was midway between London and Edinburgh. Spofforth Castle dates from the 14th century – it was more a large, fortified house than a castle. The railway path is constructed on part of the old Church Fenton to Harrogate line. The railway was opened in the late 19th century and was closed in 1966.

Starting point & parking

Old Station car park, Linton Road, **Wetherby**. Follow the A661 from the centre of Wetherby towards Harrogate. Bear left at first junction to Linton (grid reference SE 397484).

Station: Harrogate.

TIC: Wetherby, 01937 582151.

Other nearby trails: York to Overton and York to Riccall.

Useful publications & websites: OS Landranger Map 104. For more information about the route go to *www.yorkshire-guide.co.uk* then click on 'Wharfedale' then 'The Harland Way' in the drop-down list on the left. For more general information about cycling in Yorkshire, go to *www.yorkshire.com/inspire/outdoors/cycling*

Refreshments: Lots of choice in Wetherby. The Railway Inn in Spofforth.

Category
Railway path.

Distance
3$\frac{1}{2}$ miles each way (plus 1 mile to Spofforth Castle).

NB There is one busy road to cross (A661) to visit Spofforth village and its castle.

Ride 13 York to Riccall Cycle Path

13

Category
Railway path.

Distance
10 miles each way.

The trail links the cycle-friendly city of York with the village of Riccall in the Vale of York, running across a flat, arable landscape. It starts alongside the River Ouse in the heart of the city, goes past the racecourse, through the village of Bishopthorpe then over the swing bridge at Naburn, built to permit large vessels to go up the river as far as York. The ride uses the former East Coast main line which was threatened with subsidence by the development of the huge Selby coalfield in the 1970s. A new stretch of main line was paid for by the National Coal Board and opened in 1983. The old route was then converted to recreational use by Sustrans, one of their earliest projects. The path, waymarked as Route 65, is a spur off the main Trans Pennine Trail from Southport to Hull.

Starting points & parking

1. Ouse Bridge (railway station side) in the centre of **York** at the junction of Skeldergate and Micklegate (grid reference SE 602517).

2. Tadcaster Road (Askham Bar) Park & Ride (grid reference SE 582488).

3. Riccall village (grid reference SE 622385).

On your bikes!

The trail starts at Ouse Bridge and can be followed on the east or west side of the river towards Bishopthorpe.

1 (A). West side. Follow Skeldergate southwards, 'Bishopthorpe, Selby', then bear first left onto Terry Avenue to stay close to the river and pass beneath Skeldergate Bridge. This becomes a no-

through-road. Follow the red tarmac path as it swings away from the river.

1 (B). East side. Follow the traffic-free riverside path, cross the Millennium Bridge and turn left, soon bearing away from the river.

2. Cross Bishopthorpe Road, cross the racecourse and follow signs for Riccall and Selby. Join the railway path passing a series of sculptures representing the Solar System.

3. Follow the railway path for 7 miles to Riccall and turn around.

Station: York.

TIC: York, 01904 550099.

Other nearby trails: The York to Overton Route. There is another railway path in the centre of York (the Foss Island Railpath) which runs eastwards for 3 miles from the Wigginton Road (B1363) near to the hospitals to Osbaldwick.

Useful publications & websites: OS Landranger Map 105. York City Council produces an excellent cycle map for the city. Visit *www.york.gov.uk/transport/cycling/* to download a copy.

Refreshments: Lots of choice in York. Pubs in Bishopthorpe and Riccall.

York to Overton (and Beningbrough)   Ride 14

Forming part of National Cycle Network Route 65, this short ride starts near the heart of the beautiful walled city of York and runs parallel with the broad, slow-moving River Ouse. The ride crosses the grazed Rawcliffe Meadows – a managed 25 acres of wildflowers and birdlife. You will pass several curious sculptures: seats looking like horse-drawn carriages and farm implements, a weather vane with a bicycle and dog, and a metalwork globe with depictions of York Cathedral and the walled city. If you choose to go on to the National Trust property and tearoom at Beningbrough Hall you will need to use quiet lanes for a further 5 miles. For more details about the hall and opening times try *www.nationaltrust.org.uk* and search 'Beningbrough Hall'.

Starting point & parking

The River Ouse end of Marygate in the centre of **York**, on the other side of the river from the railway station (grid reference SE 597521). If you are coming from outside York it would be better to start from Rawcliffe Bar Park & Ride car park near the junction of the A19 with the Ring Road to the north of the city (grid reference SE 576548).

Distance
4 miles each way.

Category
Riverside path.

Station: York.

TIC: York, 01904 550099.

Other nearby trails: York to Riccall. There is another railway path in the centre of York (the Foss Island Railpath) which runs eastwards for 3 miles from the Wigginton Road (B1363) near to the hospitals to Osbaldwick.

Useful publications & websites: OS Landranger Map 105. York City Council produces an excellent cycle map for the city. Visit *www.york.gov.uk/transport/cycling* to download a copy.

Refreshments: Lots of choice in York. You may wish to carry on along Route 65 for a further 5 miles on quiet lanes to the teashop in the National Trust property at Beningbrough Hall (open spring to autumn).

14

297

Ride 15 Hudson Way from Beverley to Market Weighton north-west of Hull

Category
Railway path.

Distance
11 miles each way.

Explore the gently rolling hills of the southern Yorkshire Wolds on this railway path linking the historic towns of Beverley and Market Weighton. The undulating chalkland gives an impression of southern England. The handsome town of Beverley was the county town of the old East Riding of Yorkshire, and is famous for its magnificent minster and historic town walls. Market Weighton developed as a result of its strategic location on trade routes between the Wolds and the Vale of York. The Hudson Way is part of the old railway line that linked York to Hull from 1865 until 1965, when it was shut under the famous Beeching Axe.

Starting points & parking
1. Beverley. Car park just off the A1035 Beverley bypass to the north of the town (grid reference TA 028415).

2. Market Weighton. Old station site, north of Station Road, off St Helen's Square behind the parish church (grid reference SE 878420).

> **Station:** Beverley.
>
> **TIC:** Beverley, 01482 391672.
>
> **Other nearby trails:** At its western end it links to the Market Weighton to Bubwith Trail (Howdenshire Rail Trail). Two nearby trails start from Hull: one to Hornsea and the other to South Holderness.
>
> **Useful publications & websites:** OS Landranger Maps 106 & 107. Go to *www.wicstun.com/hudsonway.html* or for the *Beverley Cycle Map* go to *www.eastriding.gov.uk*, click on 'Tourism and Leisure' then 'Walking and Cycling' then 'Cycle lanes and routes'.
>
> **Refreshments:** Lots of choice in Beverley and Market Weighton. Café in Kiplingcotes station. Pubs just off the route in Goodmanham and Etton.

NB There is one busy road to cross – the B1248 north of Cherry Burton. Take care at this point.

Hull to Ride 16
Hornsea Trail

The trail follows the line of the old railway across the central part of Holderness from the centre of Hull via New Ellerby to the East Coast resort of Hornsea. A Hull timber merchant by the name of Joseph Wade was the driving force behind the building of the railway, which he hoped would develop Hornsea into a fashionable resort. The line opened in 1864 and ran for 101 years before being closed down in 1965. Hornsea Mere is the largest freshwater lake in Yorkshire, rich in birdlife.

Starting points & parking

1. Dansom Lane, off Clarence Street / Holderness Road (A165), just east of **Hull** city centre, and the bridge over the River Hull (grid reference TA 108300).

2. Skirlaugh picnic site, on the A165 to the south of the village (grid reference TA 153375).

3. The police station in **Hornsea** (grid reference TA 206475).

Station: Hull.

TIC: Hull. 01482 223559.

Other nearby trails: The Hull to Holderness Trail also starts from Hull.

Useful publications & websites: OS Landranger Map 107. *Hull Cycle Map* available from *www.hullcc.gov.uk* and search 'Cycle map' for download.

Refreshments: Hull and Hornsea. The Railway Inn near the old station in New Ellerby.

Category
Railway path.

Distance
13 miles each way.

NB You have to cross the A165 south of Skirlaugh. There are also roads to negotiate in Hull and Hornsea.

Ride 17 Hull to South Holderness

17

Category
Railway path.

Distance
13 miles each way.

NB *Patrington is 1 mile beyond the end of the railway path along the A1033 (take care).*

Starting close to the centre of Hull, the railway path runs to the north of the Humber Estuary through Hedon and Keyningham almost to the village of Patrington, with its magnificent church known as 'The Queen of Holderness'. Although mainly on a good gravel and grass track, there are rough sections at the eastern end. The Hull & Holderness Railway was built to serve the new coastal resort of Withernsea and opened in 1853. It was soon bringing thousands of people to the seaside, not only from Hull but from as far away as Nottingham and Newcastle. It was closed in 1965. Now lying a couple of miles inland, Hedon was an important port on the Humber in medieval times, exporting wool and cloth. It has many fine buildings including a magnificent church.

Starting points & parking

1. Southcoates Lane, **Hull**, north of Alexandra Dock and HM Prison, just off the A1033 Hedon / Withernsea Road (grid reference TA 125297).

2. Hedon, on the B1240 Sproatley road on the northern edge of the village (grid reference TA 190291).

3. The path ends at the A1033, about 1 mile to the west of **Patrington** (grid reference TA 300234).

Station: Hull.

TIC: Hull, 01482 223559.

Other nearby trails: The Hull to Hornsea Trail also starts in the centre of Hull.

Useful publications & websites: OS Landranger Map 107. *Hull Cycle Map* available from: *www.hullcc.gov.uk* and search 'Cycle map' for download.

Refreshments: Hull, Hedon, Patrington.

Dalby Forest Ride 18
north-east of Pickering (several routes)

D alby Forest has several waymarked trails ranging from easy family routes (Green and Blue) through to tough, technical challenges. There is also a bike hire centre offering mountain biking courses and tuition. The details of the trails provided by Forest Enterprise are as follows:

Green routes (Beginners / Family)

Name	Distance	Start
Ellerburn Cycle Trail	2.5 miles	Low Dalby
Adderstone Cycle Trail	7.7 miles	Dixon's Hollow

Blue route (Intermediate)

Name	Distance	Start
Blue Cycle Trail	8 miles	Low Dalby

The first ³/₄ mile of the Blue trail from the visitor centre is by far the hardest part, using steep and occasionally rooty singletrack. Once you have gained height it is a lot easier and uses wide tracks.

Red routes (Proficient)

Name	Distance	Start
Adderstone Bike Trail	3.3 miles	Dixon's Hollow
Jerry Noddle Bike Trail	3.6 miles	Crosscliff car park
Newclose Rigg Bike Trail	5.8 miles	Low Dalby
Riggs & Dales Bike Trail	8.6 miles	Low Dalby

Starting point & parking

The Dalby Forest Visitor Centre lies to the north-east of Pickering. Turn off the A170 in Thornton le Dale and follow signs (grid reference SE 856875).

Station: Scarborough.

TIC: Pickering, 01751 473791.

Other nearby trails: The Scarborough to Whitby Railway Path lies 12 miles to the east. Guisborough Forest is 25 miles to the north-west.

Useful publications & websites: OS Landranger Maps 94 & 101. A free map called *Dalby – The Great Yorkshire Forest MTB Trails* is available at the visitor centre (01751 460295). Also visit *www.forestry.gov.uk/england-cycling* and click on 'Dalby Forest'.

Refreshments: Low Dalby Visitor Centre.

Category
Waymarked forest routes.

Distance
3 – 21 miles.

NB There is quite a steep charge to enter the forest so be prepared for this. Call the visitor centre (01751 460295) for up-to-date tariffs.

Ride 19 **Scarborough to Whitby Railway Path North York Moors**

Category
Railway path.

Distance
20 miles each way.

The trail lies within the North York Moors National Park and follows a spectacular route along the North Yorkshire Heritage Coast from Scarborough via Scalby, Cloughton, Ravenscar, Robin Hood's Bay and High Hawsker to Whitby. For a railway path this is a tough route, with two long climbs on a mixture of good and rough stone tracks. Mountain bikes are recommended. The first climb of 625ft (190m) goes from Scarborough to Ravenscar, and the second of 250ft (75m) north from Robin Hood's Bay towards Whitby.

Starting points & parking

1. Sainsbury's car park in **Scarborough**, on West Parade Road, off the A64 Falsgrave Road / Westborough to the west of the railway station (grid reference TA 035882).

2. The trail can also be picked up in **Scalby** at the end of Lancaster Way (grid reference TA 017909), **Cloughton**, **Ravenscar** and **Robin Hood's Bay**.

3. Southend Gardens (grid reference NZ 894107), to the **west of Whitby town centre**, at the junction of Downdinner Hill, Bagdale and Chubb Hill Road.

On your bikes!

South to north, from Scarborough to Whitby

1. Exit the Sainsbury's car park past the children's playground. Follow signs for Whitby, passing under several bridges, past a cemetery and through a park.

2. After 2 miles cross Newby Farm Road (near Pornic Avenue). Briefly use Field Close Road and Lancaster Way, following signs for 'Scarborough to Whitby Trailway', and join the countryside section of the trail to the north-east of Scalby.

3. At the T-junction with the A165 (near Burniston), turn left then right at the toucan crossing.

4. At the next T-junction just after the old station at Cloughton, turn right then left. Go past the Hayburn Wyke Inn.

5. Climb to Ravenscar and follow the minor road for almost ½ mile. Immediately after a sharp left-hand bend, bear right at a sign for 'Robin Hood's Bay 5, Whitby 11'.

6. After almost 5 miles, follow signs carefully on the trail above Robin Hood's Bay. At the first road turn left then right.

At the next road, turn right then left along Station Road past the village hall and the doctors' surgery. At the T-junction at the end of Station Road by the Grosvenor Hotel, turn left then right following 'National Cycle Network Route 1' signs.

7. Long climb up from Robin Hood's Bay. Huge sea views. Cross the A171 via a toucan crossing.

8. The traffic-free path ends ³/₄ mile after crossing the large stone viaduct at a fork of tracks by a Millennium signpost and a red-brick school to the left behind green metal railings. Descend to the left here to Southend Gardens. If you wish to go into the heart of Whitby you will need to use busier roads.

Station: Scarborough or Whitby.

TICs: Scarborough, 01723 373333. Whitby, 01723 383637.

Other nearby trails: Waymarked forest trails in Dalby Forest, west of Scarborough.

Useful publications & websites: OS Landranger Maps 94 & 101. Visit *www.moortoseacycle.net*, which shows an 80-mile route including this trail.

Refreshments: Station Room Café, Cloughton. Hayburn Wyke Inn, north of Cloughton. Café in Ravenscar. Lots of choice in Scarborough, Robin Hood's Bay and Whitby.

ND There are two busy roads to cross – the A165 north of Scalby and the A171 near High Hawsker, south of Whitby – and several short sections on quiet roads through Robin Hood's Bay, Ravenscar and Scalby.

North-East Trails

Ride 15 South Tyne Trail

08

North-East Mountain Biking

Mountain biking on bridleways and byways in the North-East is spread fairly evenly from the North Pennines in County Durham right up to the border with Scotland, including several trails in the heart of the Cheviot Hills. Alwinton would be a good base for the Cheviots; Kielder for the many trails in Kielder Forest; Allendale is best for the tracks in the North Pennines. An interesting feature of the Ordnance Survey map covering the Cheviots is how all the bridleways are shown right up to the border with Scotland, then they stop: Scotland has a different Rights of Way system and although maps do not tell you where you have a right to ride, by using common sense you can use most tracks on the ground in Scotland unless signs tell you otherwise.

There is no substitute for intimate local knowledge – try to explore every bridleway, byway, unclassified road, canal towpath and Forestry Commission track near to home, sift out the good from the bad and link together the best off-road sections to form your own customised route(s). The best advice is to use the months from late spring to early autumn (May to October) to do the exploration, if possible after a spell of dry weather. The same track in winter can take twice as long or even be impassable.

Note down on the map (or colour-code with highlighter pen) the quality of the trail and whether it is better done in one direction or the other – it is normally better to climb on tarmac and descend off-road so that gravity can help you through any muddy bits. Where there are no books or leaflets describing mountain bike rides, the staff in bike shops can often put you In contact with local riders or clubs who may have done some of this research already, saving you many hours of trial and error. Bear in mind that everyone has a different view of what constitutes a good trail: hard or technical for some is easy for others, and a bit of mud for some is a quagmire for others!

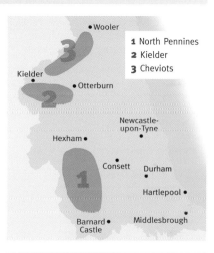

1 North Pennines
2 Kielder
3 Cheviots

Websites:

www.forestry.gov.uk – click on 'England' then click on 'Cycling and mountain biking' (under 'Explore, Experience, Enjoy') then on '1' (Kielder) for an overview of mountain biking in the forests of North East England. There are waymarked trails in Kielder, Hamsterley, Guisborough and Chopwell (south-west of Newcastle).

www.moredirt.co.uk and follow links from 'Trails & Tracks' to 'United Kingdom' to 'North East'.

http://ch.visitnortheastengland.com/mtb for details of trails in Kielder, Rothbury, Guisborough, Chopwell and Hamsterley.

North-East Forestry

The North-East has one massive forest holding at Kielder (including Wark and Redesdale), and several smaller ones lying in an arc to the south, west and north of the main centres of population around Teesside and Tyneside. To the south of Middlesbrough lies Guisborough Forest; to the south-west of Durham is Hamsterley Forest; and well to the north-west of Newcastle, up into the heart of Northumberland, there are holdings around Rothbury and into the Cheviot Hills.

Forests and woods with waymarked trails
These are shown with a corresponding ride number and page reference. There are three large Forestry Commission holdings with waymarked trails in the North-East region, and two smaller ones at Chopwell and Rothbury (see *ch.visitnortheastengland. com/mtb* for details):

1 **Guisborough Forest**, south of Middlesbrough (Ride 1, page 310)
2 **Hamsterley Forest**, south-west of Durham (Ride 4, page 313)
5 **Kielder Forest** (Ride 16, page 326)

In some forests and woods there are no waymarked routes, but you are free to explore the tracks. The relevant Ordnance Survey map is mentioned. It is highly recommended that you take a map for the larger woods as it is very easy to get lost.

The woodlands below correspond with the numbers on the map:

3. **Chopwell Wood**, south-west of Newcastle (OS Explorer Map 307)
4. **Slaley Forest,** south of Hexham (OS Explorer Map OL 43)
6. **Harwood Forest**, south of Rothbury (OS Explorer Map OL 42)
7. **Cragside Country Park**, east of Rothbury (OS Explorer Map OL 42)
8. **Harbottle Wood**, south of Alwinton, in the Cheviot Hills (OS Explorer Map OL 16)
9. **Thrunton Wood**, north of Rothbury (OS Explorer Map 322)
10. **Kidland Forest**, north of Alwinton, in the Cheviot Hills (OS Explorer Map OL 16)

It is also worth contacting the following Forest District Office for further information:

Kielder
Eals Burn, Bellingham, Hexham, Northumberland NE48 2AJ
Tel: 01434 220242
Email: enquiries.kielder@forestry.gsi.gov.uk

The Forestry Commission's website, *www. forestry.gov.uk,* is a good source of information. Click on 'Explore, Experience, Enjoy' then 'Cycling' and you can find out details of hundreds of waymarked trails throughout the UK. You can search by forest name or by the nearest town / city. The search will tell you the grade, length and waymarking details of the trails. Alternatively, by clicking on the map you can see the nearest forest to where you live.

2 Hamsterley Forest

North-East National Cycle Network

Coast & Castles Cycle Route (South)

200 miles from Newcastle to Edinburgh via Berwick-upon-Tweed, Kelso and Innerleithen. Highlights include North Tyne Cycleway to Tynemouth, the Northumbrian Coast, Warkworth Castle, Bamburgh Castle, Berwick's town walls, views of the River Tweed, Kelso town square, Floors Castle, Melrose Abbey, the Moorfoot Hills and Edinburgh.

Traffic-free sections over 3 miles long:

- North Tyne Cycleway to Tynemouth (NCN 72).
- The Innocent Railway, Edinburgh (NCN 1).

Hadrian's Cycleway

174 miles from Ravenglass on the Cumbrian coast to South Shields on the North Sea coast via Carlisle, Haltwhistle, Hexham and the Tyne Valley. Highlights include views of the Lakeland Fells, easy riding through the Solway Coast AONB, Carlisle Castle, many sections of Hadrian's Wall seen close-up, Hexham Abbey and the whole traffic-free route alongside the River Tyne beneath Newcastle's famous bridges.

Maps for these routes are available from www.sustrans. org.uk or 0845 113 0065.

Traffic-free sections over 3 miles long:

- Whitehaven to Workington Railway Path (NCN 72).
- Prudhoe to South Shields (24 miles) is almost all traffic-free (NCN 72, NCN 14 & NCN 1).

Pennine Cycleway – North Pennines

150 miles from Appleby-in-Westmorland or Penrith to Berwick-upon-Tweed. Highlights include the Eden Valley, the crossing of the Pennines, Hadrian's Wall, views of the Cheviots, Northumberland National Park, the Union Suspension Bridge and the town walls of Berwick.

Traffic-free sections over 3 miles long:

- Slaggyford to Haltwhistle (NCN 68).

Sea to Sea (C2C) Cycle Route

140 miles from Whitehaven or Workington on the West Cumbrian coast over the Pennines to Sunderland or Tynemouth on the North Sea coast. Highlights include the route through the Lake District, the riverside railway path to the east of Keswick, the crossing of the Pennines with a highpoint of 2,000ft between Nenthead and Allenheads, and the long, gentle, almost entirely traffic-free descent for the final 35 miles to Sunderland or Tynemouth.

Traffic-free sections over 3 miles long (the first three are in the North-West):

- Whitehaven to Rowrah (NCN 71).
- Whitehaven to Camerton (NCN 72).
- Keswick to Threlkeld (NCN 71).
- The Waskerley Way from Rookhope to Consett (NCN 7).
- Consett to Sunderland Railway Path (NCN 7).
- The Derwent Valley Walk from Consett to Newcastle (NCN 14).
- Newcastle to Tynemouth along Hadrian's Way (NCN 72).

Three Rivers Cycle Route

The map shows over 400 miles of signed cycle routes around the Tyne, Tees and Wear. Highlights include Newcastle's bridges, Tynemouth, North Tyne Cycleway, Derwent Walk, Consett to Sunderland Railway Path, National Glass Centre, Stadium of Light, Lanchester Valley Walk, Durham and Castle Eden Walkway Country Park.

Traffic-free sections over 3 miles long:

- Hart to Haswell Railway Path (NCN 14).
- North Tyne Cycleway (NCN 72).
- Derwent Valley Trail (NCN 14).
- Consett to Sunderland Railway Path (NCN 7).
- Lanchester Valley Walk (NCN 14).

Other good areas for lane cycling

In the southern half of the area, the best lane cycling is in the far south-west of County Durham, **around Barnard Castle** and **Upper Teesdale** or west of Corbridge in the **Tyne Valley**. Further north, once beyond Morpeth and Ashington, it is hard to go wrong: **Northumberland** is one of the least densely populated counties in England and there is a fine network of quiet lanes through big, open country. There are five busy A roads to avoid: the A1, A697, A1068, A68 and A696, but such is the network of lanes in the area that it is easy to devise routes that avoid not only these, but almost all of the B roads as well, leaving you with glorious cycling on some of the quietest lanes in the whole of England.

A map for this route is available from www.sustrans.org.uk or 0845 113 0065.

Sustrans

The Sustrans maps shown here cover various National Cycle Network routes within the region. Some of the maps may describe routes that continue into adjacent regions: these maps are mentioned in both chapters. The maps are not only useful for people wishing to ride the whole route over several days, they also show all the traffic-free sections that make good day rides.

Ride 1 **Guisborough Forest south of Middlesbrough**

Category
Railway path and forest trails.

Distance
Railway path – 3 miles each way.

Forest routes – 5 or 12 miles.

A Forestry Commission holding that stretches up the steep escarpment of the North York Moors to the south of the market town of Guisborough, once the ancient capital of Cleveland. This route combines a railway path trail with a tougher challenge in the hills. The railway path is flat with a good surface. The forest trails are steeper and rougher, and mountain bikes are recommended.

Starting point & parking

Pinchinthorpe Forest Visitor Centre, to the **west of Guisborough**, just south of the junction of the A173 with the A171 (grid reference NZ 585154). Guisborough is south-east of Middlesbrough.

On your bikes!

From Pinchinthorpe Visitor Centre, go west along the railway for 2 miles (to its junction with the existing railway) or east along the railway path and up into Guisborough Woods.

• **Blue** route (Easy / Moderate, 5 miles) – follows forest roads and grass tracks with small climbs and descents.

• **Black** route (Very Difficult / Highly Technical, 12 miles) – demanding climbs and technical singletrack descents on a combination of forest roads and grass tracks.

Station: Nunthorpe, 1 mile west of the western end of the railway path.

TIC: Guisborough, 01287 633801.

Other nearby trails: Wynyard Woodland Park (Castle Eden Walkway), north of Stockton-on-Tees. Dalby Forest lies 20 miles south-east. Scarborough to Whitby railway path.

Useful publications & websites: OS Landranger Maps 93 & 94. A map can be purchased from the Guisborough Forest Visitor Centre (01287 631132) or from the Forest Enterprise Office in Pickering (01751 472771). Also go to *www.redcar-cleveland. gov.uk* or *www.forestry.gov.uk* and search 'Guisborough Forest'.

Refreshments: None on the ride. Lots of choice in Guisborough.

Castle Eden Walkway (Wynyard Woodland Park)

Ride **2**

The Castle Eden Branch Railway ran for almost 100 years (1877 – 1968) and played an important part in the early development of Teesside. Iron and steel production required vast amounts of Weardale limestone, Durham coal and Cleveland ironstone, and the railway helped to bring these materials together. The trail rises steadily as it heads north, climbing to a highpoint of 460ft (140m) near to Station Town. Beyond here you have the option of extending the ride by linking to the Hart to Haswell Walkway near Wingate and turning east towards Hartlepool, or north to Haswell and perhaps even on to the coast, either at Ryhope or Seaham.

Starting point & parking

Wynyard Woodland Park Visitor Centre, off the A177 at Thorpe Thewles, to the **north-west of Stockton** (grid reference NZ 403244).

Station: Stockton-on-Tees.

TIC: Stockton-on-Tees, 01642 521830.

Other nearby trails: At its northern end, this trail links to the Hart to Haswell Railway Path. Guisborough Forest is south-east of Middlesbrough. There are several trails west of Durham.

Useful publications & websites: OS Landranger Map 93. For lots of background detail go to *www.wynyardwoodlandpark. org.uk*

Refreshments: Café at the Wynyard Woodland Park Visitor Centre.

Category
Railway path.

Distance
9 miles each way.

Ride 3 Hart to Haswell Walkway north of Hartlepool

Category
Railway path.

Distance
9 miles each way.

Running from Hart station on the A1086 north of Hartlepool, through Hesleden and past Shotton Colliery to Haswell, this fine railway path offers good views of the coast and the Cleveland Hills. The surface is a good gravel path from Hart to Castle Eden; beyond this point the trail is grassier and rougher – mountain bikes are recommended. There are ever more links in the network of traffic-free paths in this part of the world – for example, from South Hetton north to Seaham or Ryhope, and south from Wingate along the Wynyard Woodland Park (Castle Eden Walkway) to Stockton. Shotton Colliery was once famous for having the biggest pit heap in the UK, described by J.B. Priestley as a 'depressing smoking volcano'. The colliery was first opened in 1840, and by 1913 employed over 1,800 men producing 400,000 tons of coal. The colliery closed in 1972.

NB There are three road crossings, including the busy A181 north of Wingate.

Starting points & parking

1. Hart station, just off the A1086 between Hartlepool and Blackhall Colliery (grid reference NZ 479365).

2. South Hetton, on the A182 between Peterlee and Hetton-le-Hole (grid reference NZ 384450).

3. The trail can be followed to Ryhope, on the coast south of Sunderland (grid reference NZ 4121525) or ...

4. To Seaham (grid reference NZ 430592).

Station: Hartlepool, 4 miles south-east of Hart station.

TIC: Hartlepool, 01429 869706.

Other nearby trails: The Wynyard Woodland Park (Castle Eden Trail) links to this trail close to Wingate. The Brandon & Bishop Auckland Walk, the Auckland Way, the Deerness Valley Walk and the Lanchester Valley Walk all lie less than 10 miles to the west. The Consett to Sunderland Cycleway lies 10 miles to the north.

Useful publications & websites: OS Landranger Maps 88 & 93. This and many other traffic-free trails between Teesside and Tyneside are shown on the Sustrans *Three Rivers Cycle Route* map (£6.99), available from *www.sustrans.org.uk*. Or go to *www.durham.gov.uk* and search 'Cycle Maps'.

Refreshments: Pubs along the way in each village.

Hamsterley Forest Ride 4
south-west of Durham (4 routes)

Set in Upper Weardale, where the North Pennines meet the West Durham Moors, Hamsterley Forest covers an area of 2,000 hectares with a mixture of broadleaf and coniferous woodlands. Both the red squirrel and the roe deer are native to the forest, and there is a huge variety of birdlife. There are four waymarked trails in this popular destination. Mountain bikes are essential and there are several hills.

On your bikes!

Descriptions from the Forestry Commission website:

Grove Link Cycle Trail – 1¹/₂ miles
The Grove Link trail is ideal for families looking for a traffic-free ride along the Bedburn Valley. Weaving its way along steep hillsides, this trail gently ascends through a variety of beautiful woodlands, with majestic bridges carrying you over deep ravines.

Blue Trail – 9 miles
The surface is mainly hard and compact, although the condition of the forest roads is variable.

Red Trail – 14 miles
This trail is graded Red because it is long with a lot of hills, and is mostly at a low technical grade. It is a good trail to do if you want exercise and superb views.

Black Trail – 7 miles
This is the most strenuous and technically challenging waymarked trail in Hamsterley Forest. It sports steep technical climbs, smooth contouring singletrack and some superb rooty descents.

Starting point & parking

Hamsterley Forest Visitor Centre, 1 mile from Hamsterley Village, 15 miles south-west of Durham (grid reference NZ 092313). A toll is payable on the road from Bedburn to the visitor centre.

Station: Bishop Auckland, 9 miles to the east.

TIC: Bishop Auckland, 01388 604922.

Other nearby trails: The Auckland Walk and the Brandon and Bishop Auckland Trail start from Bishop Auckland.

Useful publications & websites: OS Landranger Map 92. A Forest Enterprise leaflet is available at the visitor centre (01388 488312) or from Kielder Forest District (01434 220242). Also visit *www.forestry. gov.uk* and search 'Hamsterley Forest'. More about mountain biking at *www.hamsterley-trailblazers.co.uk*

Refreshments: Kiosk at the visitor centre. Pub in Hamsterley Village.

Category
Waymarked forest routes.

Distance
Between 1¹/₂ and 14 miles.

Ride 5 Brandon & Bishop Auckland Walk south of Durham

Category
Railway path.

Distance
10 miles each way.

There are wonderful views over the Wear Valley on this attractive route, which was originally built to carry coal and coke for the industry in Wearside and Tyneside. It runs from the northern end of the vast Newton Cap Viaduct, just north of Bishop Auckland via Willington and Brandon, to the Broompark picnic area on the B6302, just west of Durham. It uses a gravel path, stony in places with a few gentle hills. About 3 miles north of Newton Cap there is a brief urban section through Willington. After a further 3 miles you will see Brancepeth Castle – essentially a 13th-century castle built to replace a Saxon stronghold, which was much restored in the 19th century.

Starting points & parking

1. Newton Cap Viaduct car park, just off the A689 Crook Road, on the north side of **Bishop Auckland** (grid reference NZ 204306).

2. Broompark car park **west of Durham**. From the A167 take the A690 towards Crook then turn first right on the B6302. The car park is about ³/₄ mile along this road, towards Ushaw Moor (grid reference NZ 251415).

Station: Bishop Auckland or Durham (2 miles north of the end of the route).

TIC: Durham, 0191 3843720.

Other nearby trails: The Auckland Way starts to the east of Bishop Auckland. There are links from Broompark picnic site to the Deerness Valley Walk and the Lanchester Valley Walk.

Useful publications & websites: OS Landranger Maps 88, 92 & 93. This and many other traffic-free trails between Teesside and Tyneside are shown on the Sustrans *Three Rivers Cycle Route* map (£6.99), available from *www.sustrans.org.uk*. Or go to *www.durham.gov.uk* and search 'Cycle Maps'.

Refreshments: Lots of choice in Bishop Auckland. Pubs in Hunwick, Willington and Brancepeth.

NB Take care crossing the A690 near Willington.

Auckland Walk Ride 6
south of Durham

An attractive tree-lined route with gentle gradients from Spennymoor to the outskirts of Bishop Auckland, offering fine views over the Wear Valley towards the hills of the North Pennines. Although it is a stone-based path, it is rough in places so mountain bikes are recommended. The trail passes through countryside that was once part of the Bishop's Park, as evidenced by the names of the farms along the route: 'Old Park Farm' and 'Bishop's Close', for example. Further on you pass Auckland Park, which was the Bishop's deer park and served his palace with meat, game and fish. Binchester was originally a substantial Roman Fort on Dere Street, which was built to bring supplies to the Roman armies in the north. The railway line was built in two stages. In 1841, the section between Byers Green and Spennymoor was opened as part of the Clarence Railway Company, serving Port Clarence on Teesside. This was used to carry coal from around Byers Green and Willington. In 1885, NER opened the route between Byers Green and Bishop Auckland and the whole line was then used by passengers. The line was closed in 1939.

Starting point & parking

Whitworth Road car park, near Whitworth Hall, **Spennymoor**, south of Durham (grid reference NZ 245337).

Station: Bishop Auckland.

TIC: Bishop Auckland, 01388 604922.

Other nearby trails: The Brandon to Bishop Auckland Walk starts from the north of Bishop Auckland.

Useful publications & websites: OS Landranger Map 93. This and many other traffic-free trails between Teesside and Tyneside are shown on the Sustrans *Three Rivers Cycle Route* map (£6.99), available from *www.sustrans.org.uk*. Or go to *www.durham.gov.uk* and search 'Cycle Maps'.

Refreshments: Lots of choice in Bishop Auckland.

Category
Railway path.

Distance
4 miles each way.

NB *If you choose to go from the south end of the trail into Bishop Auckland, you will need to use the busy A689 for about 1 mile.*

315

Ride 7 **Deerness Valley Walk west of Durham**

Category
Railway path.

Distance
8 miles each way.

The landscape of this area was shaped by the coal-mining industry in the 19th century, although little sign of heavy industry is left nowadays as the area has greened over. The trail runs west from Durham through Esh Winning and Waterhouses to the B6299 at Stanley Crook, crossing and re-crossing the River Deerness along a tree-lined route that reaches the edge of the Durham Dales. There is a steep climb at the Stanley Crook end of the ride. The ride uses an old railway line that was opened in 1858 and carried coal out of the valley for nearly a hundred years. The branch closed in 1951 but continued to be used one day a year for the Durham Miners' Gala.

Starting point & parking

Broompark picnic site, **west of Durham**. From the A617 take the A690 towards

Crook then turn first right on the B6302. The car park is about ³/₄ mile along this road, towards Ushaw Moor (grid reference NZ 251415).

Station: Durham Station is 2 miles from Broompark car park.

TIC: Durham, 0191 384 3720.

Other nearby trails: The Lanchester Valley Walk and the Brandon to Bishop Auckland Walk also start from Broompark car park.

Useful publications & websites: OS Landranger Maps 88 & 92. This and many other traffic-free trails between Teeside and Tyneside are shown on the Sustrans *Three Rivers Cycle Route* map (£6.99), available from *www.sustrans.org.uk*. Or go to *www. durham.gov.uk* and search 'Cycle Maps'.

Refreshments: Pubs and café in Esh Winning and Crook. Pub at Hamilton Row (west of Waterhouses).

NB If you choose to go into Durham or Crook from either end of the trail you will need to use busy roads.

Lanchester Valley Walk   Ride **8**
north-west of Durham

The trail climbs between Durham (Broompark car park) and Consett, following the River Browney to Lanchester then Backgill Burn to Hownsgill Viaduct, across predominantly arable land. Opened in 1862, the railway was built to carry iron ore to Consett Steelworks and coal from Langley Park. It was finally closed to all traffic in 1965. Located about 3 miles from the start, Langley Park has been used by film-makers to portray typical pit village life. To the left of the railway path there is a purpose-built handball wall. Handball was a popular game within the mining community. Lanchester lies on Dere Street, the Roman supply route from York to Scotland, and for centuries it has been a busy market town. The history of Consett steel-making began in 1837 when large deposits of coal and iron ore were found. They helped to transform a small village into an industrial town almost overnight. The last furnaces closed in the 1980s and now little remains of the industrial infrastructure.

Starting points & parking

1. Broompark picnic site, **west of Durham**. From the A617 take the A690 towards Crook, then turn first right on the B6302. The car park is signposted to the left (grid reference NZ 250415).

2. Langley Park (grid reference NZ 215542).

3. Lanchester (grid reference NZ 165474).

4. Hownsgill Viaduct, **south of Consett** (grid reference NZ 099494).

Station: Durham Railway Station is 2 miles from Broompark car park.

TIC: Durham, 0191 384 3720.

Other nearby trails: There are links from Broompark car park to the Deerness Valley Walk and the Brandon to Bishop Auckland Walk. From Consett you can join the Waskerley Way, the Consett to Sunderland Railway Path and the Derwent Walk.

Useful publications & websites: OS Landranger Map 88. This and many other traffic-free trails between Teesside and Tyneside are shown on the Sustrans *Three Rivers Cycle Route* map (£6.99), available from *www.sustrans.org.uk*. Or go to *www. durham.gov.uk* and search 'Cycle Maps'.

Refreshments: Lots of choice in Lanchester and Consett. Pub in Langley Park.

Category
Railway path.

Distance
12 miles each way.

317

Ride 9 **Waskerley Way south of Consett**

9

Category
Railway path.

Distance
10 miles each way.

A dramatic route that climbs 900ft (275m) from Hownsgill Viaduct, south of Consett, via Rowley and Waskerley to the Parkhead Station Café just off the B6278 at Weatherhill Summit (north of Stanhope), in the heart of the Durham Dales and with fine views across the moors and reservoirs. Mountain bikes are recommended for the stony and grassy path. The Waskerley Way mainly follows the western part of the former Stanhope & Tyne Railway, which was built in 1834 to carry limestone, lead and iron from Weardale and coal from Medomsley to the River Tyne. An old smelt wagon stands as a reminder of the nearby Consett Steel Works, which closed in 1980. The mighty Hownsgill Viaduct is made of 2¹/₂ million bricks and stands 150ft (45m) high.

Starting points & parking

1. Hownsgill Viaduct car park, signposted off the A692 **south of Consett** (grid reference NZ 099494).

2. Waskerley picnic site, south-east of Smiddy Shaw Reservoir (grid reference NZ 051454).

3. Parkhead Station Café at Weatherhill Summit on the B6278, about 3 miles **north of Stanhope** (grid reference NZ 001433).

Station: Prudhoe (to the north), Chester-le-Street or Durham (to the east), all 10-12 miles from the start, although much of this is on railway paths.

TIC: Durham, 0191 384 3720.

Other nearby trails: The trail joins three other cycle routes at Hownsgill Viaduct: the Consett to Sunderland Railway Path, the Derwent Walk and the Lanchester Valley Walk.

Useful publications & websites: OS Landranger Maps 87 & 88. This and many other traffic-free trails between Teesside and Tyneside are shown on the Sustrans *Three Rivers Cycle Route* map (£6.99), available from *www.sustrans.org.uk*. Or go to *www.durham.gov.uk* and search 'Cycle Maps'. For more information about the Sea to Sea (C2C) Cycle Route, go to *www.c2c-guide.co.uk*

Refreshments: Pubs and cafés in Consett. Parkhead Station Café at the southern end of the trail.

Consett & Sunderland Railway Path

Ride 10

The trail runs along one of Britain's oldest railways, the Stanhope & Tyne, built in 1834. The line was mainly used to carry raw materials to the Consett Steelworks and steel from Consett to the shipyards of Sunderland. When the track was lifted in 1985, Sustrans converted the path to recreational use and has since decorated the trail with many sculptures made from scrap metal and stone. There are also the famous earthwork sculptures by Andy Goldsworthy known as The Lampton Worm and The Maze. The trail runs right past the Beamish North of England Open Air Museum, which contains artefacts recovered from all over Northern England illustrating the industrial and social background of the region. Further east you pass Washington Wildfowl & Wetlands Centre (good café), then the National Glass Centre and the Stadium of Light, before arriving at Sunderland's Marina. The ride forms part of the C2C, the National Cycle Network route that runs from the Cumbrian coast to the North Sea. This may be waymarked as 'C2C' or 'National Cycle Network Route 7'.

Starting points & parking

1. Hownsgill Viaduct car park, signposted off the A692 **south of Consett** (grid reference NZ 099494).

2. The trail ends at the marina in **Sunderland** (NZ 408585).

On your bikes!

The course of the trail is as follows: Hownsgill car park off the A692 to the south of Consett via Leadgate, Annfield Plain, Stanley, Chester-le-Street and Washington to Sunderland. There is a drop of over 800ft (245m) from Consett to Sunderland, and almost all of this occurs between Annfield Plain and Washington – so plan accordingly.

Station: Chester-le-Street, Sunderland.

TIC: Sunderland, 0191 553 2000.

Other nearby trails: At Hownsgill Viaduct the trail links to the Waskerley Way, the Lanchester Valley Walk and the Derwent Valley Walk.

Useful publications & websites: OS Landranger Map 88. Sustrans' *Three Rivers Cycle Route* map (£5.99), showing this and many other traffic-free trails in the area between Middlesbrough and Newcastle, is available from Sustrans Information Service (0845 113 0065) or *www.sustrans.org.uk*. A series of maps covering the whole of Tyneside is available from *www.tyneandwearltp.co.uk*. Click 'Themes' then 'Cycling'. For more information about the Sea to Sea (C2C) Cycle Route, go to *www.c2c-guide.co.uk*

Refreshments: Lots of choice along the way.

Category
Railway path.

Distance
25 miles each way.

NB There are short road sections near Washington and in Sunderland.

Ride 11 Derwent Walk
south-west of Newcastle

11

Category
Railway path.

Distance
11 miles each way.

NB *Four busy roads are crossed and there is a short section (¹/₄ mile) on-road at Rowlands Gill.*

Running along the course of the old Derwent Valley Railway, the trail follows the River Derwent, a tributary of the Tyne, passing through meadows and broadleaf woodland as it climbs gradually south-west from Swalwell Visitor Centre (Blaydon) via Winlaton Mill, Rowlands Gill, Hamsterley and Ebchester to Hownsgill Viaduct near Consett, where there are links to several other trails. About halfway along the ride, at Pontburn and Fogoesburn viaducts, you may catch glimpses of red squirrel in the surrounding treetops. Dere Street, the old Roman Road from York to Scotland, crosses the

River Derwent at Ebchester and was once guarded by a fort (Vindomara). Shotley Bridge was once a hive of industry. In 1687, swordmakers from Solingen in Germany settled here. The swiftly flowing river provided power for the mills, local iron was available and there was plenty of timber to make charcoal for iron-smelting. The Cutlers' Hall and the Crown & Crossed Swords pub are all that remain as evidence of a once-thriving industry.

Starting points & parking

1. Swalwell Visitor Centre, beside **Blaydon Rugby Club**, signposted off the A694 and the B6317 on the east side of Blaydon, to the south of the River Tyne (grid reference NZ 197620).

2. The trail ends at Hownsgill Viaduct car park, signposted off the A692 **south of Consett** (grid reference NZ 099494).

Station: Newcastle upon Tyne.

TIC: Newcastle upon Tyne, 0191 277 8000.

Other nearby trails: From Hownsgill Viaduct car park, south of Consett, at the end of the trail, there are links to the Lanchester Valley Walk, the Waskerley Way and the Consett to Sunderland Path. From the northern (Swalwell) end the trail links to Keelman's Way, running along the south side of the Tyne.

Useful publications & websites: OS Landranger Map 88. This and many other traffic-free trails between Teesside and Tyneside are shown on the Sustrans *Three Rivers Cycle Route* map (£6.99), available from *www.sustrans.org.uk*. A series of maps covering the whole of Tyneside is available from *www.tyneandwearltp.co.uk*. Click 'Themes' then 'Cycling'.

Refreshments: Pubs in Rowlands Gill, Ebchester and Shotley Bridge.

Along the south side of the River Tyne Ride **12** from Wylam to Hebburn (Keelman's Way)

The trail runs along the south side of the Tyne from Wylam, just inside Northumberland, via Blaydon and Dunston to Gateshead and the Riverside Park in Hebburn. The route is well-signposted throughout as Keelman's Way, the South Tyne Cycleway or National Cycle Network Route 14. There are several short road sections, most notably between Blaydon and the bridge carrying the A1 over the Tyne, and then also along South Shore Road beneath the Tyne Bridge in Gateshead, but these are subject to constant improvement. As there is a traffic-free route along the north side of the river you could easily cross over then back again. If you want a shorter, completely traffic-free route, cross Newburn Bridge (4 miles east of Wylam) and return to Wylam via Hadrian's Cycleway (National Cycle Network Route 72).

Starting points & parking

1. Wylam railway station, about 10 miles west of Newcastle city centre between the A69 and the A695 (grid reference NZ 120644).

2. Hebburn Riverside Park, off Prince Consort Road on the south side of the Tyne, east of Gateshead (grid reference NZ 301647).

Station: Wylam, Blaydon, Hebburn.

TIC: Newcastle, 0191 277 8000.

Other nearby trails: The route links to the North Tyne Cycle Way (Hadrian's Cycleway) and the Derwent Valley Walk.

Useful publications & websites: OS Landranger Map 88. A series of maps covering the whole of Tyneside is available from *www.tyneandwearltp.co.uk*. Click 'Themes' then 'Cycling'.

Refreshments: All along the way.

Category
Riverside path.

Distance
14 miles each way.

Ride **13**

Hadrian's Cycleway from Prudhoe to Newcastle

13

Category
Railway path.

Distance
13 miles each way.

This section of Hadrian's Cycleway is almost entirely traffic-free and runs from Tyne Riverside Country Park Visitor Centre in Prudhoe to the Quayside, right in the heart of Newcastle upon Tyne. It could easily be followed further east along National Cycle Network Route 72 to Wallsend, North Shields and Tynemouth. One option is to catch a train from Newcastle to Prudhoe and cycle back into town with the prevailing westerly wind on your back. The path runs through Tyne Riverside Country Park past Stephenson's Cottage and along a new, wide cyclepath through Newburn Riverside. It then runs

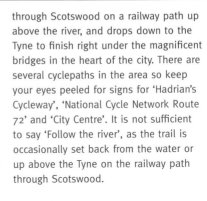

through Scotswood on a railway path up above the river, and drops down to the Tyne to finish right under the magnificent bridges in the heart of the city. There are several cyclepaths in the area so keep your eyes peeled for signs for 'Hadrian's Cycleway', 'National Cycle Network Route 72' and 'City Centre'. It is not sufficient to say 'Follow the river', as the trail is occasionally set back from the water or up above the Tyne on the railway path through Scotswood.

Starting points & parking

1. Tyne Riverside Country Park Visitor Centre in **Prudhoe**, off the A695 about 12 miles west of Newcastle (grid reference NZ 087634).

2. Newburn Leisure Centre (grid reference NZ 160656).

3. Newcastle Quayside (grid reference NZ 253637).

Station: Prudhoe, Wylam, Newcastle.

TIC: Newcastle, 0191 277 8000.

Other nearby trails: South of the Tyne, a trail runs from Wylam to Hebburn Riverside Park (west of Jarrow). You can continue along the north side of the Tyne from Newcastle city centre to Wallsend and Tynemouth on Hadrian's Cycleway. The Derwent Walk runs from near the Metro Centre south-west to Consett.

Useful publications & websites: OS Landranger Map 88. A series of maps covering the whole of Tyneside is available from *www.tyneandwearltp.co.uk*. Click 'Themes' then 'Cycling'. For more information about Hadrian's Cycleway, go to *www.hadrian-guide.co.uk* or *www.cycle-routes.org/hadrianscycleway*

Refreshments: All along the way.

Newcastle upon Tyne to Wallsend   Ride 14
along the north side of the River Tyne

This trail runs from Newcastle City Centre east to Segedunum Roman Fort, Baths & Museum in Wallsend, at the eastern end of Hadrian's Wall. Ride alongside the River Tyne then up above the river along the course of an old railway, passing the mighty cranes of the shipyards of Swan Hunter below. This trail forms part of both the Hadrian's Cycleway and the Sea to Sea (C2C) Cycle Route, each of which starts in West Cumbria and finishes at Tynemouth (or Sunderland). If you want to sample the final section of these popular trails, keep following signs for National Cycle Network Routes 1 and 72 past Royal Quays and North Shields on a mixture of streets and cyclepaths, to Tynemouth Castle and Priory at the mouth of the river.

Starting point & parking

Quayside by Tyne Bridge in the centre of **Newcastle**. Keep the river to your right and follow signs for 'C2C', 'National Cycle Network Route 72' and 'Tynemouth'. The trail takes you right to Segedunum Roman Fort, Baths & Museum off Buddle Street in Wallsend (near Wallsend Metro station).

Station: Newcastle upon Tyne.

TIC: Newcastle, 0191 277 8000.

Other nearby trails: Hadrian's Cycleway and Keelman's Way run west from the city centre on either side of the Tyne. The Derwent Walk runs from near the Metro Centre south-west to Consett.

Useful publications & websites: OS Landranger Map 88. A series of maps covering the whole of Tyneside is available from *www.tyneandwearltp.co.uk.* Click 'Themes' then 'Cycling'. For more information about Hadrian's Cycleway, go to *www.hadrian-guide.co.uk* or *www.cycle-routes.org/hadrianscycleway*

Refreshments: Lots of choice along the way.

Category
Railway path and specially-built cycle paths.

Distance
5 miles each way.

Ride 15 South Tyne Cycleway from Haltwhistle to Slaggyford

Category
Railway path with connecting road section in the middle.

Distance
10 miles each way.

The traffic-free railway path south from Haltwhistle to Slaggyford, with a diversion to visit the spectacular Lambley Viaduct, is something of a rarity in Northumberland where there are very few dismantled railways converted to recreational use. This is quite a contrast to neighbouring County Durham or the Tyne & Wear area. So, make the most of this excellent ride that climbs gently up the valley of the River South Tyne through a rolling landscape of drystone walls, pasture and copses of deciduous trees, with fine views towards the North Pennines. There is a chance of refreshment at the Wallace Arms pub at Rowfoot, either on your outward or return trip. Unfortunately, the trail is blocked at the south-west end of the Lambley Viaduct so you need to use roads – climbing and dropping down again to regain the railway path – and continue south to Slaggyford (and perhaps continue on minor lanes right into the handsome town of Alston).

Starting points & parking

1. Haltwhistle railway station (grid reference NY 705638).

2. The trail ends at **Slaggyford**, on the A689 about 5 miles north of Alston (grid reference NY 676524).

On your bikes!

1. Go out of Haltwhistle railway station, turn right then first right again, signposted 'Alston, National Cycle Network Route 68'. Cross the bridge over the river and turn right.

2. Follow this lane through a subway under the A69, then turn left through a gate onto the cyclepath parallel with and below the main road. After 1/2 mile, at the T-junction with a minor road, turn right uphill then shortly turn right again onto the start of the railway path.

3. After 2 miles go straight ahead at the first road crossing.

4. Go straight ahead at the second road crossing / car park. The Wallace Arms pub is 100yds uphill to the left.

5. At the third road crossing and car park, turn right* signposted 'NCN 68', descend to cross the bridge over the River Tyne, climb, then at the T-junction with the A689 turn left and after ¹/₂ mile turn left steeply downhill at another 'NCN 68' sign.

* It is worth going straight ahead for 1 mile to visit the spectacular Lambley Viaduct, but sadly the route is blocked at the far end. To continue south you will either need to retrace your route, or you can carry your bike down and up several sets of steps to regain the railway path.

6. At the bottom of the hill, with a red-brick house ahead, turn sharp right to rejoin the railway path and follow this for 4 miles through several gates to the end of the traffic-free section in Slaggyford.

7. If you wish to go into Alston, turn left at the end of the railway path, turn right at the junction with the A689, then after ¹/₂ mile, first left onto a minor road and keep following 'NCN 68' signs into Alston. The final mile is along the A686.

Station: Haltwhistle.

TIC: Haltwhistle, 01434 322002.

Other nearby trails: Prudhoe into Newcastle along the Tyne Valley.

Useful Publications: OS Landranger Map 87. A *South Tyne Trail* leaflet and map (£2) is available from local Tourist Information Centres or for a download go to *www. northpennines.org.uk* then search 'South Tyne Trail'. This and several other cycling options around Haltwhistle are shown on Sustrans' Hadrian's Cycleway map (£6.99), available from *www.sustrans.org.uk*

Refreshments: Lots of choice in Haltwhistle. Pubs just off the route in Rowfoot (Wallace Arms) and Knarsdale (Kirkstyle Inn). Lots of choice in Alston, about 5 miles south of the end of the trail along quiet lanes.

Ride 16 **Kielder Water & Forest Park Northumberland**

16

Category
Waymarked
forestry trails.

Distance
Up to 30 miles.

Kielder Water is the second largest man-made lake in Western Europe (the largest is Rutland Water), and Kielder Forest is the largest man-made forest in Britain, covering over 600 square kilometres. There are many waymarked routes using minor roads, forestry roads and tracks. The jewel in the crown for family cycling is the Lakeside Way, a 26-mile route around the edge of the lake. This can easily be broken up into smaller sections or you could even use the ferry for part of the journey. There are trails for all abilities and if you have done the Lakeside Way and wonder what to do next, the Castlewood Skills area gives you a taste of all the different grades of trail available in Kielder, so you can plan accordingly.

Starting point & parking

Kielder Castle Visitor Centre (grid reference NY 631933), on the minor road west from Bellingham (40 miles north-west of Newcastle upon Tyne) **OR** from Leaplish Waterside Park or Tower Knowe Visitor Centre, located along the south shore of the reservoir.

On your bikes!

There are several waymarked trails of varying length and difficulty. These are the descriptions given by the Forestry Commission:

Borderline – 7 miles
Green grade

The majority of this route follows the former Border Counties railway line, making it a relatively flat and easy ride, suitable for all abilities. The surface is mainly grassy tracks with occasional stretches on tarmac

road. The route runs parallel with the North Tyne and takes you through open countryside with fantastic views.

Lakeside Way Cycle Trail – 26 miles
Blue grade

The Lakeside Way gives access to the most scenic parts of the lake shore and the opportunity to get up close to some of Kielder's abundant wildlife. Allow plenty of time to take in the scenery and visit some of the contemporary art and architecture along the path, including the shimmering artwork known as 'Mirage' and the landmark bridge over Lewisburn inlet. It is 14 miles along the south shore from Kielder Dam to Kielder Castle Visitor Centre, passing Tower Knowe Visitor Centre and Leaplish Waterside Park. The north shore is 12 miles long (ie a total of 26 miles).

Castle Hill – 7 miles
Blue grade

This trail starts at Kielder Castle and heads up the Forest Drive. The undulating track affords views of the surrounding hills and, if you stay alert, you will catch a great view of Kielder Village.

Cross-Border Trail (Bloody Bush Trail) – 21 miles
Red grade

The Cross-Border Trail climbs up past the old Bloody Bush Toll Pillar, which is steeped in history. It is well worth stopping to read the list of fees you would have had to pay at the border. There are spectacular views of the Liddesdale Valley and the hills of the Scottish Borders. The route undulates with several long descents and links with the 7stanes bike centre at Newcastleton.

Lonesome Pine Trail – 11 miles
Red grade

The trail heads up to the top of Purdom Pike at over 1,000ft (305m), where you will be rewarded with breathtaking views of the North Tyne Valley and beyond. To help get you across the boggy terrain of Purdom Pike there is a 1,000-yd timber 'fly-over', the longest of its kind in England. From Purdom Pike the trail descends back towards Kielder Village, passing Skyspace and close to Kielder Observatory. The final stretch down Bewshaugh to the village is a thrilling, flowing descent through the forest.

Deadwater Mountain Bike Trail – 9.5 miles
Red grade

Experience one of the best singletrack trails in England, taking in the 1,900ft (580m) summit of Deadwater Fell that straddles the English / Scottish border. On a clear day it gives sensational 360° views from coast to coast. The trail plummets from the peak back down to Kielder Castle on specially constructed singletrack full of technical climbs, rock drop-offs, berms and sweeping wooden boardwalks.

Up and Over – 1.5 miles
Black grade

Gary Forrest, world-cup downhill mountain bike championship competitor, constructed this trail – which should give you an idea of the level of skill required for this route. This is a Severe-grade trail and only suitable for very experienced riders. Up and Over is accessed from the Red-grade Deadwater Trail.

Castle Wood Skills Loop

The Kielder Trail Reavers, working closely with the Forestry Commission, have built the 'Castle Wood Skills Loop' to show mountain bikers what they can expect from similar-grade trails that appear in Kielder Forest.

Station: Hexham, 20 miles to the south-east.

TIC: Bellingham, 01434 220616.

Other nearby trails: There are many waymarked cycle routes in the forest.

Useful publications & websites: OS Landranger Map 80. Leaflets are available from all the visitor centres. Also try *www.visitkielder.com/site/things-to-do (cycling / mountain biking)* or *ch.visitnortheastengland.com/mtb/trails/kielder.*

Refreshments: Café at Kielder Castle. Pub in Kielder Village.

Wales Trails

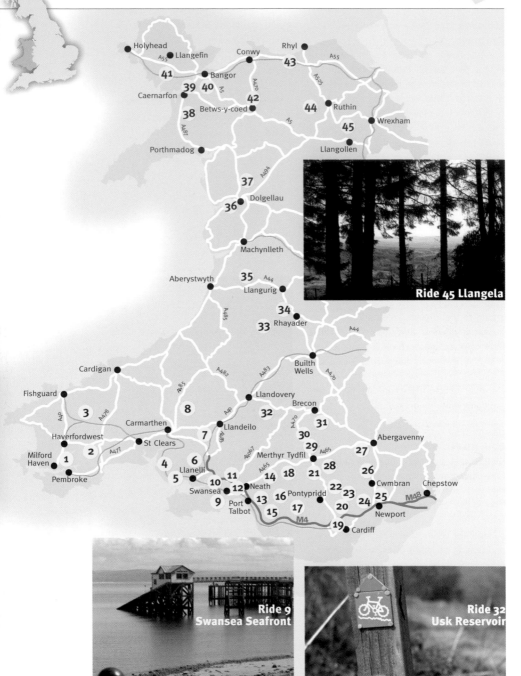

Holyhead
Llangefin
A55
41
Bangor
Caernarfon
39 40
38
A487
Porthmadog
Betws-y-coed
42
A470
A5

Conwy
Rhyl
43
A55
A55
A525
44
Ruthin
Wrexham
45
Llangollen

A5
A470

A494
37
36
Dolgellau

Machynlleth

Aberystwyth
35
A44
Llangurig
34
33
Rhayader
A485
A44

Builth
Wells
A470

Cardigan
A482
A483

Fishguard
8
Llandovery
Brecon
A40
A478
3
Carmarthen
A40
32
A470
31
Haverfordwest
7
Llandeilo
30
Abergavenny
St Clears
A48
29
Milford
Haven
2
A471
4
6
A467
Merthyr Tydfil
28
27
1
Llanelli
10 11
14 18 21
26
Pembroke
5
12 Neath
A465
22 23
Cwmbran
Chepstow
9
Swansea
13 16 Pontypridd
24 25
M48
Port
Talbot
17
20
Newport
15
M4
19
Cardiff

Ride 45 Llangela

Ride 9
Swansea Seafront

Ride 32
Usk Reservoir

328

Ride 11 Swansea Canal

Wales Mountain Biking

Wales has some of the finest mountain biking in the UK: the purpose-built singletrack Forestry Commission trails are at the cutting edge of the sport; Powys ranks as one of the best counties for the quantity and quality of byways and bridleways; there are excellent trails through the Brecon Beacons and many large Forestry Commission holdings throughout. However, the tracks and trails are not spread out evenly: with the exception of Brechfa Forest, there is very little mountain biking in the West Wales; there are no bridleways at all on Anglesey and very few on the Lleyn Peninsula. By contrast, there is a fine trail network on the Clwyd Hills, to the west of Chester, and Snowdonia has developed a successful voluntary agreement allowing mountain bikers to ride Snowdon in the early morning and early evening.

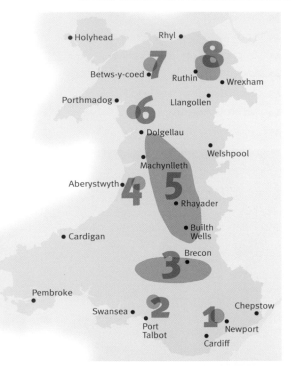

1. Cwmcarn

The Twrch Mountain Bike Trail has testing climbs, swooping descents and demanding technical sections in 9.6 miles of almost pure singletrack. The trails can be ridden all year round and vary from open and flowing hard pack to tight, technical and rooty. In places the trail hugs the sides of some very steep wooded slopes, whilst in others it sweeps along open ground with dramatic views of the Bristol Channel and the surrounding hills.

2. Afan Argoed

Twisty, rooty, rocky and in places wildly exposed, the singletrack in the Afan Valley is an enthusiast's dream. The trails have been carved out of the steep slopes transforming the valley into singletrack heaven. The Penhydd Trail takes you on an action-packed tour of the south side of the valley, with lung-bursting climbs followed by amazing singletrack descents. The Wall Trail weaves an unlikely course across the much steeper north side of the valley via superb flowing singletrack, with heart-stopping exposure and amazing views.

3. The Brecon Beacons

The best trails lie to the south of Brecon and in the Black Mountains: a challenging

6 Coed y Brenin

full-day ride south of Brecon through a pass at almost 2,000ft (600m) to the reservoirs above Merthyr Tydfil; some shorter rides around the buzzing hub of Talybont on Usk; and a series of fantastic short and long rides in the Black Mountains in the square formed by Hay-on-Wye, Talgarth, Crickhowell and Pandy.

4. Nant yr Arian

The Summit Mountain Bike Trail (10 miles) offers awesome riding on flowing, twisty singletrack. The Syfydrin Trail (22 miles) takes in the entire Summit Trail and adds to it by leading you out onto the high open hills with stunning views – it is a long and challenging ride in exposed and remote countryside, so go well prepared. The Pendam Trail (6 miles) combines sections of the Summit and Syfydrin trails to give you a taste of the fantastic riding and scenery available. Although it is the shortest route at Nant yr Arian, it includes lots of technically challenging singletrack and some hard climbs.

5. Powys

There is superb mountain biking around the Llyn Brianne Reservoir west of Llanwrtyd Wells, and from Rhayader in the Elan Valley. The border country in and around Radnor Forest offers myriad trails, and in the north there are testing challenges in the Berwyn Hills.

6. Coed y Brenin

From beautiful river valleys to wild hilltops, with forest road climbs giving way to brilliant purpose-built singletrack descents, Coed y Brenin has something to offer mountain bikers of all abilities. All the trails start and finish at the visitor centre.

7. Betws-y-Coed

The Marin Mountain Bike Trail (16 miles) is a proper mountain bike trail in every sense. Big climbs, big descents, brilliant singletrack and truly awesome scenery make this a trail to remember. Most of the climbs are on forest roads giving you time to take in views of Snowdonia. The singletrack varies from very tight, technical and rocky to wonderfully open and flowing, from dark forest to exposed ridgelines.

8. Clwyd Hills

This compact range of hills, easily accessible from Manchester and Liverpool, has a series of very satisfying loops that can be ridden singly or all linked together for a great full day out. The views out into the Vale of Clwyd are stupendous. It is one of those areas where you would do best to keep returning until you have perfected the best routes to suit your own particular requirements (see *www.ridetheclwyds.com*).

Websites:
www.forestry.gov.uk – click on 'Wales' then 'Mountain Biking'.
www.moredirt.co.uk and follow links from 'Trails & Tracks' to 'United Kingdom' then 'North Wales', 'Mid Wales' or 'South Wales'.
www.mbwales.com and choose a centre/base.
www.mtb-wales.com

5 Powys: Elan Valley

Wales Forestry

Wales has a far higher proportion of forested land than England. Ten miles either side of an imaginary north-south line from Llandudno to Porthcawl contains more forestry than all of Southern England, East Anglia and the Midlands put together. In addition, Wales has been at the forefront of developing purpose-built singletrack mountain bike trails through various of its holdings in the region. More trails are being built each year, so before visiting the forest centres it is wise to get up to date with new developments at *www.forestry.gov.uk* or *www.mbwales.com*.

In many forests and woods in Wales there are no waymarked routes, but you are free to explore the tracks. It is highly recommended that you take the relevant Ordnance Survey map and a compass for the larger woods, as it is very easy to get lost.

Forests and woods with waymarked trails

These are shown with a corresponding ride number and page reference:

1 **Canaston,** east of Haverfordwest (Ride 2, page 337)

2 **Brechfa**, north-east of Carmarthen (Ride 8, page 343)

3 **Afan Argoed & Glyncorrwg**, east of Neath (Ride 16, page 351)

4 **Cwmcarn,** north-west of Newport (*www.mbwales.com* then 'Cwmcarn')

5 **Garwnant,** north of Merthyr Tydfil (Ride 30, page 365)

6 **Nant Yr Arian**, east of Aberystwyth (Ride 35, page 370)

7 **Coed y Brenin**, north of Dolgellau (Ride 37, page 372)

8 **Gwydyr**, near Betws y Coed (Ride 42, page 378)

3 Afan Argoed

In addition to the waymarked forestry trails listed left, there are many other forestry holdings throughout Wales where it would be possible to devise your own routes on the forestry roads. There are far too many to mention them all individually. In order to find out more exact locations, look at the most recent edition of the relevant Ordnance Survey 1:50,000 Landranger Map: any of the forest areas shaded green, which also have a thin purple border around the edge, are owned by the Forestry Commission and you are allowed to ride there (forestry works permitting).

The Forestry Commission's website, *www. forestry.gov.uk*, is a good source of information. Click on 'Explore, Experience, Enjoy' then 'Cycling' and you can find out details of hundreds of waymarked trails throughout the UK. You can search by forest name or by the nearest town / city. The search will tell you the grade, length and waymarking details of the trails. Alternatively, by clicking on the map you can see the nearest forest to where you live.

It is also worth contacting the following Forest District Offices for further information:

Coed y Mynydd
(Mid & North-west Wales)
Government Buildings
Arran Road, Dolgellau
Gwynedd LL40 1LW
Tel: 0300 068 0300
Email: fcwenquiries@forestry.gsi.gov

Coed y Gororau
(Mid & North-east Wales)
Powells Place
Powells Lane
Welshpool, Powys SY21 7JY
Tel: 0300 068 0300
Email: fcwenquiries@forestry.gsi.gov

Llanymddyfri
(Mid & West Wales)
Llanfair Road
Llandovery
Carmarthenshire SA20 0AL
Tel: 0300 068 0300
Email: fcwenquiries@forestry.gsi.gov

Coed y Cymoedd
(South Wales)
Resolven, Neath SA11 4DR
Tel: 0300 068 0300
Email: fcwenquiries@forestry.gsi.gov

2 Brechfa

6 Nant yr Arian

Wales National Cycle Network

Maps for these routes are available from www.sustrans. org.uk or 0845 113 0065.

Lôn Las Cymru
(two maps: North and South)

250 miles from Holyhead to Cardiff via Caernarfon, Dolgellau, Machynlleth, Builth Wells, Brecon and Merthyr Tydfil. Highlights include the lanes across Anglesey, Caernarfon Castle, the traffic-free paths near Caernarfon, Harlech Castle, Coed y Brenin Forest, the Mawddach Trail (Dolgellau), the Centre for Alternative Technology, the Upper Wye Valley, the Brecon Beacons, the Taff Trail and Chepstow Castle.

Traffic-free sections over 3 miles long:

- Lôn Las Menai from Y Felinheli to Caernarfon (NCN 8).
- Lôn Eifion from Caernarfon to Bryncir (NCN 8).
- Mawddach Trail from Barmouth to Dolgellau (NCN 8).
- The Taff Trail south of Talybont on Usk to Cardiff (NCN 8).

A map for this route is available from www. sustrans.org. uk or 0845 113 0065.

Lôn Teifi and Lôn Cambria

This map covers two routes that can be linked to form a 183-mile ride running north-east from Fishguard on the Pembrokeshire coast to Shrewsbury.

Lôn Teifi (National Cycle Network Route 82) runs for 100 miles between Fishguard and Aberystwyth via Cardigan, Newcastle Emlyn, Lampeter and Tregaron. Highlights include the magical wooded Gwaun Valley east of Fishguard, Cilgerran Castle near Cardigan, the route through the Teifi Valley and the Cors Caron Nature Reserve north of Tregaron.

Lôn Cambria (National Cycle Network Route 81) runs for 113 miles from Aberystwyth to Shrewsbury via the spectacular Rhayader mountain road, the

Elan Valley Reservoirs, Rhayader, Llanidloes, Newtown and Welshpool. Highlights include the Ystwyth Valley, the traffic-free route past the Elan Reservoirs, the upper Wye Valley, the handsome town of Llanidloes and the fine old buildings in the heart of Shrewsbury.

Traffic-free sections over 3 miles long:

- Ystwyth Trail south-east of Aberystwyth (NCN 81/82).
- Elan Valley Trail west of Rhayader (NCN 81).

Celtic Trail (two maps: West and East*)

140 miles from Fishguard to Chepstow with several route alternatives. Highlights include the Pembrokeshire coast, St David's, the Brunel Cycle Trail (Pembroke), Tenby, the Llanelli Millennium Coastal Path, the Swansea Seafront Promenade, the Neath to Pontypridd High Level Route, Margam Country Park, the traffic-free route from Trelewis to Newport along railway paths and canal towpaths, and Chepstow Castle.

Traffic-free sections over 3 miles long:

- Brunel Cycle Trail from Neyland to Johnston (NCN 4).
- Llanelli Millennium Coastal Path (NCN 4).
- Swiss Valley Route from Llanelli to Tumble (NCN 47).
- Clyne Valley Country Park from Swansea to Gowerton (NCN 4).
- Swansea Seafront Promenade (NCN 4).
- Neath to Pontypridd High Level Route (NCN 47).
- Pyle to Tondu railway path (NCN 4).
- Trelewis to Newport via Sirhowy and Crosskeys (NCN 47).

** **The Celtic Trail – East** map shows many other traffic-free routes which lie close to but not actually on the course of the Celtic Trail. These trails tend to run alongside canals and up old mining valleys.*

Other good areas for lane cycling

With the exception of a dozen busy A roads and the densely populated, built-up triangle of South Wales between Llanelli, Abergavenny and Newport, the problem you will find in devising cycle rides in Wales is not avoiding the traffic but avoiding the hills! The island of **Anglesey** is the only large area in all of Wales where you will find a fine network of easy cycling. Elsewhere it is a case of the odd easy road along a valley, but more frequently a mix of steep climbs, fine views and thrilling descents. Some of the **attractive towns in Mid-Wales** such as Dolgellau, Machynlleth, Llanidloes, Rhayader, Presteigne, Hay-on-Wye, Brecon or Llandovery would make excellent bases for a weekend or longer.

Try also *www.cycling.visitwales.com*

Maps for these routes are available from www.sustrans. org.uk or 0845 113 0065.

Sustrans

The Sustrans maps shown here cover various National Cycle Network routes within the region. Some of the maps may describe routes that continue into adjacent regions: these maps are mentioned in both chapters. The maps are not only useful for people wishing to ride the whole route over several days, they also show all the traffic-free sections that make good day rides.

Ride 1 Brunel Trail
from Neyland to Haverfordwest

Category
Railway path and
purpose-built
cyclepath.

Distance
8 miles each way.

This ride is a gentle climb from the array of colourful yachts at Neyland Marina (north of Pembroke), up through the attractive broadleaf woodland of Westfield Pill Nature Reserve alongside the Daugleddau estuary, to Johnston. Beyond here, the trail uses a newly-built, undulating path parallel to the railway to Merlin's Bridge on the edge of Haverfordwest. The trail starts on the course of the Great Western Railway line, built between 1852 and 1856 under the direction of Isambard Kingdom Brunel, the most famous of all Victorian engineers. Neyland developed after the opening of the line as the terminus of the Great Western Railway, initially attracting passenger ships bound for southern Ireland, although this trade ceased at the end of the 19th century. The village remained a busy fishing port until the middle of the 20th century. The Cleddau Bridge, a crucial road link between the south and north banks of the waterway, was opened in 1975, replacing the ferry that used to run between Neyland and Hobb's Point.

Starting points & parking

1. Car park at the end of **Neyland Marina,** just off the B4325 to the north of Pembroke Dock (grid reference SM 968057).

2. Merlin's Bridge (Caradog's Well Road), off the roundabout at the junction of the A4076 and A487 on the south-west side of **Haverfordwest** (grid reference SM 945145).

Station: Pembroke Dock, Johnston or Haverfordwest.

TIC: Pembroke, 01437 776499.

Other nearby trails: Llys-y-Fran Reservoir to the north-east of Haverfordwest. Trails in Canaston Woods near to Narberth.

Useful publications & websites: OS Landranger Map 158. For a downloadable leaflet describing the trail, go to: *www. sustrans.org.uk* and search 'Brunel Trail'.

Refreshments: In Neyland Marina, Johnston and Haverfordwest.

Canaston Woods Ride **2**
east of Haverfordwest

There is one 'lollipop' shaped, waymarked route in this ancient 420-acre Forestry Commission woodland holding, using good, stone-based tracks appropriate for families, with a chance to explore further by using unsurfaced bridleways (which can be muddy in wet weather). The route starts from near Blackpool Mill, which has a tearoom, and runs east to the far edge of Canaston Woods, crossing the busy A4075 about halfway along. Originally part of the Slebech Estate, the woods are all that is left of a much larger forest of oak, ash and hazel. Smaller trees were used for firewood whereas the larger oaks were used for building and shipbuilding. Large amounts of wood were also converted into charcoal and used to fuel the iron foundry that existed near Blackpool Mill.

Starting point & parking

The car park near Blackpool Mill, located on the minor road leading south-west towards Minwear off the A4075, near the junction of the A4075 with the A40 at Canaston Bridge, **between Haverfordwest and Narberth** (grid reference SN 060145).

Station: Narberth.

TIC: Haverfordwest, 01437 763110.

Other nearby trails: Brunel Trail (Neyland to Haverfordwest), Llys-y-Fran Reservoir.

Useful publications & websites: OS Landranger Map 158. For a leaflet go to *www.planed.org.uk*, click on 'Greenways Walking Leaflets' (on the right-hand side) then on 'Canaston and Minwear Woods'. For more details about cycling in Pembrokeshire, and for downloads, go to: *www.pembrokeshiregreenways.co.uk* or *www. cyclepembrokeshire.com*

Refreshments: Tearoom at Blackpool Mill (summer only). Lots of choice in Narberth. If you are happy to use quiet lanes you could cycle to the Stanley Arms pub at Landshipping, about 5 miles south-west of Blackpool Mill.

Category
Waymarked woodland trails.

Distance
3 miles of surfaced tracks plus bridleways.

NB The busy A4075 has to be crossed after about 1 mile.

Ride 3 **Llys-y-Fran Reservoir north-east of Haverfordwest**

Category
Reservoir circuit.

Distance
7 miles.

An excellent route around one of the few reservoirs in West Wales. There are a couple of short, steep climbs where you may prefer to walk. Although the surface of the trail is largely stone and gravel, there are occasional muddy stretches, so mountain bikes are recommended. There are also several short hills with some steep sections.

Starting point & parking

At the visitor centre at the southern end of the lake (grid reference SN 040244). The reservoir is about 10 miles **north-east of Haverfordwest**.

Station: Clarbeston Road.

TIC: Haverfordwest, 01437 763110.

Other nearby trails: Brunel Trail (Neyland to Johnston railway path, north of Pembroke).

Useful publications & websites: OS Landranger Map 158. Go to *www.cyclepembrokeshire.com* and click on 'Llys-y-Fran' (map download available).

Refreshments: At the visitor centre.

Pembrey Country Park west of Llanelli

Ride 4

Set halfway along the long, traffic-free section of the Celtic Trail that runs from Kidwelly to Llanelli, Pembrey Country Park offers a waymarked circuit running just inside the perimeter of the grounds that takes you through the stands of pines and among the sand dunes. You will need a map / leaflet from the visitor centre, or download one from the website mentioned under **Useful publications & websites,** right. The park was once the site of a Royal Ordnance factory, producing munitions for Allied Forces during the Second World War. Llanelli Borough Council bought the site in 1977 and initiated a vast programme of land reclamation. Among other attractions at Pembrey Country Park are a dry ski slope, a toboggan run, a nine-hole pitch & putt course, an adventure playground, nature trails and an orienteering course together with a visitor centre and café. The nearby sandy beach of Cefn Sidan is 8 miles long and has won the Blue Flag Award many times.

Starting point & parking

At the **Pembrey Country Park Visitor Centre** (grid reference SN 405005), signposted off the A484 west of Llanelli.

Station: Burry Port.

TIC: Llanelli, 01554 777744.

Other nearby trails: The Celtic Trail passes through Pembrey Park. The section from Kidwelly to the Wildfowl & Wetlands Centre south west of Llanelli is one of the finest traffic-free sections of the whole route. A railway path climbs gently from Llanelli to Tumble (the Swiss Valley Trail).

Useful publications & websites: OS Landranger Map 159. Leaflet available from the visitor centre. For information about this and other country parks in Pembrokeshire, go to *www.sirgaerfyrddin.gov.uk* and follow links: English / Leisure / Coast & Countryside / Country Parks and click on 'Pembrey'.

Refreshments: Café at the visitor centre.

Category
Broad stone track around a country park.

Distance
4-mile circuit.

Ride 5 Llanelli Millennium Coastal Park
Llanelli to Kidwelly

5

Category
Coastal promenade.

Distance
18 miles each way.

Massive earth-moving equipment was deployed for over two years to create the magnificent coastal park where once there was post-industrial dereliction. The great earthworks include two award-winning earth bridges over the mainline railway. This section is one of the most popular of the Celtic Trail (National Cycle Network Route 4), stretching from Pembrokeshire to Chepstow. Enjoy the wonderful views across to the Gower Peninsula. This would be a good ride to use in conjunction with the train, catching the train from Llanelli to Kidwelly and cycling back to the start with the prevailing westerly wind on your back. Two ideas for shorter rides would be from Kidwelly to the Pembrey Forest Visitor Centre, or from the Wildfowl & Wetlands Centre to Pembrey Forest.

Starting points & parking

1. The centre of **Kidwelly** (grid reference SN 408068).

2. Pembrey Forest Country Park, off the A484 west of Llanelli (grid reference SN 405005).

3. At the Wildfowl & Wetlands Centre, off the A484 to the **south-east of Llanelli** (grid reference SS 531985).

On your bikes!

You are following the Celtic Trail and National Cycle Network Route 4 signs.

1. From the church in the centre of Kidwelly, follow the B4304 (Causeway Street) south towards the main road (A484), Burry Port and Llanelli.

2. Climb then descend. Immediately **before** the roundabout, cross the B4304 onto the pavement / cyclepath and follow this round to the right, parallel with the main Llanelli road (A484) for $^1/_2$ mile.

3. Where the pavement ends, opposite a road turning on the left to Pinged, turn right to pass under a low railway bridge and join a path along the raised embankment with the estuary to your right.

4. At the end of the track turn left down steps, cross the small bridge over the drainage ditch, turn right onto the concrete track and then bear right towards the forest, following 'Route 4' signs.

5. Follow 'NCN 4' signs for 15 miles through Pembrey Forest and past Pembrey Country Park, along the coast past the marina at Burry Port, Sandy Water Park and Llanelli to the Wildfowl & Wetlands Centre (or to Loughor Bridge).

NB You will need to use the B4304 for about 1 mile if you start in Kidwelly.

5

Station: Llanelli or Kidwelly.

TIC: Llanelli, 01554 777744.

Other nearby trails: There is a circuit in Pembrey Forest. A railway path runs north from Llanelli to Tumble (the Swiss Valley Trail).

Useful publications & websites: OS Landranger Map 159. The Sustrans map *The Celtic Trail – West* (£6.99) shows all the traffic-free trails around Llanelli plus

the course of the Celtic Trail in West Wales (Fishguard to Swansea). It is available from *www.sustrans.org.uk*. Also try *www.millenniumcoastalpark.com* or *www.sirgaerfyrddin.gov.uk* and follow links: English / Leisure / Coast & Countryside / Country Parks.

Refreshments: Lots of choice in Kidwelly. Café at Pembrey Forest Country Park. Café at the Wildfowl & Wetlands Centre.

6

Swiss Valley Trail   Ride **6**
Llanelli to Tumble

Llanelli is a focus for traffic-free trails in South Wales: it lies at a halfway point on the magnificent Millennium Coastal Park, with trails running west towards Kidwelly and east towards Swansea. This route climbs up from Sandy Water Park into the rolling hills above the town, passing high above the Lliedi Reservoirs. Beyond, its northern National Cycle Network Route 47 uses quiet lanes to reach the National Botanic Garden of Wales at Middleton Hall. There is a gentle 550ft (170m) climb from Llanelli to Tumble, so you are faced with a fantastic gravity-aided return back to the start. The route is signposted as National Cycle Network Route 47 and forms one of the options for the Celtic Trail between Llanelli and Carmarthen.

Starting points & parking

1. Sandy Water Park, **Llanelli**. This lies just off the A484 Burry Port / Kidwelly Road on the west side of Llanelli (grid reference SN 497005).

2. Tumble, just off the A476 Llandeilo road, about 10 miles north of Llanelli (grid reference SN 537115).

Station: Llanelli.

TIC: Llanelli, 01554 777744.

Other nearby trails: The Llanelli Millennium Coastal Park has a cyclepath running west to Kidwelly and east towards Swansea.

Useful publications & websites: OS Landranger Map 159. The Sustrans map *The Celtic Trail – West* (£6.99) shows all the traffic-free trails around Llanelli plus the course of the Celtic Trail in West Wales (Fishguard to Swansea). It is available from *www.sustrans.org.uk*

Refreshments: Lots of choice in Llanelli. Waun Wyllt Inn in Horeb.

Category
Railway path.

Distance
11 miles each way.

Ride 7 Llyn Llech Owain Country Park south-west of Llandeilo

7

Category
Cycle path in country park.

Distance
3 miles.

This small country park south-west of Llandeilo makes the most of the woodland and lakes within its boundaries, offering a circuit that takes you in and among the park's natural attractions. The visitor centre stands beside the lake, enjoying splendid views of Llyn Llech Owain and the surrounding area. It also houses an exhibition describing the history and natural history of the country park, as well as information on how the site is being managed. During the bird nesting season (approximately April to August), live TV pictures from nest sites are transmitted to the visitor centre.

Starting point & parking

The Country Park is located 6 miles **south-west of Llandeilo** and just to the north of the junction of the A476 and the A48 at Cross Hands (grid reference SN 566150).

Station: Llandeilo.

TIC: Carmarthen, 01267 231557.

Other nearby trails: There are several routes in Brechfa Forest to the north-west of Llandeilo.

Useful publications & websites: OS Landranger Map 159. Also try *www.sirgaerfyrddin.gov.uk* and follow links: English / Leisure / Coast & Countryside / Country Parks.

Refreshments: At the visitor centre.

Brechfa Forest Ride 8
north-east of Carmarthen (4 routes)

Lying almost 20 miles to the north-east of Carmarthen, Brechfa Forest is one of the few areas in West Wales with waymarked mountain bike routes. The four trails cater for all abilities. The start of the family trail is marked by a pair of 10ft raven wings sculpted by David Lloyd from oak and Douglas Fir from Brechfa, and scorched black to replicate the colour of the bird's feathers. They are a historical link to the ravens in the Tower of London, which are said to have come from Brechfa Forest many centuries ago. The route descriptions provided by Forest Enterprise are as follows:

Starting points & parking / the routes

Derwen Trail – Green grade – 7 miles
Enables families and beginners to enjoy the beauty of ancient natural woodland as it snakes its way through Brechfa Forest.
Start: Byrgwm car park, 3 miles south-west of Abergorlech (grid reference SN 545315).

Derwen Trail – Blue grade – 9 miles
The trail climbs a steeper bank before taking in a longer, faster descent that will have you pumping and whooping all the way to the valley bottom. The blue route is also a stepping-stone to the steeper and more technical Red-grade Gorlech route.
Start: Byrgwm car park, 3 miles south-west of Abergorlech (grid reference SN 545315).

Gorlech Trail – Red grade – 12 miles
Named after the River Gorlech, what this trail delivers in views and scenery It backs up with terrain and excitement.
Start: Aborgorlech car park on the B4310, about 17 miles north-east of Carmarthen (grid reference SN 587337).

The Raven – Black Grade – 11¹/₂ miles
A technically and physically demanding trail for expert riders only.
Start: Byrgwm car park, 3 miles south-west of Abergorlech (grid reference SN 587337).

Station: Llandeilo, 10 miles south-east of Abergorlech.

TIC: Carmarthen, 01267 231557.

Other nearby trails: Three trails in Swansea. The Afan Argoed Countryside Centre lies north-east of Port Talbot.

Useful publications & websites: OS Landranger Map 146. Go to *www.forestry.gov.uk*, click on 'Wales' then 'Mountain Biking' then 'Brechfa'. There is a trail map download available.

Refreshments: The Black Lion, at Abergorlech.

Category
Waymarked forest trails.

Distance
6 – 12 miles.

Ride 9 **Swansea Bikepath along the seafront**

9

Category
Railway path /
seafront
promenade.

Distance
5 miles each way.

The wide, curving sweep of Swansea Bay is the perfect setting for a bike path, and by good fortune and visionary planning such a path exists, running from the award-winning Maritime Quarter in the centre of the city round to Mumbles along the route of the former Mumbles railway, which carried the first passenger train in the world. The route has wonderful views across Swansea Bay to Mumbles Head, which marks the start of the Gower Peninsula. There are cafés, restaurants and pubs in Mumbles in a picturesque setting that includes the 12th-century Oystermouth Castle guarding the landward approach to Gower. The ride forms part of National Cycle Network Route 4, the Celtic Trail, which continues along the traffic-free Clyne Valley Country Park towards Gowerton and Llanelli.

Starting point & parking

The Maritime Quarter in the centre of **Swansea** (grid reference SS 654924). Parking is also available opposite the university and in Mumbles.

Station: Swansea.

TIC: Swansea, 01792 468321.

Other nearby trails: There is a cyclepath up the Clyne Valley. A section of the Swansea Canal towpath can be ridden from Clydach to Ynysmeudwy.

Useful publications & websites: OS Landranger Map 159. The *Swansea Cycling Map* is available as a download from *www. swansea.gov.uk/cycling*. This route and several other traffic-free trails to the north and east of Swansea are shown on Sustrans' *Celtic Trail – East* map (£6.99), available from *www.sustrans.org.uk*

Refreshments: In the Maritime Quarter or in Mumbles.

10

Swansea and the Clyne Valley

A spur leads off the main Swansea seafront cyclepath from Blackpill to follow a route alongside the Clyne River through Clyne Valley Country Park, providing a delightful wooded trail that runs north-west to Gowerton. The nearby Clyne Gardens are famous for azaleas and rhododendrons. The trail follows the line of the old LMS Railway, which used to link Swansea to the Midlands via Mid-Wales. The Clyne Valley bikepath forms part of the Celtic Trail, National Cycle Network Route 4, which runs from Pembrokeshire to Chepstow. There is a steady 300ft (90m) climb from the coast to the highpoint between Dunvant and Gowerton. Heading west from here, the Celtic Trail uses minor lanes then crosses the Loughor Bridge before joining the next splendid traffic-free section past the Wildfowl & Wetlands Centre to link with the Llanelli Millennium Coastal Park.

Starting point & parking

It is best to use the seafront bike path to access the start of the Clyne Valley Spur at **Blackpill (Swansea)**. There is parking in Mumbles or opposite the university on the main road (A4067) around Swansea Bay (grid reference SS 630917).

Station: Swansea or Gowerton.

TIC: Swansea, 01792 468321.

Other nearby trails: The Swansea Bikepath runs along the seafront from the Maritime Quarter to Mumbles. The Swansea Canal towpath can be ridden between Clydach and Ynysmeudwy.

Useful publications & websites: OS Landranger Map 159. The *Swansea Cycling Map* is available as a download from *www.swansea.gov.uk/cycling*. This route and several other traffic-free trails to the west of Swansea and around Llanelli are shown on Sustrans' *Celtic Trail – West* map (£6.99), available from *www.sustrans.org.uk*

Refreshments: In Dunvant and Gowerton.

Category
Railway path.

Distance
5 miles each way.

345

Ride 11   **River Tawe & Swansea Canal north-east from Swansea**

11

Category
Riverside path, canal towpath and railway path.

Distance
12 miles each way.

In their heyday, the Neath and Swansea Canals brought thousands of tons of coal down from the pits in the Swansea Valley and the Vale of Neath. Both were superseded by the railways and now plans have been drawn up to restore both waterways. This ride uses the cyclepath alongside the River Tawe from the centre of Swansea, joining the Swansea Canal towpath in Clydach through to Pontardawe then a dismantled railway to Ystalyfera. It is signposted as National Cycle Network Route 43.

Starting points & parking

1. Tawe Bridge (A483) in the centre of **Swansea** (grid reference SS 662934).

2. The trail ends on the east side of the River Tawe, to the **east of Ystalyfera**, off the A4067 Tawe valley road to the north-east of Swansea (grid reference SN 771084). It can be accessed via the bridge over the river near the A4067 / B4599 roundabout to the south of Ystalyfera.

Station: Swansea.

TIC: Swansea, 01792 468321.

Other nearby trails: Swansea seafront. Clyne Valley to Gowerton. The Neath Canal runs along the next valley to the east. There are several waymarked trails starting at the Afan Argoed Country Park (north-east of Port Talbot).

Useful publications & websites: OS Landranger Maps 159, 160 & 170. The *Swansea Cycling Map* is available as a download from *www.swansea.gov.uk/cycling*. This route and several other traffic-free trails to the north and east of Swansea are shown on Sustrans' *Celtic Trail – East* map (£6.99), available from *www.sustrans.org.uk*

Refreshments: In Clydach and Pontardawe.

Neath Canal (1) Ride 12
east of Swansea

This ride from Tonna south-west to Briton Ferry (near Neath) uses an improved section of the canal towpath that used to link the coalfields of the Neath Valley with the port at Briton Ferry, where you are still likely to see some big ships moored. The ride forms part of the northern braid of the Celtic Trail between Swansea and Pontypridd, signposted as National Cycle Network Route 47. This links in Neath to the High Level Route, a strenuous challenge for mountain bikes. In their heyday in the mid-1800s, the Neath and Tennant Canals were extremely prosperous, with up to 200,000 tons of coal alone being moved annually on the Neath Canal. However, their prosperity was short-lived and soon affected by the coming of the railway in 1851. By 1880, almost all coal traffic was being carried by rail.

Starting point & parking

The car park for Tonna Canal Basin, just off the A465 to the **north-east of Neath**. Follow signs for the B4434 to Tonna, Clyne and Melincourt, cross the River Neath and turn left immediately after the Railway Tavern into the car parking area (grid reference SS 774993). To get to the trail, cross the road and follow the canal towpath south-west towards Briton Ferry. Turn around where the canal ends.

Category
Canal towpath.

Distance
5 miles each way.

Station: Neath.

TIC: Swansea, 01792 468321.

Other nearby trails: There is another section of the canal towpath which can be followed from Resolven north-east to Glyn Neath. The Neath to Pontypridd High Level Route is a tough challenge along forest roads between the two towns.

Useful publications & websites: OS Landranger Map 170. This route and several other traffic-free trails in the Swansea / Neath / Bridgend area are shown on Sustrans' *Celtic Trail – East* map (£6.99), available from *www.sustrans.org.uk*

Refreshments: Lots of choice in Neath. Railway Tavern in Tonna.

347

Ride **13** **Port Talbot, Bryn to Goytre
(Wildbrook Estate)**

Category
Railway path.

Distance
3 miles each way.

A 3-mile section of the Cwm Dyffryn railway path through woodland that could not contrast more dramatically with the heavy industry of Port Talbot less than a couple of miles away. There is good access from Bryn – south into the adjoining Margam Forest or north into the woodlands above Afan Argoed, with its plethora of trails. There is a steady descent of almost 400ft (120m) from Bryn to Wildbrook Estate in Goytre, where the trail ends. The trail follows a stream called Ffrwd Wyllt, a name to test the language skills of all non-Welsh-speakers!

Starting point & parking

Park on the roads near to the Royal Oak pub in Bryn, on the B4282 **east of Port Talbot** (grid reference SS 818920).

Station: Port Talbot.

TIC: Swansea, 01792 468321.

Other nearby trails: There are several routes starting in Afan Argoed Country Park. Two sections of the Neath Canal are rideable: from Briton Ferry to Tonna and from Resolven to Glyn Neath.

Useful publications & websites: OS Landranger Map 170. This and many other traffic-free routes in the Swansea' / Neath / Bridgend area are shown on Sustrans' *Celtic Trail – East* map (£6.99), available from *www. sustrans.org.uk*. Also try the website of the local authority, Neath Port Talbot at *www.npt. gov.uk* and search 'Cycle Routes'. There is a basic map to download with an overall view of the routes in the area.

Refreshments: Royal Oak pub, Bryn.

Neath Canal (2) Ride 14
between Neath and Glyn Neath

There are plans for the whole length of the Neath Canal from Briton Ferry to Glyn Neath to be restored to its former glory. This section, from Blaengwrach to Resolven alongside the A465, shows what it could be like in the future. It would improve the ambience if they could build a soundproof screen between the towpath and the dual carriageway! The canal was built to transport the raw materials and manufactured goods of the valley's early industries and mines more efficiently than the packhorse and wagon routes. Cargoes included timber, coal, lime, finished iron and copper, and even gunpowder and cannonballs during the Napoleonic wars. Not all traffic was industrial. Large landowners often had pleasure boats on the canals and the favourite Sunday School outing was a trip from Neath to the beach at Jersey Marine, often completed to the accompaniment of the local brass band.

Starting point & parking

Head north-east from Neath. The start / car park is at the Resolven Basin just off the A465 to the north of **Resolven** (grid reference SN 826030). The route ends on the B4242 to the west of Glyn Neath at grid reference SN 866059.

Category
Canal towpath.

Distance
3$\frac{1}{2}$ miles each way.

Station: Neath.

TIC: Swansea, 01792 468321.

Other nearby trails: Another section of the canal can be explored south-west from Tonna to Briton Ferry. There are several waymarked trails in Afan Argoed Country Park on the A4107 to the north of Port Talbot.

Useful publications & websites: OS Landranger Maps 160 & 170. This route and several other traffic-free trails in the Swansea / Neath / Bridgend area are shown on Sustrans' *Celtic Trail – East* map (£6.99), available from *www.sustrans.org.uk*. For general information about cycling in the area go to the website of the local authority, Neath Port Talbot at *www.npt.gov.uk* and search 'Cycle Routes'.

Refreshments: Pubs in Resolven.

349

Ride **15** **Tondu to Pyle
north-west of Bridgend**

15

Category
Railway path and
specially-built
cyclepath.

Distance
6 miles each way.

This section of the Celtic Trail from Tondu Environment Centre (north of Bridgend) west to the Frogpond Wood Nature Reserve in Pyle uses some unusual wooden decking, winding its way through the Parc Slip Nature Park to keep you up above the soft ground beneath. The Nature Park has recorded 28 butterfly species, rare wading birds pass through during the migrating season, and several scarce damselfly and dragonfly species breed here. There are Scheduled Ancient Monuments at either end of the trail: Cebn Cribwr Ironworks near to Pyle and Tondu Ironworks near to Tondu. The trail could easily be linked at its eastern end to the Ogmore Valley route, taking you right up to Nant-y-moel.

Starting point & parking

Parc Slip Nature Park Visitor Centre (grid reference SS 881841), just off the B4281 between Aberkenfig and Pyle (about 2 miles west of M4, Jct 36). From the starting point the trail runs for about 1 mile to the east and 5 miles to the west.

Station: Bridgend.

TIC: Bridgend, 01656 654906.

Other nearby trails: The Ogmore Valley Community Route runs up the Ogmore Valley to Nant-y-moel. The Garw Valley Trail runs for 8 miles from Bryngarw Country Park to Blaengarw in the next valley to the west. There are several routes in Afan Argoed Country Park.

Useful publications & websites: OS Landranger Map 170. The excellent leaflet *Guide to the Tondu to Pyle Community Route* can be downloaded from *www.bridgend.gov. uk.* Click on 'Tourism' then 'Activities' then 'Cycling' then click again to download the leaflet.

Sustrans' *Celtic Trail – East* map (£6.99) covers this and many other traffic-free trails nearby and is available from *www.sustrans. org.uk*

Refreshments: In Tondu or Kenfig Hill.

Afan Argoed Countryside Centre Ride 16
north-east of Port Talbot

The Afan Argoed Visitor Centre is an excellent base for many rides in the Afan Valley. There are railway paths and waymarked forestry tracks on both sides of the valley heading south-west to Pontrhydyfen and north-east to Blaengwynfi. Spurs lead off to Efail Fach from Pontrhydyfen and to Glyncorrwg from Cymer. There are also two tough, technical mountain bike trails know as the Penhydd Trail and the Wall Trail. Two other mountain bike trails start in Glyncorrwg. The Countryside Centre has a hands-on exhibition demonstrating the landscape and history of the Afan Valley. The South Wales Miners' Museum portrays the social history of the valley's mining communities.

Mountain bike trails for experienced riders

The Penhydd Trail – Red grade – 14 miles
This is a varied trail combining forest road climbs with tight, technical, switchback trails through mixed woodland and open, flowing singletrack across open ground with great views. Not suitable for novices.

The Wall Trail – Red grade – 14 miles
This trail essentially traverses the north side of the Afan Valley on singletrack, which varies from fast, open and flowing to tight, technical and rooty.

(Glyncorrwg) White's Level – Red grade – 9 miles
Very technical, progressive riding trail with drops, step-downs and long singletrack climbs.

(Glyncorrwg) Sykline – Black grade – 28 miles
The longest all-weather trail in Britain. High-level, highly technical singletrack riding. Not to be treated lightly. Only recommended for experienced, fit riders.

(Linking route) W2 – Black grade – 27 miles
W2 links The Wall and White's Level. A high-level link connecting both these trails with some fantastic views of Afan and Neath Valleys. This trail includes two of the most demanding descents in the UK.

Starting point & parking

Afan Argoed Countryside Centre, on the A4107 north-east of Port Talbot at M4, Jct 40 (grid reference SS 821951).

Station: Maesteg or Port Talbot.

TIC: Swansea, 01792 468321.

Other nearby trails: Neath Canal north-east of Resolven. Ogmore Valley railway path from Blackmill to Nant-y-moel.

Useful publications & websites: OS Landranger Map 170. Go to *www.forestry. gov.uk*, click on 'Wales' then 'Mountain Biking' then 'Afan Forest Park'. There is a trail map download available. Also try *www. mbwales.com*

Refreshments: At the Countryside Centre. Pubs in Efail Fach, Pontrhydyfen, Cymer and Blaengwynfi.

Category
Railway path, forestry trails.

Distance
Afan Valley Cycle Route:
7 miles each way (plus optional 6-mile round trip from Cymer to Glyncorrwg).

Ride 17 Ogmore Valley north of Bridgend

Category
Railway path.

Distance
7 miles each way.

This ride up the Ogmore Vale from Brynmenyn (north of Bridgend) through Blackmill to Nant-y-moel is a splendid example of what can be done with the old railway lines that used to bring coal down from the Welsh valleys to the coast, now that the region finds itself in a post-coal-mining era. There is a steady climb from south to north, setting you up for a much easier return, leg back to the start. The southern end of the ride forms part of the Celtic Trail, which runs from Pembrokeshire to Chepstow.

Starting point & parking

NB There is a similar railway path in the next valley across to the west, running for 8 miles from Bryngarw Country Park north to Blaerngarw.

The garage / pub / post office and stores in **Blackmill**, at the junction of the A4093 and A4061, about 4 miles north of the M4, Jct 36. Park just beyond the Fox & Hounds pub and garage (grid reference SS 933867). The path starts on the other side of the river. It runs 2 miles south to Brynmenyn or 5 miles north to Nant-y-moel.

Station: Aberkenfig (north of Bridgend).

TIC: Bridgend, 01656 654906.

Other nearby trails: Tondu to Pyle. The Garw Valley Trail from Bryngarw Country Park to Blaengarw. There are waymarked trails in Afan Argoed Countryside Centre north-east of Port Talbot.

Useful publications & websites: OS Landranger Map 170. *The Guide to the Ogmore Valley Community Route* can be downloaded from *www.bridgend.gov.uk*. Click on 'Tourism' then 'Activities' then 'Cycling' then click again to download the leaflet. Sustrans' *Celtic Trail – East* map (£6.99) shows all the traffic-free sections along the National Cycle Network between Swansea and Newport. Available from *www.sustrans.org.uk*. See also *www.southernwales.com/en/cycling*

Refreshments: In Blackmill, Ogmore Vale and Nant-y-moel.

Neath to Pontypridd Ride 18
High Level Route (Celtic Trail)

The High Level Route is one of the toughest rides in the book, climbing to almost 2,000ft (600m). The route, which is part of the Celtic Trail, crosses the vast swathes of forestry that lie between Neath and Pontypridd, with fantastic views north over the Black Mountain and down into the Vale of Neath. As both Neath and Pontypridd have stations, the train could be used to complete one leg by public transport, enabling you to make the most of the prevailing westerly wind. Another option would be to take the train from either Newport or Cardiff to Neath: once you have cycled from Neath to Pontypridd you have the option of following the largely traffic-free Taff Trail down to Cardiff, or the Celtic Trail down to Newport.

Starting points & parking

1. You may choose to use the train to make this a one-way trip, in which case the ride starts from **Neath railway station** (grid reference SS 751975). Otherwise, to avoid all the urban bits ...

2. The car park at Mosshouse Wood on the minor lane to the **north-east of Neath** (grid reference SS 773982). The minor lane is called Fairylands Road, off the B4434 towards Tonna.

3. The car park by the Brynffynon Inn in Llanwonno to the **north-west of Pontypridd** (grid reference ST 031956).

Station: Neath or Pontypridd.

TICs: Swansea, 01792 468321. Pontypridd, 01443 490748.

Other nearby trails: The Taff Trail in Pontypridd. The Ogmore Vale Community Route. Routes in Afan Argoed Country Park. Neath Canal routes.

Useful publications & websites: OS Landranger Map 170. This and many other traffic free routes in the Neath / Bridgend / Pontypridd area are shown on Sustrans' *Celtic Trail – East* map (£6.99), available from *www.sustrans.org.uk*

Refreshments: Lots of choice in Neath and Pontypridd. The Brynffynon Inn at Llanwonno.

Category
Forestry roads and quiet lanes.

Distance
22 miles each way.

Ride 19 Taff Trail (1)
Cardiff to Tongwynlais

19

Category
Riverside path,
specially-built
cyclepath and
minor roads.

Distance
6 miles each way.

The 53-mile Taff Trail runs north from Cardiff to Brecon, largely traffic-free, along a mixture of riverside paths, railway paths and forestry roads. It climbs gently to Merthyr Tydfil then more steeply before dropping down into Talybont, in the Usk Valley, and turning west to Brecon. Five of the best traffic-free sections are described in the book. The most southerly part, described here, goes from Cardiff Central railway station past the Millennium Stadium north to Tongwynlais, passing through parkland alongside the River Taff on an attractive broad gravel track. The trail is signposted variously as 'The Taff Trail', 'Lôn Las Cymru' and 'National Cycle Network Route 8'. All three run together to Brecon. It is suggested you turn around in Tongwynlais at the end of the traffic-free section, but you may prefer to follow roads through the village and climb steeply to visit the fairytale Castell Coch. A good, long day ride (30 miles) for the fit would involve catching a train from Cardiff to Merthyr Tydfil and cycling back downhill to Cardiff.

Starting point & parking

From **Cardiff Central railway station** (grid reference ST 182759), head towards the Millennium Stadium, following the Taff Trail, Lôn Las Cymru or National Cycle Network Route 8 signs.

Station: Cardiff.

TIC: Cardiff, 029 2087 3573.

Other nearby trails: The Taff Trail continues north to Brecon. The next traffic-free section starts north of Castell Coch.

Useful publications & websites: OS Landranger Map 171. This and many other traffic-free trails in the area to the north of Cardiff are shown on Sustrans' *Lôn Las Cymru – South* map (£6.99), available from *www.sustrans.org.uk*. You can download a leaflet from *www.sustrans.org.uk* by putting 'Taff Trail Leaflet' in the 'Search' box. See also *www.tafftrail.org.uk* and *www.southernwales.com/en/cycling*

Refreshments: Lots of choice in Cardiff. Pubs in Tongwynlais.

Taff Trail (2) Ride 20
Castell Coch to Glyntaff

This section of the Taff Trail goes north from the fairytale castle of Castell Coch in Tongwynlais, through woodlands and along a railway path, finishing at the cemetery at Glyntaff. You are warned that there is a very steep hill at the start where you will need to push your bike through the magnificent beech woods. There is an alternative starting point from Taffs Well railway station which avoids this hill. Castell Coch was designed in the 1870s by the architect William Burges for his patron, the third Marquess of Bute, and occupies the site of a genuine medieval stronghold.

Starting points & parking

1. Castell Coch car park (grid reference ST 132827), just north of M4, Jct 32 (follow signs). The trail starts almost opposite the castle with a steep push up through beechwoods.

2. You can also start from Taffs Well railway station (grid reference ST 125833), just north of Tongwynlais.

Station: Cardiff.

TIC: Cardiff, 029 2087 3573.

Other nearby trails: The Taff Trail continues north towards Brecon. A railway path runs through Sirhowy Country Park. There are two canal towpaths starting from near Newport: one to Crosskeys and the other to Pontypool.

Useful publications & websites: OS Landranger Map 171. This and many other traffic-free trails in the area to the north of Cardiff are shown on Sustrans' *Lôn Las Cymru – South* map (£6.99), available from *www.sustrans.org.uk*. You can download a leaflet from *www.sustrans.org.uk* by putting 'Taff Trail Leaflet' in the 'Search' box. See also *www.tafftrail.org.uk* and *www.southernwales.com/en/cycling*

Refreshments: Café inside Castell Coch (you will need to pay to get in). Pubs in Tongwynlais.

Category
Woodland path and railway path.

Distance
6 miles each way.

Ride 21 Taff Trail (3) Abercynon to Merthyr Tydfil

21

Category
Railway path and quiet dead-end roads.

Distance
8 miles each way.

NB *A traffic-free section of the Taff Trail can also be followed south to the outskirts of Pontypridd, with an option to explore the railway path leading north-east from Glyncoch to Ynysybwl.*

The middle section of the Taff Trail climbs 270ft (82m) from the Navigation Inn in Abercynon north through Quakers Yard and Aberfan to the Rhydycar Leisure Centre in Merthyr Tydfil. In the northern half of the ride the path is largely up above the valley, giving wide views of the rows of terraced houses so typical of the South Wales valleys. North of Quakers Yard the trail follows the route of the Pen-y-Darren Tramroad, the scene in 1804 of the first ever steam locomotive railway journey, powered by Richard Trevithick's engine. Part of the tramroad is a scheduled ancient monument and has not been surfaced. The original trackbed and stone sleepers remain and care should be taken when riding this section. The memorial gardens in Aberfan commemorate the terrible disaster in 1966 when the tips slipped, crushing many houses and the village school, tragically killing over 100 children.

Starting points & parking

1. The Navigation Inn, **Abercynon**, near the junction of the B4275 and the A470 (grid reference ST 085949).

2. Rhydycar Leisure Centre, just south of **Merthyr Tydfil** railway station (grid reference SO 050055).

Station: Merthyr Tydfil, Abercynon North and several stations in between.

TIC: Merthyr Tydfil, 01685 379884.

Other nearby trails: The Taff Trail runs north to Brecon and south to Cardiff. A railway path runs through Sirhowy Country Park. There are two canal towpaths starting from near Newport: one to Crosskeys and the other to Pontypool. The High Level Route from Pontypridd to Neath climbs to 2,000ft (600m) as it crosses large blocks of forestry between the two towns.

Useful publications & websites: OS Landranger Maps 160 & 170. This and many other traffic-free trails in the area between Merthyr Tydfil and Cardiff are shown in Sustrans' *Lôn Las Cymru – South* map (£6.99), available from *www.sustrans.org.uk*. You can download a leaflet from *www.sustrans.org.uk* by putting 'Taff Trail Leaflet' in the 'Search' box. See also *www.tafftrail.org.uk* and *www.southernwales.com/en/cycling*

Refreshments: Lots of choice in Merthyr Tydfil. Several pubs along the way.

Hengoed Viaduct to Trelewis north of Cardiff   Ride 22

A quick glance at a map of South Wales shows how the development of the mining valleys channelled the coal down railway lines to the docks at Cardiff and Newport. Most of these lines have now gone but many have been converted to recreational use. This trail is a bit of a hybrid: for much of its length it runs parallel to an existing railway line on a specially built cyclepath. Most of the ride, starting a few miles north of Caerphilly, forms part of the Celtic Trail or National Cycle Network Route 47, and climbs gently from Hengoed Viaduct through Nelson. A spur off the Celtic Trail leads north through Trelewis to the Welsh International Climbing Centre at Taff Bargoed. There is also the chance to link to the Taff Trail from Trelewis to Quakers Yard and continue north-west towards Merthyr Tydfil.

Starting point & parking

Hengoed Viaduct, near the junction of the A472 and the B4252 in **Ystrad Mynach**, which lies 12 miles along the A469 to the north of Cardiff (grid reference ST 156949).

Station: Hengoed.

TIC: Caerphilly, 029 2088 0011.

Other nearby trails: The Taff Trail is easily accessed from Trelewis. The Sirhowy Valley Country Park lies to the east.

Useful publications & websites: OS Landranger Map 171. This and many other traffic-free trails in the area to the north of Cardiff are shown on Sustrans' *Lôn Las Cymru – South* map (£6.99) or *Celtic Trail – East* map (£6.99), available from *www.sustrans. org.uk*. See also *www.southernwales.com/en/ cycling*.

Refreshments: Trelewis.

Category
Railway path and newly-built cyclepath.

Distance
6 miles each way.

Ride 23 Sirhowy Country Park north-west of Newport

23

Category
Railway path.

Distance
5 miles each way.

The valleys of South Wales are synonymous with coal mining. Now that the pits have all closed, more and more of the old railways that used to transport coal down to the docks are being converted to recreational use. Sirhowy Valley Country Park not only has a section of railway path but also two waymarked mountain bike trails in the steep woodlands above the valley (these are shown on the leaflet that can be downloaded from the website described right). General information about the park is available from the Full Moon Visitor Centre, where there is also a small display about the industrial and natural history of the valley. The trail through the park to Wyllie is part of the Celtic Trail and can easily be linked to the route from Hengoed Viaduct to Trelewis (or from the Crosskeys end to the canal towpath down to Newport).

Starting point & parking

At the car park just off the roundabout at the junction of the A467 and A4048 to the **west of Crosskeys,** north-west of M4, Jct 28 (grid reference ST 214914).

Station: Hengoed (Ystrad Mynach).

TIC: Newport, 01633 842962.

Other nearby trails: The Newport to Crosskeys Canal lies 1 mile to the east. To the north-west the Celtic Trail crosses the Hengoed Viaduct on its way to Trelewis.

Useful publications & websites: OS Landranger Map 171. A leaflet can be downloaded from: *www.caerphilly.gov.uk.* Click on 'Leisure & Tourism' then 'Countryside and country parks' then 'Country parks' then 'Sirhowy Valley Country Park'. Alternatively, at the final stage click on 'Cycling' for an overview of the cycle routes in the area.

Refreshments: Pub in Wyllie.

24

Monmouthshire & Brecon Canal from Newport (Fourteen Locks) to Crosskeys

Ride **24**

This is one of two canals that run north from Newport. The section described here forms part of the Malpas to Crumlin branch of the main canal, which used to link Brecon to Newport. It is only to the north of Pontypool that the canal is still operational. Located in such a built-up area the canal represents a fine green corridor with an excellent wide, gravel towpath and views of hills rising to over 1,000ft (300m) at its northern end. The ride between Newport and Crosskeys forms part of the Celtic Trail that crosses Wales from Fishguard in Pembrokeshire to Chepstow.

Starting point & parking

The picnic site / visitor centre by the Fourteen Locks just off the B4591 to the north-west of M4, Jct 27, west of Newport (grid reference ST 281887).

Station: Newport.

TIC: Newport, 01633 842962.

Other nearby trails: The Newport to Pontypool Canal shares the same start. The Celtic Trail continues westwards from Crosskeys via a railway path in the Sirhowy Valley Country Park. The Taff Trail runs north from Cardiff.

Useful publications & websites: OS Landranger Map 171. This route and several other traffic-free trails in the Newport / Cardiff area are shown on Sustrans' *Celtic Trail – East* map (£6.99), available from *www.sustrans. org.uk*. Try also *www.waterscape.com* – click on 'Canals and rivers', select 'Monmouthshire and Brecon Canal' from the 'Complete list' box then click on 'Cycling'.

Refreshments: In Newport, Risca and Crosskeys, just off the canal.

Category
Canal towpath.

Distance
5 miles each way.

24

Ride 25 The Monmouthshire & Brecon Canal from Newport (Fourteen Locks) to Pontypool

25

Category
Canal towpath.

Distance
9 miles each way.

The Monmouthshire Canal, including the branch from Malpas to Crumlin (described in the previous ride), was opened in 1799 and linked with what was then known as the Brecknock & Abergavenny Canal in Pontymoile, just north of Pontypool, in 1812. Both canals were supported by horse-drawn tramroads that were mainly used to bring coal, limestone and iron ore from the hillsides. In 1880 the Monmouthshire & Brecon Canals, as they became known, were taken over by the Great Western Railway. This ride follows the course of the canal although there are sections where the canal has been built over, particularly through Cwmbran. However, as the route forms part of National Cycle Network Route 46, it is superbly signed and if you are feeling fit you could link this to the Pontypool to Blaenavon trail to create a long and enjoyable day out.

Starting point & parking

The picnic site / visitor centre by the Fourteen Locks, just off the B4591 to the north-west of M4, Jct 27, **west of Newport** (grid reference ST 281887).

On your bikes!

Go downhill along the towpath past the locks and parallel with the M4. After 1¹/₂ miles alongside the motorway, **leave** this towpath (which continues towards Newport), turn left beneath the M4 and follow the other branch of the canal towpath north towards Cwmbran and Pontypool.

Station: Newport, Cwmbran and Pontypool.

TIC: Newport, 01633 842962.

Other nearby trails: The Newport to Crosskeys Canal shares the same start. There is a railway path through the Sirhowy Valley Country Park, to the west of Crosskeys. The Pontypool to Blaenavon railway path is also part of National Cycle Network Route 46.

Useful publications & websites: OS Landranger Map 171. This route and several other traffic-free trails in the Newport / Cardiff area are shown on Sustrans' *Celtic Trail – East* map (£6.99), available from *www.sustrans. org.uk*. Try also *www.waterscape.com* – click on 'Canals and rivers', select 'Monmouthshire & Brecon Canal' from the 'Complete list' box then click on 'Cycling'.

Refreshments: In Newport, Cwmbran and Pontypool, just off the route.

Pontypool to Blaenavon

Ride **26**

This is part of National Cycle Network Route 46 that runs from Newport through Cwmbran, Pontypool and Blaenavon, then via a short section on-road to drop down into the Clydach Valley to Abergavenny. The path climbs steadily as it heads north from Pontypool to Blaenavon, meaning the trip down to Pontypool is a lot easier. Blaenavon played a significant part in the Industrial Revolution in the 19th century: the town became the home of mine owners, managers and workers of the ironworks and Big Pit Colliery when first established. Many of the schools, shops and chapels built in those early days are still standing today: the town contains 17 listed buildings, including Blaenavon Ironworks, one of the best preserved examples of 18th-century ironworks in Western Europe. At the Big Pit National Coal Museum you can experience going underground in a real colliery.

Starting points & parking

1. Hanbury Road, **Pontypool**. This lies just east of the roundabout at the junction of the A472 and A4043, at the southern end of Pontypool (grid reference SO 283007).

2. The Big Pit National Coal Museum, **Blaenavon** (grid reference SO 238087).

Station: Pontypool.

TIC: Blaenavon, 01495 742333.

Other nearby trails: The Monmouthshire & Brecon Canal from Newport to Pontypool links with this trail. You can follow NCN 46 from Brynmawr east to Llanfoist (Abergavenny).

Useful publications & websites: OS Landranger Maps 161 & 171. This route and several other traffic-free trails in the Newport / Pontypool area are shown on Sustrans' *Celtic Trail – East* map (£6.99), available from *www. sustrans.org.uk*. This trail is also described in brief, along with many others, in a Sustrans booklet. Just put 'Go Traffic Free in Wales' in the 'Search' box at *www.sustrans.org.uk*.

Refreshments: Several pubs and cafés just off the route.

Category
Railway path and specially-built cyclepath.

Distance
9 miles each way.

NB Short sections of safe, well-waymarked roads are used through Pontypool.

Ride 27 Llanfoist to Brynmawr Railway Path west of Abergavenny

Category
Railway path.

Distance
8 miles each way.

Many years of negotiation and hard work have finally allowed an almost entirely traffic-free route to be opened between Llanfoist, just to the south of Abergavenny, and Brynmawr, passing high above the Clydach Gorge. The largely wooded route climbs steadily beyond Govilon, leaving far below the Monmouthshire & Brecon Canal. One short, unavoidable section of quiet lane is used before climbing back up onto the course of the old railway. There are some splendid old mining and quarrying ruins along the course of what must have been a monumental challenge for the railway engineers. Fit and experienced cyclists can use networks of quiet but steep lanes to link through to the Big Pit National Coal Museum and join traffic-free trails all the way down through Blaenavon, Pontypool and Cwmbran to Newport.

Starting point & parking

In a road called The Cutting, by the post office in Llanfoist, just off the A465 to the **south-west of Abergavenny** (grid reference SO 286134). At the crossroads by the Llanfoist Inn turn right, then shortly after the car saleroom and a street called The Cedars on the right take the next narrow tarmac track to the right (signposted as a no-through-road). Immediately turn left onto the old railway path.

Station: Abergavenny.

TIC: Abergavenny, 01873 853254.

Other nearby trails: A railway path runs between Pontypool and Blaenavon. The Taff Trail runs through Talybont on Usk, 15 miles to the west.

Useful publications & websites: OS Landranger Map 161. This route and several other traffic-free trails in the valleys to the south-west of Abergavenny are shown on Sustrans' *Celtic Trail – East* map (£6.99), available from *www.sustrans.org.uk*

Refreshments: In Llanfoist.

NB *There is a short section on-road from the post office in Llanfoist to the start of the route.*

Cwm Darran Country Park Ride 28
south-east of Merthyr Tydfil (4 routes)

Cwm Darran Country Park is tucked away from it all in the Darran Valley, 6 miles south-east of Merthyr Tydfil. Displays in the visitor centre show the history of the park's development from mining valley to award-winning country park. There is a dismantled railway path that descends gently over four miles down to Bargoed in the Rhymney Valley, and three other waymarked mountain bike routes in the park that are tougher and steeper.

Starting point & parking

Cwm Darran Country Park, on the minor road between the A469 to the north of Bargoed and the A465 to the east of Merthyr Tydfil (grid reference SO 119030).

On your bikes!

Mountain bike routes:

Route	Distance	Waymarks
Moderate	1.7 miles	Green
Intermediate	3.0 miles	Orange
Challenging	5.5 miles	Red

Category
Railway path.

Distance
Railway path –
6 miles each way.

Mountain bike rides from 1.7 to 5.5 miles.

Station: Pontlottyn, Phillipstown.

TIC: Merthyr Tydfil, 01685 379884.

Other nearby trails: The Taff Trail runs from Cardiff to Brecon via Pontypridd and Merthyr Tydfil. There is a dismantled railway in Sirhowy Valley Country Park to the west of Risca and Crosskeys.

Useful publications & websites: OS Landranger Map 171. A leaflet can be downloaded from: *www.caerphilly.gov.uk*. Click on 'Leisure & Tourism' then 'Countryside and country parks' then 'Country parks' then 'Parc Cwm Darran'. Alternatively, at the final stage click on 'Cycling' for an overview of the cycle routes in the area.

Refreshments: At the visitor centre. Pub in Deri and several pubs in Bargoed.

NB From Bargoed there is another railway path that leads north for 3 miles through New Tredegar to Abertysswg. There are plans to extend the trail further along the Rhymney Valley.

Ride **29** **Taff Trail (4)**
Merthyr Tydfil towards Pontsticill Reservoir

Category
Railway path and purpose-built cyclepath.

Distance
5 miles each way.

It is just to the north of Merthyr Tydfil that the Taff Trail finally leaves behind the densely populated industrial area and heads for the hills, passing through woodlands and over tall viaducts to the first of the reservoirs in the Brecon Beacons at Pontsticill. There is a climb of 350ft (105m) from the Rhydycar Leisure Centre to the end of the railway path. It is suggested you only go as far as Pontsticill Reservoir – beyond here the gradients get much steeper and there are sections on roads which can get busy. Cyfartha Castle

in Merthyr Tydfil was built in 1824 for the Crawshay family, the local ironmasters. It is now a museum and art gallery, open to the public, set in 160 acres of rolling parkland.

Starting point & parking

Rhydycar Leisure Centre (grid reference SO 050055), **Merthyr Tydfil**, just south of Merthyr Tydfil railway station. Follow the Taff Trail signs carefully through Merthyr Tydfil. It largely follows the river, crossing it several times.

Station: Merthyr Tydfil.

TIC: Merthyr Tydfil, 01685 379884.

Other nearby trails: A traffic-free section of the Taff Trail runs south to Abercynon. On its way north to Brecon there is a long and challenging traffic-free section from Talybont to Taf Fechan Forest. There are waymarked forestry routes in Garwnant Forest.

Useful publications & websites: OS Landranger Map 160. This trail and many others south of Merthyr Tydfil towards Cardiff are shown on Sustrans' *Lôn Las Cymru – South* Map (£6.99), available from *www.sustrans.org.uk*. Or try *www.tafftrail.org.uk*

Refreshments: Lots of choice in Merthyr Tydfil.

NB There are several short sections of road through Merthyr Tydfil before joining the railway path off the Swansea Road (A4102) to the south of Cefn Coed Viaduct.

Garwnant Forest Ride 30
north of Merthyr Tydfil

Garwnant Forest lies just north of the old industrial town of Merthyr Tydfil, but here you are in a completely different world of woodland, lakes and reservoirs on the southern edge of the Brecon Beacons National Park. There are two waymarked loops in the forest, both starting from the visitor centre. The trails climb several hills, some of them steep, and a short section of a minor road is used in both routes. The shorter route climbs away from the visitor centre on forest roads, heading west then south to drop down to the Llwyn on-Dam before returning to the visitor centre on the road alongside the reservoir. The second, tougher loop carries on south to explore the adjacent Penmoelallt Forest. They are both graded Blue and the routes are signposted with brown waymarking discs with a bike logo.

Starting point & parking

Garwnant Visitor Centre (01685 723060), just off the A470, about 6 miles north of **Merthyr Tydfil** (grid refererence SO 005132).

Station: Merthyr Tydfil.

TIC: Merthyr Tydfil, 01685 379884.

Other nearby trails: The Taff Trail runs from Cardiff to Brecon and passes through Merthyr Tydfil.

Useful publications & websites: OS Landranger Map 160. Go to *www. cyclebreconbeacons.com* – click on 'Family Cycling' then 'Garwnant Forest'. Or try *www.forestry.gov.uk* and search 'Garwnant Cycle Trail'.

Refreshments: Café at the visitor centre.

Category
Forest trail
(Blue grade).

Distance
5 miles or
11 miles.

Ride 31 Taff Trail (5) Talybont Reservoir to Taf Fechan

31

Category
Railway path.

Distance
5^1/$_2$ miles each
way.

This is one of the toughest railway paths in the country with one long, steady climb of almost 900ft (275m) south-west from the Talybont Reservoir dam to Torpantau / Taf Fechan Forest. At 1,440ft (439m), this is the highest point on the Taff Trail with breathtaking views. From here the Taff Trail takes a downhill course almost all the way to Cardiff. If you are not aiming to do the whole of the Taff Trail and you are turning around at the top, you are rewarded with a wonderful descent. Please note, it is not worth trying to turn this into a circular ride using the road as the gradients are very steep on the narrow,

twisting lane, and will give you a fraction of the pleasure to be gained from the railway path descent.

Starting point & parking

At the picnic site on the road **south of Talybont-on-Usk** towards Pontsticill (grid reference SO 106208). Talybont lies on the B4558, about 6 miles south-east of Brecon. The trail runs along the east side of Talybont Reservoir and is joined by crossing the dam at its northern end.

Station: Merthyr Tydfil.

TIC: Brecon, 01874 622485.

Other nearby trails: The Taff Trail continues south to Merthyr Tydfil and Cardiff. A short (2^1/$_2$-mile) section of the Monmouthshire & Brecon Canal east from the Canal Basin in Brecon is designated as a cyclepath.

Useful publications & websites: OS Landranger Maps 160 & 161. This trail and many others south of Merthyr Tydfil towards Cardiff are shown on Sustrans' *Lôn Las Cymru – South* map (£6.99), available from *www.sustrans.org.uk*, or *www.tafftrail.org.uk*

Refreshments: Lots of choice in Talybont-on-Usk.

Encircling the remote Usk Reservoir, in the north-west corner of Brecon Beacons National Park, Glasfynydd Forest has an excellent 6-mile family mountain bike route. The reservoir is cradled between the stark uplands of Mynydd Myddfai and Mynydd Wysg, and is perfectly placed for great views of the dramatic sweep of the Black Mountains. The route follows clear waymarks along broad forest tracks that are bumpy in some places and muddy in others, with plenty of short climbs and descents to challenge riders. If you are looking for more mountain biking challenges, there are two small mountain bike centres north of Llandovery: Cwm Rhaeadr (go to *www.forestry.gov.uk* and search 'Cwm Rhaeadr Guide') or Coed Trallwm near Llanwrtyd Wells (*www.coedtrallwm.co.uk*). Or go to *www.mtbbreconbeacons.co.uk* for more routes in the Beacons area.

Starting point & parking

Usk Reservoir lies 5 miles west of Trecastle, off the A40 **between Brecon and Llandovery**. From Trecastle follow signs for Usk Reservoir and Talsarn. The picnic site / car park is located on the western edge of Glasfynydd Wood when travelling towards Talsarn (grid reference SN 821272).

Station: Llandovery.

TIC: Brecon, 01874 622485.

Other nearby trails: The Taff Trail at Talybont-on-Usk. Coed Trallwm Mountain Bike centre at Abergwesyn (*www.coedtrallwm.co.uk*) or Cwm Rhaeadr (*www.forestry.gov.uk*).

Useful publications & websites: OS Landranger Map 160. Go to *www.mbwales.com*, click on 'Brecon Beacons' from the 'Pick an MTB Base' box then click on 'Usk Reservoir'. Or try *www.mtbbreconbeacons.co.uk*

Refreshments: None on the route; the nearest are at Trecastle.

Category
Around reservoir route.

Distance
6-mile circuit.

Ride 33 Claerwen Reservoir west of Rhayader

33

Category
Broad stone track alongside reservoir.

Distance
6 miles each way.

The reservoirs in the Elan Valley were built at the turn of the century to collect water for the ever-expanding population of Birmingham. There are two main traffic-free rides in the area, this one and the (easier) Elan Valley Trail. Both are there-and-back routes but if you are fit and have a good map you can easily work out much tougher, circular mountain bike challenges. This ride can either start from the Elan Valley Visitor Centre or from the dam at the eastern end of the reservoir, and it then goes west for 6 miles along the north shoreline of the Claerwen Reservoir. This is a fairly exposed and remote route at over 1,000ft (305m) with several steady climbs and descents on a broad but at times rough stony surface, so it is best undertaken on mountain bikes by reasonably fit riders. It is suggested you turn around at the end of the reservoir, but you could continue west to the pub at Ffair Rhos. The wind is normally blowing from the west, which tends to help you on your return.

Starting point & parking

There is car parking space at the dam (grid reference SN 872635) at the eastern end of Claerwen Reservoir, 10 miles to the **southwest of Rhayader**. Alternatively you may wish to start from the Elan Valley Visitor Centre (grid reference SN 928647). The minor, dead-end road between the visitor centre and Claerwen carries little traffic.

Station: Llandrindod Wells.

TIC: Rhayader, 01597 810591.

Other nearby trails: The Elan Valley Trail, north from the visitor centre.

Useful publications & websites: OS Landranger Map 147. For other routes near Rhayader go to *www.cycling.visitwales.com* and click on 'Cycle Breaks' then 'Rhayader'.

Refreshments: Café at the visitor centre (seasonal). Lots of choice in Rhayader.

Elan Valley Trail Ride 34
west of Rhayader

This spectacular trail climbs past three reservoirs in the heart of beautiful Mid-Wales following the line of the old Birmingham Corporation Railway, which was built at the start of the 20th century to help construct the reservoirs to supply the growing needs of Birmingham. The ride climbs 165ft (50m) from the Elan Valley Visitor Centre past Caban Coch and Garreg Ddu Reservoirs – with their fine dams and an ornamental water tower – to the end of Pen y Garreg Reservoir, leaving you with a very fine descent back to the start. When the reservoirs are full you will be rewarded with the sight of millions of gallons of water cascading over the dam walls.

Starting point & parking

The Elan Valley Visitor Centre (grid reference SN 928647) at the end of the B4518, about 3 miles to the **south-west of Rhayader** in Mid-Wales.

Railway: Llandrindod Wells.

TIC: Rhayader, 01597 810591.

Other nearby trails: There is also a route along the north shore of Claerwen Reservoir.

Useful publications & websites: OS Landranger Map 147. To download a map go to *www.leapingstiles.com*, click on 'find me a walk' then on 'Rhayader' then on Route no. 8 (Elan Valley Trail). Or try *www.visitmidwales.co.uk* and click on 'Things to do' then 'Outdoor and Adventure' then 'Cycling and Biking'.

Refreshments: Café at the visitor centre (from mid-March to the end of October). Lots of choice in Rhayader.

Category
Railway path.

Distance
8 miles each way.

Ride 35 Nant yr Arian Forest east of Aberystwyth

Category
Three waymarked mountain bike trails.

Distance
6 – 22 miles.

As the Forestry Commission tells us: Nant yr Arian Forest offers stunning high-level wilderness riding. With trails heading out into the epic scenery of the Cambrian Mountains, this is a fantastic area for those who like their riding rugged. Be prepared for everything from true mountain climbs to river crossings and technical rocky descents. The Syfydrin Trail combines the best of the Summit Trail singletrack with back country mountain tracks for a 22-mile wilderness loop. The 10-mile Summit Trail and 6-mile Pendam Trail use twisting all-weather singletrack carved into the steep valleys and ridges of the forest to create shorter, but no less challenging, route options.

Starting point & parking

Bwlch Nant yr Arian Visitor Centre is located just off the A44 about 10 miles east of Aberystwyth and 2 miles west of Ponterwyd (grid reference SN 718813).

On your bikes!

The descriptions provided by the Forestry Commission website are as follows:

Summit Trail – Red grade – 10 miles

Superb views and awesome riding on flowing twisty singletrack make the Summit Trail something you will want to do over and over again. There are endless riding opportunities around Nant yr Arian with an unrivalled network of bridleways, byways and tracks criss-crossing the mountains.

Syfydrin Trail – Black grade – 22 miles

The Syfydrin Trail is an epic ride in epic countryside. This trail takes in the entire existing Summit trail with its fantastic swooping, flowing singletrack, and adds to it by leading you out onto the high open hills with stunning views. It is a long and challenging ride in exposed and remote countryside, so go equipped for any eventuality.

Pendam Trail – Red grade – 6 miles

This route combines sections of the 'Summit' and 'Syfydrin' trails to give you a taste of the fantastic riding and scenery available. Although it is the shortest route at Nant yr Arian, it includes lots of technically challenging singletrack and some hard climbs.

Station: Aberystwyth.

TIC: Aberystwyth, 01970 612125.

Other nearby trails: The Elan Valley Trail and Claerwen Reservoir to the west of Rhayader.

Useful publications: OS Landranger Map 135. To download a trail guide go to *www.forestry.gov.uk*, click on 'Wales' then 'Mountain Biking' then 'Nant yr Arian'. Also try *www.mbwales.com*, following links to Nant yr Arian and 'Trails'.

Refreshments: At the visitor centre.

Mawddach Trail from Dolgellau to Barmouth

Ride 36

orming part of Lôn Las Cymru or National Cycle Network Route 8, which runs from Holyhead to Cardiff, the Mawddach Trail is one of the most scenic railway paths in the country, running along the spectacular and atmospheric Mawddach Estuary. More beautiful than the Camel Trail in Cornwall with a fraction of the visitors! The trail starts right from the heart of the handsome grey stone town of Dolgellau, from the corner of the main car park by the bridge over the river. The George III Hotel at Penmaenpool is superbly located and very popular with cyclists for coffees, lunches and teas. At the western end of the trail you have to cross the wonderful old wooden railway bridge to get to Barmouth.

Starting points & parking

1. The main car park in **Dolgellau** by the bridge over the river (grid reference SH 729180).

2. Car park at **Penmaenpool** on the A493 to the west of Dolgellau (grid reference SH 695185).

3. Car park on the south side of Barmouth Bridge at **Morfa Mawddach station** (grid reference SH 628141).

4. The harbour in **Barmouth** (grid reference SH 616155).

Station: Barmouth.

TIC: Dolgellau, 01341 422888.

Other nearby trails: Forest trails in Coed y Brenin north of Dolgellau. Railway path south from Caernarfon to Bryncir.

Useful publications & websites: OS Landranger Map 124. Try www.mawddachtrail.co.uk or for a downloadable map go to the Snowdonia National Park website at www.eryri-npa.co.uk – click on 'Snowdonia for all' then 'Leisurely Walks' then 'Mawddach Trail'.

Refreshments: Lots of choice in Dolgellau. George III at Penmaenpool (also does coffees and teas). Lots of choice in Barmouth.

Category
Railway path.

Distance
9 miles each way.

NB There is a short section on road in Barmouth that has a tricky right turn if you are eastbound (ie travelling from Barmouth towards Dolgellau).

36

Ride 37 Coed y Brenin Forest north of Dolgellau (7 routes)

37

Category
Forest trails.

Distance
7 – 24 miles.

A large Forestry Commission holding in North Wales that has adopted a very positive attitude to recreational cycling, with seven waymarked trails. Only the Yr Afon Route is suitable for novices or children (over 10 years old). The trails that are graded Red or Black contain singletrack and technical sections, and are not for novices.

Starting point & parking

Coed y Brenin Visitor Centre, off the A470, about 9 miles north of Dolgellau (grid reference SH 716277).

On your bikes!

These are the descriptions provided by the Forestry Commission:

Yr Afon – Green grade – 7 miles

A route suitable for the whole family – no technical singletrack sections. Based on forest roads and contouring the hillsides, taking in the magnificent waterfalls on the Gain and Mawddach. One or two short, sharp climbs and a long, fast descent from the waterfall, so take note of the SLOW signs.

37

Dragon's Back – Red grade – 19 miles

Longer than most mountain biking trails
of this grade, the Dragon's Back has to be
one of the best mountain bike experiences
in Europe. A huge variety of terrain
from forest roads to some of the finest
singletrack, huge climbs and long sweeping
descents make this trail only suitable for
experienced mountain bikers. (Formerly the
Karrimor route.)

Temtiwr – Red grade – 6 miles

A short route giving riders a taste of what
to expect from the riding in Coed y Brenin.
It includes five sections of singletrack, from
extremely technical rock pitching to fast-
flowing swooping curves through the trees,
and of course, long climbs.

Cyflym Coch – Red grade – 7 miles

Starting from the visitor centre, this
Red-graded trail should prove an ideal
stepping stone for those riders not quite
experienced enough to take on the Black
trails in Coed y Brenin. It pieces together
some of the best fast-flowing sections in
the Forest Park, with relatively short climbs
and adrenalin-fuelled singletrack descents.

MBR – Black grade – 11.5 miles

A rocky, challenging technical trail
throughout, offering some sweeping
descents (Bugsy) as well as Coed y Brenin's
most demanding stone-pitched (Badger
and The Beginning of the End) and natural
(Cain) sections.

Beast of Brenin – Black grade – 24 miles

A combination of the Dragon's Back and
MBR routes, giving a long, gruelling
challenge using all of the best bits of the
singletrack sections.

Tarw – Black grade – 12.5 miles

A technically challenging ride with twisting,
rocky descents and forest road climbs. Tons
of singletrack including the superb 'Pins
and Needles' and the unforgettable 'R74'
(formerly the Red Bull).

Station: Barmouth.

TIC: Dolgellau, 01341 422888.

Other nearby trails: The Mawddach Trail
between Barmouth and Dolgellau lies 9 miles
south of the visitor centre.

Useful publications & websites: OS
Landranger Map 124. A Forest Enterprise
leaflet is available from the visitor centre at
Coed y Brenin. To download a trail guide go
to *www.forestry.gov.uk*, click on 'Wales' then
'Mountain Biking' then 'Coed y Brenin'. Also
try *www.mbwales.com*

Refreshments: At the visitor centre.

Ride 38 Caernarfon to Bryncir (Lôn Eifion)

38

Category
Railway path.

Distance
12 miles each way.

A good, long stretch of dismantled railway, starting near the mighty castle in Caernarfon and climbing south alongside the Welsh Highland Railway past Llanwnda and Penygroes to Bryncir, with wonderful views west out to Caernarfon Bay and east to the foothills of Snowdonia. The highpoint is reached after almost 500ft (150m) of climbing, just below the radio mast, about 2 miles south of Penygroes. The path forms part of Sustrans' National Cycle Network Route 8, known as Lôn Las Cymru, which links Holyhead to Cardiff. You may wish to break your journey with a visit to the Inigo Jones Slateworks at Groeslon, about 4 miles south of Caernarfon, to see craftsmen cut, shape and polish raw slate slabs into practical products such as steps, kitchen worktops and a multitude of craft items. There is also a café attached.

Starting point & parking

Car park by **Caernarfon Castle** (grid reference SH 478628).

On your bikes!

Follow the road from the castle past the Harbour Offices and after 300yds bear left beneath the sculptured arch onto the railway path, following signs for 'Lôn Eifion' and 'National Cycle Network Route 8'.

Station: Bangor.

TIC: Caernarfon, 01286 672232.

Other nearby trails: Lôn Las Menai (Caernarfon to Y Felinheli) starts from the north of Caernarfon.

Useful publications & websites: OS Landranger Maps 115 & 124. Go to *www. gwynedd.gov.uk* then click on 'Environment & Planning' then 'Countryside & Access' then 'Recreational Routes'.

Refreshments: Lots of choice in Caernarfon. Several pubs along the route. Café at the Inigo Jones Slateworks at Groeslon.

Caernarfon to Y Felinheli
(Lôn Las Menai)

Ride 39

This 4-mile section of dismantled railway links Caernarfon with the old slate harbour of Port Dinorwig (Y Felinheli). There are views of the Menai Straits and across the water to the island of Anglesey. Caernarfon is dominated by the towers and battlements of the mighty castle, built for Edward I in the 13th century to command the entrance to the Menai Straits. Its unique polygonal towers, intimidating battlements and colour-banded walls were designed to echo Constantinople, the imperial power of Rome and the dream castle 'the fairest that

man ever saw' of Welsh myth and legend. In 1969 the castle gained worldwide fame as the setting for the investiture of Prince Charles as Prince of Wales.

Starting points & parking

1. The Victoria Dock, **Caernarfon** (grid reference SH 478631). Follow signs for 'Lôn Las Menai' and 'National Cycle Network Route 8'.

2. In **Y Felinheli**, park by the Garddfon Inn, down by the waterside (grid reference SH 523674).

Category
Railway path.

Distance
4 miles each way.

Station: Bangor.

TIC: Caernarfon, 01286 672232.

Other nearby trails: There are two other nearby railway paths – from Caernarfon to Bryncir (Lôn Las Eifion) and from Bangor to Tregarth (Lôn Las Ogwen).

Useful publications & websites: OS Landranger Map 115. Go to *www.gwynedd. gov.uk* then click on 'Environment & Planning' then 'Countryside & Access' then 'Recreational Routes'.

Refreshments: Lots of choice in Caernarfon, café and Garddfon Inn in Y Felinheli.

Ride 40 Bangor to Llyn Ogwen (Lôn Las Ogwen)

Category
Railway path.

Distance
11 miles each way.

Lôn Las Ogwen is a superb ride, offering excellent mountain views as you climb south from the coast at Bangor (Porth Penryn) via a railway path, through mature broadleaf woodland alongside the River Cegin to the village of Tregarth. The ride continues on up through the spoils of the slate quarry on a well-designed path with ever better views of the mountains of Snowdonia ahead. The path joins a minor road that runs parallel with the busy A5 and therefore carries very little traffic. A final climb takes you to the shores of Llyn Ogwen, where there is a café

and normally several groups of outdoor enthusiasts either walking, climbing or cycling. The mountains rise to over 3,000ft (915m) on either side of the road.

Starting points & parking

1. Abercegin (Bangor), just off the A5122 (grid reference SH 592725).

2. The western edge of **Tregarth**, 4 miles to the south of Bangor on the B4409 (grid reference SH 600680).

3. Llyn Ogwen (grid reference SH 649604), on the A5 south of Bangor towards Betws-y-Coed.

Station: Bangor.

TIC: Bangor, 01248 352786.

Other nearby trails: There are two trails running north and south from Caernarfon. The Mawddach Trail links Barmouth to Dolgellau. Waymarked forest trails in Coed y Brenin.

Useful publications & websites: OS Landranger Map 115. Go to *www.gwynedd.gov.uk* then click on 'Environment & Planning' then 'Countryside & Access' then 'Recreational Routes'.

Refreshments: Lots of choice in Bangor. Pub in Tregarth. Café at Llyn Ogwen.

NB. There is a climb of almost 1,000ft (305m) from Bangor to Llyn Ogwen, so it will be considerably slower on the way up than on the way back down. For a more gentle ride, go only as far as Tregarth, which involves a climb of less than 300ft (90m).

Lôn Las Cefni Ride 41
Anglesey

Lôn Las Cefni is a traffic-free trail that runs both north and south from the town of Llangefni in the centre of the island of Anglesey. To the north, a 2-mile traffic-free trail starts from the local nature reserve known as The Dingle, and heads through broadleaf woodland past Cefni Reservoir to a woodland picnic spot just by the B5111. The much longer southern section of the route (10 miles) follows the watercourse of Afon Cefni across Malltraeth Marsh to Pont Marquis, then joins a tiny quiet lane to the village of Malltraeth. You have the chance of refreshment here before turning south to the very edge of Newborough Forest, Anglesey's largest woodland with plenty of tracks to explore and a waymarked route to the village of Newborough.

Starting point & parking

Llangefni in the centre of Anglesey, off the A5 between Bangor and Holyhead (grid reference SH 459759).

On your bikes!

North from Llangefni

1. From the far end of Dingle Reserve car park, walk your bike over the bridge then turn left on a broad track. Follow this up and down, crossing the river on an amazing wooden walkway.

2. After 1.3 miles bear right uphill on zig-zags to run parallel with the reservoir. The forest track ends after 1 mile at a picnic site by the B5111 (grid reference SH 452784).

South from Llangefni

1. Start from the car park nearest to the clocktower roundabout in the centre of Llangefni and follow blue and white bike signs on the cyclepath alongside the river, soon crossing then re-crossing the river.

2. After 2½ miles pass under the A55 and cross the A5 (take care). Follow the track between watercourses.

3. After almost 3 miles, at a T-junction with a road, turn right over the old stone bridge then left, following 'Lôn Las Cefni' signs.

4. After 2 miles on this quiet lane cross the A4080 by the Joiners pub onto a traffic-free path. Fine estuary views.

5. The signposted route takes you through Newborough Forest to Newborough, where there is a pub.

Station: Bodorgan.

TIC: Llanfair PG, 01248 713177.

Other nearby trails: Two trails start in Caernarfon and one runs south from Bangor.

Useful publications & websites: OS Landranger Map 114. For a downloadable map go to *www.visitanglesey.co.uk*, search 'Cycling' then click on 'Anglesey rural cycling network' then 'Circular Cycling Route – Lôn Las'. Also try *www.cyclingnorthwales.co.uk*, click on 'Rides & Routes' then 'Lôn Las Cefni cycle path'.

Refreshments: Lots of choice in Llangefni. Joiners pub in Malltraeth. White Lion Hotel, Newborough.

Category
Woodland trails and riverside path.

Distance
12 miles each way.

377

Ride 42 Gwydyr Forest Betws-y-Coed

42

Category
Forest trails.

Distance
6 – 16 miles.

The most well-known and popular trail in Gwydyr Forest is a tough and technical waymarked mountain bike ride called the Marin Trail, 16 miles long with almost 1,500ft (455m) of climbing and plenty of challenging singletrack. More recently the Penmachno Trail (also Red grade) has opened to the south of Betws-y-Coed. Both trails are for experienced riders. The Llyn Elsi Route is an easier trail (although there are still lots of hills), climbing up to the old reservoir to the south of Betws-y-Coed.

Starting points & parking

1. The starting point for the Llyn Elsi routes is Beics Betws (bike shop) in **Betws-y-Coed**, just north of the junction of the A470 and A5 on the western edge of Snowdonia (grid reference SH 795564).

2. The starting point for the Marin Trail is about 3 miles north of **Betws-y-Coed**,

on a minor road off the B5106 that starts opposite the link road to Llanrwst (grid reference SH 790610).

3. The starting point for the Penmachno Trail (SH 787498) is about ¹⁄₂ mile south of the small village of **Penmachno**, at the southern end of the B4406, about 5 miles south of Betws-y-Coed.

On your bikes!

Llyn Elsi route – 6 miles

It is important to pick up a leaflet from Beics Betws bike shop to help you navigate this route. Follow the A5 north through Betws-y-Coed towards Capel Curig for about ¹⁄₂ mile, then at the speed limit sign turn left and follow the waymarks.

Opposite are the descriptions of the singletrack trails provided by the Forestry Commission:

Marin Trail – Red grade – 16 miles

The Marin Trail is a proper mountain bike trail in every sense of the term. Big climbs, big descents, brilliant singletrack and truly awesome scenery make this a trail to remember. Most, but not all, of the climbs are on forest roads and tracks, giving you time to take in the views of the mountains of Snowdonia, and all of the descents are on singletrack. The singletrack varies from very tight, technical and rocky to wonderfully open and flowing, from dark forest to exposed ridgelines.

Penmachno Trail – Red grade – 13 miles

This is a challenging trail with some steady climbs, taking in some more spectacular scenery. The trail uses plenty of forest roads but also includes some decent singletrack incorporating bridge crossings, elevated wooden sections (not North Shore) and stream crossings.

Station: Betws-y-Coed.

TIC: Betws-y-Coed, 01690 710426.

Other nearby trails: Two railway paths start in Caernarfon. There are more waymarked forestry routes in Coed y Brenin Forest, 25 miles to the south.

Useful publications & websites: OS Landranger Map 115. More useful is the Forestry Commission map of Gwydyr Forest, which can be bought at the Y Stablau Information Centre. To download a Marin Trail guide go to *www.forestry.gov.uk*, click on 'Wales' then 'Mountain Biking' then 'Marin'. Also try *www.mbwales.com* and click on 'Betws-y-Coed'.

Refreshments: Lots of choice in Betws-y-Coed.

Colwyn Bay (Rhos-on-Sea) to Prestatyn Ride **43**

A superb, breezy, open ride along the seafront between Rhos-on-Sea (Colwyn Bay) in the west and Prestatyn in the east, with fine views of wooded hills rising steeply away from the coast. It is worth checking the wind on this ride: try to cycle into the wind (it is normally from the west) at the start of the ride when you are fresh, and have it behind you on the return half of the ride; or alternatively catch a train one way into the wind. The ride is part of National Cycle Network Route 5, which runs from Holyhead on the island of Anglesey to Chester. You can follow the route further west from

Ride **43** **Colwyn Bay (Rhos-on-Sea) to Prestatyn**

Category
Seafront
promenade.

Distance
16 miles each way.

Rhos-on-Sea into Llandudno, although this will involve some road sections as well.

Starting point & parking

Rhos-on-Sea (north-west of Colwyn Bay, grid reference SH 843805) or **Prestatyn** (grid reference SJ 060838).

> **Station:** Colwyn Bay or Prestatyn.
>
> **TICs:** Colwyn Bay, 01492 530478. Rhyl, 01745 355068.
>
> **Other nearby trails:** There are two railway paths starting from Caernarfon and one from Bangor.
>
> **Useful publications & websites:** OS Landranger Map 116. Go to *www.sustrans.org.uk* – put 'Denbighshire leaflet' in the 'Search' box then click on 'Layout 1' (ie a pdf of the leaflet).
>
> **Refreshments:** Lots of choice along the way.

44

Llyn Brenig & Alwen Reservoir   Ride 44
south-west of Denbigh

Set in the Denbigh Moors in North Wales, Llyn Brenig offers an attractive, largely traffic-free circuit of the water. The trail uses a mixture of forestry roads and fairly quiet minor roads. The circuit of the reservoir starts from the visitor centre. There are several gentle hills and two sections on-road, including almost 2 miles on the busier B4501 to the north of the reservoir, so take extra care on this stretch. The eastern half of the ride is completely traffic-free so if you wish, just to do this bit (about a 7-mile round trip from the visitor centre to the car park by the archaeological trail), turn left out of the visitor centre, keeping the water on your left and do the circuit anti-clockwise. It is also possible to link this ride to the Alwen Reservoir route (or to do the latter as a separate ride).

Alwen Reservoir Route
Follow forestry tracks and paths along the water's edge and up to the moorland of Mynydd Hiraethog. The scenery around the reservoir is wonderfully varied with a beautiful section along the water's edge. High on the moorland there are stunning landscape views. Along the way you will encounter illustrated panels providing information of the wildlife, culture and folk tales associated with the area, including the story of 'Freckled Fairy Cow'.

Category
Round-reservoir rides.

Distance
Llyn Brenig: 10-mile circuit.

Alwen Reservoir: 7.5-mile circuit.

These can be linked to form a 20-mile circuit (see map details under **Useful publications**).

44

Ride **44**   **Llyn Brenig & Alwen Reservoir, south-west of Denbigh**

Starting points & parking

1. At the **Llyn Brenig Visitor Centre**
on the B4501, about 6 miles north of
Cerrigydrudion, and 10 miles south-west of
Denbigh (grid reference SH 967547).

2. Alwen Dam. Follow the B4501 north
from Cerrigydrudion, then turn left into
the forest shortly after the Pont yr Alwen
junction. Follow the forest road through a
smallholding and take the first left to park
adjacent to the dam (grid reference
SH 955530).

Station: Betws-y-Coed.

TIC: Betws-y-Coed, 01690 710246.

Other nearby trails: The seafront promenade
from Prestatyn to Rhos-on-Sea.

Useful publications & websites: OS
Landranger Map 116. Go to *www.
walesdirectory.co.uk/Lakes* and click on 'Llyn
Brenig'. Visit *www.ridetheclwyds.com* – click
on 'Route maps' then 'Easy' then 'Around the
Lake'. Also try *www.mbwales.com* – click on
'Hiraethog' in the 'Pick an MTB Base' box
then at the bottom of the 'Hiraethog' page
click on 'Alwen and Brenig Map'.

Refreshments: At the Llyn Brenig Visitor Centre.

Coed Llandegla Ride 45
west of Wrexham (four routes)

Coed Llandegla is a privately owned forest covering 650 acres, where there is a visitor centre (01978 751656) with a café and four bike trails to cater for all abilities. A curious fact: 50% of the whole of the Welsh black grouse population lives within 1 mile of the forest! These are the descriptions of the trails provided by Coed Llandegla:

Family Route – Green grade – 3 miles
The route avoids major climbs and technical sections. The surfaces are generally hard-packed but there are sections which are loose, uneven or muddy at times. The trail completes a loop around the reservoir and offers views of the Clwyd Hills.

Beginners' Route – Blue grade – 7$^{1}/_{2}$ miles
There is a gradual climb up through the forest until it splits from the Intermediate (Red) route at the top of the forest. The trail offers a selection of small humps and other features on the descent back to the visitor centre to add a degree of challenge.

Intermediate Route – Red grade – 11 miles
The trail shares the same climb as the Blue route but on the descent there are a series of more technical challenges with unsurfaced singletrack, bermed switchbacks, whoops, water crossings, tabletops and boardwalk. A high level of fitness, stamina and experience is needed for this route.

Black Runs – Black grade – 13 miles
There are a series of black runs totalling 4 miles which are accessible only from the Intermediate Route. The Black Runs are predominantly steeper downhill stretches and they have much more challenging technical features including large steps, gaps and drop-offs.

Starting point & parking

The Coed Llandegla Visitor Centre is well signposted and located off a minor road to the south of the A525, about 7 miles west of Wrexham. There is a charge for the car park. The turn off the A525 onto the minor road is at grid reference SJ 227520.

Station: Wrexham.

TIC: Wrexham, 01978 292015.

Other nearby trails: Llyn Brenig. Routes from Chester.

Useful publications & websites: OS Landranger Map 117. An excellent trails map can be downloaded from *www.coedllandegla. com*. Also try *www.mbwales.com*

Refreshments: Café at the visitor centre.

Category
Forest trails.

Distance
3 – 13 miles.

Scotland Trails

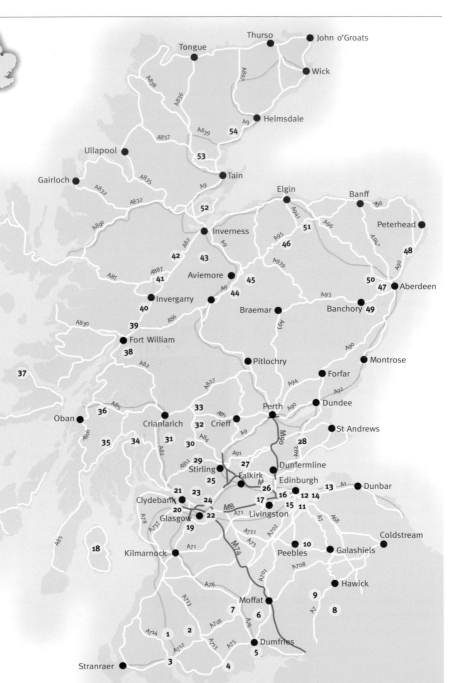

Tongue
Thurso
John o'Groats
Wick
A838
A836
A897
Helmsdale
A9
54
A837
A839
53
Ullapool
Tain
52
Gairloch
A832
A825
A9
Elgin
Banff
A838
A832
Inverness
A941
51
A96
Peterhead
A890
42
A82
43
A95
46
A947
48
A81
A887
41
Aviemore
45
A939
50
47
Aberdeen
40
44
A9
A93
Invergarry
A86
Braemar
Banchory
49
A830
39
A93
Fort William
38
A82
Pitlochry
Montrose
37
A827
Forfar
A90
36
A85
Perth
A94
A92
Dundee
Oban
35
34
31
30
Crianlarich
32
Crieff
A85
A9
St Andrews
A828
A816
A82
A84
28
33
29
M90
A91
27
Stirling
25
Falkirk
Dunfermline
A811
26
Edinburgh
21
23
Clydebank
24
M
13
A1
Dunbar
20
17
16
12
14
Glasgow
22
15
11
A78
A731
19
M8
A71
Livingston
A8
A68
A83
18
A71
Kilmarnock
10
Coldstream
Peebles
Galashiels
A73
A721
A702
A708
Hawick
9
A7
8
7
Moffat
6
A76
A713
A702
M74
A701
A712
1
2
A702
A75
Dumfries
A714
3
4
Stranraer

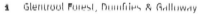

Scotland Mountain Biking

Scotland leads the way in the UK for mountain biking – not only are there ever more purpose-built trails in Forestry Commission holdings (see details of websites below), but since the Land Reform (Scotland) Act came into force, everyone has a statutory right of responsible access to most land and inland water. Find out more by visiting *www.outdooraccess-scotland.com* or call Scottish Natural Heritage on 01738 444177 for a copy of the Access Code. Be aware of the deer-stalking season from July to October (*www.snh.org.uk/hillphones*) and the grouse-shooting season (August to December).

Forestry mountain biking centres

The 7stanes project has created seven centres of mountain biking excellence in Southern Scotland, each offering a variety of purpose-built, waymarked trails of different grades. Of these, Glentress, near Peebles, is by far the most popular. The success of these trails has spurred development of centres throughout Scotland, from Carron Valley in the Central Belt up to the Highlands with centres such as Laggan Wolftrax, Highland Wildcat Trails and Moray Monster Trails. Visit the following websites:
http://cycling.visitscotland.com/mountain_biking
www.forestry.gov.uk/mtbscotland
www.7stanes.gov.uk
www.mountain-bike-scotland.com
or ask for a copy of the *Scottish Mountain Biking Guide* from Visit Scotland on 0845 2255121.

Remote riding

There are many long-distance challenges away from the forestry centres – for example, Glen Sligachan on the Isle of Skye, or coast-to-coast rides ranging from the very short – such as Ullapool to Bonar Bridge (38 miles) – to the expedition-style, 250-mile crossing from Aberdeen to Ardnamurchan Point. For more information there is a good series of guides to the Scottish Glens by Peter Koch-Osborne, published by Cicerone (*www.cicerone.co.uk*).

7G Glentress

Scotland

Forestry Commission Scotland

S cotland is by far the most forested region of the UK. National Forest Estates stretch from the south-west in Galloway right up to Wick, only a few miles from John o'Groats. There are several Forestry Commission leaflets (and many websites) describing dozens of waymarked trails in Scotland. Call the nearest Forest District office to obtain them.

Forest Districts *(see map overleaf)*

1 North Highland
The Links, Golspie Business Park, Golspie, Sutherland KW10 6UB
Tel: 01408 634063
email: northhighland@forestry.gsi.gov.uk

2 Inverness, Ross & Skye
Tower Road, Smithton, Inverness IV2 7NL
Tel: 01463 791575
email.
invernessross&skye@forestry.gsi.gov.uk

3 Moray & Aberdeenshire
Portsoy Road, Huntly,
Aberdeenshire AB54 4SJ
Tel: 01466 794161
email:
moray&aberdeenshire@forestry.gsi.gov.uk

4 Lochaber
Torlundy, Fort William, Inverness-shire
PH33 6SW
Tel: 01397 702184
email: lochaber@forestry.gsi.gov.uk

5 Tay
Inverpark, Dunkeld, Perthshire PH8 0JR
Tel: 01350 727284
email: tay@forestry.gsi.gov.uk

6 West Argyll
Whitegates, Lochgilphead, Argyll PA31 8RS
Tel: 01546 602518
email: westargyll@forestry.gsi.gov.uk

7 Cowal & Trossachs
Aberfoyle, Stirling FK8 3UX
Tel: 01877 382383
email: cowal&trossachs@forestry.gsi.gov.uk

8 Scottish Lowlands
Braidwood House, Braidwood,
Carluke ML8 5NE
Tel: 01555 660 190
email: scottishlowlands@forestry.gsi.gov.uk

9 Galloway
Creebridge, Newton Stewart DG8 6AJ
Tel: 01671 402420
email: galloway@forestry.gsi.gov.uk

10 Dumfries & Borders
Ae Village, Parkgate, Dumfries DG1 1QB
Tel: 01387 860247
email:
dumfries&borders@forestry.gsi.gov.uk

Further information

Major Trail Centres *(see map overleaf)*	7stanes Centres *(see map overleaf)*
H Drumlanrig	**7A** Glentrool
I Firetower Trails	**7B** Kirroughtree
J Witch's Trails	**7C** Dalbeattie
K Laggan Wolftrax	**7D** Mabie
L Moray Monster Trails	**7E** Ae
M Learnie Red Rock Trails	**7F** Newcastleton
N Highland Wildcat Trails	**7G** Glentress

387

Forestry Commission Scotland

The Forestry Commission's website

This is a good source of information: click on 'Explore, Experience, Enjoy' then 'Cycling' and you can find out details of hundreds of waymarked trails throughout the UK. You can search by forest name or by the nearest town / city. The search will tell you the grade, length and waymarking details of the trails. Alternatively, by clicking on the map you can see the nearest forest to where you live.

www.forestry.gov.uk

www.forestry.gov.uk/mtbscotland

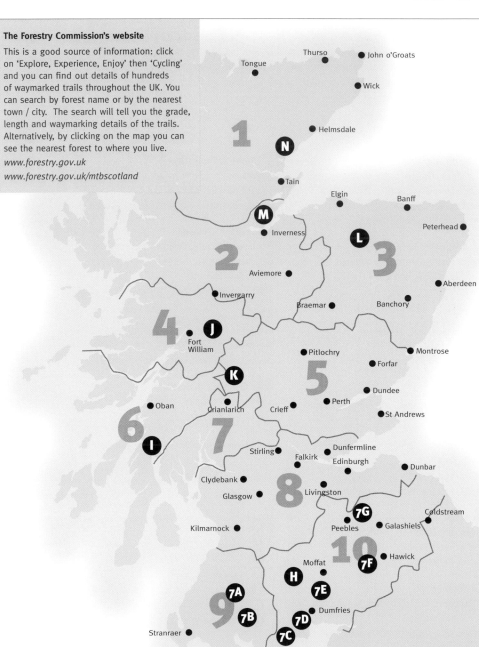

388

10 Scotland National Cycle Network

Lochs & Glens Cycle Route
(two maps: North & South)

428 miles from Inverness to Carlisle via Aviemore, Pitlochry, Callander, Glasgow, Ayr, Gatehouse of Fleet and Dumfries. Highlights include Aviemore and views of the Cairngorms, the pass of Drumochter, Pitlochry, the route alongside Loch Tay, Glen Ogle, the traffic-free route through the Trossachs, Loch Lomond, traffic-free routes through Glasgow, the Ayrshire Coast, Galloway Forest Park and the Solway Firth.

Traffic-free sections over 3 miles long:
- Killin to Kingshouse through Glen Ogle (NCN 7).
- Strathyre to Callander past Loch Lubnaig (NCN 7).
- Loch Venachar (Callander) to Aberfoyle (NCN 7).
- Loch Lomond to Glasgow Cycleway (NCN 7).
- Johnstone to Kilbirnie (NCN 7).
- Glentrool Village to Gatehouse Station via Clatteringshaws Loch (NCN 7).

Coast & Castles Cycle Route
(two maps: North & South)

372 miles from Newcastle to Aberdeen via Berwick-upon-Tweed, Kelso, Innerleithen, Edinburgh, Dunfermline, Dundee and Montrose. Highlights include the Northumbrian coast, Warkworth Castle, Bamburgh Castle, Berwick's town walls, views of the River Tweed, Kelso town square, Floors Castle, Melrose Abbey, the Moorfoot Hills, Edinburgh Falkland Palace, Tentsmuir Forest, Broughty Castle (Dundee), the coast of Angus and Aberdeenshire, the handsome town of Montrose, Dunnottar Castle, the Maritime Museum and Marischal College in Aberdeen.

Traffic-free sections over 3 miles long:
- The Innocent Railway, Edinburgh (NCN 1).
- From Dalmeny across the Forth Road Bridge (NCN 1).
- Tentsmuir Forest (Fife) (NCN 1).

Maps for these routes are available from www.sustrans.org.uk or 0845 113 0065.

Aberdeen to John o'Groats Cycle Route

501 miles from Aberdeen to John o'Groats, Orkney and Shetland via Banff, Elgin, Inverness, Tain, Tongue and Thurso. Highlights include the traffic-free Formartine & Buchan railway path, the coast of the Moray Firth, Elgin Cathedral, the ancient town of Forres, the north coast of Scotland, the Norse heritage of Orkney and Shetland.

Traffic-free sections over 3 miles long:
• Formartine & Buchan Way, north of Aberdeen (NCN 1).

Forth & Clyde Cycle Route

The map describes the two main routes between Edinburgh and Glasgow: the northern route follows the Union Canal and the Forth & Clyde Canal, joining the Clyde at Bowling; the southern route runs from Edinburgh through Livingston and Airdrie to join the River Clyde to the east of Glasgow. The map shows a route continuing west through Paisley, Greenock and Gourock to connect via ferries to the Argyll Peninsula. Highlights include the ancient city of Edinburgh, the Water of Leith, the Union Canal, the Forth & Clyde Canal (including the Falkirk Wheel), the Clyde Walkway into Glasgow and views of the Firth of Clyde from above Greenock.

Maps for these routes are available from www.sustrans. org.uk or 0845 113 0065.

Traffic-free sections over 3 miles long:
• Union Canal, Edinburgh (NCN 75).
• Water of Leith, Edinburgh (NCN 75).
• Clyde Walkway, Glasgow (NCN 75).
• Johnstone to Greenock (NCN 75).
• Johnstone to Lochwinnoch (NCN 7).
• Forth & Clyde Canal (NCN 754).
• Glasgow via Clydebank & Dumbarton to Balloch (NCN 7).

Oban to Campbeltown Cycle Route

120 miles up through the Kintyre Peninsula from Campbeltown via Tarbert, Lochgilphead and Loch Awe to Taynuilt and Oban. Highlights include stunning sea views, the Crinan Canal, the route alongside Loch Awe, Glen Lonan and the harbour at Oban.

Traffic-free sections over 3 miles long:
• The Crinan Canal north-west of Lochgilphead (NCN 78).

Round the Forth Cycle Route

134 miles between Dunbar, Edinburgh, Stirling and Kirkcaldy, plus other routes around the Firth of Forth, Fife and East Lothian. Highlights include the ancient city of Edinburgh, Forth Road Bridge and Stirling Castle.

Traffic-free sections over 3 miles long:
• Union Canal (NCN 754).
• Forth & Clyde Canal (NCN 754).
• Dunfermline to Alloa (NCN 764).
• Newbridge & the Forth Road Bridge (NCN 1).
• Innocent Railway, Edinburgh (NCN 1).

The Salmon Run Cycle Route

54 miles from Dundee to Pitlochry via Perth and Dunkeld. Highlights include The Royal Research Ship Discovery in Dundee, the Scone Palace in Perth and the stunning scenery of Strathtay between Dunkeld and Pitlochry.

Traffic-free sections over 3 miles long:
• Broughty Ferry along Dundee waterfront to Invergowrie (NCN 1).
• Perth to Almondbank (NCN 77).

Sustrans

The Sustrans maps shown here cover various National Cycle Network routes within Scotland. Some of the maps may describe routes that continue into England: these maps are mentioned in both chapters. The maps are not only useful for people wishing to ride the whole route over several days, they also show all the traffic-free sections that make good day rides.

Other good areas for lane cycling

Unsurprisingly for such a vast area, Scotland offers a wide variety of cycling from easy rolling country up the east coast to expedition-style trips linking the various islands of the Outer Hebrides on the west coast. Almost all the population of Scotland is concentrated in the Central Belt from the Clyde to the Forth around the two hubs of Glasgow and Edinburgh. To the south of the Central Belt there are thousands of miles of quiet lanes through Dumfries & Galloway and the Scottish Borders, with any number of fine little towns which could be good bases for a few days: big enough to offer a variety of accommodation and refreshments but small

enough for you to be in the countryside in less than 10 minutes' cycling. North of the Central Belt there is a big east / west divide: the west is more spectacular, mountainous, wetter and broken into hundreds of islands linked by ferries to the mainland; the east is less mountainous, drier, with a much more extensive lane network but less extraordinary by Scottish standards. Take your pick! The other warning is about midges: less troublesome for cyclists than for walkers, they are nevertheless pretty unpleasant during the summer months. Late spring or early autumn may be better times of year to appreciate the beauty of Scotland.

Also try:

http://cycling.visitscotland.com

www.sustrans.org.uk, click on 'Sustrans near you' then 'Scotland' then 'Maps and Leaflets'.

A map for this route is available from www.sustrans.org.uk *or 0845 113 0065.*

Ride **1** # Glentrool Forest
Dumfries & Galloway (four routes)

Category
Waymarked forest trails.

Distance
4 – 36 miles.

Glentrool is the westernmost of the 7stanes – seven centres of mountain biking excellence spread out across Southern Scotland. Five of the seven centres are located in Dumfries & Galloway, a sparsely populated and heavily forested region of South-West Scotland. For the most up-to-date information about Glentrool it is worth going to the 7stanes website at *www.7stanes.gov.uk* then click on 'Glentrool'.

Starting point & parking

Glentrool Visitor Centre, off the A714 about 8 miles **north of Newton Stewart.** Turn off at Bargrennan and after passing through Glentrool take the right fork (grid reference NX 372786 / OS Landranger Map 77).

The rides

The Glen

Distance	Grade	Waymarks
4 miles	Easy	Green

Follow the same gentle singletrack as the Blue route around the Pulnagashel Glen before dropping back down on forest tracks that lead back to the visitor centre.

Palgowan

Distance	Grade	Waymarks
8 miles	Easy	Green

A circular route running to the north of Glentrool Visitor Centre on forest roads, and returning on quiet back roads. There are some small hills but no big climbs, and surfaces are either on good forest roads or public roads, making this route a good family cycle.

Green Torr Blue Route

Distance	Grade	Waymarks
6 miles	Moderate	Blue

The purpose-built singletrack is wider than the trails at nearby Kirroughtree and has none of the rocks and roots found there, so it should not prove intimidating to less experienced riders. It is not without its challenges though, as it climbs 715ft (218m) to the Green Torr overlooking Loch Trool, before descending quickly back to the visitor centre.

Big Country Route CTC Ride

Distance	Grade	Waymarks
36 m:es	Strenuous	Purple

Unlike the other 7stanes trails, the whole of the route is on minor public and forest roads, without any singletrack. With magnificent views of lochs and hills contrasting with sheltered woodlands, and some testing climbs and big descents, it is a challenging but rewarding day out.

Other cycle trails in Galloway Forest Park

The Carrick Cycle Trail is a 14-mile Blue-grade (moderate) trail on the north side of Galloway Forest Park that takes you around Loch Braden. There is also the option of cycling across the hill to Loch Doon. The route is located south of Dalmellington (grid reference NX 476942).

Round Clatteringshaws Loch Cycle Route

is also a 14-mile Blue-grade (moderate) route with no major climbs or descents. The route follows tarmac roads and forest roads, and is located on the A712 between Newton Stewart and New Galloway (grid reference NX 552764).

Station: Dumfries or Girvan.

TIC: Dumfries, 01387 253862.

Other nearby trails: The other 7stanes centres are at Kirroughtree, Dalbeattie, Mabie, Ae, Newcastleton and Glentress / Innerleithen (www.7stanes.gov.uk). There are also easy trails at Drumlanrig Castle (www.drumlanrig. com).

Useful publications & websites: OS Landranger Maps 77 & 83. For maps of all the trails go to www.7stanes.gov.uk, click on 'Glentrool' then click on 'Download the trail map here' (in a green box at the top of the page).

Refreshments: At the Glentrool Visitor Centre (seasonal – call 01671 840302 for opening times).

Glentrool to Gatehouse Station along the Lochs & Glens Cycle Route Ride **2**

Dumfries and Galloway is one of the least populated and most densely forested regions of the whole of Great Britain, with a fine network of quiet roads and hundreds of miles of forestry tracks. Excellent news for every kind of cyclist. This route uses a section of the Lochs & Glens Cycle Route (National Cycle Network Route 7) through forests and past lochs, with two climbs – the first through Glentrool between Loch Trool and Loch Dee, and the second to the south of Clatteringshaws. The route runs from Glentrool Village east to Gatehouse Station (north-west of Gatehouse of Fleet) via Loch Dee, Clatteringshaws Loch and Meikle Cullendoch Moss. It is an alternative to

the main Lochs & Glens Cycle Route which stays closer to the coast, passing through Creetown and Newton Stewart.

Starting points & parking

1. In Glentrool Village, off the A714 **between Newton Stewart and Girvan** (grid reference NX 371786 / OS Landranger Map 77).

2. At Clatteringshaws Loch Visitor Centre, on the A712 **between Newton Stewart and New Galloway** (grid reference NX 552764 / OS Landranger Map 77).

3. The visitor centre at Dromore, off the northern end of the B796, and the old Gatehouse Station, 7 miles **north-west of Gatehouse of Fleet** (grid reference NX 556638).

Category
Minor roads and forestry tracks.

Distance
Up to 25 miles each way.

Ride **2** Glentrool to Gatehouse Station along the Lochs & Glens Cycle Route

Station: Barhill (Cairnlea) south of Girvan.

TIC: Newton Stewart, 01671 402431.

Other nearby trails: Nearby 7stanes centres are at Kirroughtree, Glentrool, Dalbeattie, Mabie and Ae *(www.7stanes.gov.uk)*. There are also easy trails at Drumlanrig Castle *(www.drumlanrig.com)*.

Useful publications & websites: OS Landranger Map 77. Sustrans' *Lochs & Glens Cycle Route – South* map (£6.99) includes many traffic-free sections between Glasgow and the Ayrshire coast as well as this trail, and is available from *www.sustrans.org.uk*. Try also *www. visitdumfriesandgalloway.co.uk/cycling*

Refreshments: Tearoom in the Clatteringshaws Loch Visitor Centre.

Ride **3** Kirroughtree Forest east of Newton Stewart (four routes)

Category
Waymarked forest trails.

Distance
4 – 19 miles.

The second of the 7stanes mountain bike centres described in the book, Kirroughtree lies to the south of Glentrool and is home to some of the best technical singletrack in the country. However, it is also a favourite family venue with a wide range of trails, a seasonal café and a great kids' play area. For more details go to *www.7stanes.org.uk*, click on 'Kirroughtree' then click on one of the trails mentioned below.

Starting point & parking

Kirroughtree Visitor Centre, off the A75 about 4 miles **east of Newton Stewart** (grid reference NX 452644 / OS Landranger Map 83).

The rides

Bargaly Wood

Distance	Grade	Waymarks
4 miles	Easy	Green

Uses a mixture of minor public roads, wide tracks and one short section of easy singletrack to take you around the scenic Bargaly Glen.

Larg Hill & Doon Hill extension

Distance	Grade	Waymarks
9 miles	Moderate	Blue

Long sections of narrow, flowing singletrack ending in a superb plunge through stunning woodland. Great views from the Doon Hill extension.

The Twister

Distance	Grade	Waymarks
10.5 miles	Difficult	Red

More demanding with rock step-ups, drops, berms and jumpable sections, all on the tight and twisting trail that is typical of Kirroughtree.

Black Craigs (includes The Twister)

Distance	Grade	Waymarks
19 miles	Severe	Black

For many, the highlight is 'McMoab' – huge slabs and ridges of exposed granite, linked by boulder causeways. Skill and bags of nerve required.

Station: Barhill.

TIC: Dumfries, 01387 253862.

Other nearby trails: Other nearby 7stanes centres are at Glentrool, Dalbeattie, Mabie and Ae *(www.7stanes.gov.uk)*. There are also easy trails at Drumlanrig Castle *(www.drumlanrig.com)*.

Useful publications & websites: OS Landranger Maps 77 & 83. For maps of all the trails go to *www.7stanes.gov.uk*, click on 'Kirroughtree' then click on 'Download the trail map here' (in a green box at the top of the page).

Refreshments: At the Kirroughtree Visitor Centre (seasonal – call 01671 840302 for opening times).

Ride 4 Dalbeattie Forest south-west of Dumfries

Category
Waymarked forest routes.

Distance
2.4 – 10.6 miles.

Dalbeattie is another 7stanes mountain bike centre. As well as the challenging Hardrock Trail, Dalbeattie has a choice of easier rides including the Ironhash Trail and the Moyle Hill Trail. The Forestry Commission describes the Hardrock Trail in the following terms: 'This amazing route offers a riding style unlike anything else in the UK. The 7stanes trailbuilders have carved out feature-filled singletrack that seems to go on forever undulating up and down, weaving in and out of trees and over and around Dalbeattie's famous granite rock. It is a physically long and challenging ride but all the tricky rock features include easier options – always ride within your ability.'

Starting point & parking

Richorn car park on the A710 about 2 miles **south of Dalbeattie**, to the south-west of Dumfries (grid reference NX 836592 / OS Landranger Map 84).

The rides

Ironhash Trail

Distance	Grade	Waymarks
7.1 miles	Easy	Green

The trail provides an easy ride deep into the heart of the forest, mainly on forest roads, and is ideal for getting a flavour of what mountain biking can offer.

Moyle Hill Trail

Distance	Grade	Waymarks
8.7 miles	Moderate	Blue

The trail is a good introduction to riding 7stanes singletrack – and to the granite

rock that gives Dalbeattie a character all of its own – offering some cracking views and fun riding.

Hardrock Trail

Distance	Grade	Waymarks
16 miles	Difficult	Red

This is a classic Red-grade route that includes miles of singletrack and some very challenging Black-grade features. The hard, granite surface makes the trail one of the most resilient in the country and provides good grip in the wet, so the route is fantastic to ride all year round.

Station: Dumfries.

TIC: Dumfries, 01387 253862.

Other nearby trails: Other nearby 7stanes centres are at Kirroughtree, Glentrool, Mabie and Ae *(www.7stanes.gov.uk)*. There are also easy trails at Drumlanrig Castle *(www. drumlanrig.com)*.

Useful publications & websites: OS Landranger Map 84. For maps of all the trails go to *www.7stanes.gov.uk*, click on 'Dalbeattie' then click on 'Download the trail map here' (in a green box at the top of the page).

Refreshments: Dalbeattie.

Mabie Forest Ride 5
south of Dumfries (five routes)

Mabie Forest, the original mountain biking venue in South-West Scotland, lies just a few miles south of Dumfries and now caters for beginners right through to the most expert of riders. The Green-grade Big Views Loop and the Blue-grade Woodhead Loop are great introductions to mountain biking and to Mabie's striking surroundings. The Lochbank Loop is a longer route but with no technical features, offering a fine exploration of the wider area. The Red-grade Phoenix Trail has testing climbs, fast descents, berms and water splashes. Mabie's Kona Dark Side is for experts only.

Starting point & parking

The car park by Mabie House Hotel, off the A710 about 4 miles **south-west of Dumfries** (grid reference NX 950708 / OS Landranger Map 84).

The rides

Big Views Loop

Distance	Grade	Waymarks
5 miles	Easy	Green

You are rewarded with some great views over the Solway Firth and the Nith Estuary without too much climbing. The route, mostly on forest road, has been laid out to keep to the shallowest gradients in the forest, giving you an easy, enjoyable ride.

Woodhead Loop

Distance	Grade	Waymarks
6.2 miles	Moderate	Blue

Following the early part of the green route you climb around the hill behind

Marthown of Mabie. A couple of sections of singletrack take you across one road to join the next for an easy spin past Hill Head and the Long Wood before descending to just above Lochanhead.

Lochbank Loop

Distance	Grade	Waymarks
14.3 miles	Moderate	Purple

There is no singletrack on this route, so it is ideal for riders with less technical ability but with a reasonable level of fitness. The trail is exactly what you want to make it: a race round as quick as you can, or a chance to take your time and enjoy the views.

Phoenix Trail

Distance	Grade	Waymarks
10.6 miles	Difficult	Red

Category
Waymarked forest routes.

Distance
2.4 – 14.3 miles.

397

Ride 5   Mabie Forest, south of Dumfries (five routes)

A mixed cross-country route in stunning woodland, with 'natural' trails complementing classic 7stanes singletrack.

Mabie's Kona Dark Side

Distance	Grade	Waymarks
2.4 miles	Severe	Black

Offers one of the most severe tests for any mountain biker and is **for experts only**. The circuit is made up mostly of North Shore timber trails – and they are among the most technical to be found anywhere.

Station: Dumfries.

TIC: Dumfries, 01387 253862.

Other nearby trails: The other 7stanes centres are at Kirroughtree, Glentrool, Dalbeattie, Ae, Newcastleton and Glentress / Innerleithen *(www.7stanes.gov.uk)*. There are easy trails at Drumlanrig Castle *(www.drumlanrig.com)*.

Useful publications & websites: OS Landranger Map 84. For maps of all the trails go to *www.7stanes.gov.uk*, click on 'Mabie' then click on 'Download the trail map here' (in a green box at the top of the page).

Refreshments: Only in Dumfries.

Ride 6   **Forest of Ae north of Dumfries**

Category
Waymarked forest routes.

Distance
6 – 15 miles.

Located only 20 minutes from the M74 motorway, the Green- and Blue-grade trails in the Forest of Ae are ideal for entry-level riders and families, while its Red-grade and downhill routes are for more experienced riders.

Starting point & parking

Ae Forest lies around 8 miles **north of Dumfries,** just off the A701 Dumfries to Moffat road. The trailhead is just past Ae village, roughly 3 miles from the A701 turn-off (grid reference NX 982901).

The rides
Ae Valley Route

Distance	Grade	Waymarks
6 miles	Easy	Green

An entry-level mountain bike trail, the Green-grade route is aimed mainly at families with young children. It runs up the Ae Valley to a lovely viewpoint overlooking the Water of Ae. A beautiful place to stop and picnic with lots of rocks around the river.

Larch View Route

Distance	Grade	Waymarks
8.4 miles	Moderate	Blue

This Blue-grade ride shares much of its route with the Green trail – the difference is a 3-mile section on forest road. It is suitable for those families looking to take in a little bit more of the forest than just the short Green-grade valley route.

6

Ae Line – Scottish Power Renewables Trail

Distance	Grade	Waymarks
15 miles	Difficult	Red

The Red-grade trail is a challenging, high-quality ride through quiet coniferous forest. This route has an aggressive freeride style to it with some large and sometimes intimidating trail features in addition to very steep climbs and descents. Ridden at speed, things get very exciting, but if you are more cautious you can keep your wheels on the ground all the way round. For many, the highlight of the route is the final descent of Omega Man, with its multiplicity of jumps.

Station: Dumfries.

TIC: Dumfries, 01387 253862.

Other nearby trails: Other nearby 7stanes centres are at Kirroughtree, Glentrool, Dalbeattie and Mabie *(www.7stanes.gov. uk)*. There are easy trails at Drumlanrig Castle *(www.drumlanrig.com)*.

Useful publications & websites: OS Landranger Map 84. For maps of all the trails go to *www.7stanes.gov.uk*, click on 'Ae' then click on 'Download the trail map here' (in a green box at the top of the page).

Refreshments: Ae Bike Shop and Café. The café and bike shop are open 7 days a week, 9.00am – 5.00pm. See *www.Ae7.co.uk* for details. Nearby Dumfries also has plenty of options.

Ride 7 **Drumlanrig Castle north of Dumfries**

7

Category
Waymarked forest routes.

Distance
1.9 – 12.4 miles.

Magnificent Drumlanrig Castle, constructed from distinctive pink sandstone, was finished in 1691 by architect William Douglas – the first Duke of Queensberry – and represents one of the first and most important Renaissance buildings in Scotland. Choose from a selection of bike trails to suit every ability and interest, from gnarly 'old school' technical singletrack routes, to swooping family trails through the beautiful Drumlanrig woodlands and quiet country back roads. The trails are constantly evolving with new sections of singletrack being added to extend the overall distance and improve the experience. Go to *www. drumlanrig.com* for the most up-to-date information.

Starting point & parking

Drumlanrig Castle lies about 15 miles **north of Dumfries**, on the A76 road towards Kilmarnock (grid reference NX 852994).

The rides

The Policy

Distance	Grade	Waymarks
1.9 miles	Easy	Green

A short ride on country roads around Drumlanrig Castle.

Burnsands

Distance	Grade	Waymarks
8 miles	Easy	Green

This pleasant ride takes you through the quaint hamlet of Burnsands. You are rewarded with superb views of the Lowther Hills above the Nith Valley, which sprawls out beneath you.

Rocking Stone

Distance	Grade	Waymarks
3.1 miles	Easy	Green

A gentle trail through mixed woodlands that will lead you past three lochs and an erratic boulder area known as 'The Rocking Stone'.

Low Gardens

Distance	Grade	Waymarks
5 miles	Easy	Green

A meandering ride past lochs, burns and rivers, heading towards the old kitchen gardens known as Low Gardens.

Copy Cat

Distance	Grade	Waymarks
5.6 miles	Moderate	Blue

This trail at times follows the red way-marked route on bumpy forest tracks, narrowing to a 1m-wide woodland trail. This is an ideal route for groups with different riding abilities.

The Old School

Distance	Grade	Waymarks
12.4 miles	Difficult	Red

A technical, swooping trail using natural singletrack less than 40cm wide with narrow wooden structures, drop-offs, berms and roots galore.

7

Hell's Cauldron

Distance	Grade	Waymarks
5 miles	Severe	Black

This is an unforgiving trail with very narrow tracks, steep climbs and descents with technically challenging obstacles and terrain, testing the best of riders.

Station: Dumfries.

TIC: Dumfries, 01387 253862.

Other nearby trails: The 7stanes centres at Kirroughtree, Glentrool, Dalbeattie, Mabie and Ae (*www.7stanes.gov.uk*).

Useful publications & websites: OS Landranger Map 84. Go to *www.drumlanrig. com* or *http://cycling.visitscotland.com* – click on 'Mountain biking' then 'Mountain Bike Centres' then on 'Drumlanrig'.

Refreshments: Tearoom at the castle.

8

Newcastleton & Hyndlee Forest Trails Ride **8**
south of Hawick in the Scottish Borders

Located close to the Scotland-England border, Newcastleton has trails for all levels. There is plenty of fun to be had here on routes that are shorter than most of those found at the other 7stanes. The Skills Area is reached via a short but stiff forest road climb from the trailhead. With Blue- and Red-grade loops and features, it offers lots of fun whatever your riding level, and is an excellent place to practise your skills before heading out onto the routes proper.

Starting point for Newcastleton routes

Newcastleton – halfway between Carlisle and Hawick. From Canonbie or Bonchester Bridge take the B6357, then take the unclassified road at the southern end of Newcastleton village and follow the signs for Dykecrofts (grid reference NY 503874).

Caddrouns Blue

Distance	Grade	Waymarks
3.4 miles	Moderate	Blue

Ideal for first-timers, families and novices, the Caddrouns route is short and sweet with excellent views across the Liddel Valley and beyond. The final section is a gentle downhill ride, running alongside the Priesthill Burn. The ponds make an ideal spot for some wildlife-watching or a picnic.

Linns Blue

Distance	Grade	Waymarks
5 miles	Moderate	Blue

The longer of the two Blue-graded routes on offer at Newcastleton. It sticks to forest roads and takes you further into the forest, with some great scenery along the way.

Category
Forest trails.

Distance
2 – 10 miles.

Ride 8 Newcastleton & Hyndlee Forest Trails, south of Hawick in the Scottish Borders

8

Red trail

Distance	Grade	Waymarks
10 miles	Difficult	Red

Newcastleton's Red route provides fast, narrow singletrack, bridge crossings and boardwalks. Its exhilarating descent of Swarf Hill is the ideal finish, while the North Shore section will test your skills.

Starting point for Hyndlee route

Located **between Hawick and Newcastleton**. From Hawick, head to Bonchester Bridge on the A6088. Turn right onto the B6357 south towards Newcastleton for approximately 4 miles, past Hell's Hole, Hyndlee Forest entrance and Piet's Nest car park. Lower Cheviot car park is on the left-hand side (grid reference NT 591033).

Hyndlee Circular

Distance	Grade	Waymarks
6.2 miles	Moderate	Blue

This circular route is suitable for all those who enjoy solitude and stunning views. The path is mostly forest roads and tracks, making for easy riding. It is exposed on the tops, so be prepared for the weather.

Starting point for Cauldron Trail

Located **between Hawick and Newcastleton**. From Hawick, head to Bonchester Bridge on the A6088. Turn right onto the B6357 south towards Newcastleton for approximately 2 miles. Hell's Hole is the first access point to Hyndlee and is on the right-hand side (grid reference NT 590071).

Cauldron Trail

Distance	Grade	Waymarks
2 miles	Moderate	Blue

Take a steady spin up the forest road that will bring you to the downhill section. Enjoy the swoopy singletrack and beware of the quarry!

Station: None nearby.

TIC: Hawick, 0870 608 0404.

Other nearby trails: Kielder Water (North-East chapter, page 326) or Glentress near Peebles.

Useful publications & websites: OS Landranger Map 79 for Newcastleton trails and OS Landranger Map 80 for Hyndlee & Cauldron trails. Go to *www.7stanes.gov.uk* for the Newcastleton routes and to *www.forestry. gov.uk* and search 'Hyndlee' and 'Cauldron' for the other trails. A 'Hyndlee' leaflet showing the trails may be available: call the Borders Forest District Office (01750 721120).

Craik Forest Ride 9
south-west of Hawick, Scottish Borders

Craik Forest covers 10,000 acres and rises to almost 1,500ft (455m) on the boundary of Dumfries & Galloway and the Scottish Borders. Riders with a reasonable degree of fitness will find the narrow paths fast and fun. The trail heads west from Craik Village on forest roads and tracks before swinging north across Wolfcleuch Burn and onto Crib Law. Here you choose between the stiff climbs and flowing Red-grade singletrack, or an easy spin alongside the Aithouse Burn on a Blue-grade route. The trails converge south of Hunter Holes and share a grassy hill track back to base.

Starting point

The hamlet of Craik lies at the end of the minor road that leads south-west from the B711 Hawick to Ettrick road, 12 miles **west of Hawick** in the Scottish Borders (grid reference NT 347079).

Crib Law Trail

Distance	Grade	Waymarks
11 miles	Difficult	Red

The outward leg of the Crib Law trail offers intermediate mountain bikers a real workout. The 820ft (250m) of climbing on forest roads and cyclepaths is rewarded with magnificent views of the Borthwick Valley, and a fantastic singletrack descent.

Station: Lockerbie.

TIC: Hawick, 0870 608 0404.

Other nearby trails: The nearest 7stanes centres are at Newcastleton and Glentress / Innerleithen *(www.7stanes.gov.uk)*. Kielder Water lies due south of Hawick (see North-East chapter, page 326).

Useful publications & websites: OS Landranger Map 79. Go to *www.forestry.gov.uk*, click on 'Scotland' then search 'Crib Law Trail'. A Craik Forest leaflet showing the trails may be available: call the Borders Forest District Office (01750 721120).

Refreshments: The nearest are in Hawick.

Category
Waymarked forest trail.

Distance
11 miles.

Ride 10 Glentress Forest near Peebles (four routes)

10

Category
Waymarked forest routes.

Distance
3 – 18 miles.

Glentress is probably the best biking centre in Britain, with brilliant trails of all grades, a fantastic café, an excellent bike shop with bike hire, changing and showering facilities, and a great atmosphere. For the beginner the skills area has sections of different grades to help you get started. Once you are ready for the next step, the Green route offers 'real' mountain biking but with none of the scary stuff found on the harder routes. In addition to the routes listed below, there are also two orienteering Trailquest historic trails following information boards.

NB The trails in nearby Innerleithen are Red or Black grade, so only for fit and experienced riders.

Starting points

The Osprey car park, Glentress Forest, off the A72, about **2 miles east of Peebles** in the Scottish Borders, south of Edinburgh. This is the lower of the two car parks (grid reference NT 287402 / OS Landranger Map 73). There is also an upper car park for the easier routes known as the Buzzards Nest car park, approached through the lower car park. Follow signs.

Green route

Distance	Grade	Waymarks
3 miles	Easy	Green

The trail starts and finishes at the Buzzards Nest car park. Along the way it takes in some stunning views of Peebles, the Tweed Valley and the surrounding hills.

Blue route

Distance	Grade	Waymarks
9 miles	Moderate	Blue

The route has had extra sections of singletrack added over time. This makes climbing from the trailhead to the Buzzards Nest car park a much easier, more enjoyable experience, and the descent back down a whole lot of fun!

Red route

Distance	Grade	Waymarks
10.5 miles	Difficult	Red

The red route boasts some fine singletrack climbs as well as massive, fast descents with jumps and berms in good measure.

Black route

Distance	Grade	Waymarks
18 miles	Severe	Black

With over 2,600ft (800m) of vertical climbing this is a truly epic ride. Long, challenging singletrack climbs combine with equally long and testing singletrack descents that take riders into remote parts of the forest.

Station: No nearby railway.

TIC: Peebles, 0870 608 0404.

Other nearby trails: Newcastleton. Craik. The Innerleithen Cross Country (XC) is a tough 12-mile Red-grade trail.

Useful publications & websites: OS Landranger Map 73. Go to *www.7stanes.gov. uk* or *www.forestry.gov.uk/mtbscotland*

Refreshments: Café in the forest. Lots of choice in Peebles and Innerleithen.

Dalkeith to Penicuik south of Edinburgh   Ride 11

This is the longest of the dismantled railways near to Edinburgh and the most scenic, passing through many beautiful wooded cuttings. Starting at Eskbank on the south-west edge of Dalkeith, the trail climbs steadily through Bonnyrigg and Lasswade to Penicuik (pronounced 'Pennycook'). Away to the right lie the Pentland Hills*. The prettiest section of the trail runs alongside the tumbling waters of the River North Esk. After passing through two short tunnels, you emerge at the A701 in Penicuik near to the distinctive octagonal church tower. Roslin Mills was the biggest gunpowder mill in the country until it closed in 1954 due to mining subsidence. It supplied munitions from Napoleonic times right through to the Second World War, as well as explosives for mining and quarrying. When the gunpowder mill was manufacturing, the railway ran through a 200-yd corrugated iron tunnel built to ensure no sparks from trains would reach and ignite the gunpowder!

* Cycling in the Pentland Hills *is a leaflet showing you where cycling is allowed in these hills to the south-west of Edinburgh. The map can be downloaded from* www.edinburgh.gov.uk/phrp *then click on* 'Cycling'.

Starting points & parking

1. The Eskbank Post Office, Lasswade Road, on the south-west edge of **Dalkeith**, just off the 6-road roundabout at the junction of the A768 and A6094 (grid reference NT 324664).

2. The octagonal church at the junction of the A701 and B6372 on the south-east edge of **Penicuik** (grid reference NT 236596).

Station: Musselburgh.

TIC: Newtongrange, 0845 2255121.

Other nearby trails: The Pencaitland Railway Walk starts 3 miles north-east of Dalkeith. The Water of Leith runs south-west from Edinburgh through Balerno.

Useful publications & websites: OS Landranger Map 66. To download a route map go to *www.sustrans.org.uk* and search 'Penicuik to Dalkeith'. An excellent cycling map of Edinburgh and surrounds can be purchased from SPOKES: visit *www.spokes.org.uk*. Also try *www.midlothian.gov.uk*, click on 'Roads & Transport' then 'Walking & Cycling', then scroll down for a map download. Sustrans' *Coast & Castles – South Cycle Map* (£6.99) shows this and several other traffic-free trails in the Edinburgh / Lothians / Borders area *(www. sustrans.org.uk)*.

Refreshments: Lots of choice in Dalkeith and Penicuik.

Category
Railway path.

Distance
8 miles each way.

NB The busy B704 needs to be crossed in Lasswade.

Ride 12 **Pencaitland Railway Walk east of Edinburgh**

12

Category
Railway path.

Distance
6 miles each way.

One of several railway paths lying to the south and east of Edinburgh, the Pencaitland Railway Walk runs from West Saltoun past Pencaitland and Ormiston to Crossgatehall, across predominantly arable land where there were once open-cast coal mines. Passenger services ceased in 1933 and the line closed in 1964 when the last mine in the area closed. The trail could easily be linked at its western end to the railway path from Dalkeith to Penicuik, or to form part of a longer ride using the network of quiet lanes that abound to the north of the Lammermuirs. If you want to find out more

about the coal-mining history of the area it is worth visiting the Scottish Mining Museum near Prestonpans, set in the Lady Victoria and Prestongrange Collieries. For details of opening times go to *www. scottishminingmuseum.com.*

Starting point & parking

The car park in **Pencaitland**, just off the A6093 between Haddington and Dalkeith (grid reference NT 437686). This is about two-thirds of the way along the trail so you can do two rides: one south-east to the West Saltoun Road, and one west to Crossgatehall.

Station: Prestonpans.

TIC: Edinburgh, 0845 2255121.

Other nearby trails: The Dalkeith to Penicuik Trail starts 3 miles to the west of the end of the Pencaitland Railway Walk. There is another railway path between Haddington and Longniddry.

Useful publications & websites: OS Landranger Map 66. *The Edinburgh Cycle*

Map (£4.95) shows all the cycle routes in and around Edinburgh. It is available from SPOKES: visit *www.spokes.org.uk*. Sustrans' *Round the Forth Cycle Map* (£3.99) shows this and several other traffic-free trails in the Edinburgh area *(www.sustrans.org.uk)*. Also try *www.visiteastlothian.org/cycling.asp*

Refreshments: None on the route; the nearest are in Dalkeith.

Ride 13 **Haddington to Longniddry east of Edinburgh**

13

Category
Railway path.

Distance
4$\frac{1}{2}$ miles each way.

This is just one of several railway paths lying close to Edinburgh. East Lothian is a very, progressive authority and year by year, progress is being made on a safe cycling link from Longniddry along the coast to Musselburgh, and thence into the centre of Edinburgh. This trail runs from the west side of Haddington (Alderston Road) to

Longniddry railway station. Haddington is a handsome town with wide streets, dating from the 12th century. The Town House was built in 1748 and the church in the 15th century. The town was the home of the reformer John Knox and also Thomas Carlyle, whose house has a fine façade. Longniddry was a mining village for 500 years until the 1920s. Gosford House,

13

the seat of the Earl of Wemyss, was designed by Robert Adam.

Starting points & parking

1. Alderston Road, on the west side of **Haddington**, near to the hospital. From the centre of Haddington, follow signs for Edinburgh. Alderston Road is a street on your right towards the end of the village (grid reference NT 502740).

2. Longniddry railway station (grid reference NT 446762).

Station: Longniddry.

TIC: Edinburgh, 0845 2255121.

Other nearby trails: The Pencaitland Railway Walk lies 7 miles to the south-west. Dalkeith to Penicuik is a little further west.

Useful publications & websites: OS Landranger Map 66. SPOKES *Edinburgh Cycle Map* (£4.95) can be purchased from SPOKES: visit *www. spokes.org.uk*. Also try *www.visiteastlothian. org/cycling.asp*. Sustrans' *Round the Forth Cycle Map* (£3.99) shows this and several other traffic-free trails in the Edinburgh area. Available from *www.sustrans.org.uk*

Refreshments: Haddington and Longniddry.

14

Innocent Railway   Ride **14**
Edinburgh

The Innocent Railway offers a good exit from the heart of Edinburgh out to the east, passing beneath the towering mound of Arthur's Seat, rising to over 800ft (245m). The trail starts from St Leonard's Bank, on the western edge of the magnificent Holyrood Park in the centre of this beautiful city, and heads through a tunnel near the start towards Duddingston Loch, Bingham and Brunstane. Holyrood Park itself is closed to traffic on Sundays from 1000 – 1600 hrs. The Innocent Railway lies at the start of the southern section of the Coast & Castles Cycle Route (National Cycle Network Route 1) that links Edinburgh to Newcastle via the Scottish Borders and the Northumbrian coast. There are long-term plans to create a traffic-free route from the end of the Innocent Railway path through Dalkeith Country Park and along another disused railway to Gorebridge and North Middleton.

Starting point & parking

St Leonard's Bank, Newington, near the Royal Commonwealth Pool, at the south-west edge of **Holyrood Park in Edinburgh** (grid reference NT 266727).

Station: Waverley, Edinburgh or Musselburgh.

TIC: Edinburgh, 0845 2255121.

Other nearby trails: There are several trails in or near Edinburgh – Water of Leith, Union Canal, Newbridge & Forth Road Bridge, Dalkeith to Penicuik, Pencaitland Railway Walk.

Useful publications & websites: OS Landranger Map 66. SPOKES *Edinburgh Cycle Map* (£4.95) can be purchased from SPOKES: visit *www.spokes.org.uk*. Sustrans' *Round the Forth Cycle Map* (£3.99) shows this and several other traffic-free trails in the Edinburgh area *(www.sustrans.org.uk)*.

Refreshments: Lots of choice at the Edinburgh end.

Category
Railway path.

Distance
4 miles each way.

Ride 15 **Water of Leith west of Edinburgh**

15

Category
Canal towpath.

Distance
6 miles each way.

Although the Water of Leith wends its way right through the heart of Edinburgh to the Docks, the inner-city stretch is not easy to follow on a bike and there are frequent road sections. The best part for cyclists runs from Kingsknowe, south-west of the city centre (off the Lanark Road), to Balerno, passing the many old mills which used the water from the river as a source of power. There were over 70 mills in its heyday, producing flour, paper, spices and snuff. The famous Scott's 'Porage' Oats were made in Colinton from 1909 to 1947. If you wish to cycle from the centre of Edinburgh, you can follow National Cycle Network Route 75 from the Meadows, soon joining the Union Canal towpath. Shortly after crossing the aqueduct carrying the canal over the Water of Leith, you turn off to the left onto a continuation of Route 75. The traffic-free trail stops at Bridge Road, Balerno, just off the A70 Lanark Road.

Starting points & parking

1. The Union Canal Bridge, on the Lanark Road (A70) just to the east of Kingsknowe railway station on the **west side of Edinburgh** (grid reference NT 216704).

2. Bridge Road, **Balerno**, just off the A70 on the north side of the village (grid reference NT 164670).

Station: Edinburgh, Currie.

TIC: Edinburgh, 0845 2255121.

Other nearby trails: The Union Canal also runs into the east side of Edinburgh. There is a cyclepath between Newbridge and the Forth Road Bridge.

Useful publications & websites: OS Landranger Map 66. SPOKES *Edinburgh Cycle Map* (£4.95) can be purchased from SPOKES: visit *www.spokes.org.uk*. Also *www.cycling-edinburgh.org.uk/escape.htm*

Refreshments: Lots of choice all along the route.

Newbridge and the Forth Road Bridge west of Edinburgh

Ride **16**

R iding across the Forth Road Bridge is one of the most extraordinary cycling experiences in Scotland. You cross from South Queensferry to North Queensferry in complete traffic-free safety along the cycle lanes that run either side of the bridge, hundreds of feet above the waters of the Firth of Forth, with views to the east of the magnificent Forth Rail Bridge (the one where, as the saying goes, they start painting at one end the moment they have stopped at the other!). Starting from Newbridge, on the A8 to the west of Edinburgh, you follow a dismantled railway north through Kirkliston and Dalmeny to pass under the Forth Rail Bridge before climbing through Queensferry, named after Queen Margaret who used the ferry to cross the Forth in the 11th century. After crossing the bridge you have the choice of returning on the other side or dropping down into North Queensferry for refreshments, a visit to Deep Sea World

and a train trip back to Edinburgh across the Forth Bridge.

Starting point & parking

East of Newbridge, just off the A8 to the west of Edinburgh (grid reference NT 125726). You can cycle along both sides of the Forth Road Bridge.

Station: North Queensferry or Dalmeny.

TIC: Edinburgh, 0845 2255121.

Other nearby trails: The Water of Leith from Balerno to Edinburgh.

Useful publications & websites: OS Landranger Map 65. Much better is the *West Lothian Cycle Map* (£4.95) which can be purchased from SPOKES: go to *www.spokes. org.uk*. This trail and many others are shown on Sustrans' *Coast & Castles North Cycle Route Map* (£6.99) available from *www. sustrans.org.uk*

Refreshments: In Kirkliston, Queensferry and North Queensferry.

Category
Railway path and bridge over Firth of Forth.

Distance
7 miles each way.

NB There is a cyclepath alongside the A89 and A8 enabling you to get safely from Newbridge onto the footbridge over the M9 to the start of the railway path.

Ride 17 Airdrie to Bathgate Railway Path east of Glasgow

17

Category
Railway path.

Distance
15 miles each way.

NB For updates on progress go to www.airdrie bathgate raillink.co.uk

Having been shut to passengers for over 50 years and freight for the last 25, the Airdrie to Bathgate Junction Railway is being reopened for rail traffic. The new cyclepath will run alongside the new railway and it is planned to open in 2010 / 2011. The Airdrie to Bathgate path forms part of National Cycle Network Route 75. There is a gentle climb from both Bathgate and Airdrie up to Hillend Reservoir, which is at the highest point, in the middle of the ride. Originally built in the 1850s, the Airdrie to Bathgate Junction Railway carried coal, ironstone and limestone to the numerous works in the Monklands district. All along the route there are remains of these old industries: quarries, coal mines and mining villages. The route is accompanied by a sculpture trail which closely identifies with the communities through which it passes.

Starting points & parking

1. Drumgelloch railway station, on the east side of **Airdrie**, just off the A89 Armadale Road to the east of the roundabout with the A73 (grid reference NS 776654).

2. Guildiehaugh, south of **Bathgate**, at the roundabout on the B792 (grid reference NS 987677).

Station: Airdrie or Bathgate.

TIC: Glasgow, 0141 204 4400.

Other nearby trails: The Union Canal and Forth & Clyde Canal lie to the north.

Useful publications & websites: OS Landranger Maps 64 & 65. This trail plus many others in Central Scotland is covered by the *Forth & Clyde Cycle Routes Map* (£6.99) available from *www.sustrans.org.uk*

Refreshments: Airdrie, Caldercruix, Blackridge and Bathgate.

Forest trail Ride 18
from Dyemill to Kilmory, Isle of Arran

Arran is the largest island in the Firth of Clyde, about 19 miles long and 10 miles wide. It is often claimed that the Isle of Arran is like Scotland in miniature, with the Highlands in the north (Goat Fell rises to 2867ft / 874m) and the Lowlands in the south. This must make this forest trail in the south-east corner of the island a ride across the Scottish Borders! Following forest roads all the way, it is certainly not a flat ride, climbing from the coast to a highpoint of 850ft (260m). However, your efforts are rewarded with spectacular views – with visibility as far as Ireland on clear days. There is also a waymarked 4-mile route in the woods to the north of Brodick Castle. For other ideas for mountain bike rides on Arran go to http://cycling.visitscotland.com – click on 'Mountain Biking' then 'Mountain Bike Centres' then on 'Arran Mountain Biking'.

Starting point & parking

The car park in Dyemill south west of **Lamlash**. Take the A841 south from Lamlash, then after 1 mile turn right at Monamore Bridge onto the minor road signposted 'Kilmory'. The entrance is on the left-hand side, ½ mile along the road (grid reference NS 015298).

Ferry: The start is about 6 miles south of the ferry port at Brodick.

TIC: Brodick, 01770 303776.

Other nearby trails: Plenty on the mainland around Ardrossan.

Useful publications & websites: OS Landranger Map 69. Go to www.visitarran.net/cycling or www.arranbikeclub.com. A Forestry Commission leaflet, *The Forests of the Isle of Arran*, may be available: call the Lowlands Forest District (01555 660190).

Refreshments: In Lamlash or Kilmory.

Category
Forest trails.

Distance
9 miles each way.

Johnstone to Kilbirnie Ride 19
west of Glasgow

There are two dismantled railways that run west from Johnstone: the trail to Greenock is described in the next ride. This one takes a more southerly direction, passing Castle Semple Loch, Barr Loch and Kilbirnie Loch along its course. The colour-washed houses in Lochwinnoch date from the early 19th century. The village was a centre for cask and barrel making. The trail is part of the Lochs & Glens Cycle Route (National Cycle Network Route 7) that runs from Glasgow to Carlisle. There are long-term plans to extend the traffic-free section along the valley of the River Garnock from Kilbirnie to Kilwinning, thus bringing the dream one step closer of creating a traffic-free path all the way from central Glasgow to the Ayrshire coast.

Starting points & parking

1. Johnstone, 1 mile to the west of the B789 / A761 roundabout at the point where Old Road passes beneath the railway (grid reference NS 444635).
2. Castle Semple Visitor Centre in Lochwinnoch (grid reference NS 363595).
3. Kilbirnie (grid reference NS 319537).

Category
Railway path.

Distance
11 miles each way.

Ride 19 Johnstone to Kilbirnie, west of Glasgow

19

Station: Johnstone, Kilbirnie.

TIC: Glasgow, 0141 204 4400.

Other nearby trails: The trail links with the Johnstone to Greenock route.

Useful publications & websites: OS Landranger Maps 63 & 64. Sustrans provide a downloadable leaflet of the ride: go to *www.sustrans.org.uk* and put 'Lochwinnoch Loop Line' into the 'Search' box. Sustrans' *Forth & Clyde Cycle Routes Map* (£6.99) contains details of this and many other traffic-free trails in the Glasgow and Edinburgh area. Available from *www.sustrans.org.uk*. See also *www.routes2ride.org.uk/scotland* and search 'Lochwinnoch'.

Refreshments: Johnstone, Lochwinnoch, Kilbirnie.

Ride 20 Johnstone to Greenock west of Glasgow

20

Category
Railway path.

Distance
14 miles each way.

Although there is a waymarked National Cycle Network route starting right in the heart of Glasgow, it is very bitty between Bell's Bridge and Johnstone and uses several sections of roads. By contrast, the Johnstone to Greenock route is almost entirely on the course of an old railway line. It runs from Johnstone via the Bridge of Weir, Kilmacolm and Port Glasgow to the Lady Octavia Recreation Centre above Greenock. There are splendid views across the Firth of Clyde to the hills above Helensburgh on the north shore. Greenock is famous for ships, sugar and as the birthplace of James Watt, improver of the steam engine. The Comet, Britain's first passenger steamboat, was built at nearby Port Glasgow in 1812. A replica is on show at Port Glasgow railway station. The ride forms part of the Forth & Clyde Cycle Route (National Cycle Network Route 75), which runs from Gourock through Glasgow and Edinburgh to Leith Docks.

Starting points & parking

1. The ride starts in **Johnstone**, 1 mile to the west of the B789 / A761 roundabout at the point where Old Road passes beneath the railway (grid reference NS 444635).

2. The western start / finish is at the Lady Octavia Recreation Centre in **Greenock**, off the B788 Kilmacolm Road up to the south-east of town (grid reference NS 295747).

20

Station: Johnstone or Whinhill, Greenock.

TIC: Glasgow, 0141 204 4400.

Other nearby trails: Links with the Johnstone to Kilbirnie route.

Useful publications & websites: OS Landranger Maps 63 & 64. Sustrans provide a downloadable leaflet of the ride: go to *www. sustrans.org.uk* and put 'Paisley & Clyde

Coast' into the 'Search' box. Sustrans' *Forth & Clyde Cycle Routes Map* (£6.99) contains details of this and many other traffic-free trails in the Glasgow and Edinburgh area. Available from *www.sustrans.org.uk*. See also *www.routes2ride.org.uk/scotland* and search 'Paisley & Clyde'.

Refreshments: Johnstone, Bridge of Weir, Kilmacolm, Port Glasgow, Greenock.

21

Glasgow to the banks of Loch Lomond   Ride **21**

O ne of several traffic free routes in and near Glasgow, this one links the Lowlands with the start of the Highlands on the banks of Loch Lomond. Starting at Bell's Bridge in central Glasgow, you pass John Brown's shipyard in the centre of Clydebank, where the great ships The Queen Mary, The Queen Elizabeth and The Queen Elizabeth II were built. Beyond Clydebank the route joins the Forth & Clyde Canal on a broad, well-maintained towpath. The canal, built in 1790, was the main route across Scotland linking the Clyde at Bowling, west of Glasgow, with the Forth near to Falkirk / Grangemouth. The ride becomes more open with green views of the Kilpatrick Hills behind Erskine Bridge. A second railway path starting at the end of

the canal takes you through woodland and rocky outcrops to the outkirts of Dumbarton, the ancient fortress-capital of the Kingdom of Strathclyde. The route through Dumbarton is on quiet roads and soon you join the waterside path alongside the River Leven, which leads to Balloch and the bonny banks of Loch Lomond. It is worth stopping to read the information boards along the river, which include interesting background detail about the history and wildlife of the riverside.

Starting point & parking

The path starts at Bell's Bridge (grid reference NS 578652) in central **Glasgow** (near to the Scottish Exhibition & Conference Centre, just west of the M8, Jct 20).

Category
Railway path,
canal towpath,
riverside path.

Distance
19 miles each way.

NB North of Balloch, the West Loch Lomond Cycle Route is a 17-mile traffic-free cyclepath parallel with the A82 as far as Tarbert. There are fine views of the loch and its islands, although you are rarely free of the traffic noise (for more information go to www.lochlomond-trossachs.org then search 'West Loch Lomond Cyclepath').

Ride 21 Glasgow to the banks of Loch Lomond

Station: Railway stations all along the way.

TIC: Glasgow, 0141 204 4400.

Other nearby trails: This is part of the Lochs & Glens Cycle Route (National Cycle Network Route 7). At Bell's Bridge in Glasgow, you can link to the Johnstone to Greenock and Johnstone to Kilbirnie routes.

Useful publications & websites: OS Landranger Maps 63 & 64.

Download a leaflet from *www.sustrans.org.uk* by searching 'Clyde & Loch Lomond'. Visit *www.gobike.org/map.php* for details about the Glasgow Cycling Map. Try *www.cyclingscotland.org* and go to 'Routes'. Go to the council's website at *www. glasgow.gov.uk* and type 'Cycling' in the search box. Try *www.routes2ride.org.uk/ scotland*

Refreshments: Lots of choice along the way.

Ride 22 East from Glasgow along the Clyde

Category
Riverside path.

Distance
9 miles each way.

NB There are three short mountain bike rides in Pollok Country Park, just south of Glasgow city centre: go to http://cycling. visitscotland. com, click on 'Mountain Biking' then 'Mountain Bike Centres' then 'Pollok Country Park'.

The route runs from Bell's Bridge in the heart of Glasgow alongside the River Clyde as it meanders east towards Uddingston. It forms part of National Cycle Network Route 75, which connects Glasgow and Edinburgh. The trail passes the People's Palace Museum, Glasgow's social history museum, offering you the chance to see the story of the people and city of Glasgow from 1750 to the present. When the People's Palace and Winter Garden opened in 1898 the surrounding area of Glasgow's old centre and East End was an unhealthy and extremely overcrowded place. Glasgow Green was the only large area for recreation nearby. Lord Rosebery, speaking to a crowd of about 3,500 at the opening, declared it 'open to the people for ever and ever' and characterised it as 'a palace of pleasure and imagination'.

Starting point & parking

The path starts at Bell's Bridge (grid reference NS 578652) in central **Glasgow** (near to the Scottish Exhibition & Conference Centre, just west of the M8, Jct 20).

Station: Glasgow or Newton.

TIC: Glasgow, 0141 204 4400.

Other nearby trails: West from Bell's Bridge to Clydebank, Dumbarton and Loch Lomond.

Useful publications & websites: OS Landranger Map 64.

Download a leaflet from *www.sustrans.org.uk* by searching 'Clyde Corridor'.

Visit *www.gobike.org/map.php* for details about the Glasgow Cycling Map.

Try *www.cyclingscotland.org* and go to 'Routes'.

Go to the council's website at *www.glasgow. gov.uk* and type 'Cycling' in the search box.

Try *www.routes2ride.org.uk/scotland*

Refreshments: All along the way.

23

Strathblane to Kirkintilloch Ride 23
(Strathkelvin Walkway), north of Glasgow

There is a plethora of traffic-free tracks in and around Glasgow. Some use riverside paths, some use canal towpaths and others, like this trail, use dismantled railways. This is one of the most spectacular, running parallel with the dramatic Campsie Fells, which rise to almost 2,000ft (610m) on Earl's Seat to the north of Strathblane. The tree-lined trail uses the course of the old Kirkintilloch to Gartness Railway. It is worth diverting $1/2$ mile off the railway path to visit the Clachan of Campsie where there is a craft village, a coffee shop and a bike shop. Kirkintilloch was originally Caerpentulach, meaning 'the fort on the ridge', the fort being part of the Roman Antonine Wall. It developed dramatically after the arrival of the Forth & Clyde Canal in 1773 and was soon operating as Scotland's first inland port, linked to the Forth by the canal.

Starting points & parking

1. Strathblane, 10 miles north of Glasgow on the A81. The trail starts just to the east of the junction of the A81 with the A891 (grid reference NS 565794).

2. Kirkintilloch, 8 miles north-east of Glasgow on the A803. The trail starts on the north side of town on the B757 towards Milton of Campsie (grid reference NS 655746).

Station: Milngavie, south of Strathblane or Auchinloch, south of Kirkintilloch.

TIC: Glasgow, 0141 204 4400.

Other nearby trails: The Forth & Clyde Canal runs through Kirkintilloch. Carron Valley Forest Trails.

Useful publications & websites: OS Landranger Map 64. Sustrans' *Forth & Clyde Cycle Routes Map* (£6.99) shows this and many other traffic-free trails in the Glasgow / Edinburgh area and is available from *www.sustrans.org.uk*. Try also *www.eastdunbarton.gov.uk*, put 'Strathkelvin Railway Path' into the 'Search' box then click on 'Where to Cycle'.

Refreshments: Strathblane, Lennoxtown, Milton of Campsie and Kirkintilloch.

Category
Railway path.

Distance
8 miles each way.

Ride 24 Forth & Clyde Canal between Glasgow and Falkirk

24

Category
Canal towpath.

Distance
34 miles each way.

The Forth & Clyde Canal towpath starts to the west of Glasgow and ends in the east, just beyond Falkirk. It was one of the great engineering projects of the late 18th century: construction of a canal to create an east-west shortcut through Central Scotland had been suggested as early as the reign of Charles II, but a route was not properly surveyed until the early 1760s. Work began at the Grangemouth end in 1768 and Kirkintilloch was operating as Scotland's first inland port by 1773. It was a further 17 years before it was completed in 1790. The full course of the route is from Bowling and Clydebank along the northern edge of Glasgow passing

Kirkintilloch, Kilsyth and Bonnybridge to Falkirk and Grangemouth. The Union Canal joins Falkirk to Edinburgh. The two canals are linked by the engineering marvel of the Falkirk Wheel, which lifts boats from one level to the next.

Starting points & parking

1. The canal joins the Clyde at **Bowling** (grid reference NS 450736), just off the A82 between Clydebank and Dumbarton, 1¹/₂ miles west of Erskine Bridge (A898).

2. Its eastern end is located **between Falkirk and Grangemouth,** just to the west of the M9, Jct 6 (grid reference NS 905816).

Stations: There are railway stations on or close to the route along its entire length.

TIC: Falkirk, 0845 2255121.

Other nearby trails: The towpath links with the Glasgow to Loch Lomond Trail at its western end, crosses the Strathblane to Kirkintilloch Path (Strathkelvin Railway Path) in Kirkintilloch, and links to the Union Canal in Falkirk by the Falkirk Wheel.

Useful publications & websites: OS Landranger Maps 64 & 65. Sustrans' *Forth* *& Clyde Cycle Routes Map* (£6.99) contains details of this and many other traffic-free trails in the Glasgow and Edinburgh area, and is available from *www.sustrans.org.uk*. Visit *www.waterscape.com* – click on 'Canals & rivers' then 'Glasgow' on the map to open up the page on the Forth & Clyde Canal. Also *http://cycling.visitscotland.com* – click on 'Find a route' then 'Greater Glasgow' then 'Glasgow to Falkirk Wheel'.

Refreshments: All along the way.

Ride 25 Forest trails in Carron Valley north of Glasgow

25

Category
Forest trails
(Red grade).

Distance
6$\frac{1}{2}$ miles.

Carron Valley Forest, managed by Forestry Commission Scotland (FCS), has long been a popular spot for mountain biking, although traditionally this has been restricted to the many established forest tracks and smaller paths. Thanks to local mountain bikers and the support of FCS, the professionally designed trails are suitable for a wide range of abilities. Fast, fun and purpose-built for year-round use – the Carron Valley mountain bike trails are guaranteed to entice you back for more. The natural beauty of the area, combined with panoramic views, offers 'big country' biking in the heart of Scotland within easy reach of the major population centres of Glasgow, Edinburgh, Stirling and Perth. The 6$\frac{1}{2}$ miles of Red-grade trails have something for everyone. Linked trail sections provide the option of a short, fun route, or something longer and more challenging on singletrack and forest road.

25

Starting point & parking

The Carron Valley Mountain Bike Trails are in the Carron Valley Forest, lying at the eastern edge of the Campsie Fells to the **south-west of Stirling**. Access is from the Carron Valley car park, just off the B818 Denny – Fintry road (grid reference NS 721839).

Station: Stirling or Croy.

TIC: Stirling, 0845 2255121.

Other nearby trails: Forth & Clyde Canal. Strathblane to Kirkintilloch railway path.

Useful publications & websites: OS Landranger Map 57. Go to *www.forestry. gov.uk/mtbscotland*, click on 'Carron Valley Trails' then download a map of the Carron Valley mountain bike trail map. Also try *http:// cycling.visitscotland.com* – click on 'Mountain Biking' then 'Mountain Bike Centres' then on 'Carron Valley Mountain Bike Trails'.

Refreshments: The nearest are in Denny or Kilsyth.

Ride **26** **Union Canal west of Edinburgh**

Category
Canal towpath.

Distance
30 miles each way.

The Union Canal, waymarked as National Cycle Network Route 754, is one of two waterways that enters Edinburgh from the west, the other being the Water of Leith. The canal was opened in 1822 to link Edinburgh and Falkirk. It was built to follow the 240ft contour so it needed no locks except for a flight of 11 to join it to the Forth & Clyde Canal at Falkirk. The contour method increased the distance but saved the time and water needed for lock operation. The Forth & Clyde Canal and the Union Canal were re-opened to navigation via the dramatic Falkirk Wheel that raises and lowers boats almost 80ft (24m) between the two canals. The regeneration included the upgrading and improvement of the towpath. The canal runs from the centre of Edinburgh through Ratho, Broxburn, Winchburgh and Linlithgow to Falkirk.

Starting point & parking

The towpath starts in **Edinburgh** at the junction of Gilmore Park and Dundee Street, Fountainbridge, south-west of the castle (grid reference NT 242727).

Stations: Edinburgh, Slateford, Kingsknowe, Linlithgow, Polmont and Falkirk.

TIC: Edinburgh, 0845 2255121.

Other nearby trails: The Water of Leith also has a towpath. There is a cyclepath between Newbridge and the Forth Bridge. The Union Canal links to the Forth & Clyde Canal at the Falkirk Wheel.

Useful publications & websites: OS Landranger Maps 65 & 66. The excellent *Edinburgh Cycle Map* (£4.95) can be purchased from SPOKES: visit *www.spokes.org.uk*. Try also *www.waterscape.com* – click on 'Canals & rivers', scroll down to 'Union Canal' in the 'Complete list' box and click on 'Cycling'.

Refreshments: All along the way.

West Fife Way: Ride 27
Dunfermline to Clackmannan

Forming part of the Kingdom of Fife Millennium Cycleways, the old railway path between Dunfermline and Clackmannan is the longest unbroken stretch of traffic-free trail in the whole project. Dunfermline was a favourite residence of Queen Margaret who married King Malcolm III of Scotland in 1070. The town's 19th-century church contains the grave of Robert Bruce, the 14th-century king of Scotland. The railway was opened in 1849 linking Dunfermline to Alloa and the Stirling line. It closed in 1968.

Starting point & parking

The car park at the junction of William Street and Baldridgeburn (the A907 Alloa Road) on the west side of **Dunfermline** (grid reference NT 081881).

Station: Dunfermline Town.

TIC: Dunfermline, 01383 720999.

Other nearby trails: Forestry routes in Fife's forests – Blairadam, Devilla, Tentsmuir and Pitmedden.

Useful publications & websites: OS Landranger Maps 65 & 58. Go to *www.fife-cycleways.co.uk* and *www.routes2ride.org.uk/scotland* (search 'Dunfermline'). Sustrans' *Round the Forth Cycle Routes Map* (£3.99) shows this and several other traffic-free trails in the Edinburgh and Fife areas, and is available from *www.sustrans.org.uk*

Refreshments: Plenty of choice in Dunfermline. Pubs just off the route in Carnock, Oakley, Comrie and Blairhall.

Category
Railway path.

Distance
11 miles each way.

Ride 28 Fife Forests (12 routes in 4 forests)

Category
Waymarked forest trails.

Distance
2 – 9 miles.

As part of the Kingdom of Fife Millennium Cycleways Project, three short routes have been waymarked in each of the four small forests that lie within the boundaries of Fife, namely Tentsmuir to the north of St Andrews; Pitmedden to the south-west of Newburgh, Blairadam to the north of Dunfermline and Devilla Forest to the east of Kincardine. Go to *www.fife-cycleways.co.uk* and click on 'Get Cycle Maps' for more details.

Devilla Forest (three routes)

The forest has a long history of occupation and use. Prehistoric coffins, stone circles and Roman urns have been found in different parts of the forest. In 1038, King Duncan fought the (Danes who were camped at Moor Loch) at the Battle of Bordie, near Bordie Loch.

Starting point for the three routes

Devilla Forest car park, just off the A985 about 9 miles **west of Dunfermline** (grid reference NS 964872 / OS Landranger Map 65).

Distance	Grade	Waymarks
2.7 miles	Easy	Yellow
3 miles	Easy / Moderate	Blue
5.5 miles	Moderate	Purple

Station: Dunfermline.
TIC: Dunfermline, 01383 720999.
Refreshments: In Kincardine.

Blairadam Forest (three routes)

The Scottish architect, Sir William Adam, planted Blairadam in the early 18th century. Most of the original forest was felled during the two World Wars and the

Forestry Commission replanted with Sitka and Norway spruce. One of the ways to tell the difference between a spruce and a pine is to remember that S is for spruce and single needles, and P is for pine and paired needles!

Starting point for the three routes

Blairadam Forest car park, 7 miles **north of Dunfermline**. Leave the M90 at Jct 4, follow the B914 towards Saline for 1/4 mile then turn right onto the forest road for almost 1 mile to the car park (grid reference NT 130947 / OS Landranger Map 58).

Distance	Grade	Waymarks
2.2 miles	Easy / Moderate	Yellow
3 miles	Moderate	Blue
6.5 miles	Moderate	Purple

Station: Cowdenbeath.
TIC: Dunfermline, 01383 720999.
Refreshments: In Kelty.

Pitmedden Forest (three routes)

Pitmedden means the middle part, but it is not known what it was the middle part of! Nearby Auchtermuchty was part of the hunting ground for the Kings and Queens of Scotland when they stayed at Falkland Palace. It is likely that Pitmedden was part of this hunting land, too. In 1917 large parts of the forest were felled to supply wood for the war effort. It was replanted with spruce trees like those you can see today.

Starting point for the three routes

Pitmedden Forest car park, 4 miles **south-west of Newburgh**. From the A913 between Abernethy and the A912 / 913 roundabout (south-east of M90, Jct 9), take the minor

road towards Strathmiglo. Go through Glenfoot, climb steeply for 1¹/₂ miles and the forest car park is on your left (grid reference NO 188139 /OS Landranger Map 58).

Starting point for the three routes

Kinshaldy Beach car park, Tentsmuir, at the end of the minor road to the **north-east of Leuchars** (grid reference NO 499242 / OS Landranger Map 59).

Distance	Grade	Waymarks
2.2 miles	Moderate	Yellow
4.2 miles	Moderate	Blue
9 miles	Moderate / Hard	Purple

Distance	Grade	Waymarks
2.7 miles	Easy	Yellow
4.5 miles	Easy	Blue
5.2 miles	Easy	Purple

Station: Ladybank.

TIC: Kinross, 01577 863680.

Refreshments: In Abernethy.

Station: Leuchars.

TIC: St Andrews, 01334 472021.

Refreshments: In Leuchars or Tayport.

Tentsmuir Forest (three routes)

This is the flattest Forestry Commission holding in all of Scotland with many miles of easy tracks. During Malcolm Canmore's reign (1058-93), courtiers from Leuchars Castle hunted in the forest. Medieval chroniclers believed that it was a marshy area inhabited by diaboli (devils), and at one time there was even a colony of shipwrecked sailors living in the forest.

Other information

Other nearby trails: Dunfermline to Clackmannan railway path. Forth Road Bridge cyclepath.

Useful publications & websites: OS Landranger Maps 58, 59 & 65. *Kingdom of Fife Millennium Cycleways Forest Routes* available from Tourist Information Centres. Also visit the website: *www.fife-cycleways. co.uk* and click on 'Get Cycling Maps'.

Ride **29** **Aberfoyle to Callander in the Trossachs**

29

Category
Forest trails, specially-built lochside route, quiet lane.

Distance
14 miles each way.

Aberfoyle is an ideal base for exploring the Trossachs. Located on National Cycle Network Route 7, the Lochs & Glens Cycle Route from Glasgow to Inverness runs north and south from Aberfoyle on forestry roads. This ride follows the route north from Aberfoyle, climbing steeply on the waymarked route through Achray Forest then dropping down to the track along the south side of beautiful Loch Venachar, with views across the water to the towering bulk of Ben Ledi,

rising to almost 2,900ft (885m). A quiet lane east from Invertrossachs takes you into Callander, an attractive and popular tourist destination, with the option of extending your ride northwards on a traffic-free path past the Falls of Leny and Loch Lubnaig to Strathyre.

Starting point & parking

The Queen Elizabeth Forest Park Visitor Centre, on the A821 just to the **north of Aberfoyle** (grid reference NN 520014).

Station: Dunblane, east of Callander.

TIC: Aberfoyle, 0845 2255121.

Other nearby trails: National Cycle Network Route 7 continues north from Callander to Strathyre. There are two waymarked trails in Queen Elizabeth Forest Park in Loch Ard Forest to the west of Aberfoyle.

Useful publications & websites: OS Landranger Map 57. A better map is produced by the Forestry Commission and can be purchased from Forest Enterprise, Aberfoyle

(01877 382383). Sustrans' *Lochs & Glens Cycle Route Map – North* (£6.99) shows this and several other traffic-free sections on National Cycle Network Route 7 and is available from *www.sustrans.org.uk*. Try *www.lochlomond-trossachs.org*, click on 'Visiting' then under 'Things to do' click on 'Cycling' or try *www.incallander.co.uk* and click on 'Cycling & Mountain Bike'.

Refreshments: Lots of choice in Aberfoyle and Callander. Pub just off the route in Brig o' Turk.

NB There is a ¹/₂-mile section on the A81 at the northern end of the ride and a longer section on a minor road west of Callander.

29

30

Queen Elizabeth Forest Park in the Trossachs — Ride 30

Queen Elizabeth Forest Park covers three forests in the Aberfoyle / Callander area: Strathyre, Achray and Loch Ard. The Lochs & Glens Cycle Route (National Cycle Network Route 7) uses tracks through Achray Forest and alongside Loch Lubnaig in Strathyre Forest on its way north to Callander and Killin. In Loch Ard Forest there are two waymarked circular routes. First designated as a Forest Park by the Forestry Commission in 1953 to mark the coronation of Queen Elizabeth II, the park attracts over a million visitors a year. From the east shore of Loch Lomond to the rugged terrain of Strathyre, the park encompasses mountain and moorland, forest and woodland, rivers and lochs. It is home to a rich variety of animal and plant life.

Starting points & parking

1. The Loch Ard Route starts at Milton, about 1½ miles **west of Aberfoyle** along the B829 (grid reference NN 503014).

2. The Orbital Circular Route starts from Manse Road, near **Aberfoyle Tourist Information Centre** (grid reference NN 520010).

The rides

Loch Ard Route

Distance	Grade	Waymarks
10 miles	Easy	Red

An easy route near to the loch. Fairly flat with fine views, it is an excellent option for young children.

The Orbital Circular Route

Distance	Grade	Waymarks
25 miles	Hard	Yellow

A more challenging ride with stiff climbs and steep descents. On the way there are excellent views towards Stirling and the Lake of Menteith (Scotland's only lake), and Ben Venue to the north.

Station: Balloch, Milngavie or Dunblane.

TIC: Aberfoyle, 0845 2255121 or the David Marshall Lodge Visitor Centre in Queen Elizabeth Forest Park on 01877 382258.

Other nearby trails: The Lochs & Glens Cycle Route (National Cycle Network Route 7) passes through Aberfoyle and Callander. There is a traffic-free road along the north side of Loch Katrine.

Useful publications & websites: OS Landranger Map 57. A Forestry Commission leaflet called *A Guide to the Forest Park*, shows the routes. It is available from the Visitor Centre (01877 382258) and Tourist Information Centres or from Cowal & Trossachs Forest District (01877 382383). Also try *www.incallander.co.uk* and click on 'Cycling & Mountain Bike', or for a map, go to *http://cycling.visitscotland.com* – click on 'Find a Route' then 'Loch Lomond' then 'Loch Ard Forest' then 'Route Map'.

Refreshments: In Aberfoyle, Callander and Strathyre.

Category
Waymarked forest routes.

Distance
10 or 25 miles.

Ride **31** **Loch Katrine**
the Trossachs, north of Glasgow

Category
Route along the
shoreline of the
loch.

Distance
10 miles each way
(ie this is **not** a
circuit).

This exploration of Loch Katrine is one of the loveliest in the whole book – there is a delightful tarmac track, which is shut to traffic but open to walkers and cyclists, along the north side of the loch and part of the south side as far as Stronachlachar. There is not a complete circuit of the lake. If you wish to go on from Stronachlachar to Loch Lomond and the Inversnaid Hotel for refreshments, you will need to use a road that carries some traffic. The road is much busier in the high season as it is a popular day trip for vehicles from Aberfoyle to Loch Lomond. There has been some talk of completing the circuit by building the missing 2-3 miles at the south-east corner of the loch on the northern slopes of Ben Venue, although this is probably some years away. It would create one of the best and most popular lakeside circuits in the whole of the country.

Starting point & parking

The pier car park at the eastern end of Loch Katrine at the terminus of the A821, to the **west of Callander** and to the north of Aberfoyle (grid reference NN 496073).

Station: Nowhere nearby – Glasgow and Dunblane are both more than 20 miles distant.

TIC: Aberfoyle, 0845 2255121.

Other nearby trails: There are two waymarked forestry tracks in the Queen Elizabeth Forest Park in the vicinity of Aberfoyle and Callander. There is a traffic-free route from Aberfoyle to Callander, and another from Callander to Strathyre.

Useful publications & websites: OS Landranger Maps 56 & 57. Also try *www. incallander.co.uk* and click on 'Cycling & Mountain Bike'.

Refreshments: At the Captain's Rest Café at the start. The Inversnaid Hotel, on the east shore of Loch Lomond, lies 5 miles to the west of Stronachlachar (ie this would add another 10 miles to the trip).

32

Callander to Strathyre north-west of Stirling   Ride **32**

You should enjoy spectacular views of Ben Ledi and Loch Lubnaig along the course of this dismantled railway, which links Callander with Strathyre via the Falls of Leny and the west side of Loch Lubnaig. This forms part of the Lochs & Glens Cycle Route from Glasgow to Inverness (National Cycle Network Route 7). There are several short climbs where the route leaves the course of the railway path to join forestry tracks. Strathyre is 200ft (60m) higher than Callander. The trail uses the course of the old Caledonian railway line, which until 1965 used to run from Stirling to Oban. Passing through broadleaf woodland alongside the swift waters of the River Leny, the ride runs a parallel course to the A84 through the Pass of Leny, known as the entrance to the Highlands. It is said that 2,000 years ago the Druids lit fires at the top of Ben Ledi to celebrate the changing of the seasons.

Starting point & parking

The central car park in **Callander** (grid reference NN 627099). The route starts at the western end of the car park. Follow signs for Strathyre and Balquhidder, or for National Cycle Network Route 7. There is also car parking off the A84 at the Falls of Leny and in Strathyre.

Station: Dunblane.

TIC: Callander, 0845 2255121.

Other nearby trails: South to Aberfoyle from Callander along the banks of Loch Venachar. Two waymarked routes in Queen Elizabeth Forest Park. North from Kingshouse along National Cycle Network Route 7 through Glen Ogle to Killin.

Useful publications & websites: OS Landranger Map 57. Also try *www.incallander. co.uk* and click on 'Cycling & Mountain Bike'.

Refreshments: Lots of choice in Callander and Strathyre.

Category
Railway path and forest tracks.

Distance
10 miles each way.

Ride 33 Killin to Kingshouse via Glen Ogle north of Callander and the Trossachs

33

Category
Railway path, woodland path and old military road.

Distance
9 miles each way.

NB *Care should be taken crossing the A85 near Glen Ogle Cottages.*

The route through Glen Ogle on a mixture of old military road, woodland paths and a disused railway has been one of Sustrans' greatest triumphs in the creation of the National Cycle Network in Scotland, as the alternative was a very unpleasant ride along the busy A84 and A85. There is a climb of over 500ft (150m) from Killin south along the railway line, then up through the forestry to reach the highpoint and the pass just to the south of Lochan Lairig Cheile. You cross the spectacular Glen Ogle Viaduct and then you can enjoy a 500ft (150m) descent down to Kingshouse, where there are refreshments at the hotel. Glen Ogle has, over the centuries, been used by Roman and English armies as the easiest way to get to and from the Highlands. Queen Victoria even called it the 'Khyber Pass of Scotland'!

Starting point & parking

The Breadalbane Folklore Centre in **Killin**, on the A827 about 20 miles to the north of Callander (grid reference NN 570322).

Station: Pitlochry.

TIC: Killin, 08707 200 627.

Other nearby trails: The continuation of the Lochs & Glens Cycle Route to the south has traffic-free sections between Strathyre and Callander, then south of Callander via Loch Venachar and Achray Forest to Aberfoyle. There are also mountain bike trails at Comrie, west of Crieff: go to *www.comriecroftbikes.co.uk*

Useful publications & websites: OS Landranger Map 51. Sustrans' *Lochs & Glens Cycle Route – North Map* (£6.99) shows this and many other traffic-free trails between Glasgow and Inverness and is available from *www.sustrans.org.uk*

Refreshments: In Killin, Lochearnhead and Kingshouse.

Argyll Forest Park Ride 34
Cowal Peninsula

The park lies on the Cowal Peninsula to the west of the Firth of Clyde and Loch Long, and is approached either by ferry from Gourock to Dunoon or the A82 / A83 via Arrochar. There are seven waymarked trails through this spectacular part of Scotland: three from Ardgartan and four from Glenbranter.

Starting point for Ardgartan routes

Ardgartan Visitor Centre, A83 **west of Arrochar** (grid reference NN 2710382 / OS Landranger Map 56).

Cat Craig Loop

Distance	Grade	Waymarks
5 miles	Moderate	Green

A circular trail that includes some spectacular views over Loch Long, Arrochar, Cobbler and Glen Croe.

Ardgartan Shore Cycle Route

Distance	Grade	Waymarks
7 miles	Moderate	Blue

Follow blue waymarkers down to the shore, then climb back up to Coilessan Glen crossing the Ardgartan Peninsula Circuit route. Go past the Coilessan Events car park to return to Ardgartan Visitor Centre.

Ardgartan Peninsula Circuit

Distance	Grade	Waymarks
20 miles	Difficult	Red

A grand tour of the wild, rugged and remote Ardgartan Peninsula, with excellent views of the Clyde and surrounding mountains. Best done clockwise.

Starting point for Glenbranter routes

Glenbranter on the A815, **south of Loch Fyne** (grid reference NS 110978 / OS Landranger Map 56).

Loch Eck Shore Trail

Distance	Grade	Waymarks
18 miles	Easy	Green

The trail uses forest roads that stay close to the west shore, giving attractive views across the hills of Cowal. The tearoom at Benmore makes a welcome destination. The round trip can be completed by taking the path and forest road on the east side of Loch Eck, or by the use of the public road.

Glenshellish Loop

Distance	Grade	Waymarks
8 miles	Easy	Blue

The ride provides a good introduction to the delights of off-road cycling for the family and novice riders. At the head of the glen is a ford that may be impassable after heavy rain, so care will be required. The

Category
Waymarked forestry routes.

Distance
5 – 20 miles.

Ride 34 Argyll Forest Park, Cowal Peninsula

34

ride downhill back to the start will give you plenty of time to admire the views of Beinn Bheula and Beinn Laggan across the glen.

Glenbranter Splash

Distance	Grade	Waymarks
6 miles	Difficult	Red

A demanding circular route that provides a variation in terrain and challenges, with two fords to be crossed. Expect to get muddy!

The Twister

Distance	Grade	Waymarks
4 miles	Difficult	Red

Flowing, purpose-built descent with fire trails to climb to high points.

Station: Tarbet.

TIC: Inveraray, 0845 2255121.

Other nearby trails: Waymarked forest trails in Queen Elizabeth Forest Park, Aberfoyle.

Useful publications & websites: OS Landranger Map 56. Go to www.forestry.gov.uk, click on 'Explore, Experience, Enjoy' then with map of Britain showing click on 'Oban'. As you hover the mouse over the red dots you will find 'Argyll Forest Park' (it is in the middle). A Forestry Commission leaflet, *Cycling in the Forest: Argyll Forest Park* may be available: call the Cowal & Trossachs Forest District (01877 382383).

Refreshments: At Ardgartan Visitor Centre. Hotel at Lochgoilhead. Tearooms at Benmore, south of Glenbranter.

Ride 35 Forest trails near Lochgilphead south of Oban

35

Category
Waymarked forestry routes.

Distance
3½ – 12 miles.

With Lochgilphead as a base, there are several waymarked forest trails accessible within a 10-mile radius. Some explore Knapdale Forest to the west with excellent views of Loch Sween and the Sound of Jura, also offering a chance to ride along the Crinan Canal. Just to the north of Lochgilphead there is the only Red-grade trail – the Firetower Trail – for which there is a Forestry Commission trail guide download. To the east, two trails give fine views over Loch Fyne.

Starting point for Ardnoe/Faery Isles trails

Gleann a Gealbhan car park, off the B8025 Tayvallich road, 8 miles **west of**

Lochgilphead, off the A816 (grid reference NR 777910 / OS Landranger Map 55).

Ardnoe

Distance	Grade	Waymarks
12 miles	Moderate	Blue

From Gleann a Gealbhan car park, this trail follows forest roads into the forest of West Knapdale to reach viewpoints looking down on the picturesque Crinan harbour. The trail then takes you to some of the finest views on the western seaboard, encompassing Islay, Jura – with its famous Paps – the Gulf of Corryvreckan, Scarba, Lunga, Mull, Luing, the Craignish Peninsula, and many smaller islands and skerries in the Sound of Jura. Refreshments can be found at the Tayvallich Inn or the Tayvallich coffee shop. Return along the quiet public road running beside the sea loch of Caol Scotnish.

Faery Isles (linear route)

Distance	Grade	Waymarks
6 miles	Easy	Red

Ride through the broadleaf woodland of the Faery Isles Caledonian Forest Reserve with stunning views of Loch Sween, and a chance of seeing otters, seals and herons.

Starting point for Lochan Buic trail

Dunardry car park, near Cairnbaan on the B841, about 4 miles **west of Lochgilphead**, off the A816 (grid reference NR 822908 / OS Landranger Map 55).

Lochan Buic

Distance	Grade	Waymarks
10 miles	Moderate	Green

From the car park by the Crinan Canal, the trail follows the forest road through the mixed conifer and broadleaf woodland of Dunardry Face. Openings amongst the trees give views down to boats negotiating the canal locks. The trail passes Dunans Farm, where you can take in great views west over the forest. About 1 mile beyond Dunans there is a fork in the trail. Turning right leads you to the beautiful Lochan Buic, where a wealth of wildlife including dragonflies, moorhens and divers can often be seen. Soon the trail brings you to the public road. Here you have the option of

turning left to reach the small village of Achnamara. At the far end of the village the trail returns to the forest, bringing you back through Dunans to Dunardry. A right turn onto the public road takes you to Barnluasgan Information Centre, where display panels interpret the life of the forest, its history and its wildlife. From Barnluasgan the road takes you to Bellanoch where you meet the Crinan Canal, which you follow to the east to take you back to Dunardry.

Starting point for Fire Tower trail

Follow the A816 **north of Lochgilphead** (towards Oban). After 2¹/₂ miles, turn right onto the unsurfaced forest road, which will take you about 500yds before another right turn into Achnabreac car park (grid

Ride 35   Forest trails near Lochgilphead, south of Oban

35

reference NR 852909 / OS Landranger Map 55).

Fire Tower Trail

Distance	Grade	Waymarks
10 miles	Difficult	Red

A compact, Red- and Black-grade trail that has it all! Flowing singletrack, drop-off slabs, downhill rushes through berms and some optional technical sections to try out your skills. It wouldn't be the same without a few desperate climbs, so they are in as well. All in a really wild setting with stunning views out towards Jura and Scarba.

A Fire Tower Trail map download is available: go to *www.forestry.gov.uk*, click on 'Scotland' then 'Mountain Biking in Scotland' then 'Fire Tower Trail'. Fire Tower Trail maps are available free of charge from the leaflet dispenser in the Achnabreac car park; from Crinan Cycles in Lochgilphead and from the Forestry Commission office (9.00am – 5.00pm Monday to Friday). The office is in Lochgilphead, just around the corner from the Esso filling station on the Inverary Road.

Starting point for Ardcastle Cycle Trail

Located on the A83 **between Lochgilphead and Inverary**, the Ardcastle car park is 2 miles north-east of Lochgair and 3$^1/2$ miles south-west of Minard (grid reference NR 942919 / OS Landranger Map 55).

Ardcastle Cycle Trail

Distance	Grade	Waymarks
3.5 miles	Easy	Green

This easy route takes you through mixed forest to stunning views of Loch Fyne. Stop for a picnic by the pebble beach – if you are lucky, you might see an otter searching for food along the shoreline.

Starting point for Loch Glashan Trail

Follow the A83 **north-east of Lochgilphead** towards Inverary and through Lochgair. The road leading to Glashan is on the left about 200yds beyond Lochgair power station (grid reference NR 923922 / OS Landranger Map 55).

Loch Glashan Trail

Distance	Grade	Waymarks
10 miles	Moderate	Red

Forest roads take you right round Loch Glashan and through Kilmichael Forest without having to climb too many hills. The Add Ponds make a great halfway point to stop and have a picnic. Old quarry pits next to the River Add were landscaped and then flooded, and now provide a great habitat for wildlife. During the summer months, 10 species of dragonfly and damselfly can be found as well as many other insects. The insects in turn attract birds and bats, which go there to feed.

TIC: Lochgilphead, 0845 2255121.

Useful publications & websites: OS Landranger Map 55. Go to *www.forestry.gov. uk*, click on 'Explore, Experience, Enjoy' then 'Oban' on the UK map, then 'Cycling' then any of the red dots around Lochgilphead. Two useful Forestry Commission leaflets may be available: *Knapdale Forest Up Close* and *Ardcastle & Glashan Forest Up Close*. Call the West Argyll Forest District (01546 602518).

Forest trails Ride 36
near Oban

Oban is one of the main tourist centres on the West Coast of Scotland, and a hub for many of the ferries serving the islands. It is also a convenient centre for exploring many of the forest trails that lie within 10 miles of the town (and many more a little further south towards Lochgilphead, or north towards Fort William).

Starting point for Loch Awe and Loch Avich routes, south-east of Oban

Barnaline car park, north of Dalavich, on the minor road on the west side of Loch Awe, at the road junction east of Loch Avich, **south-east of Oban** (grid reference NM 969138 / OS Landranger Map 55).

Two Lochs Cycle Trail

Distance	Grade	Waymarks
9 miles	Easy	Red

The Two Lochs Cycle Trail takes you along the shores of Loch Awe and Loch Avich, and into the heart of Inverinan Forest. If you are lucky, you might see one of the rare capercaillie that make Inverinan Glen their home.

Loch Avich Trail

Distance	Grade	Waymarks
14 miles	Moderate	Green

This trail takes you out through the forests of Barnaline, rising to a view over Loch Avich. Using forest roads and public roads the trail circles the loch. Dorlin Point, halfway along the north shore, makes a great place to stop for a picnic. Look out for red squirrels, pine martens, buzzards and eagles throughout the year. During the summer months you may see osprey fishing on the lochs.

Starting point for Kilmaha & New York routes, south-east of Oban

Kilmaha car park, on the west side of Loch Awe, about 4 miles south-west of Dalavich, **south-east of Oban** (grid reference NM 940085 / OS Landranger Map 55).

Category
Forest trails.

Distance
4 – 14 miles.

NB You can download a leaflet showing the trails to the north of Oban. Go to www.forestry.gov.uk and put 'North Argyll Cycling' into the 'Search' box.

36

Ride **36**   **Forest trails near Oban**

Kilmaha & New York

Distance	Grade	Waymarks
10.5 miles	Moderate	Blue

This route takes you along the shore of Loch Awe and climbs into the heart of Inverliever Forest.

Starting point for Fearnoch & Glen Lonan routes, north-east of Oban

Quarry car park in the forest east of Fearnoch village on the A85 between Connell and Taynuilt, **north-east of Oban** (grid reference NM 969322 / OS Landranger Map 49).

Fearnoch & Glen Lonan

Distance	Grade	Waymarks
4 or 5 miles	Easy	Green & Blue

(a) A circular 5-mile route within the forest (green waymarks), passing through an area of native woodland and the village of Fearnoch before returning back to the quarry. At the right time of year, glow worms can be seen in the dusk just before reaching the village of Fearnoch.

(b) A linear 4-mile route (blue waymarks) that leads through the forest, past the deserted settlement of Barglass, to Glen Lonan where a quiet, singletrack public road can take you back to Taynuilt or on to Oban.

Starting point for Am Maoilean route, north-east of Oban

Forest car park 1 mile south of Barcaldine, on the B845 towards Bonawe, **north-east of Oban** (grid reference NM 964404 / OS Landranger Map 49).

Am Maoilean

Distance	Grade	Waymarks
6 miles	Moderate	Blue

This elevated loop gives you magnificent views over Loch Creran and the Firth of Lorn Special Area of Conservation (SAC).

Starting point for Glen Dubh routes, north-east of Oban

Sutherland's Grove car park, ¹/₂ mile north-east of Barcaldine on the A828 **north-east of Oban** (grid reference NM 966424 / OS Landranger Map 49).

Glen Dubh

Distance	Grade	Waymarks
5 miles	Easy	Green
8 miles	Moderate	Blue

Two routes: one shorter, for families (green waymarks); one longer and more challenging (blue waymarks). The reservoir provides water for the alginate factory which processes seaweed into valuable food compounds. In the winter you may be able to make out Loch Creran through the broadleaf trees lining the route to the west.

Station: Oban.

TIC: Oban, 01631 563122.

Useful publications & websites: OS Landranger Maps 49 & 55. Go to *www. forestry.gov.uk*, click on 'Explore, Experience, Enjoy' then 'Oban' on the UK map, then 'Cycling' then any of the red dots around Oban. Two Forestry Commission leaflets may be available: for *Cycle the Forests of North Argyll* call the Lorne Forest District (01631 566155); for *Loch Awe Forest Up Close* call West Argyll Forest District (01546 602518).

37

Routes near Tobermory on the Isle of Mull — Ride 37

The Isle of Mull has become a favourite destination for road cyclists looking for tough challenges in a spectacular setting on one of the more accessible islands of the Inner Hebrides. There are also three easy forest trails close to Tobermory, which give you a taste of the area.

Starting point for the Lettermore & Loch Frisa routes

Aros Forest Office, off the A848, about 10 miles **south-east of Tobermory** (grid reference NM 564452 / OS Landranger Map 48).

Lettermore & Loch Frisa

Distance	Grade	Waymarks
5 mile loop	Easy	Blue
8 mile (linear)	Easy	Red

The Ledmore Circular Route (5 miles) goes through woodland and fields, passing the traditional burying place of the Clan MacQuarrie. The Ledmore to Lettermore Through Route (8 miles one way) runs along the east side of Loch Frisa to the B8073.

Starting point for the Ardmore & Glengorm routes

Forest car park, 2 miles along the minor road from Tobermory towards Glengorm

(grid reference NM 486558 /OS Landranger Map 47).

Ardmore & Glengorm

Distance	Grade	Waymarks
4 miles	Easy	Green

A route through the forest and along the coast, returning by the county road. Fine views of the Ardnamurchan Peninsula. The fastest-growing Sitka spruce trees in Britain are here, near the shore at Penalbanach. Further along the road, views of Coll, Tiree and Ardnamurchan open out where the trees have been dwarfed by the salt-laden winds. The road once again enters close forest until you come to the gate into the fields of Glengorm estate. Cross the fields for 300yds and you return to the county road. Turn left to Tobermory (4 miles away).

TIC: Tobermory, 08707 200 625.

Useful publications & websites: OS Landranger Maps 47 & 48. Go to *www. forestry.gov.uk*, click on 'Explore, Experience, Enjoy' then 'Oban' on the UK map, then 'Cycling' then on the red dots around Tobermory. A Forestry Commission leaflet, *The Forests of the Isle of Mull*, may be available from Lorne Forest District (01680 300346).

Category
Forest trails.

Distance
4 – 8 miles.

38

The Witch's Trails Fort William — Ride 38

There are many miles of tracks to explore in Leanachan Forest, with spectacular views of Ben Nevis and the Great Glen throughout. Legend has it that the Witch of Leanachan ('lee-nach-an') fled to the hills of Aonach Mor in the 1800s. Keeping her spooky spirit alive, the world-famous Witch's Trails continue to

Category
Forest trails.

Distance
4.3 – 6.2 miles.

bewitch mountain bikers. Leanachan Forest also has plenty of non-waymarked forest roads for you to explore. All the forest roads are indicated on the trail map: go to *www.forestry.gov.uk*, click on 'Scotland' then 'Mountain biking in Scotland' then 'Witch's Trails'.

Starting point & parking

Aonach Mor ski facility, 6 miles **north-east of Fort William** (grid reference NN 172773 / OS Landranger Map 41).

Broomstick Blue

Distance	Grade	Waymarks
4.3 miles	Moderate	Blue

Bubbling around the River Lundy – a great trail to start. Plenty of flowing singletrack.

10 under the Ben

Distance	Grade	Waymarks
6.2 miles	Difficult	Red

A mix of dedicated singletrack and forest road – not forgetting Nessie, a real black monster of a descent.

Witch's World Champs

Distance	Grade	Waymarks
5.2 miles	Difficult	Red

The loop includes almost 900ft (270m) of climb and descent. Watch out for some technical features and hard climbs as well as exhilarating descents on fast singletrack.

Station: Fort William.

TIC: Fort William, 0845 2255121.

Other nearby trails: The Caledonian Canal (Great Glen Cycle Route). There are two easy forestry routes at Glenachulish (grid reference NN 048590), near Glencoe about 10 miles to the south of Fort William, and two more near Lochaline (grid reference NM 682505) about 40 miles south-west of Fort William along the A884. For more details go to *www. forestry.gov.uk*, click on 'Explore, Experience, Enjoy' then 'Fort William' on the UK map, then 'Cycling' then the red dots south and south-west of Fort William. For the Lochaline routes also try *www.sunartoakwoods.org.uk*, click on 'Get Active' then 'Cycling'.

Useful publications & websites: OS Landranger Map 41. A Forestry Commission leaflet, *Ride the Witch's Trails,* may be available: call the Lochaber Forest District (01877 382383). Also try:

www.mtb-highland.com

www.ridefortwilliam.co.uk

www.greatglenbikes.com

http://cycling.visitscotland.com, click on 'Mountain Biking' then 'Mountain Bike Centres' then 'Fort William'.

Refreshments: Café at Nevis Range base station.

Great Glen Cycle Route (1)   Ride 39
Banavie/ Fort William to Gairlochy

The Great Glen Cycle Route is one of the most spectacular long distance routes in the country, using a mixture of canal towpath, minor roads and forestry tracks, passing alongside several lochs. The route is broken down into the traffic-free sections. This section follows the Caledonian Canal north-west from Banavie, near Fort William, to Gairlochy. There is one short climb, alongside the locks of Neptune's Staircase, where on fine days you will see Ben Nevis to your right. The route is waymarked with a series of white on brown 'Great Glen Cycle Route' signs. Beyond Gairlochy the route follows the relatively quiet B8005 for 4 miles to Clunes before joining the next traffic-free section alongside Loch Lochy.

Starting point & parking

The car park at Neptune's Staircase off the A830 to the **north-east of Fort William** (grid reference NN 113768). The towpath runs along the south side of the canal – ie keep the water to your left as you head away from Fort William.

Station: Fort William.

TIC: Fort William, 0845 2255121.

Other nearby trails: Witch's Trails in Leanachan Forest.

Useful publications & websites: OS Landranger Map 41. An excellent map, *The Great Glen Cycle Route* (£4.95), is produced by Stirling Surveys and available from *www.footprintmaps.co.uk*. Also try:
www.mtb-highland.com
www.ridefortwilliam.co.uk
www.greatglenbikes.com
http://cycling.visitscotland.com, click on 'Mountain Biking' then 'Mountain Bike Centres' then 'Fort William'.

Refreshments: In Banavie and Gairlochy.

Category
Canal towpath.

Distance
7 miles each way.

Ride 40 Great Glen Cycle Route (2) Clunes to Kilfinnan (Laggan)

Category
Forestry track alongside loch.

Distance
10 miles each way.

The second traffic-free section of the Great Glen Cycle Route follows the north shore of Loch Lochy from Clunes north-east to the historic Kilfinnan graveyard, passing the ruins of Glas Dhoire. This section of the trail involves some climbs with great views across to the hills on the east side of Loch Lochy. If you are lucky you may glimpse red deer and even a golden eagle. A minor road continues beyond Kilfinnan towards Invergarry. Steep forest roads lead onto the next easy section.

Starting point & parking

The car park at **Clunes** on the B8005, off the A82 / B8004 to the   of Fort William (grid reference NN 205885).

Station: Fort William.

TIC: Fort William, 0845 2255121.

Other nearby trails: Other sections of the Great Glen Cycle Route.

Useful publications & websites: OS Landranger Map 34. An excellent map, *The Great Glen Cycle Route* (£4.95), is produced by Stirling Surveys and available from *www.footprintmaps.co.uk*. Also try:

www.mtb-highland.com

www.ridefortwilliam.co.uk

www.greatglenbikes.com

http://cycling.visitscotland.com, click on 'Mountain Biking' then 'Mountain Bike Centres' then 'Fort William'.

Refreshments: None on route, lots of choice in Invergarry.

Great Glen Cycle Route (3) Ride 41
Oich Bridge to Fort Augustus

This easy section of the Great Glen Cycle Route follows the Caledonian Canal from the Bridge of Oich to Fort Augustus, where there is a wide choice of refreshments. The canal joins Loch Oich to Loch Ness. The scenic Kytra Lock lies in the shadow of the ancient Torr Dhuin hill fort. Fort Augustus was built after the 1715 Jacobite uprising and named after Prince William Augustus, the Duke of Cumberland. Local history is covered in the Great Glen Heritage Centre. The link to the section alongside Loch Lochy is via a steep climb through forestry, passing through Invergarry.

Starting points & parking

1. Bridge of Oich on the A82 south west of Fort Augustus (grid reference NH 338035).

2. Fort Augustus on the A82 halfway between Fort William and Inverness (grid reference NH 378092).

Station: Fort William or Inverness.
TIC: Fort Augustus, 0845 2255121.
Other nearby trails: Other sections of the Great Glen Cycle Route.
Useful publications & websites: OS Landranger Map 34. An excellent map, *The Great Glen Cycle Route* (£4.95), is produced by Stirling Surveys and available from *www. footprintmaps.co.uk*. Also try:
www.mtb-highland.com
www.ridefortwilliam.co.uk
www.greatglenbikes.com
http://cycling.visitscotland.com, click on 'Mountain Biking' then 'Mountain Bike Centres' then 'Fort William'.
Refreshments: Lots of choice in Fort Augustus.

Category
Canal towpath.

Distance
5 miles each way.

Great Glen Cycle Route (4) Ride 42
Fort Augustus to Drumnadrochit

This final traffic-free section of the Great Glen Cycle Route is the hardest of the four sections described with several demanding climbs, rewarded by wide-ranging views over woodland, water and mountains. Who knows, you may be rewarded with a wave from the Loch Ness monster! Starting at Allt na Criche car park to the north-east of Fort Augustus, the trail goes through Invermoriston along the north side of Loch Ness. The final 4 miles are on a minor lane dropping you steeply right down into Drumnadrochit, where you have a chance of refreshment. From Drumnadrochit to Inverness the Great Glen Cycle Route is all on-road, albeit quiet lanes until almost reaching Inverness where you have to join the busy A82.

Starting points & parking

1. The Allt na Criche car park and picnic site, about 1 mile **north-east of Fort Augustus** along the A82 (grid reference NH 391107).

2. Invermoriston at the junction of the A887 and A82. By starting here you could break the route into two: a south and a north section (grid reference NH 419165).

3. Drumnadrochit on the A82 between Fort Augustus and Inverness (grid reference NH 513290).

Category
Challenging forestry roads with fantastic views over Loch Ness.

Distance
19 miles each way.

NB Quiet lanes take you into and out of Invermoriston, but the busy A82 is joined for a few hundred yards through the village.

Ride 42 — Great Glen Cycle Route (4) Fort Augustus to Drumnadrochit

Station: Inverness.

TIC: Inverness, 0845 2255121.

Other nearby trails: The other sections of the Great Glen Cycle Route. There is also a small mountain bike centre at Abriachan, between Drumnadrochit and Inverness. Go to *www. abriachan.org.uk* for more details.

Useful publications & websites: OS Landranger Maps 26 & 34. An excellent map, *The Great Glen Cycle Route* (£4.95), is

produced by Stirling Surveys and available from *www.footprintmaps.co.uk*. Also try:

www.mtb-highland.com

www.ridefortwilliam.co.uk

www.greatglenbikes.com

http://cycling.visitscotland.com, click on 'Mountain Biking' then 'Mountain Bike Centres' then 'Abriachan'.

Refreshments: Invermoriston.

Ride 43 — Laggan Wolftrax forest trails south of Inverness

Category
Forest trails.

Distance
3 – 9 miles.

Join the pack at Laggan Wolftrax! An exciting, purpose-built singletrack mountain bike centre with over 20 miles of trails for all-year-round use. Take in the stunning views of Loch Laggan, the hill fort at Dun da-Lamh and the natural beauty of Strathmashie. Whichever route you choose to ride, you will understand why Laggan Wolftrax is something special. Wolftrax provides a Green-grade beginners' trail, the thrills of a big-and-bermy bike park, a fast Red-grade route packed with features and a Black-grade trail that is possibly the most technical of its type in Scotland. Bike wash, bike hire and shower facilities are also available.

Starting point & parking

Lying about 30 miles **south of Inverness** and 30 miles north-west of Fort William, Laggan Wolftrax trails are in Strathmashie Forest, just off the A86 Laggan to Spean Bridge road. The trailhead is at Base Camp MTB, just off the A86 (grid reference NN 594925 / OS Landranger Map 35).

Green Trail

Distance	Grade	Waymarks
3 miles	Easy	Green

For novices and young children, the Green trail, featuring real singletrack, is a perfect introduction to mountain biking. This easy, low-level route links with a Sustrans trail to form a circular route between the Laggan Wolftrax hub and the community-owned Gorstean car park. It has been built with the very young and the more inexperienced in mind.

Red Trail

Distance	Grade	Waymarks
9.3 miles	Difficult	Red

43

Designed to be fast and flowing, the Red Trail is a fantastic experience in two sections, enjoyably testing and rideable. The upper part of the Red Trail uses the existing Black-grade singletrack climb and exit. With a fast descent and a choice of 'opt in' features, you will find the views that open up quite stunning. Much of the lower part of the Red Trail is narrow black shale with embedded rock obstacles, drop-offs, rock causeways, boardwalk and lots of tough little technical climbs.

Black Trail

Distance	Grade	Waymarks
4 miles	Severe	Black

Watch out for serious drop-offs, boulder fields, stone staircases and rock slabs. Aimed at the expert riders, the black route is a demanding, tight, testing and technical trail.

Bike Park

Novices can trundle or freewheel from top to bottom, but more skilled riders will find 'big air' opportunities all the way down. Not recommended for very young children. The trail is wide, sealed-surface singletrack with big berms, tabletops and gap jumps. It is a lot of fun whatever your skill level, twisting and turning through open ground and pine forest.

Station: Dalwhinnie and Newtonmore.

TIC: Newtonmore, 01540 670157.

Other nearby trails: Trails in Aviemore.

Useful publications & websites: OS Landranger Map 35. Go to *www.forestry. gov.uk*, click on 'Scotland' then 'Scotland Mountain Biking' then 'Laggan Wolftrax' for more information and trail downloads.

Refreshments: Base Camp MTB Café.

Ride 44 Aviemore to Slochd

44

Category
Forest trails and railway path.

Distance
15 miles.

Aviemore is a real outdoors centre, both summer and winter, located at the base of the Cairngorms, on the banks of the River Spey. It is surrounded by Forestry Commission woodland and big estates that have taken a positive attitude towards cycling, namely Rothiemurchus, Glenmore and Glenlivet. This ride follows the off-road alternative to National Cycle Network Route 7 (the Lochs & Glens Cycle Route) north from Aviemore to Boat of Garten, parallel with the Strathspey Steam Railway line, then on a steep woodland climb to Carrbridge. From here, a short section on a quiet dead-end road passes under the railway and the A9, soon turning off the road onto a track which crosses the historic, grass-covered Sluggan Bridge and leads on to Slochd. National Cycle Network Route 7 can also be followed on a parallel, waymarked road route, although some

sections can be busy. Mountain bikes are recommended for the off-road route.

Starting point & parking

The railway station in Aviemore (grid reference NH 896124). The route follows the Speyside Way as far as Boat of Garten.

Station: Aviemore or Kingussie.

TIC: Aviemore, 0845 2255121.

Other nearby trails: Rothiemurchus Estate, the Speyside Way, Laggan Wolftrax.

Useful publications & websites: OS Landranger Maps 35 & 36. For the leaflet go to *www.sustrans.org.uk* and put 'Aviemore to Slochd leaflet' in the 'Search' box. Try also *www.visitaviemore.com/onabike* or *http://cycling.visitscotland.com*, click on 'Mountain Biking' then 'Mountain Bike Centres' then 'Glenmore'.

Refreshments: Lots of choice in Aviemore. Cafés and pubs in Boat of Garten and Carrbridge.

NB It makes good sense to download from www.sustrans.org.uk the Aviemore to Slochd leaflet as it shows various links to other nearby routes.

45

Rothiemurchus Estate south-east of Aviemore Ride 45

There are three trails that start from Rothiemurchus Visitor Centre to the south-east of Aviemore. They all start using the road that heads east towards Loch Morlich and Glenmore, then climb up on estate roads into the forested hills at the foot of the mighty Cairngorm mountains. The main types of tree you will see are Scots pine and birch, and you may also spot the shrub juniper. This is a typical Caledonian forest habitat, important as a home to a wide variety of wildlife such as capercaillie, crossbill, crested tit, red squirrel and pine marten.

Starting point & parking

Rothiemurchus Visitor Centre (01479 812345) on the B970 about 1 mile to the **south-east of Aviemore** (grid reference NH 902109).

Rothiemurchus trails

Lochan Deo – 5 miles
A chance to glimpse the stunning, secluded, small sparkling loch.

Loch an Eilein – 6 miles
Translated as 'the loch of the island', a beautiful ruined castle is marooned on an island in the middle of this magical loch.

Ancient Forest – 10 miles
Experience the best of the ancient Caledonian pine forest.

Station: Aviemore.

TIC: Aviemore, 0845 2255121.

Other nearby trails: The Aviemore to Slochd Cycle Route (National Cycle Network Route 7). There are trails from Glenmore Visitor Centre and also on the Glenlivet Estate.

Useful publications & websites: OS Landranger Map 36. A map, *Biking Map of Rothiemurchus* (£2), shows the three routes. It is available from the visitor centre. Also visit *www.rothiemurchus.net*

Refreshments: At the Rothiemurchus Visitor Centre.

Category
Minor roads and estate tracks.

Distance
5 – 10 miles.

NB There are other, similar trails on the Glenlivet Estate centred around Tomintoul and Tomnavoulin to the north-east of Aviemore. Visit the website: www. glenlivetestate. co.uk/cycle.html

46

Speyside Way east of Inverness Ride 46

The Speyside Way is predominantly a walking route that follows the River Spey – famous for its fishing and whisky distilleries – from Aviemore to the coast at Spey Bay. From a cyclist's point of view there is a long, rideable middle section largely on the course of an old railway line between Ballindalloch (Cragganmore) and Craigellachie, with

a spur to Dufftown. It would also be possible to continue north along the Speyside Way for a further 13 miles from Craigellachie to Fochabers, but you should be warned that it contains some hillier and rougher sections through the forest. The trail described runs close to the river for much of its length, passing the famous distilleries of Tamdhu and Knockando.

Category
Riverside path and railway trail.

Distance
16 miles each way.

Ride 46   Speyside Way, east of Inverness

Starting points & parking

1. The visitor centre in **Craigellachie**, at the junction of the A95 and A941, south-east of Elgin (grid reference NJ 292454).

2. Cragganmore, at the end of the B9137, off the A95 between Grantown and Aberlour (grid reference NJ 167367).

NB There is a short road section from the end of the railway path on the A941 to get right into Dufftown.

Station: Elgin or Keith.

TIC: Elgin, 01343 542666.

Other nearby trails: There are easy forest trails in Culbin Forest north-east of Nairn. Moray Monster Trails. Trails around Aviemore, Glenmore and Rothiemurchus. Also on the Glenlivet Estate – for more details go to *www.glenlivetestate.co.uk/cycle.html*

Useful publications & websites: OS Landranger Map 28. More information about the trail can be obtained by calling the Ranger Service on 01340 881266, or visit *www.speysideway.org* and scroll down to 'Cycling on the Speyside Way'.

Refreshments: In Fochabers, Craigellachie and Ballindalloch.

Deeside Way from Aberdeen to Banchory
Ride 47

The Deeside Way offers an attractive wooded exit from the centre of Aberdeen west to Banchory, with views across the wide valley of the River Dee. Aberdeen is known as 'Granite City' because of the speckled grey stone used in so many of the city's buildings. Duthie Park has floral displays in all seasons including the spectacular 'rose mountain'. The Winter Gardens house exotic plants, flowers, birds, fish and turtles. The route makes its way out past the remains of stations at Pitfodels, Cults, Bieldside, Murtle, Milltimber, Peterculter (or Culter, as it is more commonly known by locals), Drum, Park, Mills of Drum, Crathie and finally Banchory some 16 miles later. The Deeside railway opened in 1853 with a service between Aberdeen and Banchory. The line was planned originally to end at Braemar but Queen Victoria was afraid her privacy would be disturbed by hordes of tourists at Balmoral, so she bought land along the route between Ballater and Braemar to prevent this. Its fate, like so many other railways, was decided by the Beeching Report of 1963. The final service ran from Ballater in 1966.

Starting point & parking

The route starts at the Polmuir Road entrance to Duthie Park, just behind the David Welch Winter Gardens to the south of **Aberdeen** city centre (grid reference NJ 938044).

Category
Railway path.

Distance
16 miles each way.

Station: Aberdeen.

TIC: Aberdeen, 01224 288828.

Other nearby trails: The Aberdeen & Peterhead Lines (Formartine & Buchan Way).

Useful publications & websites: OS Landranger Map 38. Go to *www.cyclegrampian.co.uk* and click on 'Trail' then 'Deeside Way'.

Refreshments: Lots of choice in Aberdeen, Peterculter and Banchory.

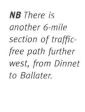

NB There is another 6-mile section of traffic-free path further west, from Dinnet to Ballater.

Ride 48 Formartine & Buchan Way (Aberdeen and Peterhead Lines)

48

Category
Railway path.

Distance
25 miles each way from Dyce to Maud.

15 miles each way Maud to Fraserburgh.

13 miles each way Maud to Peterhead.

NB *Care should be taken crossing the A920 near Ellon and the A948 in Auchnagatt.*

This is the longest railway path in the whole country, stretching north for 40 miles from Aberdeen to the coast at either Fraserburgh or Peterhead. It can easily be broken down into much shorter sections. The closer you are to Aberdeen, the better the surface. From Dyce railway station (next to Aberdeen Airport) the trail heads north past Newmachar, Ellon and Auchnagatt to Maud, with spurs beyond to Fraserburgh and Peterhead. There is a gentle 300ft (90m) climb north from Dyce to Newmachar. Just south of Newmachar is the highest embankment and one of the deepest cuttings of the line. In the 1940s a train was stuck in the snow here for many weeks. Beyond Newmachar you will see the distinctive outline of Bennachie, far to the west. The Formartine & Buchan Way passes through many places of interest including Aden Country Park, Drinnies Wood Observatory, Strichen Stone Circle and Deer Abbey.

Starting point & parking

The railway station at Dyce, 6 miles **north of Aberdeen** on the A947 (grid reference NJ 885127).

> **Station:** The route starts at Dyce railway station to the north of Aberdeen.
>
> **TIC:** Aberdeen, 01224 288828.
>
> **Other nearby trails:** The Deeside Way. Trails in Pitfichie and Kirkhill Forests.
>
> **Useful publications & websites:** OS Landranger Map 38. Go to *www. cyclegrampian.co.uk* and click on 'Trail' then 'F&B Way'.
>
> **Refreshments:** In Dyce, Newmachar, Udny Station, Ellon, Auchnagatt and Maud (and at Strichen / Fraserburgh or Mintlaw / Peterhead).

49

Scolty to Shooting Greens Trail | Ride 49
Banchory, south-west of Aberdeen

This waymarked route is on good-quality forest roads all the way. You can go from Scolty through the forest to Shooting Greens at the west end of Blackhall, or you can do a slightly longer circular loop that brings you back to Scolty. There are excellent views over Deeside and Feuchside, and to the hills beyond.

Starting point & parking

Take the B976 south from the traffic lights in **Banchory**, cross over the River Dee, take the first public road to the right, then the next public road to the left. Near the top of the hill turn right along a track past the Scolty signboard, and take the next track to the right, again past a sign board. The car park is on your left roughly 30yds along this track (grid reference NO 691950).

Station: Aberdeen.

TIC: Banchory, 01330 822000.

Other nearby trails: The Deeside Way.

Useful publications & websites: OS Landranger Map 45. For a download of the trail go to *www.forestry.gov.uk* and put 'Scolty Trail Map' in the 'Search' box.

Refreshments: Lots of choice in Banchory.

Category
Forest trail.

Distance
7 miles.

50

Pitfichie & Kirkhill Forest Trails | Ride 50
west of Aberdeen

There are many small forest holdings in a wide arc around Aberdeen. The two described here have the additional benefit of good maps that can be downloaded from the Forestry Commission website.

Starting point for Pitfichie trails

Pitfichie car park, south-west of Monymusk, 16 miles **west of Aberdeen**, near the junction of the B993 and A944 (grid reference NJ 656133 / OS Landranger Maps 37 & 38).

Pitfichie Forest Trail

Distance	Grade	Waymarks
9.3 miles	Moderate	White

Moderate with some steeper sections, mostly on forest road with about 10% on rough track, rewarded with panoramic views of Bennachie and over the Vale of Alford.

Cairn William Trail

Distance	Grade	Waymarks
4.3 miles	Difficult	Red

Steep gradients, narrow tracks, some rocky sections with berms and a stone staircase. Amazing summit views.

Starting point for Kirkhill trail

Mountjoy car park, on the north side of the A96 near the junction of the B979 and A96, about 6 miles **west of Aberdeen** (grid reference 854114 / OS Landranger Map 38).

Category
Forest trails.

Distance
4 – 9 miles.

Ride **50** Pitfichie & Kirkhill Forest Trails, west of Aberdeen

NB There is also a Mountain Bike Fun Park to try out.

Kirkhill Loop Forest Trail

Distance	Grade	Waymarks
4.2 miles	Moderate	Red

This route encircles the heart of Kirkhill Forest. It is on forest road for most of the way and gives terrific views over Bennachie and to the north. There are only a few steep gradients, making this an ideal family cycle. The loop is waymarked from the southern car park.

Station: Aberdeen.

TIC: Aberdeen, 01224 288828.

Other nearby trails: Deeside Way. Formartine & Buchan Way.

Useful publications & websites: OS Landranger Maps 37 & 38. Map downloads for the trails are available from *www.forestry.gov.uk* and search 'Kirkhill Loop Trail' or 'Pitfichie Cycle Map'. Also try *http://cycling.visitscotland.com*, click on 'Mountain Biking' then 'Mountain Bike Centres' then 'Kirkhill' or 'Pitfichie'.

Refreshments: In Blackburn for Kirkhill and Monymusk for Pitfichie.

Moray Monster Trails   Ride **51**
Fochabers

With almost 20 miles of fun-packed singletrack mountain bike routes, there is something here to feed the monster in everyone! Whether you are totally new to off-road mountain biking or a seriously expert rider looking for big thrills, there is a trail here that is just right for you – from an easy Green-grade track to severe Black-grade trails and Orange-grade downhill and Northshore sections. The main Moray Monster Trails work as three independent sites but are linked to each other, so for those with a truly monster appetite and stamina to match, try all three sites end to end from Fochabers to Craigellachie. The easy Green-grade trail is at Quarry Wood, near Elgin.

Category
Forest trails.

Distance
Various.

449

Ride 51 Moray Monster Trails, Fochabers

NB If you are interested in gentle gradients there are many miles of easy tracks in Culbin Forest, located on the coast between Elgin and Nairn.

Starting points & parking

The Moray Monster Trails run between **Fochabers** and **Craigellachie** down the Spey Valley to the east of Elgin. Access points are at Ordiequish and Whiteash, both near Fochabers; at Ben Aigan near Craigellachie; and at Quarry Wood near Elgin. Fochabers and Elgin both lie on the A96 Inverness to Aberdeen road. Craigellachie is on the A95 to the south.

1. Ordiequish, south of Fochabers

Turn south off the A96 by the chip shop in the middle of Fochabers (look for the blue sign). Stay on this road for ³/₄ mile, going through Ordiequish and Upper Ordiequish until you reach the car park (grid reference NJ 341562 / OS Landranger Map 28).

2. Whiteash (Winding Walks), east of Fochabers

Follow the A98 out of Fochabers towards Buckie for ³/₄ mile. The Winding Walks car park is on the right (south) side of the road (grid reference NJ 358586 / OS Landranger Map 28).

3. Ben Aigan, north-east of Craigellachie

Turn off the A95 Craigellachie to Keith road about 5 miles north-east of Craigellachie (near Mulben). The car park is on the left (grid reference NJ 334492 / OS Landranger Map 28).

4. Quarry Wood, west of Elgin

(a) For the Brumley Brae car park, leave the A96 at Eight-Acres Hotel, on the west side of Elgin, and turn onto Morriston Road. Continue for about ¹/₂ mile then turn left at the road signposted 'Pet Centre' on to Brumley Brae. The car park is on the left-hand side about 400yds uphill (before the pet centre).

(b) For the Leggat car park, turn off the A96 about 3 miles west of Elgin onto the minor road signposted to Rosebrae. Look out for the car park about 300yds along on the right.

Choosing a trail

Start at Ordiequish if you are looking for moderate-graded routes, the skills area and the infamous Black-grade Gully Monster. Whiteash offers Red- and Orange-grade routes, including the Fochabers Freeride. At Ben Aigan there are sustained Red- and Black-grade routes with a big hill feel, as well as The Bunny. The route most suitable for families is an easy Green-grade taster cross-country route in Quarry Wood to the west of Elgin.

Station: Keith or Elgin.

TIC: Elgin, 0845 2255121.

Other nearby trails: The Speyside Way. There are plenty of easy, flat tracks in Culbin Forest, between Elgin and Nairn – for more details go to *www.forestry.gov.uk* and search 'Culbin Forest Trail Guide'.

Useful publications & websites: OS Landranger Map 28. For more details (including a trail map download) go to *www.forestry.gov.uk*, click on 'Scotland' then 'Mountain Biking in Scotland' then 'Moray Monster Trails'. A Forestry Commission *Moray Monster Trails* leaflet may be available: call Moray Forest District (01343 820223).

Refreshments: There are local cafés and shops in Fochabers, Elgin and Craigellachie.

52

Learnie Red Rock Trails Ride 52
on Black Isle, north of Inverness

The Red Rock trails at Learnie offer 10 miles of trails for all skill levels, combined with some of the best views from any mountain bike trail anywhere! There are Green-, Blue- and Black-grade trails, with a bike park and a dirt jump area (both Orange). Even the Green-grade singletrack is not 'billiard table' smooth – it gives a sufficient challenge for those wanting more than just forest road-type mountain biking.

Starting point & parking

The Learnie Red Rock Trails are in Learnie Forest on the Black Isle, to the **north of Inverness**. Access to the trailhead is from the Red Rock car park, which lies just off the A832 Fortrose – Cromarty road about 3 miles past Rosemarkie village (grid reference NH 736614). Right beside the car park is the dirt jump area. From the car park, a stretch of forest road takes you to the start of the trails. At the fork in the forest road, turn right to get to the start of Home Green and Callachy Hill, or bear left for the start of the Muirhead Climb.

The rides

Green Trail

Distance	Grade	Waymarks
2 miles	Easy	Green

A combination of forest roads and a nice link back to the car park make this suitable for beginners and novices of mountain biking.

Callachy Hill, Callachy Descent, Muirhead Climb & Firth Views

Distance	Grade	Waymarks
6 miles	Moderate	Blue

Category
Forest trails.

Distance
2 – 6 miles.

NB Mention should also be made of the Morangie Trail, a Blue-grade 12-mile trail to the south of Tain with fine views across the Dornoch Firth (grid reference NH 758793).

451

Ride **52**   **Learnie Red Rock Trails on Black Isle, north of Inverness**

The trail winds its way through Larch trees which provide plenty of variety all year round. Near the top, look out for the Bronze Age burial cairn in the cleared area. The descent twists and turns down Callachy Hill before climbing and crossing over to Learnie, where the trail enjoys magnificent views of the Moray Firth.

Learnie Hill

Distance	Grade	Waymarks
2 miles	Severe	Black

The Black-grade trail is one that leads you over two hills that are full of technical surprises! It has the lot – swoopy sections, rock features and Northshore.

Station: Inverness.

TIC: Inverness, 0845 2255121.

Other nearby trails: The Great Glen Cycle Route. There is also a cross-country mountain bike route at Contin Forest, on the A835 towards Ullapool, about 20 miles north-west of Inverness. Go to *http://cycling.visitscotland. com*, click on 'Mountain Biking' then 'Mountain Bike Centres' then 'Strathpeffer – Contin Forest'.

Useful publications & websites: OS Landranger Maps 21 & 26. For more details and a route map to download, go to *www. forestry.gov.uk*, click on 'Scotland' then 'Scotland Mountain Biking' then 'Learnie Red Rock Trails'. A Forestry Commission leaflet, *Learnie Red Rock Trails – Ride the Divide,* may be available from Inverness Forest District (01463 791575).

Refreshments: In Rosemarkie and Cromarty.

Kyle of Sutherland Trails north of Inverness
Ride 53

With stunning views over the Kyle of Sutherland, the inner Dornoch Firth and Bonar Bridge, the Kyle of Sutherland Mountain Bike Trails offer 10.5 miles of trail for a range of skills. There are Blue-, Red- and Black-grade trails combining technical features and forest roads.

Starting points & parking

The Kyle of Sutherland Trails lie about 10 miles **west of where the A9 crosses the Dornoch Firth** on the Dornoch Bridge (about 30 miles north of Inverness).

(a) The Balblair trails are accessible just off the A836 about 1 mile past Bonar Bridge, heading towards Lairg. Look for the car park and trailhead on the right (grid reference NH 604929).

(b) For Carbisdale, carry straight on past Culrain station before joining the road up to the youth hostel, on the left. The car park and trailhead are about 200yds along this road on the left-hand side (grid reference NH 578952).

The rides

The trails are split between the Carbisdale trails on the west side of the Kyle, and the Balblair trails on the east.

Carbisdale Blue

Distance	Grade	Waymarks
1.6 miles	Moderate	Blue

Perfect for intermediate mountain bikers: optional rock features, wonderful views and technical descents, such as Goldie Rocks and Hissing Sid. This route is a great introduction to the trails and is ideal for improving your skills in preparation for riding the Red route.

Carbisdale Red

Distance	Grade	Waymarks
3 miles	Difficult	Red

This route has some technical features, such as Little Red Riding Wood and What Big Teeth along with forest road sections. The viewpoint overlooking the lochan provides the perfect rest point when you get to the top of the hill. Soak in the view while you regain your energy for the cycle ahead.

Balblair Blue

Distance	Grade	Waymarks
1.9 miles	Moderate	Blue

A great route if you want a quick spin. Enjoy the in-forest feel of the Whoopy-do section and the smooth descent on the Ceilidh Trail.

Balblair Black

Distance	Grade	Waymarks
4.7 or 7 miles	Severe	Black

There is plenty on the Balblair Black to test even the most experienced cyclist, with rock slabs such as Rock Hard and Candy Mountain, timber trails and lung-busting uphill sections. Not for the faint-hearted, but the view from the top of the hill at the mast is well worth the effort.

Category
Forest trails.

Distance
$10^{1}/_{2}$ miles.

Ride 53 Kyle of Sutherland Trails, north of Inverness

Station: Ardgay or Culrain.

TIC: Tain, 0845 2255121.

Other nearby trails: The Morangie Trail is a 12-mile Blue-grade trail south of Tain (go to *www.forestry.gov.uk* and search 'Morangie cycle route').

Useful publications & websites: OS Landranger Map 21. Go to *www.forestry.gov.uk*, click on 'Scotland' then 'Scotland

Mountain Biking' then 'Kyle of Sutherland Trails' for more information and trail downloads. Also try *http://cycling.visitscotland.com,* click on 'Mountain Biking' then 'Mountain Bike Centres' then on 'Balblair Trails' or 'Carbisdale'.

Refreshments: The nearest are in Bonar Bridge and Ardgay.

Ride 54 Highland Wildcat Trails Golspie

Category
Forest trails.

Distance
4 – 8 miles.

Highland Wildcat is the most ambitious community-led mountain bike development in the UK. Since being established in 2005, over 11 miles of trail have been constructed at a cost of £600,000. The aim has been to build quality trails and to complement the wonderful natural environment of Sutherland. The trails have been designed with everyone in mind and are 'stacked' so that the more difficult routes can only be reached by cycling up through the easier sections. Families of mixed ability and novice riders may find it easier to start from the Big Burn car park just outside the village to the north. From here there is the option of going via Big Burn mixed woodlands towards Ben Bhraggie on a Blue-grade route, or otherwise into Dunrobin Wood on an easy Green-grade route, joining paths and tracks in the wider countryside or coast. For inexperienced riders keen to reach the summit of 'The Ben', there is a double track all the way from the Blue trail that leads off at

the crossroads in the forest. For more information, go to the excellent website at *www.highlandwildcat.com*

Starting point & parking

Golspie lies on the coast in the far north-east of Scotland, halfway between Tain and Wick (grid reference NH 830000). The car park for the cycle trails is at Rhives Farm, Golspie. If driving up from the South, turn left in the centre of Golspie Village onto Fountain Road and follow it to the end, over the crossroads by the fountain, under the stone arch of the railway bridge and the car park is on the right.

Blue Trail

Distance	Grade	Waymarks
4 miles	Moderate	Blue

This trail is great for novices or families who want some relatively easy, sociable cycling on gentle slopes. The trail starts at the Highland Wildcat car park near Big

Burn (accessed via the turn-off to Backies, just north of Golspie), and follows a wide path through young broadleaf woodland to the public road at Big Burn Cottage. As it winds through semi-mature Scots pine and open space on the forest margin, there is a gradual gain in height until the forest road is reached above Golspie Tower. A gradual climb through the forest and out into an open glade offers wonderful views across the Moray Firth.

Red Trail

Distance	Grade	Waymarks
4.7 miles	Difficult	Red

The singletrack starts from the car park at Rhives Farm and enters a mature broadleaf wood, climbing steadily up into the forest. Minor stone features along the way add interest and a warm-up for things to come. On joining the forest road, the Red Trail turns downhill and then up a fairly steep section to the start of the serious fun with drop-offs, bomb holes, ski jumps, a canyon jump and other stone features en-route to a seriously fast section of narrow swoopy singletrack within closely planted pinewood. More details on the website.

Black Trail

Distance	Grade	Waymarks
8.4 miles	Severe	Black

The Black Trail shares the course of the Red-grade route until the main forest road is reached at the top of 'Cat's Climb'. This provides an excellent warm-up for entering 'Fox Farm', a narrow singletrack climb with stone features. At 'Stone Circle' there is

a choice of remaining inside the forest on 'Treeline', or emerging onto the open hill to experience one of the most full-on and testing technical climbs to be found in the UK. Stone slabs abound, creating many difficult features as you climb rapidly through a series of tight switchback corners. More details on the website.

Station: Golspie.

TIC: Dornoch, 01845 2255121.

Other nearby trails: There is a 12-mile Blue-grade forest trail in Morangie Forest to the south of Tain – go to *www.forestry.gov.uk*, click on 'Scotland' and search 'Morangie Cycle Route'. Consider also the trails at Balblair and Carbisdale near Bonar Bridge.

Useful publications & websites: OS Landranger Maps 17 & 21. Try the excellent website covering the trails at *www.highlandwildcat.com* or email for a leaflet.

Refreshments: In Golspie.

Index

459

Notes